NetWare™ 3.12 System Administrator's Reference

Doug Archell

NetWare 3.12 System Administrator's Reference

Copyright© 1994 by Que® Corporation.

Library of Congress Catalog No.: 94-67942

ISBN: 1-56529-925-6

96   95   94   6   5   4   3   2   1

Interpretation of the printing code: the rightmost double-digit number is the year of the book's printing; the rightmost single-digit number, the number of the book's printing. For example, a printing code of 94-1 shows that the first printing of the book occurred in 1994.

Screen reproductions in this book were created with Collage Plus from Inner Media, Inc., Hollis, NH.

Publisher: David P. Ewing

Associate Publisher: Joseph B. Wikert

Publishing Managers: Brad R. Koch and Steven M. Schafer

Product Marketing Manager: Greg Wiegand

Dedication

This book is dedicated to my parents, Gail and Bob Archell. It is with their guidance that I have learned that the boundaries of one's success are only restricted by that with which they desire.

Credits

Acquisitions Editor
Fred Slone

Acquisitions Coordinator
Patricia J. Brooks

Product Director
C. Kazim Haidri

Production Editor
Susan Ross Moore

Copy Editors
Patrick Kanouse
Julie McNamee

Editorial Assistant
Michelle Williams

Technical Editors
Peter Kuo, Ph.D.
David Shinn

Book Designer
Paula Carroll

Cover Designer
Dan Armstrong

Production Team
Steve Adams
Angela Bannan
Aren K. Howell
Bob LaRoche
Beth Lewis
Erika Millen
Wendy Ott
G. Alan Palmore
Nanci Sears Perry
Kaylene Riemen
Clair Schweinler
Michael Thomas
Robert Wolf

Indexer
Charlotte Clapp

Composed in *Stone* and *MCPdigital* by Que Corporation

About the Author

Doug Archell is an independent network consultant located just east of Toronto, Ontario. For over five years, he has supported and implemented Novell NetWare servers and workstations in ARCnet, Token Ring, and EtherNet environments. As a Certified NetWare Administrator, Certified NetWare Engineer, and Enterprise Certified NetWare Engineer, Doug has assisted many others with their networking problems through various electronic messaging systems such as CompuServe NetWire, the Internet, and NANET:Networks, where he is a moderator. Previously, his writing experience has resulted in articles in *LAN Magazine, NetWare Connection* magazine, and the *CNEPA Network News* as well as being a contributing author for *NetWare Unleashed* and *Using NetWare 3.12: Special Edition*. Doug can be reached on CompuServe at 70751,767 or through the Internet at DOUG.ARCHELL@CANREM.COM.

Acknowledgments

While I have written magazine articles before and acted as a contributing author for two other books, I never really realized how much work was actually involved in writing an entire book on your own, until now. As I look back over the past three gruelling months of being locked in front of my PC into the wee hours of the morning after a full day at work, I cannot forget all of the people who have made this book happen. I may have written the book on my own, but without the assistance of several people backing me up, you would not be reading this book today.

First and foremost, I must thank Angie Lee, formerly of Que Publishing, for taking the time to listen to my idea and taking my proposal forward to get this book approved. Without her assistance, this book may never have become more than a thought in my mind. But Angie was not the only one from Que who has made this book a reality. Brad Koch, Patty Brooks, and Fred Slone have all been there to answer any questions I might have and listen as I preached to them that two hours' sleep in one night is sufficient...honest.

Systems books can be interesting, but reading them over and over again, poring over each word can be, well, boring. This usually thankless task fell upon Susan Ross Moore, Chris Haidri, Stephanie Gould, and a team of others. Their keen eyes have been responsible for correcting several layout and grammatical problems throughout this book.

To ensure this book provides you with the wealth of NetWare information that is intended, and that it is accurate, two skilled systems professionals have spent a lot of their time poring over the techno-jargon and command syntax, checking every detail. During the past three months, David Shinn and Peter Kuo have kept me honest and accurate and have provided a few great ideas for this book. In addition to technical editing, Peter was also kind enough to find time in his already too-busy schedule to provide his technical expertise in the Basic MHS section of this book.

Before I started writing this book, I consulted with various systems professionals throughout the Internet and CompuServe, looking for ideas and suggestions. Ron Eisner, Gene Hertel, John Howell, Steve Meyer, Frank

Ramsey, and Frank Schneider were all kind enough to reply to my requests and provided some valuable insight and information.

There are those outside of the networking and writing worlds who also have played a crucial role in bringing this book to print. Of all the women in the world, my girlfriend Michelle has got to be one of the most understanding and considerate. While not in the systems field, she has patiently listened as I rambled on about low-quality systems components and made a valiant attempt at pretending to be excited when I found a new way of improving the performance of a workstation. Next, my close friend Craig has provided the support and that imaginary "countdown to completion" clock that has kept me going. Then, not only a friend but also my brother, Bryan, has definitely put up with a lot throughout our years together. His sense of humor and personality were a real help for getting through many of the difficult times that are in the past and will be of great help for the hurdles that await. Finally, my longtime friend Steve. While we have not had the opportunity to get together that often in the recent year, his support in the past and future is appreciated.

Trademark Acknowledgments

All terms mentioned in this book that are known to be trademarks or service marks have been appropriately capitalized. Que Corporation cannot attest to the accuracy of this information. Use of a term in this book should not be regarded as affecting the validity of any trademark or service mark.Contents at a Glance

Contents at a Glance

Installation

Environment Setup

Environment Management

Security Management

File/Directory Management

Network Printing

Console Management

Console Management

Troubleshooting

Troubleshooting

Appendixes

Appendixes

Contents

III Environment Management

IV Security Management

VI Network Printing

VII Console Management

22 Console Commands   347

Introduction

Since I first began working with NetWare I have accumulated quite a stack of papers with notes and tips that I have learned. My library of networking books has grown each and every year. NetWare may not be the most difficult operating system in the world, but there is lots to know and plenty of "gotchas." Then, approximately six months ago, I started looking at the stacks of paper and my assortment of books and thought how nice it would be to have all the information I need about NetWare in one simple book. The result of this thought is the book you are holding right now.

This book may not be a monster-sized 1,000+ page book, but don't let the size fool you for there is *lots* of information packed into these pages. Before I started writing I had several objectives for this book that had to be met, these being:

- *The book must provide as much information about NetWare as possible in the least amount of space as possible.* Basic theories of networking are not covered in this book. Here, you find almost everything you need to know about installing and managing your NetWare V3.12 server.

- *The readers of this book must be warned of any pitfalls they may encounter with NetWare.* Throughout this book, you find text, known as a "Caution," that stands out from all other text. As topics are being discussed, these "Cautions" are used whenever there is something you must know about, which could cause a potential problem for you.

- *Tips and tricks should be shared with the readers.* Before consulting, my position was as a Network Administrator for a large financial institution. During this time, I had the opportunity to uncover various ways of performing different tasks. To bring this "real world" experience to you, you find numerous tips and shortcuts throughout this book.

- *The book must be usable.* One of my primary goals was to create a book the reader could actually use. During my discussions with various networking professionals, the one thing I found is that many of them spent hundreds of dollars on a variety of books only to leave them on their bookshelves at home, collecting dust. Hopefully, if I have met my goal, that is not the case with this book. The generous use of tips, notes, cautions, and valuable reference material should keep you coming back for more!

■ *The book must have something for everyone.* Instead of trying to target a specific audience, whether that be the beginner or the advanced reader, this book has been written to provide valuable information for readers of all experience levels. Whether you are brand new to NetWare or an experienced veteran, this book gives you what you need to know!

Based on these objectives, Que Publishing and I now present this book to you. Hopefully, you will enjoy reading this book as much as I did writing it. If you have any comments or suggestions that could be used in later revisions, please feel free to contact me on CompuServe at 70751,767. Thank you. Doug Archell.

How This Book Is Arranged

One of the key features of this book is that it is task oriented. Each of the sections and chapters has been broken down into specific tasks, not based on a specific utility. By doing so, instead of having to remember which utility performed what task, by using the index you can look up the task you want to perform. Following is a summary of each of the parts contained within this book:

Part I: Installation covers the various aspects of installing your LAN, such as topology and architecture selection, and file server and workstation installation and configuration.

Part II: Environment Setup covers the various steps you must take to access the server such as logging in, and creating user IDs, login scripts, and menus.

Part III: Environment Management covers a variety of commands you will use to manage your NetWare environment such as MAP, SESSION, FILER, and a host of others.

Part IV: Security Management covers everything you need to create and implement a secure NetWare file server.

Part V: File and Directory Management covers the various utilities Novell provides to manage your file and directory structures.

Part VI: Network Printing covers printing in the NetWare environment with detailed information on creating and using your print servers and queues.

Part VII: Console Management covers the console commands and utilities you use to manage your file server from the console.

Part VIII: Troubleshooting covers some of the more common problems you run into when using NetWare and the steps you should take to resolve them.

As you read through this book, there are a few things you should know regarding the different typefaces:

1. Whenever a command is being presented to you that you must type, the command is shown in **BOLD** letters. For example, **USERLIST /A**.

2. Unless noted otherwise, the square brackets used within the command syntax signify an optional parameter. The information contained in the square brackets can be used at your discretion, and when used, you should *not* enter the square brackets in your command.

3. Throughout this book, you find instances where you are asked to type a command on the server console or the workstation. To save space and to be as concise as possible, occasionally you are asked to "enter the following command." Whenever you see examples such as this, unless noted otherwise, you should press the Enter key after entering the command.

Chapter 1

The Basis of Networking

Compared to the history of computing, LANs may seem fairly new, but a lot of work has gone into their production and development. To understand how LANs have gotten where they are now, you need a basic understanding of some of the "Who's Who" of the networking world.

In this chapter, you read about:

- Different Standards Organizations
- The OSI Reference Model

Standards Organizations

Large corporations like Novell, Microsoft, and IBM have all played a crucial role in determining the fate of LANs, but in many cases, they have received guidance from outside their walls. Standards organizations have helped the industry by setting and/or recommending guidelines about how hardware and software should communicate.

In the past, many manufacturers produced proprietary hardware and software. The big problem with proprietary systems is that they are not always fully compatible with other manufacturers' systems. By adhering to generic standards, manufacturers have a better chance of making sure their products will work with other vendors' products. Organizations such as the Consultative Committee for International Telegraph and Telephone (CCITT), the Institute of Electrical and Electronics Engineers (IEEE), and the International Standards Organization (ISO) have worked hard for a number of years to promote their research and the open systems environment.

Consultative Committee for International Telegraph and Telephone

One of the best known standards organizations, the Consultative Committee for International Telegraph and Telephone (CCITT), is responsible for many of the communications standards we have today, such as Asynchronous Transfer Mode, the V series (V.24, V.32, V.42) of modem standards, and X.25, a common packet switching architecture.

The Institute of Electrical and Electronics Engineers

The largest professional organization in the world is the Institute of Electrical and Electronics Engineers (IEEE). In 1980, the IEEE embarked on a new task: to develop a series of standards to govern how LANs should operate. Their work resulted in the 802 series of standards.

When the IEEE began working on the 802 series, they realized one standard governing all aspects of LANs and WANs would not suffice. Consumers want standards, but they also want a choice as to what product best suits their requirements.

In keeping with this spirit, the IEEE established separate workgroups to provide standards for different areas of the 802 series. Each workgroup is charged with a certain task they should fulfill. These workgroups are noted in Table 1.1. Should you want a further description of a particular workgroup, you can look in the Glossary, found at the back of this book.

Table 1.1 IEEE workgroups.	
Workgroup	**Responsibility**
802.1	Interoperability
802.2	LLC
802.3	CSMA/CD /100BaseX (Fast Ethernet)
802.4	Token Bus
802.5	Token Ring
802.6	Metropolitan Area Networks
802.7	Broadband Technology
802.8	Fiber-Optics
802.9	Integrated Voice and Data
802.10	LAN Security
802.11	Wireless Communications
802.12	100VG-AnyLAN

International Standards Organization

The International Standards Organization (ISO) was formed in 1977 to develop standards on a wide range of topics. With offices throughout the world, the ISO has a presence in approximately 100 countries. In the United States, the ISO's representative is known as the American National Standards Institute (ANSI). The ISO is most famous for its development of the OSI Reference Model.

The Open Systems Interconnection (OSI) Reference Model is one of the best-known recommendations from any standards committee. This model is unique because it does not detail any specific communications standard that must be used. Instead, the OSI model gives developers a set of rules or guidelines to follow. Unlike some standards that only govern one portion of the networks communications, the OSI Reference Model looks at everything from the electrical characteristics of the cabling all the way to the manner in which an application is presented to the user.

Visually, the OSI Reference Model is a tower of building blocks (see fig. 1.1). Split into seven different layers, the operation of the model begins at the bottom block, or layer, and works its way to the top.

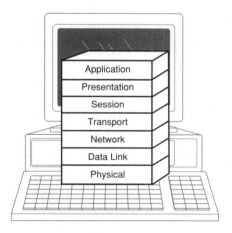

Fig. 1.1 The Open Systems Interconnection Reference Model.

Each layer in the model has a specific focus, such as electrical specifications of the cabling, packet addressing, and encryption. Below, a brief description of each layer is provided to give you an idea how the model works.

- *Layer 1—Physical:* The Physical layer deals with issues such as the electrical specifications of the cabling, how data is accessed from the cable, and how the network interface cards connect with the cabling. At the Physical layer, data is referred to as bits.

- *Layer 2—Data Link:* The Data Link layer is capable of reading the source and destination physical addresses contained in a packet. Based on this information, the Data Link layer can determine for what node the packet is destined.

- *Layer 3—Network:* The Network layer of the OSI model examines the network layer address and directs the data to the appropriate network. Information passed by the Network layer is referred to as a *packet.*

- *Layer 4—Transport:* The Transport layer ensures data is sent and received properly over the network. At this layer, acknowledgments are generated from the receiving station to confirm a packet was received properly.

- *Layer 5—Session:* The Session layer of the OSI model establishes and terminates connections between nodes on the network. After a connection has been established, the Session layer manages what occurs between the two nodes and directs problems from the upper layers.

- *Layer 6—Presentation:* The Presentation layer translates data into a format the sending and receiving stations can read. In addition to translation, the Presentation layer also manages services such as data compression and encryption.

- *Layer 7—Application:* You probably are most familiar with the Application layer. This layer provides the communications interface between the computer and the user. Examples of Application layer services are electronic mail, network management, and file transfers.

Unofficial Standards

It may seem contradictory to call something a standard, yet not an official standard, but this happens in the world of computing. Not all standards are formed by official standards bodies. Instead, they may be a result of widespread user acceptance—or by government legislation.

Two terms to know are *de jure* (By Law) and *de facto* (By Fact). When something has become a standard based on widespread use, such as TCP/IP, it is known as a *de facto* standard. If it has become a standard solely due to government legislation or some other law, it is known as a *de jure* standard.

Chapter 2

The Network's Platform

Now that you know some of the standards that have been developed for networking, we can look at the foundation of a network—the network's platform.

NetWare is a very complex operating system that has a lot of "bells and whistles," but on its own, it's nothing. Consider networking as a pyramid of building blocks carefully balanced on each other. If one block is not placed just right, the entire pyramid comes tumbling down. In any structure, the most important part is the platform that supports it.

In this chapter, we look at:

- Topologies and how they are used

- Architecture restrictions

- The different types of cabling

- Installing your network architecture

Topologies

The meaning of the word *topology*, as it pertains to networking, is frequently confused with the meaning of the word *architecture*. While new architectures pop up from time to time (such as FAST Ethernet and ARCnetPLUS) and current architectures improve, there are five topologies that have not changed. The topology defines how the network is physically laid out. Within a topology, there are no specifications that provide details on the types of cabling that can be used or how fast it will run.

The Bus Topology

The simplest of all topologies is the bus (see fig. 2.1). Unlike other topologies that make use of additional hardware, the bus is extremely simple. In a bus, each node is wired onto a length of cable that connects each station in sequence. The ends of the cable do not connect with each other and usually are terminated in some fashion. While the bus is easy to install, it does provide some additional headaches when troubleshooting cabling and network problems. Since each workstation is wired in succession, a failure anywhere on the bus brings that segment to a grinding halt.

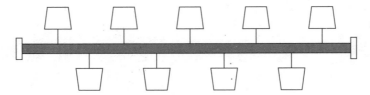

Fig. 2.1 The bus topology.

The Hybrid Topology

The hybrid topology is the most complex of all the topologies. While the other topologies have a single definition to describe the layout, describing the hybrid is not that easy. Essentially, the hybrid is a mixture of two or more topologies in the same network. For example, if a network has a bus segment, a star segment, and a ring segment, the overall network topology is said to be a hybrid (see fig. 2.2).

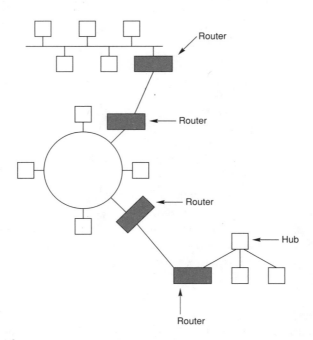

Fig. 2.2 The hybrid topology.

The Mesh Topology

The mesh topology is the most fault tolerant of the five shown here. In the mesh (see fig. 2.3), each node is wired to every other node in the mesh. If one connection fails, data can be rerouted through another connection to reach the desired destination. While the mesh topology provides a high degree of reliability, it is an extremely expensive system to implement and is usually only used in large packet switching networks such as X.25.

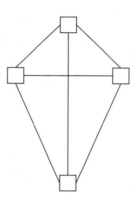

Fig. 2.3 The mesh topology.

The Ring Topology

A ring topology is one with nodes wired together in succession (see fig. 2.4). In this topology, the ends of the wiring segment are closed together to form the actual ring. Like the bus, a break anywhere along the common cabling causes the entire segment to go down.

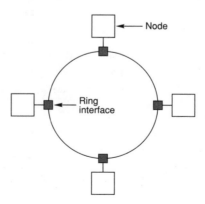

Fig. 2.4 The ring topology.

The Star Topology

The star topology defines a network where each node is directly connected to a central point such as a hub or concentrator (see fig. 2.5). Overall, the star provides a certain degree of protection because each node is directly connected to the hub. When a failure occurs on one of these dedicated links, the hub usually can reroute the electrical signals to ensure that the rest of the network will continue to function. The main fault with the star topology is that the hub or concentrator acts as a single point of failure for the LAN.

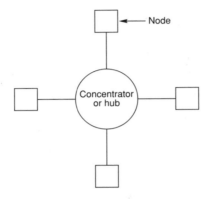

Fig. 2.5 The star topology.

Architectures

Choosing the architecture that best suits your needs is an extremely important task when designing your LAN. Before making any decisions, you first must determine what the LAN is used for and the required type of response.

The LAN's architecture defines restrictions such as the overall size and speed at which your LAN will operate. Depending on your circumstances, you may require only a low-speed solution such as ARCnet, yet, maybe you need something a lot faster such as FDDI or 16Mbps Token Ring; only you will know.

This section describes what each of these architectures is, and some of the things you should look out for when installing them.

> **Caution**
>
> There may be only three key networking architectures, ARCnet, Ethernet, and Token Ring, but there are hundreds of companies involved in producing associated equipment. While this section provides information about the installation and configuration of your hardware, *always* read the manuals that come with your hardware.

ARCnet

ARCnet is a 2.5Mbps networking solution designed in 1977 by Datapoint Corporation. While electrically operating as a token-passing bus, ARCnet is physically wired as either a bus or star topology with a passive or active hub at the center of the star. One of the key benefits to using ARCnet as your architecture is its low cost. Compared to other solutions, ARCnet is very afford-able and fairly easy to install.

Components Required for a Standard ARCnet Installation

When installing the ARCnet LAN, you need several components to get everything up and run-ning. The first item is cabling. In most cases, ARCnet is run on coaxial RG-62 cabling, but there are ARCnet cards available that use unshielded twisted pair (UTP) or even fiber-optic cabling. Each type of cable has its own little quirks (refer to the heading "Cabling," later in this chapter); you must assess each for your specific application.

Next, you need ARCnet Network Interface Cards (NICs) to install in each node attached to the network. There are several manufacturers of ARCnet cards, such as Datapoint or Standard Micro Systems.

> **Note**
>
> Before purchasing equipment, make sure it is all compatible. Just because it is possible to use ARCnet with UTP or fiber-optic cable does not mean every vendor's NIC or hub will. Check with your local vendor about any compatibility issues.

With the type of cabling and NIC you will be using in mind, you then require a passive or active hub. While they both serve the same purpose, they operate differently.

When using a passive hub, your overall network size is reduced. As described in the next section on restrictions, the maximum distance between a node and passive hub is 1/20 that of the maxi-mum distance between a node and an active hub. The main reason for this restriction is that the passive hub merely passes the signal through the LAN, while the active hub amplifies the signal it receives, so the signal can travel a longer distance. Depending on your LAN, this may immedi-ately eliminate the possibility of using a passive hub.

Finally, if you are using a passive hub, make sure you have available a few terminators that corre-spond to the type of cabling you plan to use. When using RG-62, you need a 93 Ω terminator, while UTP installations are terminated at 100 Ω.

Restrictions when Installing ARCnet

Like everything in life, there are rules and regulations you must know before proceeding. ARCnet is no different. In Table 2.1, several restrictions regarding the maximum distances are shown. Be careful not to go beyond these ranges. Failure to comply with these restrictions will result in in-termittent network problems that are not always easy to isolate.

Table 2.1 ARCnet restrictions.

Restriction	Value
Maximum distance between nodes	2,000 feet
Maximum distance between two farthest nodes	20,000 feet
Maximum distance between node and passive hub	100 feet
Maximum distance between node and active hub	2,000 feet
Maximum distance between passive hub and active hub	100 feet
Maximum distance between two active hubs	2,000 feet

Aside from the restrictions shown previously, there are four more you should know:

1. Any unused ports on a passive hub *must* be terminated.

2. Two passive hubs cannot be connected together in succession.

3. A passive hub can only connect a node to an active hub; the passive hub cannot connect two active hubs.

4. You should *never* set two stations to the same physical address.

Installing ARCnet

Unlike other network architectures like Ethernet or Token Ring, which have the physical addresses burned into the chips, ARCnet NICs require you to set the physical address, using dip switches on the card, to a value between 1 and 255. Before you set the station addresses, you should first install the cabling and the hubs. Addresses should be set in an orderly fashion to ensure the optimal performance of your LAN and make life easier when you're troubleshooting.

Tip
When setting the workstation addresses, you should leave a bit of a space between each number. For example, if your LAN has ten workstations, number the interface cards in increments of five or ten—the first workstation's address would be 1, the second 5, and so on. This makes life easier when you add workstations down the road.

I

Installation

Communications on your ARCnet LAN are based on a process called the ARCnet reconfiguration process (referred to as *RECON*). Here's how it works:

When a node wants to join the network, the RECON process is initiated. Each node on the network has a table containing two addresses, a Source Identifier (SID) and a Next Identifier (NID). Each node's SID is equivalent to its physical address you set with the dip switches. The NID is the physical address of the next station (in numerical order) attached to the network. For example, assume your node's SID is 1. If the node with the physical address 5 is turned off, but the node with the physical address of 10 is on, your node's NID would be set to 10.

The RECON process determines which nodes are attached to the network and the order in which their requests should be processed. When a node first joins the network, it issues a RECON request that disrupts the normal flow of the token. At this point, the node with the highest SID releases a new token onto the network. The first node then determines where its NID should be set by polling stations with a higher SID value. When its NID is determined, the token is passed to the node at this NID, which repeats the process. Once the RECON process is over, normal operation of the network will be returned and nodes will pass tokens to the workstations shown as being their NIDs.

If care is not taken when setting the physical addresses of your LAN, the network communications may follow a path like the one in Figure 2.6. In this diagram, an ARCnet LAN is configured with five stations using a mixture of the star and bus topologies. As you can see, data is not flowing in the logical order of the cabling.

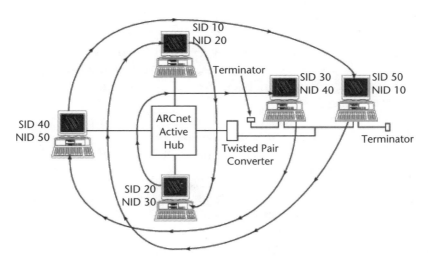

Fig. 2.6 The ARCnet reconfiguration process on a LAN where station physical addresses have not been set in an orderly fashion.

Now take a look at Figure 2.7. The person who set the physical addresses on this network took the time to plan where each node would be physically located and set the addresses accordingly.

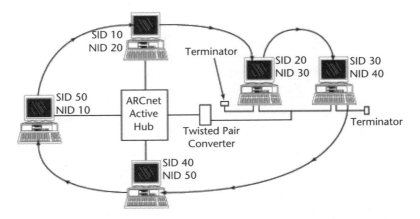

Fig 2.7 The ARCnet reconfiguration process on a LAN where station physical addresses have been set in an orderly fashion.

Based on figures 2.6 and 2.7, you should have a clear understanding of the importance of proper planning. Certain situations may require you to rush through a specific job, but planning the basis of your LAN is no place for sloppy work. Any installations you do should be well thought out and planned even *before* you buy any equipment.

10Base2 Ethernet

One of the most popular networking solutions is a version of Ethernet known as 10Base2. Operating as a 10Mbps bus topology network, 10Base2 is easy to install and reasonably priced. Based on the IEEE's 802.3 specifications, 10Base2 uses the Carrier Sense Multiple Access with Collision Detection (CSMA/CD) protocol.

Components Required for a Standard 10Base2 Installation

Of all the available flavors of Ethernet, 10Base2 is the simplest to install. To install your 10Base2 LAN, there are several basic things you need.

To start with, 10Base2 uses RG-58 A/U coaxial cabling, a thin coaxial cable with an impedance of 50 Ω, hence its nickname: *Thinnet*. Depending on the size of the LAN you are installing, you may want to purchase the cabling in rolls and cut the cabling to the desired length. For small installations, precut cabling would be an easier solution.

Next you need one Ethernet interface card for every node connecting to the LAN. Most Ethernet cards today have several ports on the back: a coaxial connector and a DB-9 (nine-pin connector), and maybe one for RJ-45 cabling. Make sure the card you are using has a coaxial connection.

Caution

Most cards that have multiple ports—a coaxial and a DB-9—require you to set a jumper on the card to signify which port you are using. Make sure you check the NIC's manual for a description of the proper configuration.

To connect the workstations to the cabling, you need a connector known as a T-Connector. T-Connectors are fairly inexpensive, so you should always have a few extras on hand. While reasonably sturdy, there is always a possibility a connection will short. A failure at the T will cause the attached station to lose its connection to the file server and may bring the entire network segment down.

The only other thing you need to get your 10Base2 LAN up and running is a 50 Ω terminator for each end of the segment. Since 10Base2 operates as a bus topology, where the ends of the cabling segment do not connect, the ends must be capped in some fashion. This is where the terminator comes in. The terminator ensures signals are not reflected or echoed down the segment, which would make data transmissions difficult if not impossible. In addition to terminating the bus, one end of the segment must be grounded. Grounding terminators are available for roughly the same price (as non-grounding terminators) and have a wire that comes out the side and attaches to a suitable ground. Always have a few extra terminators on hand in case one fails.

Restrictions when Installing 10Base2

Although the installation of a 10Base2 LAN is fairly simple, there are several potential hot spots you should be aware of before tackling this architecture. The most important thing to look out for during installation is the length of cabling being used. Cabling-related problems can be costly and time-consuming to resolve.

Table 2.2 details the physical limitations that must be observed while you are installing or upgrading your 10Base2 LAN. Within this table, you may notice two terms that are new to you: taps and populated segments. A *tap* is a fairly basic term that signifies any location where a piece of hardware has been added directly to the network. For example, if your network has five PCs and one printer attached directly to the network cabling, you are using six taps. A *populated segment* is a segment that has PCs, printers, or any other type of node directly wired to it. If you are now asking yourself why you can have five segments, yet only three can be populated, don't worry—that's a common question. The additional two segments enable you to expand your network over a greater distance.

Table 2.2 Physical limitations of a 10Base2 network.	
Restriction	**Value**
Minimum distance between stations	.5 meters (1.5 feet)
Maximum segment length	185 meters (607 feet)
Maximum network length	925 meters (3,035 feet)
Maximum node separation	5 segments/4 repeaters
Maximum taps per segment	30
Maximum populated segments per LAN	3

Aside from the restrictions shown previously, there are two more you should know:

■ Nodes must be connected directly to the network cabling with a T-Connector attached to the NIC. Drop cables are *not* allowed.

> **Note**
>
> A "drop cable" is merely a cable used to attach the workstation to the main segment of the network cabling. It is called a "drop cable" because in many installations, the main network cable is run through the ceiling so the cable attaching the workstation to the main network cable "drops" from the ceiling.

■ Each end of the segment *must* be terminated. Failure to terminate one end will result in a network that doesn't work!

Installing 10Base2

Installing any bus topology LAN is easy, but requires much advance planning; 10Base2 is no exception. Because each node is wired in succession, you should determine where each PC will be before cutting any cabling.

> **Note**
>
> Remember, a node is any piece of equipment that is attached directly to the network. Therefore, the maximum restriction of 30 nodes per segment includes workstations, repeaters, file servers, and printers connected directly to the network's cabling (such as an HP LaserJet Printer with a JetDirect card).

Once you know where each node is situated, plan your cabling accordingly. If you have 50 nodes to attach to the LAN, a repeater is required somewhere to split the LAN into at least two segments. Whatever you do, *plan ahead*. If there is a reasonable possibility you will be adding more nodes in the near future, try to predict where they might end up. While no one can be a mind reader, it will make your life a lot easier if you are prepared. For example, a LAN with 50 nodes requires at least two segments connected by one repeater. These 50 nodes could be split up as 30 nodes on one segment and 20 on another *or* 25 nodes on each. By going the latter route, you are giving yourself a little leeway to add a node to either segment. If you went with the 30/20 split, and someone on the first segment wanted to install a JetDirect card in their HP LaserJet IV, this would force you to rewire several areas on the LAN to ensure that no more than 30 nodes were connected to any segment; such rewiring is not a fun task.

Caution

Since 10Base2 operates as a bus topology, adding or removing nodes from the LAN requires you to bring down the entire system. Therefore, by planning ahead, you make your life easier by minimizing the amount of changes needed down the road, and you will reduce the amount of down time to which your users are subjected.

When connecting the workstation to the network cabling, you should attach one T-Connector to the NIC and then attach the cables from the station upstream and the station downstream to the two ends of the T. If this is the last node on the segment, a terminator should be attached to one side of the T.

Caution

Never attach the cabling directly to the network interface card. The only thing that should ever connect to the NIC is the T-Connector.

After cabling the stations together, terminating both ends of each segment, and grounding one end, your LAN should look something like the one shown in Figure 2.8.

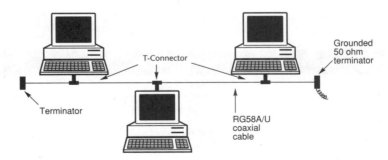

Fig. 2.8 Physical layout of a 10Base2 network.

10Base5 Ethernet

Like 10Base2, 10Base5 is a bus topology LAN operating at 10Mbps. As an IEEE 802.3 standard, 10Base5 uses the CSMA/CD protocol to transfer data back and forth on the LAN. While 10Base5 is a little more expensive than 10Base2, and requires more work to install, it offers a lot more flexibility for growth and upgrades than 10Base2 offers.

Components Required for a Standard 10Base5 Installation

Along with the added complexity that comes with 10Base5, there are a few additional pieces of equipment you need to get your LAN up and running. Let's start at the beginning.

First, while 10Base5 still uses coaxial cabling, it's not the same type. For this architecture, you need RG-8 or RG-11 coaxial cabling. These thicker and more expensive types of coaxial cable have been given the nickname "garden hose" because of their thickness.

Again, as with 10Base2, you need a 50 Ω terminator for each segment's end. One should be a grounding terminator.

Next, a network interface card is required for each node attached to the LAN. Unlike 10Base2, which uses the coaxial connector on the Ethernet card, 10Base5 uses the DB-9 connector (also called the DIX connector).

Finally, there are two new components you need for your 10Base5 installation—a transceiver, also called a Medium Attachment Unit (MAU); and a transceiver cable, also called an Attachment Unit Interface (AUI) cable. The transceiver is used as a wire tap into the common cabling system. The workstation then connects to the transceiver using the transceiver cable. 10Base2 does not use an external transceiver, but rather an internal transceiver, since the card must be attached directly to the network cabling.

Restrictions when Installing 10Base5

Table 2.3 lists the various restrictions you should consider when installing or upgrading your 10Base5 LAN. As with any other architecture, it is important that you stay within the established guidelines to ensure your LAN runs as smoothly as possible. Going beyond these limits could result in intermittent problems that are difficult to troubleshoot.

Table 2.3 Physical limitations of a 10Base5 network.	
Restriction	**Value**
Minimum length between transceivers	2.5 meters (8 feet)
Maximum transceiver cable length	50 meters (164 feet)

Restriction	Value
Maximum segment length	500 meters (1,640 feet)
Maximum network length	2,500 meters (8,200 feet)
Maximum node separation	5 segments/4 repeaters
Maximum taps per segment	100
Maximum populated segments	3

Note

When determining the number of nodes per segment, you must include any repeaters, file servers, print servers, or gateways in addition to the workstations being used.

Installing 10Base5

Compared to 10Base2, 10Base5 is a far more physically robust LAN architecture. Not only is the physical size of your LAN increased, but there is more room to grow because the maximum number of nodes per segment has more than tripled!

Nodes within the 10Base5 LAN do not connect directly to the network cabling, but instead use transceivers and transceiver cables to tap into the main segment, sometimes called the 10Base5 backbone. This makes life a lot easier for you when adding stations to, or removing stations from, the LAN because the amount of rewiring is minimized compared to that on a 10Base2 LAN.

Even though adding nodes to, or removing nodes from, the 10Base5 LAN may be a little easier, this does not mean less planning is required. There are still restrictions on the maximum number of nodes and on cable lengths. Before installing your LAN, plan, plan, plan.

These are additional things to keep in mind when installing your 10Base5 LAN:

- When attaching repeaters to a segment with an external transceiver, make sure you disable the SQE test on the transceiver.

- Both ends of the segment's backbone must be terminated with a 50 Ω terminator and one end must be connected to a suitable ground.

Once you have installed your cabling, network interface cards, and transceivers, your LAN will look something like the one shown in Figure 2.9.

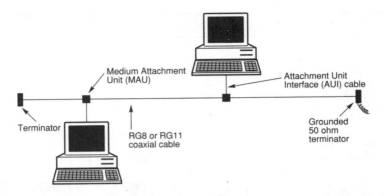

Fig. 2.9 Physical layout of a 10Base5 network.

10BaseT Ethernet

Several years after 10Base2 and 10Base5 hit the market, users were looking for more flexibility in Ethernet LANs. To meet these requirements, a new version of Ethernet, called 10BaseT, was introduced. Unlike the initial versions of Ethernet that relied on the bus topology, 10BaseT makes use of the star topology while still keeping with the CSMA/CD protocol operating at 10Mbps.

Components Required for a Standard 10BaseT Installation

There are few differences between the hardware used for 10BaseT and the older versions of Ethernet. Instead of using coaxial cable, 10BaseT uses UTP, which is lighter and cheaper.

Next, you need a hub or concentrator. Since 10BaseT operates as a star topology, a hub (or concentrator) is required to act as the LAN's wiring center.

One of the benefits to using 10BaseT is that it is a flexible network architecture. If you are upgrading from 10Base2 or 10Base5, you can integrate your current cabling and network interface cards. With 10BaseT, you can either upgrade your cards, or use your existing IEEE 802.3 NICs as long as you purchase a 10BaseT transceiver for each one. The 10BaseT transceiver converts the electrical signals from the DB-9 (DIX) connector to 10BaseT's UTP cabling.

Unlike 10Base2 and 10Base5, 10BaseT does not require any terminators to be installed along the cabling.

Restrictions when Installing 10BaseT

As with the other flavors of Ethernet, it is important to keep a watchful eye on the nodes of your network and cable lengths. Table 2.4 notes the most important restrictions.

Table 2.4 Physical limitations of the 10BaseT network.	
Restriction	**Value**
Maximum workstation to concentrator length	100 meters
Maximum nodes per segment	512
Maximum concentrators in sequence	4
Maximum node separation	5 segments/4 repeaters

Aside from these restrictions, the only other thing to remember is that if you connect a repeater to a transceiver, the transceiver's SQE test must be disabled.

Installing 10BaseT

One of 10BaseT's key selling points is that it is easy to install. Each node can be wired directly to the hub or concentrator using UTP cabling with RJ-45 connectors.

> **Note**
>
> If you are not using cards specifically designed for 10BaseT, your wiring will be slightly different. In these cases, the node is first wired into a 10BaseT transceiver which is then connected to a port on the hub or concentrator.

Once your hubs have been installed, and the workstations have been connected to one of their ports, your LAN should look something like the one shown in Figure 2.10.

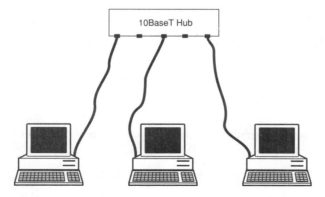

Fig. 2.10 Physical layout of a 10BaseT network.

Token Ring

Initially developed by IBM, Token Ring is a 4 or 16Mbps architecture wired as a star topology, but operates electrically as a ring. Using a central wiring center known as a Multi Station Access Unit (MSAU), Token Ring has nodes connected to the MSAU where internal circuitry creates the actual ring. While slight modifications were made (such as the maximum number of supported nodes), the IEEE has included Token Ring in its 802 series of standards within the 802.5 workgroup.

Components Required for a Standard Token Ring Installation

With Token Ring, you have two primary cabling options: shielded twisted pair (STP) or unshielded twisted pair (UTP). STP cable uses UDC connectors (also referred to as IBM data connectors), while UTP uses RJ-45 connectors (see fig. 2.11).

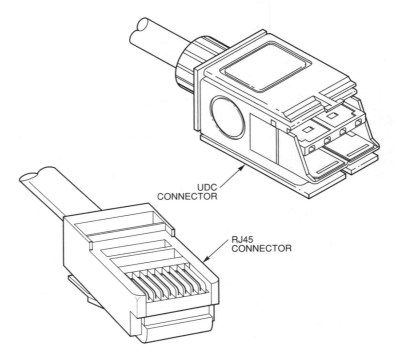

Fig. 2.11 UDC and RJ-45 connectors.

Next, you require a network interface card for every node attached to the LAN. Token Ring cards are not as readily available as Ethernet or ARCnet cards, and they cost more, so be prepared.

Now, you need an MSAU or Token Ring hub. There is a wide variety of products on the market, ranging from "dumb" MSAUs (such as IBM's Model 8228) and newer, "intelligent" MSAUs or hubs. Unless money is really tight, look into the intelligent MSAUs or hubs. These systems offer varying levels of diagnostic capabilities that can be a real asset when troubleshooting problems on your LAN.

Finally, when using multiple MSAUs, you need some Token Ring patch cables. These cables connect multiple MSAUs together to form one larger ring.

Restrictions when Installing Token Ring

As with any architecture, you must consider some guidelines regarding cable lengths and the maximum number of nodes. Table 2.5 shows the variables you should be aware of about the standard Token Ring LAN.

Table 2.5 Physical specifications for Token Ring.	
Restriction	**Value**
Maximum number of nodes	96
Maximum number of MSAUs	12
Maximum patch cable distance between two MSAUs	150 feet
Maximum patch cable distance connecting all MSAUs	400 feet
Maximum distance between MSAU and node	150 feet

Installing Token Ring

Token Ring is one of the more expensive LAN architectures on the market. Even though it offers improved diagnostic facilities and performance over systems such as Ethernet or ARCnet, many users shy away from it solely due to its cost. In most cases, the power of Token Ring is reserved for larger LANs and internetworks (a series of LANs interconnected to form one large network).

When installing Token Ring, many users choose to run STP cabling that contains several pairs of wires. By doing so, an installer can run one cable per station that is usable for both Token Ring communications and the user's phone, thus reducing the amount of work required and the cost of an additional cable for the phones.

Providing instructions on implementing a large scale Token Ring LAN is beyond the scope of this book, but knowing the basics is not.

To illustrate a small installation, let's assume we are setting up a LAN with nine workstations and one file server. Once the cabling has been pulled to each of the workstations and the file server, it then must be connected together in some fashion. Since Token Ring is physically wired as a star, this is where MSAUs come in. An MSAU uses its internal circuitry to form the actual ring. Confused? Don't worry, it gets easier.

The first thing to consider is that the standard MSAU has 10 ports on it. Eight of them are used for node connections and the other two are called the Ring-In (RI) and the Ring-Out (RO) ports. We'll get to these in a minute.

Because we must install 10 stations in all, assume we will be using two MSAUs. The first eight stations are wired to MSAU #1 and the other two are wired to MSAU #2.

> **Note**
>
> When you first install your MSAUs, you must initialize each of the ports using an initialization tool (if they are unpowered). This tool is a small gadget that plugs into each of the ports and emits a small electrical current. This current resets the relay inside the MSAU port. When you hear a click from the port, you know the relay has been reset.

Now that the stations have been connected to the MSAUs, we must link the two MSAUs together in some fashion. By running a cable from the Ring-In port of MSAU #1 to the Ring-Out port of MSAU #2 and running a second cable from the Ring-Out port of MSA #1 to the Ring-In port of MSAU #2, we have finished creating the logical ring. Figure 2.12 shows you what we just did.

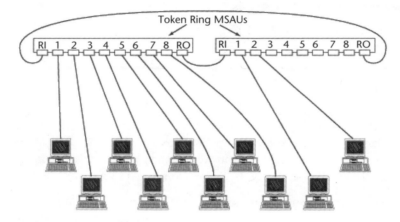

Fig. 2.12 The basic Token Ring network.

Cabling

Assuming you aren't running a wireless system, the cabling is one of the most important parts of any network. Cabling for your network is as important as tires on your car, for just as the tires on your car carry you from place to place, the cabling carries your data from place to place.

Depending on the network architecture or topology you use, your cabling options may be restricted. Therefore, you must choose with care the perfect blend of architecture, topology, and cabling to ensure they are all compatible.

> **Caution**
>
> Always make sure the type and classification of cabling you choose are 100 percent compatible with your network. Using the wrong type of cable can result in a completely unusable network, or one that suffers from intermittent problems. Cabling can be the toughest point in the network to troubleshoot.

There are three main types of cabling you may use in your network: coaxial, twisted pair, and fiber-optic. Each of these varieties is discussed in the following section, along with detailed information on finer points such as the different certified versions and some of their electrical characteristics.

Coaxial Cable

Coaxial cabling (also called *coax*) was the cabling of choice for the first network architectures. While Token Ring has always relied on twisted pair cables, architectures like ARCnet and Ethernet started off with coaxial, and to this day still have specifications that call for it.

The coaxial cable is made up of four parts. At the center of the cable is a stiff copper conductor that acts as the medium for the data being sent from node to node. Surrounding the core, a thick layer of plastic is used as insulation and to protect the cable from breaking. The third layer is a type of wire mesh protecting the electrical signals from being distorted by electrical interference. Finally, the whole cable is surrounded by a durable layer of plastic or PVC that keeps everything in a tight bundle and protects the cable from wear and tear—cuts, nicks, and so on. If you strip off the layers, the coaxial cable would look something like the one shown in Figure 2.13.

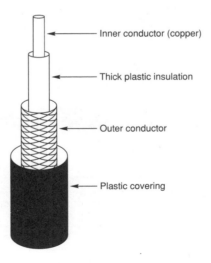

Inner conductor (copper)

Thick plastic insulation

Outer conductor

Plastic covering

Fig. 2.13 The coaxial cable.

Things to Know Before Choosing Coaxial Cable

While coaxial cable is durable and long lasting, it is important to know it is susceptible to electro-magnetic interference (EMI). EMI is generated by heavy machinery, fluorescent lighting, and various types of office equipment such as photocopiers. When running your cabling, it is best to avoid placing the cable too close to any of these potential hot spots.

Another area for concern is the cost associated with coaxial. For the small- to medium-sized net-work, the overall cost involved with using coaxial may not be much of an issue. But for larger networks, the cost of running coaxial to each station may be too steep. Compared to twisted-pair cabling, coaxial can run you almost twice as much per foot. Buy in bulk when you can to save money.

One final problem you should consider before choosing coaxial cabling is its weight. Compared to twisted-pair cabling, coaxial cabling is heavy and a lot bulkier. Depending on your specific application, this may affect your decision.

Even with these drawbacks to coaxial cabling, one thing in its favor is that it is readily available. Since coaxial is used for a wide variety of applications, even smaller electronics stores often carry it in bulk.

Types of Coaxial Cable You Can Use

Earlier, you read about the importance of making sure you choose the right cabling for the job. Unfortunately, it's not as easy as just saying that you will use coaxial. There are several varieties of coaxial cabling, each with differing electrical characteristics. Luckily, instead of having to know detailed information such as the cable's impedance, all you need to know is the "type" of coaxial to use.

Table 2.6 shows the different types of coaxial, the typical application, and the type of terminator you need when using this cabling. Make sure you pick the proper one when designing your net-work. A few of these coaxial types look almost identical, yet their electrical specifications differ.

Table 2.6 Types of coaxial cable.		
Cable Type	**Architecture**	**Terminator**
RG-8	10Base5	50 Ω
RG-11	10Base5	50 Ω
RG-58A/U	10Base2	50 Ω
RG-59/U	CATV	75 Ω
RG-62/U	ARCnet	93 Ω

> **Tip**
>
> If you don't know what type of cable you have, examine the writing on the cable's outer sheath. The manufacturer's name, a part number, and the cable type usually are imprinted every few feet.

Installing Coaxial Cabling

Installing coaxial cabling requires a certain degree of skill, but overall it is a fairly simple task. Once you have your cable, you must determine whether to use a crimp-on or a screw-on BNC connector, as shown in Figure 2.14. Both are within the same price range, but the screw-on cables are a little easier to put on and require fewer tools.

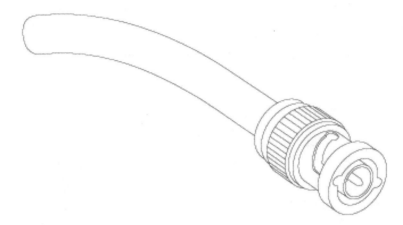

Fig. 2.14 Screw-on and crimp-on BNC connectors for coaxial cabling.

Following are the basic steps to installing your coaxial cable. The only tools you really need are something to cut the cable, a cable stripper to remove the sheath, and a crimper (if using crimp-on connectors).

1. Run the raw cabling from point to point.

> **Tip**
>
> It is always best to run the length of cabling between the two nodes before attaching any connectors or cutting the cabling. This way, you are assured you won't fall too short or too long. Falling short means having to run a whole new stretch of cable (which gets expensive) and if the cable is too long, you have to cut it back, thus wasting cable and forcing you to reattach connectors.

2. Strip the ends of the cabling. When stripping the coaxial cabling, be very careful, because stripping too much results in unreliable cable. Many of the crimpers on the market have details about the amount to strip directly on their handles!

3. Place the BNC connector on the end of the cable and make sure there is a good, tight fit.

> **Caution**
>
> It is extremely important to have a good solid connection between the cable's inner conductor and the BNC connector. A loose connection will result in intermittent network problems.

4. Once a solid connection has been established, twist or crimp the connector into place.

> **Caution**
>
> If you are using crimp-on connectors, be sure you do not crimp them too tightly. While each connection should be snug and secure, a connector that has been crimped too hard might cut into the inner conductor and result in intermittent network errors.

Twisted-Pair

Twisted-pair (TP) cabling is probably the most widely used cabling for network applications. Unfortunately, while TP may be widely used, it can be a bit confusing when determining what type you should use for your network architecture.

As discussed earlier, there are two general classifications for TP, unshielded twisted-pair (UTP) (see fig. 2.15), and shielded twisted-pair (STP) (see fig. 2.16). Both types are made up of one or more pairs of wire twisted a certain number of times per foot (the value changes depending on the cable) contained within a plastic or PVC sheath to protect the cable from nicks and cuts. The key physical difference between the two is that the STP cable has a layer of shielding wrapped around the pairs beneath the outer sheath, to provide additional protection from external influences such as EMI.

Fig. 2.15 Unshielded twisted-pair cable.

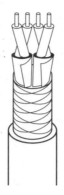

Fig. 2.16 Shielded twisted-pair cable.

Things to Know Before Choosing Twisted-Pair

Like anything, there are pros and cons when making a decision about using twisted-pair cabling. Overall, the cable is durable, light, and fairly inexpensive. The main problem you must consider is that twisted-pair is very susceptible to the effects of EMI. With this in mind, you should assess your proposed installation site for potential sources of EMI. As with coaxial cabling, you should avoid placing twisted-pair cable anywhere near these sources.

If there is an excessive amount of EMI at your site, you should stick with STP. Versus UTP, STP offers improved protection against EMI.

Another issue to consider is the proposed size of your network. STP can support a greater number of users and greater distances than UTP. The actual numbers regarding maximum users and distances vary between architectures.

Types of Twisted-Pair You Can Use

Coaxial cabling makes life a little easier by only having five varieties with which you must concern yourself. With twisted-pair, you have two general varieties (STP and UTP) and then several classifications for each.

Due to TP's widespread use, standards are required to ensure electrical specifications of the cabling match those required by the architecture. With TP, there are three main bodies that certify and standardize TP cabling: Underwriters Laboratories, EIA/TIA, and IBM.

Underwriters Laboratories (UL). Aside from UL's work with certifying cabling for safety standards, the organization also provides performance certifications of TP cabling. Using a test called the Data Transmission Performance Level Marking test, the laboratory classifies TP within one of five groups called "levels." Cable classified within this program can be used for applications such as voice or data transmission.

- *Level 1:* Intended for voice transmissions and not suitable for data. At this level, there are no set performance requirements.

- *Level 2:* Can be used for voice transmissions or data transmissions up to 1Mbps. Because current network architectures range in speeds from 2.5Mbps to 20Mbps, Level 2 cable should not be used in a network.

- *Level 3:* Intended for voice or data transmission up to 10Mbps. Typically used for 10BaseT networks, Level 3 cable is tested up to 16 MHz.

- *Level 4:* For 16Mbps Token Ring networks or large Ethernet 10BaseT LANs. Tested up to 20 MHz, it is comparable to Category 4 cabling certified by the EIA/TIA.

- *Level 5:* Tested up to 100 MHz and intended for use in high-speed networks operating up to 100Mbps, such as CDDI, TCNS, or the 100Mbps Ethernet proposals.

EIA/TIA. The Electrical Industries Association and ANSI published a report in 1991 called EIA/TIA-568. This report certified cabling within five groups known as "categories" covering both voice- and data communications-grade cable. Each category in the report is downwardly compatible. For example, an installation requiring Category 3 wiring could also use Category 4 or 5 cable.

- *Category 1:* Low-speed data and voice.

- *Category 2:* Low-speed data and voice.

- *Category 3:* Used for voice or data communications. Tested up to 16 MHz, this cable usually is used for 10BaseT or 4Mbps Token Ring.

- *Category 4:* Tested up to 20 MHz, this cable is for voice communications or 16Mbps Token Ring.

- *Category 5:* For 16 Mbps Token Ring or FDDI over UTP, this cable is tested up to 100 MHz and also can be used for voice communications.

IBM's Twisted-Pair Standards. IBM's specifications are the only ones geared toward a specific architecture. When Token Ring was introduced into the marketplace, IBM felt there was a need for a certification program to ensure the cabling being used was up to par for Token Ring's requirements. With this in mind, IBM came out with a cable certification program for its Token Ring environment. Aside from one exception, IBM's specifications are for shielded and unshielded twisted-pair cabling.

- *Type 1:* For use in networks up to 16Mbps with a maximum of 260 nodes. This shielded cable contains four wires (two pairs) of 22 AWG (American Wire Gauge) cable.

- *Type 2:* For use in networks up to 16Mbps. Contains 12 wires, two shielded pairs of 22 AWG plus four pairs of 26 AWG cable between the insulating sheath and shield.

- *Type 3:* For transmission up to 4Mbps when a media filter is used, with a maximum of 72 nodes. Intended as a voice grade telephone cable, this unshielded cable contains four pairs of 24 AWG wire.

- Type 4: No published specifications.

- *Type 5:* A fiber-optic cable (100/140 microns).

- *Type 6:* Used in patch cables to connect ports on the MSAU. This shielded cabling contains two pairs of 26 AWG cable.

- Type 7: No published specifications.

- *Type 8:* A flat cable (no twists) with two parallel pairs of 26 AWG wire intended for use under carpeting.

- *Type 9:* Shielded cabling intended for use in building plenums (the area in between the ceiling and the floor above used for air conduits, piping, and cables).

Installing Twisted-Pair Cabling

Installing twisted-pair cabling is a little more complex than installing coaxial. There are different types of connectors—RJ-11 and RJ-45, as shown in Figure 2.17—that must be taken into account and depending on the category, level, or type you choose, there are varying numbers of pairs. Unfortunately, detailed information on cabling pinouts is out of the scope of this book, but you may want to check your local bookstore or vendor for any literature on wiring.

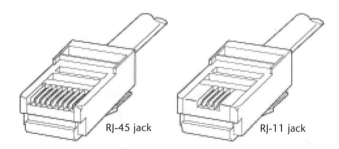

RJ-45 jack   RJ-11 jack

Fig. 2.17 RJ-11 and RJ-45 unshielded twisted-pair connectors.

Fiber-Optic Cable

The newest type of cabling to enter the network arena is fiber-optic cable (see fig. 2.18). Made of a glass or plastic core, fiber-optic cable uses pulses of light rather than electricity to transmit data. Surrounding the inner core a thick layer of *cladding* is used to reflect the pulses of light down the cabling. Although fiber-optic cabling is expensive, it offers increased security (to tap into the network, someone must actually cut the cable) and problems are minimized due to its immunity to EMI and other outside interference.

During installation, extreme care must be taken if you are cutting your own cable lengths. Precision tools designed specifically for this type of cable must be used. If you have never worked with fiber-optics before, you would be wise to consult a professional in this field. Because both the cable and the required tools are so expensive, learning by trial and error can put a huge dent in your pocketbook.

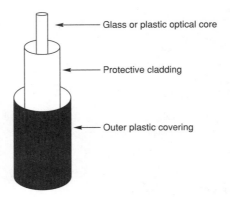

Glass or plastic optical core

Protective cladding

Outer plastic covering

Fig. 2.18 Fiber-optic cable.

Conclusion: Advice for the Do-It-Yourselfer

There are all types of do-it-yourselfers in the world. Some like doing things on their own to learn more about what they are working with. When they're stuck, they seek out more experienced people for assistance.

Then, there are those who try to do everything on their own without asking for advice. Unfortunately, this philosophy and networking do not mix well.

Designing and building the platform of any LAN is an involved task requiring much patience and planning. A LAN that has been designed without these factors will not perform as it should.

In this chapter, the main networking architectures, cabling, and topologies were discussed. While instructions and tips were given regarding the installation and configuration of your network's platform, depending on the proposed size of your LAN, there is a great deal more to know. When in doubt, ask. There are many qualified LAN and cabling specialists around who would be happy to help you out. And, remember that designing a small LAN is one thing, but a big LAN—well, that's a whole different ball game.

Chapter 3

Installing NetWare on the File Server

Novell has made the NetWare installation process easier with each new release. In previous versions, the installation was a prolonged process that was tedious if nothing else. In NetWare 3.12, Novell has taken most of the "grunt" work and made it the responsibility of the installation program, where it belongs!

Even though the process of installing NetWare has become far easier with recent versions, the method you use will vary depending on your environment. While it is not possible to cover every type of installation, this section discusses:

- Preparing the file server for NetWare

- Selecting an installation method

- Installing NetWare using CD-ROM and diskette

- Basic configuration procedures for the server

Pre-Installation Setup

Before you install the NetWare operating system, you must weigh your options regarding the initial configuration and the steps you follow to complete the installation. Primarily, there are three questions you must ask yourself:

- How will the hardware be set up?

- Will I use a DOS partition on the server hard disk or will I use a floppy boot diskette?

- From where will I be installing NetWare?

File Server Hardware

Before setting up the file server hardware, there are a few NetWare requirements of which you should be aware. If you have already purchased your server hardware, make sure you can meet these requirements; otherwise, you may want to consider upgrading your components. The file server hardware should:

- Be a 386 or 486 with an SX or DX processor.

- Have at least a 50M hard disk installed.

- Have a minimum of 4M of RAM. This minimum will change, depending on several variables (refer to the following heading, "Memory Requirements").

- Have at least one Network Interface Card (NIC).

While detailed instructions for installing your hardware are beyond the scope of this book, there are three key areas we can address to some degree: Memory Requirements, Disk Configuration, and Network Interface Cards. For information on installing the server's NIC, refer to the heading "The Workstation's Network Interface Card," in Chapter 4, "Installing Workstations."

Memory Requirements

When calculating the amount of memory required in the file server, there are several considerations that must be taken into account, such as how much disk space will be installed and if you will be supporting multiple name spaces. To determine the minimum amount of memory you need, follow these guidelines:

1. The server should have a minimum of 4M of RAM.

2. Add 2M if you are running the print server on the file server (PSERVER.NLM).

3. Add 2M if you are running BTRIEVE.NLM, STREAMS.NLM, or CLIB.NLM.

4. Add 2M for each additional NetWare product on the server—such as NetWare for Mac.

5. Multiply the total system disk space (in M) by .008 and add this amount—for example, 1Gig Drive x .008 = 8M of RAM.

6. Add a minimum of 1M, preferably 4M or more, of RAM for caching.

When the file server is up and running, you can use the MONITOR.NLM utility to see how the memory is being used. Depending on whom you speak to, the available cache buffers should be between 60 percent and 80 percent, but the exact value in this range is more or less a judgment call. If the server is operating with 65 percent cache buffers and it is performing fairly well, don't worry. Ideally though, try keeping the cache buffers at a minimum of 70 percent. Chapter 23, "The MONITOR Console Management Utility," discusses the MONITOR.NLM utility and the different types of memory pools in more detail.

Installing Disk Drives

NetWare enables you to protect your data by using one of two features: *disk mirroring* or *disk duplexing*. With disk mirroring, a single hard drive controller is used with drives installed as pairs. Data stored on the file server will be maintained on both disk drives. If one drive fails, the server continues to function by using the second drive until you replace the faulty drive.

Disk duplexing is an enhancement to mirroring. While in theory the two operate in a similar manner, disk duplexing makes use of two hard drive controllers instead of one. Where the drive pairs were installed on the same controller when mirrored, duplexed drives are installed on opposite controllers. For example, assume there are two controllers we will call Controller A and Controller B, and two hard disks called Disk A and Disk B. When duplexing, you would install Disk A on Controller A and Disk B on Controller B. Should any single drive or controller fail, the server will continue to function.

Using a DOS Partition on the Server

With your NetWare installation, you can run the server with or without a DOS boot partition. While using a DOS partition on the server reduces the overall space available to NetWare, there are several benefits for having one:

■ Booting the file server is much faster when the boot files are stored on the hard drive as opposed to using a floppy disk.

■ Floppy disks are more prone to failure than hard drives and they can be lost.

■ Floppy disks hold considerably less than hard drives. You can allocate sufficient space to the DOS partition on the hard drive for diagnostic tools in preparation for hardware problems.

■ If enough space is allocated to the DOS partition, it can be used as a storage area for debug information should the server ever have an abend error. When there is no DOS partition, dumping debug data to floppy disks can take a considerable amount of time and requires numerous diskettes.

Hopefully, based on the points above, you have decided to use a DOS partition on the server's hard disk. Creating the actual partition requires a minimal amount of work on your part. The basic steps are as follows:

1. Boot the soon-to-be NetWare server with a DOS system diskette.

2. Using the FDISK DOS utility, create a DOS partition of at least 5M on the server.

3. Within FDISK, flag the partition as Active. This means the server can boot from this partition.

4. After exiting FDISK, the server reboots. Keep the DOS system disk in the floppy drive and when the DOS prompt comes up, format your new partition using the FORMAT utility with

the /S option to copy DOS system files (for instance, type **FORMAT C:\ /S**). Once the formatting is complete, you can remove the diskette and, after rebooting the server, the c:\ prompt should appear.

Tip

While 5M is the minimum partition size that should be used, consider increasing this minimum to be 5M + 1M for every M of RAM installed in the server + 2M. For example, if your server has 48M of RAM, create a 55M DOS partition. This gives you 5M for the basic NetWare files, 2M for any extra files you want to place on there, and 48M of free space available to perform a dump of DEBUG information if your server crashes.

Using a Boot Diskette

If you decide to use a floppy boot disk instead, you need to create a DOS boot diskette and manually copy at least the following files to the diskette:

- SERVER.EXE

- INSTALL.NLM

- *.NAM; the boot disk must contain the name space files for any additional name spaces on the server, such as MAC.NAM

- ????????.DSK; where ???????? is the name of your disk driver. If you bought NetWare on diskette, you can find the disk drivers on the SYSTEM_2 diskette, but if you bought NetWare on CD-ROM, you can copy the appropriate driver from the directory \NetWare.312_____\DISKDRV

After you have created the boot diskette, you then can boot the soon-to-be NetWare server using this diskette. When the A:\DOS> prompt appears, type **SERVER** to run the SERVER.EXE program. NetWare then starts to load.

If you are following this book to do your installation, and you are booting the server from a floppy diskette, you should skip ahead to the heading "Installing Your NetWare Operating System—Phase 2," as the Phase 1 section will not apply to you.

Note

Before you can proceed to Phase 2, NetWare requires you to enter the file server's name and IPX internal network address. Refer to these specific sections in the Phase 1 instructions that follow for information about picking a server name and IPX internal network address.

Determining From Where to Install

The final aspect you need to determine is where you are going to install the server from. Depending on your environment, and the package you purchased—CD or diskette—there are three options:

- Install from Diskette

- Install from CD-ROM

- Install from Another Server

Installing from Diskette

Installing NetWare from diskettes takes longer than the other methods, but it is the easiest to prepare. To start the installation procedure from diskette, you first can boot the server with DOS, then insert the diskette labeled INSTALL, and run the batch file INSTALL.BAT.

Installing from CD-ROM

If you are installing from a CD-ROM, besides having a CD-ROM device on your server, you need the NetWare CD-ROM and the SYSTEM_1 floppy diskette. To start the installation from CD-ROM, insert the CD into the drive, make the CD-ROM drive your default drive (if the CD-ROM is assigned to drive E:, type **E:** from the DOS prompt), change directories to NETWARE.312\ENGLISH, and run the batch file INSTALL.BAT.

Installing from Another Server

Instead of using diskettes or a CD-ROM drive to install your new NetWare server, you can install NetWare from another file server on your network. There are a few benefits to installing NetWare from another server:

- If you purchased NetWare on CD-ROM, you can copy the CD-ROM to another server from a workstation on the network that has a CD-ROM drive; therefore, you will not require a CD-ROM in the new server.

- If you purchased NetWare on diskette and are installing multiple servers, you won't have to switch diskettes for every install.

Before you can proceed, you must first copy your NetWare disks or CD-ROM to the server that will be the source for your installation. The following steps will get you set up:

1. Log in to the source file server from a workstation on the network. If you bought NetWare on CD-ROM, log in from a workstation that has a CD-ROM device.

2. Once you are logged in, make the F: drive your default.

3. Make a directory called NWINSTAL by typing **MD NWINSTAL**. You can call this directory anything you want.

4. If you bought NetWare on CD-ROM, type **XCOPY** *drive:****.* F:\NWINSTAL /S /E /V**. Replace *drive:* with the drive letter assigned to the CD-ROM device.

5. If you bought NetWare on diskette, you must first make a subdirectory within NWINSTAL based on the DOS label of each diskette except the SYSTEM_1 disk. For example, if you insert a diskette in the drive and run a directory on the disk, it may tell you the disk is labeled SYSTEM_2. Therefore, beneath the NWINSTAL directory, make a subdirectory called SYSTEM_2. Then, copy the contents of each diskette into the appropriate subdirectory.

Once you have completed the steps above, you can start the installation process by:

1. Logging into the source file server from the soon-to-be NetWare server.

2. From the F:\NWINSTAL\NETWARE.312\ENGLISH directory, typing **INSTALL** to run the batch file INSTALL.BAT.

Installing NetWare on the Server—Phase 1

The first portion of the installation procedure is initiated by using a batch file called INSTALL.BAT. If you are not sure how to start the INSTALL.BAT file, refer to the previous section, "Determining From Where to Install," for detailed instructions. If you already have loaded INSTALL.BAT, your initial screen should be like the one shown in Figure 3.1.

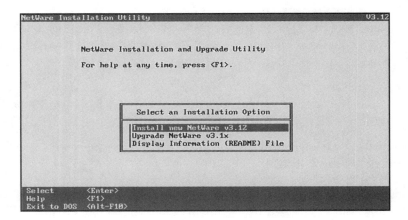

Fig. 3.1 The INSTALL.BAT main menu screen.

Within the initial screen, three options are presented to you: Install new NetWare v3.12, Upgrade NetWare v3.1x, and Display Information (README) File. If this is your first time installing NetWare, you should take the time to read the README files. These files contain some recent information regarding any installation quirks you should know about and some other basic information on installation.

Depending on your specific installation, upgrading your file servers from previous versions of NetWare can be a fairly in-depth procedure that is beyond the scope of this book. Refer to the installation and upgrade instructions that accompany your NetWare software for detailed information.

Creating a Disk Partition

After you select Install new NetWare v3.12 from the main menu of INSTALL.BAT, you are presented with an option to create a new disk partition or maintain your current disk partitions on the server. If you have been following the installation instructions from the beginning, you may already have a DOS partition on your server. In this case, you should select Retain current disk partitions from the Disk Partition Options menu (see fig. 3.2).

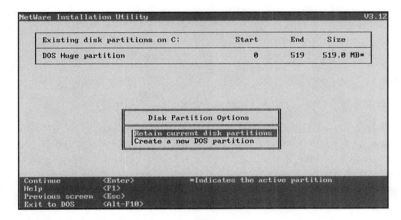

Fig. 3.2 Choosing between using the current disk partitions or creating a new disk partition.

If you did not create a DOS partition on the server, and you want to do so, select Create a new DOS partition from the Disk Partition Options menu.

Caution
Choosing the second option to create a new DOS partition deletes any data currently stored on the hard disk. Be absolutely sure this is what you want to do before you proceed.

Selecting a File Server Name

Before selecting a name for your file server, consider setting some sort of standard naming convention. Depending on your organization, there could be only one server, or there could be 100. Using a standard naming convention makes it easier to determine what the server is actually used for and by whom. For example, if you are naming a server to be used by the accounting department on the fourth floor of your Toronto office, you could call the server

FS-TOR4-ACCOUNTING; where FS stands for File Server, TOR4 stands for Toronto, fourth floor, and ACCOUNTING is the name of the department.

Whatever naming convention you select, the server name must be between 2 and 47 characters and cannot include any of the following characters:

" * [ ] < > ? . = ; : + , / | \

Setting the IPX Internal Network Number

Every NetWare 3.12 server on your LAN/network must have a unique internal IPX network number. As shown in Figure 3.3, the NetWare install program randomly generates one that includes alphanumeric characters for you. At this point, you can either accept the value that INSTALL generated, or you can type in your own. If you select your own IPX internal network number, follow these guidelines:

- The IPX internal network number must contain one to eight characters

- You can use any number between 0 and 9 or any character between A and F

- The IPX internal network number must *not* be equal to 0 or FFFFFFFF

- The IPX internal network number must *not* be equal to the IPX internal network number of another file server

- The IPX internal network number must *not* be equal to the physical network number used by any connected network

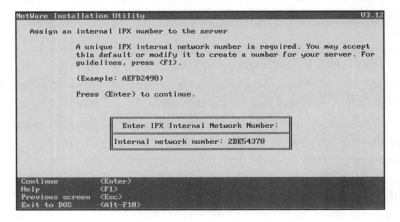

Fig. 3.3 NetWare installation—Generating the IPX internal network number.

> **Tip**
>
> By creating your own numbering scheme, you can have more control over your LAN/WAN and at the same time, make network management easier. For example, IPX internal network addresses starting with AAAAA could be for servers in one building while addresses starting with BBBBB could be in another. Just make sure that, overall, each address is unique.

Copying the Server Boot Files to the DOS Partition

The next step is to install the file server's boot files to a DOS partition on the file server. As shown in Figure 3.4, the INSTALL program presents you with two boxes, one for the Source path, and the other for the Destination path. By default, INSTALL wants to copy the boot files to a directory called C:\SERVER.312; if this directory does not exist, INSTALL creates it.

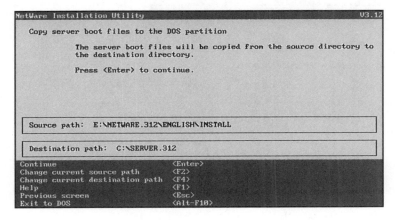

Fig. 3.4 NetWare installation—Selecting the directory to install the boot files.

If the values shown in these boxes are acceptable, press the Enter key to continue. Otherwise, you can change them to suit your specific requirements.

> **Note**
>
> Unless you have some particular reason for not using the default parameters, accept them as shown. Where possible, it is best to stick with the system defaults.

Once you press Enter, INSTALL asks you to insert the SYSTEM-1 diskette into the A: drive.

Caution

Make sure you have not used the same SYSTEM-1 diskette for any other file server on your LAN/WAN. Serialization information is stored on this diskette and if you *do* use it, the file server broadcasts copyright violation messages across the network.

Selecting the File Server Locale

After the boot files are installed, INSTALL asks you some questions regarding the file server's "locale." As shown in Figure 3.5, you are presented with three options: Country Code, Code Page, and Keyboard Mapping. If these values are not acceptable, you can select each one and scan through the listing of what is available.

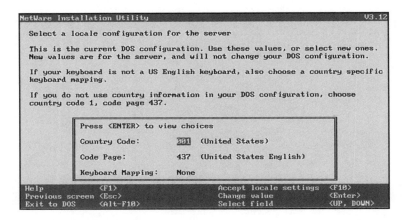

Fig. 3.5 NetWare installation—Selecting the file server's locale.

Note

Until this point, INSTALL asked you to use the Enter key to continue. On this screen, however, the continue key has been switched to F10.

Selecting a File Name Format

In previous versions of NetWare, it was possible to create files using certain characters that were not acceptable by DOS. On this screen (see fig. 3.6), INSTALL asks you if you want to use the DOS file format or the NetWare file format. Unless you are upgrading a file server that has files stored with the characters that are unacceptable to DOS, you should stick with the default option: DOS Filename Format.

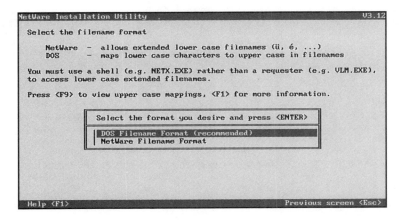

Fig. 3.6 NetWare installation—Selecting the filename format to be used on the server.

Specifying Special Commands for the STARTUP.NCF

Next, the INSTALL.BAT program asks you to specify if you want to include any special commands in the STARTUP.NCF file. The STARTUP.NCF file runs when the server is first booted and contains information such as the load commands for your disk controllers and several other settings. For a complete listing of these settings, please refer to the heading "SET" in Chapter 22, "Console Commands."

> **Note**
>
> It is not mandatory to enter anything at this point, as the STARTUP.NCF file can easily be changed later.

Running the File Server Automatically

The last step in the INSTALL.BAT program is to specify if you want the server's AUTOEXEC.BAT file to be edited to automatically run the SERVER.EXE program. If you want the server to automatically boot when the server is turned on, select Yes; otherwise, select No.

Whether you select Yes or No, INSTALL.BAT then loads the SERVER.EXE program. SERVER.EXE is the NetWare operating system program loaded to start your file server. Once SERVER.EXE has finished loading, you then are presented with the file server console prompt SERVERNAME:, where servername is the name specified at the beginning of the INSTALL.BAT program.

> **Tip**
>
> If you are not prepared to continue installing the NetWare file server, you can type **DOWN** at the console prompt to shut down the server. The server will then initiate the shutdown process. Once completed, you then can type **EXIT** to go back to DOS.

Caution

If you want to shut down the file server, *never* just turn it off as problems will arise with the files on your hard disk. *Always* use the DOWN command.

If you shut down the server at this point, you can restart the installation procedure later from where you left off. To do so, from the DOS prompt, change directories to where the boot files were installed—the directory name and location were specified earlier in the INSTALL.BAT process—and then type **SERVER**. The NetWare operating system then loads and you are presented with *two* mandatory prompts:

```
FILE SERVER NAME:
IPX INTERNAL NET:
```

Either type in the same values you specified in the INSTALL.BAT procedure, or select new ones; just make sure you still comply with the rules specified earlier regarding the server naming and IPX numbering.

Installing NetWare on the Server—Phase 2

The final phase to get your NetWare server up and running involves configuring the hard drives, loading the NetWare utilities, and loading any necessary NLMs. While each of the steps is discussed in the following sections, listed below is a brief rundown of what is required to complete the installation:

- Create the NetWare partition(s)
- Configure disk mirroring/duplexing if required
- Create one or more volumes
- Copy the NetWare utilities onto the server
- Load any necessary NLMs or drivers (such as NIC drivers)
- Create and configure your boot files, STARTUP.NCF and AUTOEXEC.NCF
- Reboot the file server

Activating the File Server's Hard Disks

Before you can install the NetWare utilities or create a NetWare partition, you must inform the operating system about the types of drives you are using. You tell the OS what disks you are using by loading a disk driver module.

Disk driver modules are included with your NetWare software and are placed in the boot directory during the initial installation procedure. You should scan through the listing of DSK files to find one that matches your hard drive controller. If there is nothing suitable, you should contact the manufacturer of your controller to see if it has a driver that is suitable for NetWare 3.12.

Caution

Some disk drivers that worked with NetWare 3.11 will *not* work with NetWare 3.12. If you are using a driver that was not supplied with your NetWare 3.12 software, consult the driver manufacturer to ensure it will work properly.

Once you know the name of the driver you will be using, you can load it from the server colon prompt by typing:

```
LOAD driver [parameter(s)]
```

Based on the syntax above, replace:

> *driver* with the name of the disk driver you are using. If the disk driver is not stored in the boot directory, you also must specify the full path leading to the driver.

> *parameter(s)* with one or more of the parameters found in Table 3.1. If you do not specify any of the parameters, NetWare prompts you for the ones it needs. In some cases, there may be additional parameters that are available with your specific driver. Consult the documentation that came with your disk controller for further information.

Table 3.1 Parameters used when loading the disk drivers.

Parameter	Example	Description
DMA=*number*	**LOAD AHA1540 DMA=5**	Specifies the disk controller's DMA setting.
INT=*interrupt*	**LOAD ISADISK INT=3**	Specifies the disk controller's interrupt setting.
MEM=*memory address*	**LOAD AHA1740 MEM=CC000**	Specifies the RAM and ROM addresses for the disk controller.
PORT=*I/O port*	**LOAD DCB PORT=330**	Specifies the I/O port address used by the disk controller.
SLOT=*slot #*	**LOAD DCB SLOT=3**	Specifies the slot in which the disk controller board is installed.

> **Note**
>
> You can use more than one parameter from the table above in the load command. For example, if you were using an AHA1740 disk controller in slot 5 of the computer using interrupt 11, you could load the driver by typing **LOAD AHA1740 SLOT=5 INT=11**.

> **Note**
>
> You must load a disk driver for each controller installed in your server. Even if the two controllers are the same, you must load the same driver a second time and specify the different configuration settings when asked.

Preparing the File Server's Disks

Before you can install any NetWare programs and utilities, you first must prepare the server's disks by using the INSTALL.NLM console utility. You access this utility by typing **LOAD INSTALL** from the file server's colon prompt.

Next, from the Installation Options main menu of INSTALL.NLM, select the first option, Disk Options. Once selected, you are presented with the Available Disk Options menu shown in Figure 3.7. The following sections provide you with detailed information on each of the available options and the tasks you can perform with them.

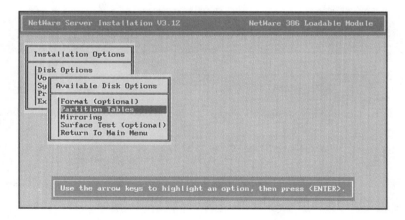

Fig. 3.7 INSTALL.NLM's Available Disk Options menu.

Formatting the Disk

The first option, Format (optional), is used to format the hard disk. Most drives today come preformatted and are ready for NetWare to use. Before you choose this option, first check the instructions that came with your disk drive. This option performs a low-level format that could destroy your disk, rendering it unusable.

If you decide to choose this option, NetWare shows you a listing of the available drives where you then must select the drive you want to format.

Caution

Formatting the disk deletes *all* the data on the hard disk. Make sure you are positive you do not need anything stored on this disk before proceeding.

The NetWare Partition—Creating, Deleting, and Changing

If you do not need to format the drives, your first step is to create a partition on the server's hard disk. To do so, select the Partition Tables option and you are presented with another window entitled Partition Options (see fig. 3.8).

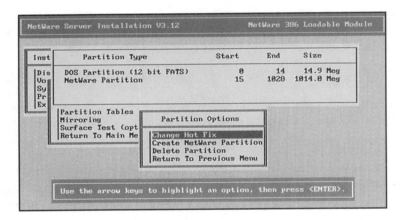

Fig. 3.8 The Partition Options screen of INSTALL.NLM used to create, delete, or modify the NetWare disk partition table.

Creating the Partition

To create the NetWare partition, select Create NetWare Partition from the Partition Options menu. At this point, you are presented with three options pertaining to this partition:

■ *Partition Size:* NetWare needs to know how big you want the partition. By default, the maximum available free space is selected, but you can manually change this value to change the size of the partition. Unless there is some reason why you do not want to use all the available space for the NetWare partition, stick with the default. The only way to change the size of the partition is to re-create it and you *cannot* have more than one NetWare partition per disk.

■ *Data Area:* The data area is the amount of space NetWare allocates for data storage within the NetWare partition. By default, this option is 98 percent of the NetWare partition size. Changing this value automatically adjusts the amount of space allocated in the redirection area.

■ *Redirection Area:* The redirection area is the amount of space allocated for Hot Fix. Hot Fix is a NetWare feature that automatically remaps bad blocks found in the data area. While the default value of 2 percent is more than sufficient for almost all implementations, if you decide to adjust this parameter, the data area will be reduced.

After setting these options, you can create the partition by pressing the Esc key. When asked if you want to create the partition, answer Yes. If you are not happy with the values you set, you can answer No and start over.

Changing Partition Information. While you cannot change the size of the NetWare partition on a disk, you can change how the space within the partition is allocated for data and Hot Fix by selecting the option Change Hot Fix from the Partition Options window. Once selected, INSTALL presents you with a window where you can modify the size of the data area (the amount of space available for data) and the redirection area (the amount of space allocated to Hot Fix). After making the desired changes, press Esc to return to the Partition Options window.

Caution
Any changes to the Hot Fix information require that you delete the NetWare volumes, thus losing all data stored on these volumes. Unless there is some critical reason for you to increase the Hot Fix size, don't.

Deleting a Partition. If the drive you are using is old, or if you made a mistake when creating the NetWare partition, you can delete a partition by selecting Delete Partition from the Partition Options window. INSTALL then presents you with a listing of the available partitions on the drive. By selecting one of these partitions, INSTALL will remove the partition from the disk.

Caution
Once a partition is removed, data stored on the partition will not be available. The only way to recover the data would be to restore it from the latest backup.

Mirroring Hard Disks

To mirror or duplex the hard drives in the file server, select Mirroring from the Available Disk Options menu. Once you select this option, you are presented with a screen entitled Partition Mirroring Status. Mirroring the drives is achieved by:

1. Selecting the first drive in the listing to be used as the primary drive in the mirrored pair. A window entitled Mirrored NetWare Partitions appears, showing the device you just selected (see fig. 3.9).

2. Pressing the Insert key and selecting the partition of the second disk to which you want to mirror the primary disk.

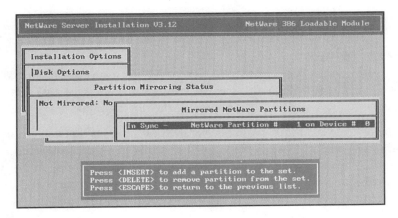

Fig. 3.9 Configuring disk mirroring/duplexing on the server.

When you first configure the mirroring, NetWare proceeds to duplicate the primary drive onto the secondary drive. Depending on the amount of data and the size of the drives, this can take several minutes to more than an hour.

Running a Surface Test

The fourth option on the Available Disk Options menu is called Surface Test. Previous versions of NetWare forced you to use a utility called COMPSURF that tested the hard drive for defects. While drives used in the earlier days of NetWare were prone to media defects, the architecture of modern drives has drastically reduced the number of potential problems, and therefore, the testing of the drive has become optional.

If you decide to run the surface test, NetWare asks you if you want to run a Destructive or a Non-Destructive test. If you choose a Destructive test, NetWare performs a read-write test for each block on the disk, destroying any data currently on the disk.

> **Note**
>
> Depending on the size of your hard drive, the surface test could take anywhere from a few minutes to several hours. Therefore, judge your time accordingly.

Tip
Most people do not run the surface test since modern drives are fairly reliable and the test can take some time to run, *but* defects are still possible, even with the most advanced drives. If this is a new server install and you are not pressed for time, you may want to run the surface test. It is better to isolate any potential drive problems now, instead of when the server has been running in a production environment for several weeks or months.

The NetWare Volumes

After a NetWare partition has been created, the next step is to create one or more volumes. NetWare enables you to span a single volume over as many as 32 physical disk drives. When spanning, you are using several disk drives to provide the single volume.

One of the key benefits to spanning a volume over multiple drives is that you can improve the performance of your server by enabling NetWare to search multiple drives when performing a read or write request. The following sections provide you with the information that you will need to create, delete, or modify your NetWare volumes. These tasks are achieved using the INSTALL.NLM utility. If INSTALL.NLM is not already loaded, you can load it by typing **LOAD INSTALL** from the file server prompt.

Caution
If you are creating a volume that spans more than one drive, seriously consider using disk duplexing or disk mirroring in your file server. Otherwise, if a single drive containing one of the volume's segments fails, the entire volume will be unusable.

Tip
For optimal performance, you can span your volumes *and* duplex the drives.

Creating a Volume

To create a volume, select Volume Options from the Installations Options main menu of INSTALL.NLM and INSTALL presents you with a new window called Volumes. If this is a new server, INSTALL.NLM does not show any volumes in this box. By pressing the Insert key to create your first volume, you are presented with a screen like the one in Figure 3.10. On this screen, there are three options you must complete:

■ *Volume Name:* If this is the first volume on the server, it must be called SYS; otherwise, you can select a different name, such as VOL1.

- *Volume Block Size:* The volume block size determines the smallest size block it will use to store a file. If the server primarily is made up of smaller files, choose a maximum 4K or 8K block size, but if your server contains large database files, choosing 16K or higher for your block size improves performance.

> ### Caution
>
> Once the block size has been chosen, it cannot be changed unless you delete the volume, thereby losing all of the data stored on the volume.

- *Initial Segment Size (BLOCK):* The initial segment size tells NetWare how big you want the volume to be. By default, NetWare chooses the entire NetWare partition for the volume. You can select the default, or specify a new one.

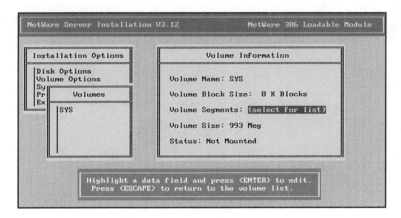

Fig. 3.10 The Volume Information screen in INSTALL.NLM for creating a NetWare volume.

> ### Note
>
> Once the volume has been created, you can increase its size as needed, but you *cannot* decrease the size of the volume without deleting it, thereby losing all data stored on the volume.

When you are finished, press the Esc key to continue. NetWare then asks you if you want to create this volume. If the parameters you chose are acceptable, say Yes; otherwise, answer No and start over.

Adding More Space to a Volume

If a volume currently on your file server is running out of room, you can add additional space by following the steps below:

1. From the Installation Options main menu of INSTALL.NLM, select Volume Options.

2. Choose the volume to which you want to add space by selecting it and pressing the Enter key.

3. Next, you are presented with a screen entitled Volume Information. Cursor down to the Volume Segments option and press the Enter key.

4. The Volume Segments screen displays the segments currently in use by the volume. To add additional space, press the Insert key to view and insert space from any NetWare partition not already allocated to a volume.

> **Note**
>
> You will only be able to add additional space to a volume from a valid NetWare partition. If you added a new drive to the server for the purpose of increasing the size of a volume, you must first create the NetWare partition on that drive. For detailed information on creating a NetWare partition, refer to the heading "Creating the Partition" earlier in this chapter.

Renaming a Volume

As the administrator, at some point, you may want to rename a volume on your file server. Using the INSTALL utility, you can do so by following the steps below:

1. From the Installation Options main menu of INSTALL.NLM, choose Volume Options and press Enter.

2. Select the volume you would like to rename from the listing of Volumes.

3. On the Volume Information screen, dismount the volume by selecting Status and then Dismount Volume.

4. Once the volume is dismounted, choose the first option, Volume Name, and press Enter. Once the cursor appears after the volume name, change the name as required.

5. After changing the name, complete the name change by pressing Esc and confirming that you want to change the volume's name.

6. Remount the Volume by selecting Status and then Mount Volume from the Volume Information screen.

> **Caution**
>
> You should not change the name of a volume when people are logged into the server, nor should you change the name of the SYS: volume unless you are intending to add a new drive that will become SYS:. Every server *must* have a SYS: volume; it will not boot properly without one.

Deleting a Volume

If there is a volume you no longer want currently on your server, or if you created a volume that was too big, you easily can delete it using INSTALL.NLM by following the steps below:

1. Select Volume Options from the Installation Options main menu of INSTALL.NLM.

2. Next, INSTALL.NLM displays a listing of the currently configured volumes on the server. Select the volume you want to delete and then press Delete.

3. Finally, when asked, confirm the deletion process.

Loading the NetWare Utilities

For the server to be fully functional, you must install all of the utilities and other programs that were provided with your NetWare software. During the loading procedure, NetWare creates the basic directory structure and places each file in the appropriate area. Depending on the method you are using to install your file server—such as from diskette, from CD-ROM, or from another server—the method you use varies. The following sections will provide you with the detailed instructions you will need to install the NetWare utilities and programs using the INSTALL.NLM utility. If INSTALL.NLM is not already loaded, you can load it by typing **LOAD INSTALL** from the file server prompt.

Installing from Diskette

To install the necessary NetWare programs and utilities from diskette, follow these steps:

1. From the Installation Options main menu of INSTALL.NLM, select System Options.

2. Next, you are presented with a screen entitled Available System Options. From this screen, select Copy System and Public Files.

3. Insert the INSTALL diskette into drive A: and press Enter to continue.

4. Insert the remaining diskettes as requested.

> **Caution**
>
> While copying the diskettes, there is one disk, the UNICODE disk, that takes an especially long time. Don't worry; your server is not stalled. This diskette can take up to an hour depending on the type of server you are using!

Installing from CD-ROM

Until this point, the programs you were running to install the server—such as INSTALL.NLM or SERVER.EXE—were located on the boot partition you created during Phase 1. Now, NetWare requires you to make the CD-ROM accessible so it can copy all the necessary files from the

CD-ROM to the server's hard disk. Before you can access files from the CD, you first must make it accessible to NetWare by following these steps:

1. From the server colon prompt, load the driver ASPICD.DSK from the boot partition you created earlier (for instance, C:\SERVER.312) by typing **LOAD C:\SERVER.312\ASPICD.DSK**.

2. Load CDROM.NLM from the same directory by typing **LOAD C:\SERVER.312\CDROM.NLM**.

3. Once CDROM.NLM is loaded, there is a new command-line option, called CD, available to you. This option can be used to view and change the status of your CD-ROM systems. To view the CD-ROMs currently available, type **CD DEVICE LIST**.

4. If all is well, NetWare displays the volume name of the CD currently installed in the server; you should see a CD with the volume name NetWare_312. You must mount this CD by typing **CD MOUNT NetWare_312**. After you press Enter, it could take 10 minutes or more to actually mount the CD, so be patient.

Once completed, the CD is available to NetWare as a mounted volume. Now, to load the system and public files, follow these steps:

1. From the Installation Options main menu of INSTALL.NLM, select System Options.

2. From the next menu, Available System Options, select Copy System and Public Files.

3. INSTALL.NLM then asks you to insert the INSTALL disk in drive A: or press F6 to install from another location. Press F6 so you can install the files from the CD-ROM.

4. When asked to specify the location of the files, type **NETWARE_312:\NETWARE.312\ENGLISH** and then press Enter.

NetWare then copies all the necessary files from the CD-ROM to the server's hard disk.

From Another File Server

If you have been installing NetWare from another file server, you can copy all the necessary files by following these steps:

1. From the Installation Options main menu of INSTALL.NLM, select System Options.

2. Next, from the Available System Options screen, select Copy System and Public Files.

3. INSTALL.NLM then asks you to either insert the INSTALL disk in drive A: or press F6 to specify another location. Since you are installing your server from another server, press F6.

4. Finally, type the path where the files are located, **drive:\directory\NETWARE.312\ENGLISH**; where *drive:* is the drive letter of the drive

from which you ran INSTALL.BAT, *directory* is the name of the subdirectory on the other server where you copied the disks or CD-ROM, and *NETWARE.312\ENGLISH* is the path requested by INSTALL.NLM.

Activating the Server Network Interface Cards

To activate the server's Network Interface Card(s), you must load a driver that tells NetWare what card is installed and how it is configured. Depending on your card, you may be able to use a driver supplied with your Novell software, or you may have to use a driver supplied by the vendor. The actual name of the driver varies from card to card, but their naming scheme is usually self-explanatory. For example, 3C503.LAN is the driver for the 3COM 3C503 network interface card. You can load the driver by typing the following from the file server prompt:

```
LOAD driver [parameter(s)]
```

Based on the syntax above, replace:

driver with the name of the LAN driver you are using.

parameter(s) with one or more of the parameters shown in Table 3.2.

Table 3.2 Parameters used from the command line when loading the network interface card drivers.

Parameter	Example	Description
DMA=*number*	**LOAD 3C503 DMA=5**	Specifies the NIC's DMA setting.
FRAME=*frame type*	**LOAD 3C503 FRAME= ETHERNET_802.3**	Specifies the frame type used with the NIC.
INT=*interrupt*	**LOAD 3C503 INT=3**	Specifies the NIC's interrupt setting.
MEM=*memory address*	**LOAD 3C503 MEM=CC000**	Specifies the RAM and ROM address for the NIC.
NAME=*board name*	**LOAD 3C503 NAME=BCKBONE**	Gives the board a recognizable name.
NODE=*node address*	**LOAD 3C503 NODE=101**	Sets a locally administered addresses for the NIC. This address overrides the address burned into the card.
PORT=*I/O port*	**LOAD 3C503 PORT=330**	Specifies the I/O port address used by the NIC.
RETRIES=*#*	**LOAD 3C503 RETRIES=10**	Specifies how many times the NIC will retry a failed transmission.
SLOT=*slot #*	**LOAD 3C503 SLOT=3**	Specifies the slot in which the board is installed.

Note

You can use more than one parameter from the preceding table in the load command. For example, if you were using a 3C503 NIC with a port address of 300 and a memory address of CC000, you could load the driver by typing **LOAD 3C503 PORT=300 MEM=CC000**.

Note

Before loading your NIC driver, make sure the NIC is connected to the network cabling system. Some drivers/cards, such as Token Ring cards, will not initialize properly when the cabling is not set up.

Binding a Protocol to the Network Interface Card

The last step in activating the NIC is to bind the protocol it uses. By binding the protocol, you actually tell NetWare which protocol the NIC can use. The format you use for the BIND command will differ depending on whether you have one or more NICs.

Binding a Protocol when You Only Have One NIC. When only one NIC is installed in the file server, you bind the protocol by following this syntax:

```
BIND protocol TO driver or board name NET=network number
```

Based on the syntax above replace:

> *protocol* with the name of the protocol being bound, such as IPX.
>
> *driver or board name* with the driver name, for example, 3C503, or the name you assigned with the NAME parameter during the load command, as in BCKBONE.
>
> *network number* with the number of the physical network to which the server is attached, *not* the IPX internal network number that is unique to each file server.

An example of a bind command when there is only one NIC installed is:

> BIND IPX TO 3C503 NET=10

Binding a Protocol when You Have Several NICs

When there are several NICs installed in the file server, binding the protocol requires a little more work on your part. Since there are multiple NICs, you must tell NetWare which NIC you are referring to. To actually bind the protocol, the format is:

```
BIND protocol TO driver or board name [config information] NET=network number
```

Based on this syntax, replace:

protocol with the name of the protocol, such as IPX, being bound.

driver or board name with the driver name, such as 3C503, or the name you assigned with the NAME parameter during the load command, as in BCKBONE.

[config information] with the configuration information specific to the card to which you want to bind. **This information *must* be enclosed in square brackets!**

network number with the number of the physical network to which the server will be attached, *not* the IPX internal network number that is unique to each file server.

An example of a bind command when there is more than one NIC installed is:

```
BIND IPX TO 3C503 [PORT=300 FRAME=ETHERNET_802.3] NET=10
```

The above command tells NetWare to bind the IPX protocol to the 3C503 board using the I/O port 300 with a frame type of Ethernet_802.3 to the physical network 10.

Using More Than 16M of RAM in an ISA Server

When your file server uses an ISA bus, you must specifically inform NetWare when you are using more than 16M of RAM. The ISA bus does not automatically recognize the memory above the 16M limit.

This process of notification is known as Registering the Memory. To complete this task, use the following syntax (the values used must be in hexadecimal):

```
REGISTER MEMORY start_of_memory_segment length_of_memory_segment
```

For example, assuming you have an ISA server that has 32M of RAM, the correct syntax to register the memory would be:

```
REGISTER MEMORY 1000000 1000000
```

The above example shows you that the start of the memory segment is 16M (1000000 is the HEX value for 16M), and the length of the segment is 16M, therefore a total of 32M.

> **Note**
>
> If you need to register memory in your file server, insert the command within your AUTOEXEC.NCF file so you don't have to type it every time your server is booted.

You can check in Appendix C, "Hexadecimal Memory Conversion Table," for your specific requirements.

Creating the Server Boot Files

On your NetWare server, there are two boot files that must be created, AUTOEXEC.NCF and STARTUP.NCF. The STARTUP.NCF file resides on the DOS boot partition of the file server and contains the load commands for the disk drivers as well as several other parameters that affect the way the server is configured. The AUTOEXEC.NCF file is stored in the SYSTEM directory on the file server and is used in a similar fashion to your workstation's AUTOEXEC.BAT file. In the AUTOEXEC.NCF file, the commands needed to load and bind your NIC, mount volumes, load other drivers, and set certain parameters that affect the server's configuration are used. For a complete listing of the different settable environment variables, refer to the SET parameter in Chapter 22, "Console Commands."

Using the INSTALL.NLM utility, you can create or edit these file by following the steps below (if INSTALL.NLM is not loaded, you can load it by typing **LOAD INSTALL** from the file server prompt):

1. From the Installation Options main menu of INSTALL.NLM, select System Options.

2. Next, you are presented with a screen entitled Available System Options. To create the AUTOEXEC.NCF and STARTUP.NCF files, select Create AUTOEXEC.NCF File and Create STARTUP.NCF File.

    When you are installing NetWare 3.X, the commands you typed from the server prompt—such as LOAD and BIND—are automatically shown on-screen when you create the files previously named. At this point, you can add any additional commands you want or you can press Esc on each screen to save your changes.

Rebooting the File Server

Once you have completed the installation process, reboot the server to make sure all your hard work paid off. Type **DOWN** at the file server colon prompt to shut down the operating system and ensure all files are closed properly. From there, type **EXIT** to get back to the DOS prompt.

If you enabled NetWare to edit your AUTOEXEC.BAT file to automatically load SERVER.EXE (this was done during the INSTALL.BAT routine), you can cold- or warm-boot your server and it should load all the necessary files. But, if your AUTOEXEC.BAT does not include SERVER.EXE, you can start the server manually by first changing directories to where you installed the boot files and then typing **SERVER** from the DOS prompt.

If your server does not boot properly, the problem may be attributed to the parameters you included in your STARTUP.NCF or AUTOEXEC.NCF files. Since both files are loaded automatically by SERVER.EXE, you can use a command-line switch to override the loading of these files.

To start the file server without loading the STARTUP.NCF file, type **SERVER -ns**, where -ns stands for No STARTUP.NCF.

To start the file server without loading the AUTOEXEC.NCF file, type **SERVER -na**, where -na stands for No AUTOEXEC.NCF.

Installation

Chapter 4

Installing Workstations

Getting a workstation up and running on the LAN can be a simple process, or it can be quite lengthy and require a great deal of attention to detail. While it would be almost impossible to cover every possible workstation configuration, this section provides you with valuable information to get the job done.

In this section, you find detailed information on:

- Installing ODI/NETX
- Installing the DOS Requester
- Configuring your NET.CFG file
- Advanced configuration options

Configuring the Workstation's Network Interface Card

When it comes to connecting your workstations to the network, you must ensure that each one has a network interface card properly installed and configured. Physically installing the card into the workstation is fairly straightforward and only requires that the card is firmly seated in the bus and that it is screwed in tightly. The one part of installing your NIC that requires the utmost care is the actual configuration.

Note

Not all workstations use NICs installed within the computer. There are some products on the market, such as the XIRCOM Pocket Adapter, that connect to the external parallel port of your workstation. In cases like this, the same theory applies; make sure there is a good, tight fit between the adapter and the port.

Caution

Always screw the adapter board into place. If you have lost the screw, find it or get another one. When the board is not screwed in, it is possible the board can become dislodged from the workstation's bus, thereby causing intermittent communications problems, or possibly damage to the board itself.

Depending on the type of NIC you are using, it may use jumpers, dip switches, or a program to establish the required settings. While the method will vary from card to card, there are four settings you should know about when configuring your NICs:

■ *DMA Channel:* The NIC uses the DMA (Direct Memory Access) channel to access memory directly without having to go through the workstation's CPU. If the card requires the use of a DMA channel, care should be taken *not* to use a channel already occupied by another device. Table 4.1 provides you with a listing of the commonly used DMA channels.

Table 4.1 Commonly used DMA channels in an 80X86-based PC.

DMA	Used for
0	Available
1	Available
2	Floppy disk controller
3	Available
4	First DMA controller
5	Available
6	Available
7	Available

■ *IRQ:* The NIC uses the IRQ (Interrupt ReQuest) to request a service from the workstation's CPU. Since most adapter cards and other services such as the workstation's parallel or serial port use an IRQ, it is not always possible to assign a dedicated IRQ to the NIC. While you should try not to use the same IRQ for more than one NIC, it is possible to use the IRQ typically assigned to another device, if the device is not present. For example, if the serial ports are not being used on the file server, you can assign their IRQs to your NIC. Table 4.2 shows you a listing of the most common IRQ assignments for your PC hardware.

Table 4.2 Commonly used IRQs in an 80X86-based PC.	
IRQ Level	**Used for**
0	System RAM
1	Keyboard
2	Cascade to IRQ 9 (available)
3	COM 2/4
4	COM 1/3
5	LPT2
6	Floppy Controller
7	LPT1/3
8	System Clock
9	Available (redirected from IRQ2)
10	Available
11	Available
12	Motherboard mouse port
13	Co-Processor
14	ISA Hard Disk
15	Available

Caution

Avoid using IRQ 15 in the file server for the NIC or any other hardware for that matter. There is a known problem when using this interrupt that could result in intermittent file server abends.

■ *I/O Port:* The CPU uses I/O ports to communicate with hardware devices such as NICs, printing ports, and other adapters. I/O ports *cannot* be shared within the workstation; therefore, care must be taken when setting the NIC's I/O port to ensure it does not conflict with any other settings.

■ *Memory Address:* Many NICs on the market have their own memory (ROM) installed directly on the card; this memory is used to store low-level information about the card and how it should operate. When your NIC uses on-board memory, you must allocate a portion of the

PC's memory for interaction with the on-board memory. This memory address *cannot* be shared with other devices; therefore, care must be taken to ensure there are no conflicts.

Tip

If you are using EMM386 or another memory manager on your workstation, you may encounter problems accessing the network if your NIC uses a memory address. This problem occurs frequently with Token Ring cards. If you encounter such a problem, try adding an exclude parameter to your memory manager for the memory address of the NIC being used.

Tip

If you are noticing that your workstation freezes when loading the network drivers, the problem could also be caused by QEMM. If QEMM is being run in STEALTH mode, some drivers will not operate properly. Consult your QEMM documentation on how to disable STEALTH mode.

After you have spent the time configuring and installing the NICs, do yourself a favor: *Document your work*. Knowing the specifics on how each workstation is configured makes things easier down the road when you troubleshoot or upgrade.

Tip

Once the workstation hardware is fully configured, write the NIC Physical Layer address and the location of the user's desk on a small sticker. Place the sticker around the associated cable in your wiring room. This tiny sticker can save you hours trying to figure out which cable goes where.

ODI and the DOS Requester

When NetWare 3.0 first came out, getting the workstation to actually connect with the LAN was something of a chore. To start with, two files were used, IPX.COM and the shell (such as NET3.COM, NET4.COM, or NET5.COM). After a year or two, Novell decided to do away with the NET3, NET4, and NET5 files by replacing them with a new shell called NETX.EXE. Unlike the previous programs—that were dependent on the version of DOS you were running—NETX.EXE didn't care about your DOS version.

While this made the administrator's life a little easier, there was still IPX.COM. IPX.COM could not be run straight from the box. Instead, the administrator actually created this file using a utility called WSGEN that took two files—IPX.OBJ and a NIC driver—and combined them into one command file. While IPX.COM offered many functions in one compact file, it made things difficult for the administrator when changes were needed. It was especially difficult when NICs from several different vendors were in use; since IPX.COM included a NIC driver, multiple versions of IPX.COM also had to be used.

After a while, Novell released the Open DataLink Interface (ODI) method for network access. Instead of using one file to handle many functions, ODI broke the tasks up into three separate files (LSL.COM, a NIC driver, and IPXODI.COM). When Novell did so, upgrades, installations, and modifications were simplified for the administrator. When updates were required, instead of having to regenerate the IPX.COM file for each brand of interface card, the administrator could just copy the updated program over the old version. In addition to easier management of the workstation, ODI gave the administrator a lot more freedom by supporting multiple frames and protocols on the same interface card.

When NetWare 4.X first came out, Novell decided to further enhance the modular nature of ODI by introducing the Virtual Loadable Module (VLM) architecture, otherwise known as the DOS Requester. While the initial versions of ODI used NETX, EMSNETX, or XMSNETX as the workstation shell (hereafter referred to as ODI/NETX), the DOS Requester has done away with these three files in favor of one executable file (VLM.EXE) and 15 modules known as VLMs.

> **Note**
>
> The number of modules might be increased from time to time as Novell releases updates to the DOS Requester.

With the DOS Requester, the workstation's interaction with DOS and NetWare has been changed radically. Instead of acting as a front end to DOS as NETX did, the Requester blends with DOS to share common tables and functions. Because it does so, the utilization of memory and system performance is improved.

Whether you use the older ODI/NETX implementation or the new DOS Requester is up to you, but depending on which one you choose, the manner in which you configure your workstation differs. The first difference we look at lies in the files you use on the workstation.

> **Note**
>
> Using the DOS Requester is *not* mandatory with NetWare 3.12, but if your LAN contains NetWare 4.X servers, you must use the DOS Requester if you want to take full advantage of the Directory Services facilities of NetWare 4.X. You also must use the DOS Requester if you want to take advantage of NetWare 3.12's Large Internet Packet Exchange and Packet Bursting features.

With ODI and the DOS Requester, there are several common files used on the workstation: LSL.COM, the MLID, IPXODI.COM, and NET.CFG. Descriptions of these files are found in Table 4.3.

Table 4.3 Files used with ODI and the DOS requester.

File	Description
LSL.COM	The LSL.COM (Link Support Layer) file manages communications between the Network Interface Card (NIC) and the workstation protocols currently in use.
MLID	The MLID (Multiple Link Interface Driver) is used by the NIC. This driver supplies configuration information about the card and handles requests from other processes for its services. The actual name of the MLID will vary from card to card as the drivers are usually supplied by the manufacturer; NetWare, however, comes with several MLID drivers such as TOKEN.COM (for IBM Token Ring cards).
IPXODI.COM	The IPXODI.COM file allows the workstation to communicate with the network using the IPX/SPX protocols. As the primary protocol used on the NetWare LAN, this file is used with the older ODI/NETX implementations as well as the Requester installs.
NET.CFG	Unlike the other programs shown above, NET.CFG is a standard ASCII text file that can be created with any text editor. This file stores configuration information such as frame types, protocols used, and preferred server names.

The program used next depends on your decision whether you use the older ODI/NETX implementation or the DOS Requester. As shown in Table 4.4, four different programs can be used.

Table 4.4 Programs that determine whether you are using the ODI/NETX implementation or the DOS requester.

File	Description
NETX.EXE	NETX.EXE acts as a front end to DOS by intercepting requests and determining if they should be handled by DOS or itself. While NETX.EXE can be loaded into upper memory, it is primarily designed for use in conventional RAM. This file loads after IPXODI under the ODI/NETX implementation.
EMSNETX.EXE	While the functions of EMSNETX are the same as those for NETX.EXE, EMSNETX.EXE was designed for use in the expanded memory region of the workstation.
XMSNETX.EXE	While the functions of EMSNETX are the same as those for NETX.EXE, XMSNETX.EXE was designed for use in the extended memory region of the workstation.
VLM.EXE	VLM.EXE is a replacement for the older NETX.EXE configuration. Instead of acting as a front end to DOS (like NETX), VLM.EXE blends with DOS to handle the workstation's requirements. Both DOS and VLM.EXE can share table information, thereby improving performance and memory utilization. This file loads after IPXODI when using the DOS Requester/VLM architecture.

If you use the DOS Requester, several other programs unique to the Requester also are loaded (see Table 4.5). For the most part, these files are loaded automatically by the VLM.EXE program, but there are a few exceptions, mainly RSA.VLM, AUTO.VLM, and NMR.VLM. These files are loaded, depending on the manner in which you set up your NET.CFG file. The options included in this file are covered later in this chapter under the headings "Installing the DOS Requester" and "Configuring And Customizing Your NET.CFG File."

Table 4.5 Files used only with the DOS Requester.

Module	Loaded with Default NET.CFG?	Description
AUTO.VLM	No	Restores the connection between the workstation and file server after a critical error has occurred (for instance, the server has crashed). Once the file server has been brought back on-line, AUTO.VLM handles tasks such as reestablishing the connection, driver mappings, and printer assignments.
BIND.VLM	Yes	Logs into the bindery servers such as NetWare 2.X or NetWare 3.X. BIND.VLM is not required in the NetWare 4.X environment.
CONN.VLM	Yes	Acting as the connection table manager for the workstation, this module maintains a table of server connections—up to fifty—and informs the other VLMs of your current connections. This module can also supply APIs to check a current connection handle or gather statistics.
FIO.VLM	Yes	The FIO.VLM (File Input/Output) manages features such as packet bursting, caching, and NetWare's Large Internet Packet facility. FIO also accesses files stored on the NetWare file server.
GENERAL.VLM	Yes	The GENERAL.VLM does not have any specific responsibility focus, hence the name GENERAL. One example of what the GENERAL.VLM controls is management of NetWare drive mappings and first drive assignments. This module is used mostly to supply information to other modules.
IPXNCP.VLM	Yes	Handles communication between incoming and outgoing IPX/SPX packets from the network and the workstation's DOS Requester. Builds IPX packets with the proper NCP headers. *Note:* IPXNCP is *not* a replacement for the IPXODI file.
NDS.VLM	No	The NDS.VLM is only required for installations involving NetWare 4.X. NDS.VLM allows the workstation to access directory services features of the NetWare 4.X environment. *Note:* When a NET.CFG file is *not* found, VLM.EXE automatically loads the NDS.VLM module.
NETX.VLM	Yes	This module is optional within the NetWare 4.X environment. NETX.VLM manages the communications and function calls associated with the NetWare 2.X and 3.X operating system as well as programs and utilities designed for these versions of NetWare.

(continues)

Table 4.5 Continued.

Module	Loaded with Default NET.CFG?	Description
NMR.VLM	No	NMR is the NetWare Management Responder module that acts as an agent on the workstation for Windows or OS/2. This module can be used to gather and supply configuration and diagnostic information.
NWP.VLM	Yes	Known as a multiplexor, or parent VLM, NWP.VLM handles the communications between BIND.VLM or NDS.VLM and other modules within the VLM suite.
PRINT.VLM	Yes	As the name implies, the PRINT module is responsible for redirecting print jobs from the workstation to the network printers.
REDIR.VLM	Yes	The REDIR module is known as the DOS Redirecter and handles the requests for files and directories stored on the NetWare file server.
RSA.VLM	No	An optional VLM, RSA is another security type of VLM that authenticates and encrypts when used in the NetWare 4.X NDS environment. This VLM is required if you are using the auto reconnect feature of the VLMs.
SECURITY.VLM	Yes	SECURITY.VLM manages security-related features of NetWare such as packet signing.
TRAN.VLM	Yes	Known as a multiplexor or parent VLM, TRAN.VLM manages the communications between the DOS Requester and protocol VLMs such as IPXNCP.VLM.
VLM.EXE		VLM.EXE is the executable file run in place of NETX.EXE, EMSNETX.EXE, or XMSNETX.EXE. Manages and loads the Virtual Loadable Modules—files with the extension .VLM—used to connect and communicate with the network.

Note

The various ODI/NETX and DOS Requester files are updated by Novell from time to time. Unfortunately, the versions that came with your 3.12 software are already outdated. The latest versions are always placed on CompuServe in two files, DOSUP*x*.EXE and WINUP*x*.EXE where *x* increements with each release. At the time of writing, the latest files to download were DOSUP9.EXE and WINUP9.EXE.

Installing the Workstation Files

Before you install the workstation files, you first must determine if you are going to use the older ODI/NETX implementation or the DOS Requester. While ODI/NETX has proven itself to be quite stable and reliable, it doesn't offer as many benefits as the Requester, including packet bursting and large internet packets (the ability to send packets larger than 576 bytes through routers). The choice is really up to you, but unless there is some particular reason, such as company standards, why you cannot use the Requester, you should choose it over the ODI/NETX implementation. In addition to the added benefits of the Requester, Novell is pushing this method the most. Eventually, Novell probably will stop supporting ODI/NETX, so it may be best to plan ahead.

The following headings show you how to install the ODI/NETX and DOS Requester workstation files. To review how you can configure how these files operate, refer to the heading "Configuring and Customizing Your NET.CFG" later in this chapter.

Installing ODI/NETX

Since Novell is moving away from the ODI/NETX implementation, installing these files takes a little more work on your part. Unlike the DOS Requester, that has a spiffy little installation program, this installation process is completely manual.

Finding the Necessary Files

When you are sourcing the ODI/NETX files, the most difficult part is finding them—actually, many people don't even know they're there! Table 4.6 shows the files you need and where they are located:

Tip
You can view a file called FILES.DAT to find out what directory or disk a specific file is on. If you bought NetWare on CD-ROM, the FILES.DAT file is located in the directory \NETWARE.312\ENGLISH\INSTALL; and if you bought NetWare on diskette, the FILES.DAT file is located on the INSTALL disk.

Table 4.6 Locations of files you need from the CD-ROM or Diskettes to use the ODI/NETX implementation.

Filename	Directory on CD-ROM	Diskette
LSL.COM	\CLIENT\DOSWIN	WSDOS_1
MLID FILES	\CLIENT_____\WSDRV_2\DOS	WSDRV_2
IPXODI.COM	\CLIENT\DOSWIN	WSDOS_1
NETX.EXE	\NetWare.312_____\3	SYSTEM_2

(continues)

Table 4.6 Continued.		
Filename	**Directory on CD-ROM**	**Diskette**
EMSNETX.EXE	\NetWare.312_____\3	SYSTEM_2
XMSNETX.EXE	\NetWare.312_____\3	SYSTEM_2
NLUNPACK.EXE	\CLIENT\DOSWIN	WSDOS_1

Creating an Installation Disk

If you are going to use ODI/NETX, you should make an installation disk containing all the necessary files. It may take you a bit longer at the beginning, but it makes life easier down the road. To create an installation disk, copy the following files to a floppy diskette:

> **Note**
>
> If you bought NetWare on diskette, you will not be able to copy the NETX, EMSNETX, or XMSNETX files directly from the diskette as they are compressed. To uncompress them, follow these steps:
>
> 1. From the INSTALL disk, type **NWXTRACT drive: file destination**, replacing drive with the letter of the floppy drive, file with the name of the file you want to extract (such as NETX.EXE), and destination with the drive and directory to which you want the file extracted.
>
> 2. After entering this command, you are presented with the prompt Place a master data file diskette in Drive A: and press Enter. At this point, you should leave the INSTALL disk in the drive and press Enter.
>
> 3. When prompted, insert the SYSTEM_2 diskette in the drive.

LSL.COM

IPXODI.COM

NETX.EXE

EMSNETX.EXE

XMSNETX.EXE

Next, you need your MLID file. If your NIC did not come with a driver diskette, you can check the directory to see if Novell has supplied one (see Table 4.6). The drivers on the CD-ROM are packed (compressed) with an extension of CO_ (for example, TOKEN.CO_), so they must be uncompressed before they can be used. To uncompress a file, you must use the NLUNPACK.EXE program stored in the \CLIENT\DOSWIN directory. The syntax is:

```
NLUNPACK path\driver_filename destination
```

For example, if you want to unpack the file TOKEN.CO_ that is on the CD-ROM drive (in this case, drive E) directly to the floppy drive A, type:

NLUNPACK E:\CLIENT_____\WSDRV_2\DOS\TOKEN A:

Once you have the necessary files on the floppy disk, you can copy them onto each workstation of your LAN. While the ODI/NETX installation does not create a default NET.CFG file as the Requester installation does, you can create your own. Refer to the heading "Configuring and Customizing Your NET.CFG File" later in this chapter for further information.

Tip
When installing files, place them in a subdirectory off the root. Placing them in their own directory minimizes the chance the user will delete them by accident, and makes future upgrades easier.

Installing the DOS Requester

Installing the DOS Requester is a fairly straightforward procedure that can be completed by the administrator as a new installation, or by a current network user who is running an older version of the shell. Depending on your circumstances, you will be running the install from one of the following locations:

- NetWare 3.12 CD-ROM

- NetWare 3.12 diskettes

- A directory on the file server

- Requester installation disks

Loading the Install Program

To assist you with initiating the installation procedure, the following headings provide you with detailed instructions for each method.

The actual installation is the same from each location, but the manner by which you get into the installation program differs.

Loading Install from the NetWare 3.12 CD-ROM. If your workstation is equipped with a CD-ROM drive, you can start the installation process directly from the CD. To do so, just follow these steps:

1. Insert the CD into the CD-ROM drive.

2. Change drives to the CD-ROM (for instance, E:).

3. Change directories to \CLIENT\DOSWIN.

4. Run the install batch file by typing **INSTALL** from the DOS prompt.

Loading Install from the NetWare 3.12 Diskettes. If you did not purchase NetWare 3.12 on CD-ROM but instead opted for the disk-based version, you should have received several diskettes pertaining to the DOS Requester. To start the install program, you should:

1. Insert the WSDOS_1 disk into the floppy drive.

2. Make this drive current (such as by typing **A:**).

3. Run the install batch file by typing **INSTALL** from the DOS prompt.

Loading Install from a File Server Directory. To run the install program from a file server directory, you must first copy the required files from your 3.12 disks onto the file server. While you can copy the programs into any directory, it is recommended that you install them in a directory called SYS:\PUBLIC\CLIENT\DOSWIN. If you have not already done so, you can create the installation directory by:

1. Logging in to the file server as a SUPERVISOR or SUPERVISOR-EQUIVALENT from a work-station with a CD-ROM.

2. Mapping a drive to the root of the SYS: volume (for instance, by typing **MAP G:=SYS:**) and making this your current drive (for example, by typing **G:**).

3. Creating the installation directory by typing **MD \PUBLIC\CLIENT\DOSWIN**.

4. With the server prompt still at G:, changing the prompt to the drive with the CD-ROM (for example, E:) and then, from the E:\ prompt, typing **XCOPY CLIENT\DOSWIN*.* G:\PUBLIC\CLIENT\DOSWIN /S /E /V**. This command copies all files and sub-directories from the CLIENT\DOSWIN directory on the CD-ROM to the file server directory you created. The /V switch is used to verify that each file was copied correctly.

Tip
While the /V switch—used to verify the copy was done correctly—is not mandatory, and increases the time it takes to copy a file, you should use it when creating a directory from which many users will be copying files.

Once all the files have been copied over to the server, you then can make SYS:\PUBLIC\CLIENT\DOSWIN your current directory and run the installation batch file by typing **INSTALL** from the command line.

Note

Only workstations that can currently access the file server—those running the old shell programs—can use this method.

From the Requester Installation Disks. Instead of using the file server as your installation base, you can make a set of install disks from your CD-ROM. This scenario is ideal for situations where you will be installing new workstations that do not have older shells loaded, or if you will be traveling around to different sites doing installs and/or upgrades. To prepare your installation disks, first make sure you have four high density formatted diskettes available, then:

1. Insert the NetWare 3.12 CD into the workstation's CD-ROM.

2. Make the CD-ROM drive current (such as by typing **E:**).

3. Change directories by typing **CD\CLIENT\DOSWIN**.

4. Run the program MAKEDISK.

This process creates each of the disks necessary to run the installation program and also tells you what to label each one. Once completed, insert the disk labeled WSDOS_1 into the floppy drive, and after making the floppy drive your current default drive, type **INSTALL** to initiate the DOS Requester installation.

Using the INSTALL Program

No matter what method you use to run the INSTALL program, the result will always be the same. Once you run INSTALL, you are presented with a screen like the one shown in Figure 4.1.

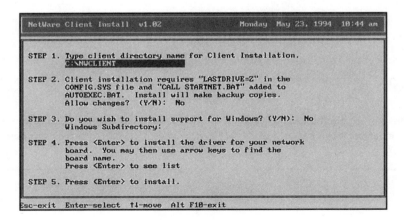

Fig. 4.1 NetWare Client Installation screen for installing the DOS requester.

Step 1: Client Directory Name. The first step asks you what you want the client directory name to be. Unless there is some particular reason why you must choose something other than the default C:\NWCLIENT directory, don't. Where possible, it is always best to stick with the default settings.

Step 2: Allow Changes. The second step asks if you want the INSTALL program to make the necessary modifications to the workstation's CONFIG.SYS and AUTOEXEC.BAT files. If you choose YES, INSTALL makes the following changes:

- A line that says LASTDRIVE=Z is added to the CONFIG.SYS. This change is mandatory if you want to use the Requester.

- A line that says @CALL C:\NWCLIENT\STARTNET.BAT is added to the AUTOEXEC.BAT. This command calls a batch file called STARTNET.BAT that contains the commands to load all the necessary files.

Note

If you do *not* allow the INSTALL program to make the necessary changes, you must, at a minimum, insert the command LASTDRIVE=Z in the workstation's CONFIG.SYS file.

If you choose not to allow INSTALL to make these changes, it creates two files in the directory specified in Step 1: CONFIG.NEW and AUTOEXEC.NEW. These files contain the same information stored within the current versions *plus* the changes that INSTALL would have made.

Step 3: Install Support for Windows. If the workstation where you are installing the Requester uses Microsoft Windows, answering Yes to this option will make several changes to your WINDOWS directory and the configuration file such as WIN.INI and SYSTEM.INI. After answering Yes, INSTALL then asks you for the name of the directory where you installed Windows.

By telling INSTALL to install Windows support, you are authorizing the following changes to be made to the workstation's Windows installation:

Caution

These changes only work with the DOS Requester and do not operate properly if you are using the ODI/NETX implementation. Make sure you make a backup copy of your \WINDOWS directory *before* installing the requester.

■ Install new files in the \WINDOWS directory:

> SYSTEM.BNW
>
> WIN.BNW
>
> ET.INI
>
> NOVELL.BMP
>
> NOVLOGO1.BMP
>
> NWADMIN.INI
>
> NWCALLS.DLL
>
> NWIPXSPX.DLL
>
> NWLOCALE.DLL
>
> NWNET.DLL
>
> NWPSRV.DLL
>
> NWRCON.PIF
>
> NWUSER.EXE
>
> TASKID.COM
>
> TBMI2.COM
>
> NWUTILS.GRP

■ Create a new directory called \WINDOWS\NLS with 75 files known as *unicode tables*. These tables are used for such things as language support.

Tip
If you do not require language support beyond ENGLISH, you can delete all the files in this directory except for the ones with the extension .001.

■ Create a new directory called \WINDOWS\NLS\ENGLISH with the following files:

> TASKID.MSG
>
> TBMI2.MSG
>
> NETWARER.DRV
>
> NETWARE.HLP

■ Install new files in the \WINDOWS\SYSTEM directory:

>   NETWARE.DRV
>
>   NETWARE.HLP
>
>   NWPOPUP.EXE
>
>   VIPX.386
>
>   VNETWARE.386

■ Make modifications to the \WINDOWS\WIN.INI file:

Section	Original Line	New Line
[windows]	load =	load= nwpopup.exe

■ Make modifications to the WINDOWS\SYSTEM.INI file:

Section	Original Line	New Line
[boot]	network.drv=	network.drv=netware.drv
[boot.description]	network.drv=	network.drv=Novell NetWare (V 4.0)
[386Enh]	network=*dosnet,*vnetbios TimerCriticalSection=10000	network=*vnetbios, vipx.386, vnetware.386 ReflectDOSInt2A=TRUE UniqueDOSPSP=TRUE PSPIncrement=5 OverlappedIO=OFF

Step 4: Install a Driver for the NIC. In this step, the INSTALL program is asking you what type of network interface card is installed in the workstation. You are presented with an additional menu like the one shown in Figure 4.2, which lists several NICs currently on the market. You can scroll through this listing or, if you can't find your NIC, you can select the last option in the list, Other Driver. If you select Other Driver, you must have a driver diskette supplied by the NIC's manufacturer.

Once a driver has been selected from the listing, you are presented with another screen (see fig. 4.3) asking for more specific information such as the frame type to be used and hardware configurations—Interrupts and Port Addresses. The actual options you see will vary from driver to driver.

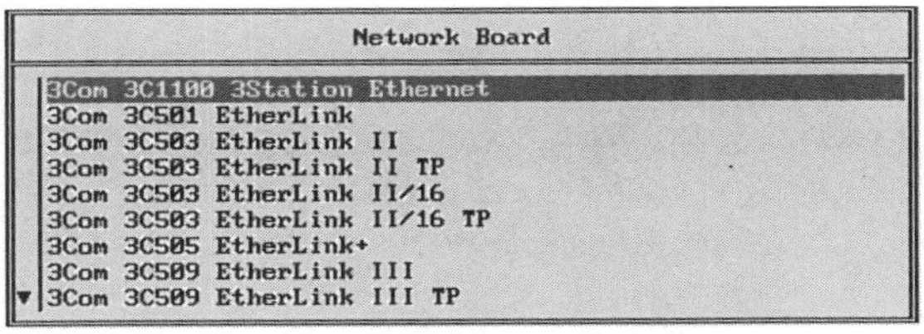

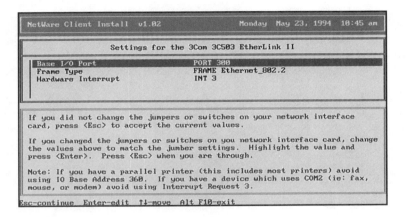

Fig. 4.2 Network board selection for the DOS requester.

Fig. 4.3 Network board configuration settings.

Newer Ethernet drivers default to the 802.2 format. If your LAN still uses the older 802.3 format, you must manually select this within the Frame Type option.

Step 5: Install the Requester. The final step is to actually run the installation. If you are happy with the selections you have made up to this point, the INSTALL program makes the changes shown in Steps 1–4 and creates a basic NET.CFG file in the directory specified in Step 1. This file then can be customized even further for your installation, as described in the next section.

Configuring and Customizing Your NET.CFG File

Once ODI/NETX or the DOS Requester has been installed on your workstation, you have the opportunity to run it "as is" or to fine-tune the NET.CFG file—to try loading ODI/NETX or the Requester, refer to the heading "Loading the Workstation Files and Command Line Options" later in this chapter. NET.CFG is a standard ASCII text file that acts as a central location where other programs such as LSL.COM and VLM.EXE can read any configuration options you have set.

Note

If you are using the ODI/NETX implementation, you do not have a default NET.CFG. Based on the information in this section, you can create your own NET.CFG, if required, with a standard text editor.

The NET.CFG file created upon installation will look something like the one shown in Figure 4.4. This file was created using the information supplied during the DOS Requester installation.

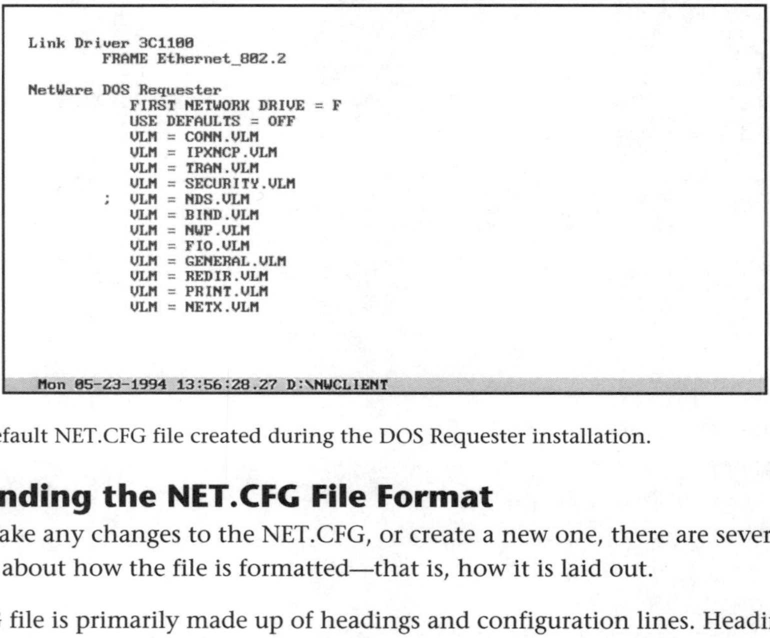

```
Link Driver 3C1100
        FRAME Ethernet_802.2

NetWare DOS Requester
           FIRST NETWORK DRIVE = F
           USE DEFAULTS = OFF
           VLM = CONN.VLM
           VLM = IPXNCP.VLM
           VLM = TRAN.VLM
           VLM = SECURITY.VLM
        ;  VLM = NDS.VLM
           VLM = BIND.VLM
           VLM = NWP.VLM
           VLM = FIO.VLM
           VLM = GENERAL.VLM
           VLM = REDIR.VLM
           VLM = PRINT.VLM
           VLM = NETX.VLM

 Mon 05-23-1994 13:56:28.27 D:\NWCLIENT
```

Fig. 4.4 The default NET.CFG file created during the DOS Requester installation.

Understanding the NET.CFG File Format

Before you make any changes to the NET.CFG, or create a new one, there are several things you should know about how the file is formatted—that is, how it is laid out.

The NET.CFG file is primarily made up of headings and configuration lines. Headings break up the NET.CFG into logical sections with a specific focus. As shown in Table 4.7, there are seven main headings used in the NET.CFG, shown in the order in which they are usually organized.

Whether you are changing your current NET.CFG file or creating a new one, there are several rules you should follow. They are:

- Section headings are placed flush against the left margin
- Configuration options for each section are indented with one tab directly beneath the appropriate heading; there should be no space after the section heading
- A single space should be left empty between sections
- Each comment line to be inserted in the NET.CFG should be preceded by a semicolon

Table 4.7 Headings used within the NET.CFG file.

Heading	Used For
Link Driver	Configuration options used by the MLID (such as the NIC Driver).
Link Support	Configuration options used by the LSL.COM file.
NetBIOS	Configuration options used by NETBIOS.EXE.
NetWare DOS Requester	Configuration options used by VLM.EXE, the DOS Requester.
NETX	Configurations options used by NETX.EXE.
PROTOCOL IPXODI	Configuration options used by IPXODI.COM.
TBMI2	Configuration options used by the TBMI2.COM file.

Tip

As well as comment lines, there may be actual configuration lines you want to remark out temporarily. Precede these also with a semicolon.

NET.CFG Options You Can Use

The following sections provide you with the various parameters that can be used in the NET.CFG file. Where possible, examples have been provided to demonstrate how the parameters are used.

Link Driver Options

The LINK DRIVER section of the NET.CFG file groups the configuration options for your network interface card. The heading for this section is called LINK DRIVER XXXXXXXX where XXXXXXXX is the name of the network board that you are referring to (such as LINK DRIVER 3C503). Table 4.8 details the options available for this section.

Note

If the workstation has two NICs installed, you will have two different Link Driver sections. For example, if you are using a 3C503 and IBM Token Ring Card, you would have one section called LINK DRIVER 3C503 and another called LINK DRIVER TOKEN.

Table 4.8 Available LINK DRIVER options to be used in the NET.CFG file.

Option	Example	Description
ALTERNATE	ALTERNATE	Specifies Token Ring parameters for another adapter.
DMA *channel #*	DMA 5	Specifies the Network Interface Card's DMA channel. The default value is 1.
FRAME *frame name*	FRAME Ethernet_II	Specifies the frame type used by the NIC. Multiple FRAME parameters can be included to make use of more than one frame type per NIC. *Note:* Make sure your server is configured to support the frame type you specify here; otherwise, you will not be able to connect to the server. In NetWare 3.12, the default Ethernet frame type is 802.2, yet many of the older NICs and current installations are still using the old default, 802.3. Keep an eye out for this!
INT *interrupt #*	INT 2	Specifies the interrupt, or IRQ used by the NIC.
LINK STATIONS #	LINK STATIONS 3	When using the IBM LANSUP.COM program, you must specify the number of LINK STATIONS. The value changes depending on the number of applications using the LANSUP program. The default value is 1 and the maximum varies depending on the type of network board being used.
MAX FRAME SIZE *frame size*	MAX FRAME SIZE 4216	In Token Ring, specifies the maximum frame size that can be sent. The following formula will help you determine the valid number to insert: bytes of data + 6 bytes for NIC overhead + 114 bytes for the header. Therefore, if you wanted to use a 4K packet, the formula is 4096 + 6 + 114 = 4216. *Note:* The total number must be divisible by 8; if it's not, you miscalculated. *Note:* When using Windows in enhanced mode, the VIPX.386 driver will not operate properly when the maximum frame size is greater than 8,000 bytes.
MEM *memory address [length]*	MEM D8000	Specifies the ROM address of the NIC in HEX. The memory address is usually five HEX digits with the last digit usually being a 0. *Note:* The length is rarely, if ever, needed.

Option	Example	Description
NODE ADDRESS *node address*	NODE ADDRESS 10005AC29415	You can use this option to override the burned-in address of your NIC. *Do not change the station's address without a valid reason.* For example, assume you have an application that is configured to allow only a specific node address to have access. If the NIC with the burned-in address fails, you are not able to access the application. Using this parameter fools the application into thinking the station is authorized. Changing the address from the burned-in value makes administration more difficult.
PORT *I/O port address*	PORT 300	Specifies the I/O port in use by the NIC.
PROTOCOL *protocol name hex_id frame type*	PROTOCOL ABC 806B Ethernet_802.3	Allows you to use a protocol besides IPX/SPX with your existing drivers. For example, the new protocol ABC with the HEX ID of 806B would be able to use the Ethernet_802.3 frame type.
SAPS #	SAPS 40	When using the LANSUP.COM program, this option specifies the number of SAPs available. This value should be equal to the total requirement of all running applications. The default value is 1.
SLOT #	SLOT 3	When using an EISA or MCA workstation, this parameter specifies the bus SLOT in which the NIC is physically installed. You also can use this parameter when there are more than two NICs in the computer. The default value is SLOT 1.

Installation

Link Support Options

The LINK SUPPORT section of the NET.CFG file provides configuration information to LSL.COM. This section is usually included when there is more than one protocol running at any given time. Table 4.9 provides the configuration options available for this section.

Table 4.9 Available LINK SUPPORT options to be used in the NET.CFG file.			
Option	**Default**	**Example**	**Description**
BUFFERS # [size]	0 buffers, 1130 bytes	BUFFERS 10 2108	When packets are being transmitted and received, they are first stored in the station's memory. While IPX and SPX do not require the use of buffers, some protocols may (as in TCP/IP requires at least two). When setting the buffer size, it should be configured to be equal to the maximum packet size used on the network. The minimum buffer size that can be used is 618 bytes.
MAX BOARDS #	4	MAX BOARDS 2	Defines the maximum number of boards that can be installed within the workstation. This is a cumulative number that includes every physical board installed and every additional frame type added per board. The maximum value is 16.
MAX STACKS #	4	MAX STACKS 2	Defines the maximum number of protocol stack buffers allocated from memory. Each protocol you will use on your workstation uses a minimum of one stack. The maximum value is 16.[1]
MEMPOOL pool size		MEMPOOL 4096	Defines the size of the memory pool buffers required by some protocols; IPX and SPX do not require this setting. When using TCP/IP, you should use a MINIMUM of a 4K MEMPOOL size.

1 If you are trying to load a protocol stack and get an error stating an "out of resource" condition, try increasing the MAX STACKS setting.

NetBIOS Options

The NetBIOS section of your NET.CFG file is for configuration options that will be used by NETBIOS.EXE. Table 4.10 details these options and how they can be configured.

Table 4.10 Available NetBios options to be used in the NET.CFG file.

Option	Default	Values Allowed	Description
NETBIOS ABORT TIMEOUT = # of ticks	540		Determines the number of ticks. NetBIOS waits to receive a packet before terminating the connection.
NETBIOS BROADCAST COUNT = # of ticks	2 or 4	2 to 65535	Sets the maximum delay to broadcast a name resolution packet. The default setting is determined by the NetBIOS Internet setting. When set to ON, the default setting is 4; when set to OFF, the default setting is 2.
NETBIOS BROADCAST DELAY = # of ticks	18 or 36	2 to 65535	Determines the time, measured in ticks, it takes to transmit a name resolution packet across the network. The default value is determined by the NetBIOS Internet setting. When ON, the default is 36; when OFF, the default is 18.
NETBIOS COMMANDS = # of commands	12	4 to 250	Determines the maximum number of NetBIOS commands an application is allowed to use at any one time.
NETBIOS INTERNET = ON or OFF	ON	ON or OFF	Specifies if NetBIOS is running over a internetwork or one physical network. ON is used for an internetwork, OFF is used for a single network.
NETBIOS LISTEN TIMEOUT = # of ticks	108	1 to 65535	Sets the number of ticks—18 ticks is roughly 1 second—a station will wait without receiving a response before transmitting a watchdog packet.
NETBIOS RECEIVE BUFFERS = # of buffers	6	4 to 20	Used by NetBIOS to set the number of IPX receive buffers allocated for incoming packets.

(continues)

Installation

Table 4.10 Continued.

Option	Default	Values Allowed	Description
NETBIOS RETRY COUNT = # of retries	10 or 20	10 to 65535	The default setting is determined by the value set for the NetBIOS Internet setting. When set to ON, the default is 20; when set to OFF, the default is 10. The NetBIOS RETRY COUNT determines the number of unacknowledged packets that may be sent before the connected station is deemed inactive.
NETBIOS RETRY DELAY = # of ticks	10	10 to 65535	Specifies the amount of ticks that must pass before an unacknowledged packet is resent.
NETBIOS SEND BUFFERS = # of buffers	6	4 to 20	Used by NetBIOS to set the number of IPX send buffers allocated for outgoing packets. You should increase this option from the default when the stations are using several NetBIOS connections.
NETBIOS SESSIONS = # of sessions	32	4 to 250	Determines the number of NetBIOS sessions the workstation can run.
NETBIOS VERIFY TIMEOUT = # of ticks	54	4 to 65535	Specifies the number of ticks that must pass without receiving a packet from a connected station before requesting verification that the connected node is still on-line.
NPATCH = offset, value			Used when applying patches for NetBIOS supplied by Novell. *Always* read the accompanying documentation thoroughly for the correct settings.

NetWare DOS Requester Options

Several options can be used in your NET.CFG file under the heading NetWare DOS Requester. Table 4.11 details the options currently available. While this listing is complete at the time of writing, new options may be available when file updates come out for the DOS Requester.

Table 4.11 Available NetWare DOS requester options to be used in the NET.CFG file.			
Option	**Default**	**Values Allowed**	**Description**
AUTO LARGE TABLE = *ON or OFF*	OFF	ON or OFF	Establishes a large table of 178 bytes (ON) or a small table of 34 bytes (OFF) per bindery server connection. Whenever a connection has been broken (such as due to server failures), the workstation can automatically reattach to the server and reestablish drive mappings and printer assignments. Using a small table saves memory but decreases your chances of a successful reattachment. You should set this value to ON if your username and password are more than 16 characters. *Note:* You must include BIND RECONNECT = ON in your NET.CFG for this to work.
AUTO RECONNECT = *ON or OFF*	ON	ON or OFF	Allows you to reconnect to a NetWare 4.X file server if/when your connection has been lost— when the server goes down. By setting this value to ON, your connection, printer assignments and all drive mappings will be restored. You must include the line VLM=AUTO.VLM in your NET.CFG for this option to work.
AUTO RETRY = *# of seconds*	5	0 to 3640 seconds	Specifies the amount of time the AUTO.VLM should wait before attempting to reestablish the network connection after receiving a critical network error.
AVERAGE NAME LENGTH = *# of characters*	48	2 to 48	Using this option, you may be able to save yourself a little bit of memory. The requester automatically reserves 48 bytes for each server name in your connection table. For optimal memory utilization, you should set this value to the size of the largest server name on your network.

(continues)

Table 4.11 Continued.

Option	Default	Values Allowed	Description
BIND RECONNECT = *ON or OFF*	OFF	ON or OFF	When set to ON, this option automatically restores drive mappings, printer assignments, and your connection after a server failure. When set to ON, this option requires that you set AUTO RECONNECT = ON and VLM=AUTO.VLM in your NET.CFG.
CACHE BUFFERS = *# of buffers*	5	0 to 64	Sets the number of cache buffers used to cache files open on the server.[1]
CACHE BUFFER SIZE = *# of bytes*	See Description	64 to 4096	Sets the size of the local cache buffers to get the best performance by setting this value to match your packet size minus 64 bytes. The default value for this option is the maximum for your media minus 64. For example, an Ethernet packet is 1,500 bytes long, therefore 1,500 minus 64 would make the default 1,436 bytes.
CACHE WRITES = *ON or OFF*	ON	ON or OFF	When set to ON, your PC reports writes to the cache buffer to the Requester *before* they are com-pleted. Setting to OFF will only report when the write is completed. Setting this value to off provides the highest degree of integrity while the ON setting improves performance.
CHECKSUM = *value*	1	0 to 3	Determines if checksums are embedded within an IPX packet. 0=Do Not Use Checksums, 1=Use Checksums Only When Re-quested, 2=Use Checksums With Any Device Capable Of Using Checksums, 3=Always Use Checksums.
CONNECTIONS = *# of connections*	8	2 to 50	With NetWare 4.X, you can connect to more than eight file servers at a time. Setting this value higher than neccessary wastes memory. *Note:* Setting this value greater than 8 when using NetWare 3.X or NetWare 2.X servers does not work properly.

Option	Default	Values Allowed	Description
DOS NAME = *name*	MS_DOS	Any Name, Maximum 5 Characters	Overrides the autodetection of the DOS version you are running.
FIRST NETWORK DRIVE = *drive*	First Available Drive	Any Drive Between A: and Z:	Sets the first drive letter to be used when accessing the network; usually it is F:.
HANDLE NET ERRORS = *ON or OFF*	ON	ON or OFF	Setting this option to ON causes network errors to be viewed as DOS error codes and will be dealt with by the DOS error handler. Setting this option to OFF uses the NetWare error code. *Note:* Some applications will not work properly when this value is set to OFF.
LARGE INTERNET PACKETS = *ON or OFF*	ON	ON or OFF	If your router can transmit packets greater than 576 bytes, set this value to ON; otherwise, set it to OFF. *Note:* Some routers are programmed to use 576 byte packets only; in cases like this, the DOS Requester will only use 576 byte packets regardless of this setting.
LOAD CONN TABLE LOW = *ON or OFF*	OFF	ON or OFF	This option first came about with NetWare 4.0 and does basically the same thing LOAD LOW CONN does except the default for this one is OFF.
LOAD LOW CONN = *ON or OFF*	ON	ON or OFF	Leaving this value set as ON loads CONN.VLM in conventional memory; it uses 3K of RAM. By keeping your server connection table in conventional memory, your PC will operate faster than loading it high.
LOAD LOW IPXNCP = *ON or OFF*	ON	ON or OFF	Leaving this value set to ON loads IPXNCP.VLM in conventional memory; it uses 4K of RAM. When packets are received and sent from the station, IPXNCP must examine each one. When loading IPXNCP in conventional memory, your PC operates faster than loading it high.
LOCAL PRINTERS = *# of printers*	3	0 to 9	Sets the number of local printers you have attached to your PC. A setting of 0 means you have no printers attached.[2]

Installation

(continues)

Table 4.11 Continued.

Option	Default	Values Allowed	Description
LONG MACHINE TYPE = *name*	IBM_PC	Any name up to six characters	Sets the machine name associated with the PC. The value can be referenced by the MACHINE login script variable.
MAX TASKS = *# of tasks*	31	5 to 254	Your PC uses up one task for every process running at any given time, including opening and closing files. This option defines the maximum number of tasks your PC can work on at once; Microsoft Windows workstations may require you to increase from the default.
MESSAGE LEVEL = *value*	1	0 to 4	Specifies what the requester should display when loading the VLMS. 0=Copyright, version and critical errors, 1=Level 0 plus warnings, 2=Level 1 plus name and version of each loaded VLM, 3=Level 2 plus configuration information for each loaded VLM, 4=Level 3 plus diagnostic messages.
MESSAGE TIMEOUT = *# of ticks*	0	0 to 10000	Determines the number of processor ticks required before a broadcast message is cleared from the workstation's screen. A value of 0 means the user must clear this messages manually. *Note: 10,000 ticks is roughly 6hrs.*
MINIMUM TIME TO NET = *# of milliseconds*	0	Any value specified in milliseconds.	Overrides the value set by the router during a connection. Used when connections are made through satellite links when the default restricts a station from making a connection when the transfer rate is less than 2400 baud or when the NetWare 2.X or NetWare 3.X server on the other side of the link is not using packet bursting.
NAME CONTEXT = *name*	"ROOT"	"Any Context"	Sets the starting context when logging into directory services. Context should be enclosed in double quotes. This option is not required for a NetWare 3.X LAN.

Option	Default	Values Allowed	Description
NETWORK PRINTERS = *# of printers*	3	0 to 9	Sets the maximum number of parallel (LPT) ports that can be captured. A setting of 0 restricts PRINT.VLM from loading.
NETWARE PROTOCOL = *protocol*		BIND or NDS	Allows you to specify which order you want to load the protocol VLMs without having to set USE DEFAULTS=OFF and then specifying all of the VLMs within your NET.CFG file.
PB BUFFERS = *# of buffers*	3	0 to 10	Determines whether the workstation can use packet bursting. A value of 0 turns packet bursting off; any other value uses packet bursting, when supported on the LAN.
PBURST READ WINDOW SIZE	16		*There is no reason to change this parameter. Doing so could cause serious network problems.*
PBURST WRITE WINDOW SIZE	10		*There is no reason to change this parameter. Doing so could cause serious network problems.*
PREFERRED SERVER = *server name*		Any Server	Establishes what server your workstation will try to connect to first when loading the Requester. Do not use this parameter when logging in to your network as an NDS client. Doing so may result in authentication problems.
PREFERRED TREE = *tree name*		Any Valid Directory Tree Name	Establishes the NDS directory tree you will be placed in when first loading the requester.
PRINT BUFFER SIZE = *# of bytes*	64 BYTES	0 to 256 bytes	Sets the size of the print buffer used to cache print spooling between the software and the packet driver. When redirected printing is spooled, the size of the packets is very small. By increasing buffer size, you reduce the number of packets; therefore, the printing is sped up.[3]
PRINT HEADER = *# of bytes*	64 BYTES	0 to 1024 bytes	Sets the size of the print header to be used. The header holds setup information such as printer initialization strings.

(continues)

Table 4.11 Continued.

Option	Default	Values Allowed	Description
PRINT TAIL = *# of bytes*	16 BYTES	0 to 1024 bytes	Sets the size of the print tail to be used. The print tail resets the printer after each job.
READ ONLY COMPATIBILITY = *ON or OFF*	OFF	On or OFF	Set this value to ON if you are trying to use an application that insists on trying to open a file in READ/WRITE mode.
SEARCH MODE = *value*	1	0 to 7	Specifies how an executable file will be able to search for other files (such as the CAPTURE.EXE command opens the file PRINTCON.DAT when run). 0=No special instructions. DOS searches the path for COM, EXE, or BAT files. Executables will only search based on the locations encoded within the program. 1=Executables first search the encoded locations within the program and will then scan the path. 2= Only searches the working directory and ignores encoded locations. 3=Searches hard coded location except read-only executables that will search encoded locations, working directory, and then the path. 4=Not used. 5=Searches working directory and path—this is the option commonly used for CAPTURE.EXE. 6=Not Used. 7=Read-only executables searches working directory and path regardless of the encoding.
SET STATION TIME = *ON or OFF*	ON	ON or OFF	Determines if your workstation synchronizes its clock with the server's when first connecting to the server.
SHORT MACHINE TYPE = *name*	IBM	Any name up to four characters	Can be used to override the short machine name used when using overlay files. Can be used by the SMACHINE login script variable.

Option	Default	Values Allowed	Description
SHOW DOTS = *ON or OFF*	OFF	ON or OFF	Unlike DOS, NetWare does not use a "." to symbolize the current directory or a ".." to symbolize the parent directory. Setting this value to ON will force the requested to insert a "." and a ".." in the directory listing. This option is required when using Windows prior to version 3.1.
SIGNATURE LEVEL = *value*	1	0 to 3	Packet signing can be used on the Novell LAN to prevent anyone from trying to "crack" into the server or network. Using this option, you can set the degree of protection required. 0=Do Not Use Packet Signatures, 1=Use Packet Signatures Only When Requested, 2=Using Packet Signatures If The Server Can Sign Packets, 3=Require Packet Signatures For All Packets.
TRUE COMMIT = *ON or OFF*	OFF	ON or OFF	Setting this value to ON ensures that an application does not receive an acknowledgment of a successful write to the server disk until the data is actually written. While using ON decreases the overall performance, it provides the highest degree of integrity.
USE DEFAULTS = *ON or OFF*	ON	ON or OFF	Determines if VLM.EXE loads all default VLM files. When set to OFF, the VLM= option is used to specify which VLMs should be loaded.
VLM = *[path]\name*		Any .VLM file	Specifies what .VLM file should be loaded, including path, unless stored in the current directory.

1 *You will get the best performance by setting the CACHE BUFFERS equal to the number of files that are open at any one time, but you will use up more memory.*

2 *If you have no locally attached printers, and you have not captured to a print queue, setting the LOCAL PRINTERS to 0 prevents your PC from freezing if you press Shift+Print Screen.*

3 *When you usually print large graphics jobs, increasing the PRINT BUFFER SIZE can increase performance.*

NETX Options

The NETX section of the NET.CFG file provides configuration information when using the NETX shell. Table 4.12 provides a listing of the available options.

Note

Some of the parameters shown in the DOS Requester section are also valid for NETX. If both sections exist in your NET.CFG, NETX scans through the DOS Requester section and uses any settings it considers valid. Remember though, you cannot use NETX and the DOS Requester at the same time.

Table 4.12 Available NETX options to be used in the NET.CFG file.

Option	Default	Values Allowed	Description
ALL SERVERS = *ON or OFF*	OFF	ON or OFF	When this value is set to ON, an End Of Task (EOT) will be sent to all currently attached file servers.
ENTRY STACK SIZE = *value*	10	5 to 40	Confirms if a program running in expanded memory should be visible in the memory frame page. *Do not change this value unless required.*
ENVIRONMENT PAD = *# of bytes*	17	17 to 512	Determines how many bytes should be added to a program's environment space before the program is executed. By increasing this parameter, you can allow a NetWare utility to update the workstation's path variable when adding search drives.
EOJ = *ON or OFF*	ON	ON or OFF	Specifies if a files should be closed automatically at the end of a job.
FILE HANDLES= *# of open files*	40		Determines how many files a workstation can have open on the network at any given time. *Note:* The value set here has no bearing on files stored locally to the workstation; for this, you must use the FILES parameter in your CONFIG.SYS.
HOLD = *ON or OFF*	OFF	ON or OFF	Specifies if workstation files should be held open when they have been accessed until the application is exited.
LOCK DELAY = *# of ticks*	1		Specifies how long the shell (NETX) should wait before trying to lock a file. You may want to increase this value if the station is getting frequent errors when accessing a file.

Option	Default	Values Allowed	Description
LOCK RETRIES = *# of retries*	3		Specifies how many times the shell (NETX) should attempt to get a lock on a file. You may want to try increasing this value if the station is getting frequent errors when accessing a file.
MAX CUR DIR LENGTH = *# of bytes*	64	64 to 255	Specifies the maximum number of bytes that can be returned by DOS to specify the current directory.
MAX PATH LENGTH = *# of bytes*	255	64 to 255	Specifies the size of the maximum path excluding the server's name and file names.
SHARE = *ON or OFF*	ON	ON or OFF	When set to ON, allows a process to use the same resources that its parent can, such as files or RAM.
SIGN 386 MODE = *value*	1	0 to 2	Used for NCP packet signatures when using the NETX shell if Windows is loaded in enhanced mode from the network. 0=Enable interrupts, 1= disable interrupts, 2= force 16 bit signing.

Installation

PROTOCOL IPXODI Options

The PROTOCOL IPXODI section of the NET.CFG file provides in-depth configuration options for the IPX protocol being run from the workstation. Table 4.13 provides a listing of the valid parameters for this section.

Table 4.13 Available PROTOCOL IPXODI options to be used in the NET.CFG file.

Option	Default	Values Allowed	Example	Description
BIND *board #*			BIND 3	When IPX/SPX loads, by default, it attempts to bind to the first NIC installed in the workstation. When multiple NICs are installed, you must include a statement informing the requester to bind IPX to any additional boards other than the first one installed.

(continues)

Table 4.13 Continued.

Option	Default	Values Allowed	Example	Description
CONFIG OPTION #	0		CONFIG OPTION 3	Overrides the value chosen when generating your IPX.COM file.
INT64 = ON or OFF	ON	ON or OFF	INT64 = OFF	Enables the workstation to use interrupt 64 when accessing services from IPX. If you have an application that worked on earlier versions of NetWare but does not work on your NetWare 3.11 or 3.12 server, try setting this value to OFF.
INT7A = ON or OFF	ON	ON or OFF	INT7A = OFF	Enables the workstation to use interrupt 7A when accessing services from IPX. If you have an application that worked on earlier versions of NetWare but does not work on your NetWare 3.11 or 3.12 server, try setting this value to OFF.
IPATCH = byte offset, value				When patches are available for IPX, this option is used to actually apply the patch to IPX. Before doing so, carefully read the text file or document that accompanies the patch.
IPX PACKET SIZE LIMIT = # of bytes	4160	576 to 6500	IPX PACKET SIZE LIMIT = 1500	Reduces the maximum size allowed for the packet. If you are getting errors about insufficient memory, you can try reducing this number; but for optimal performance, your should use the largest possible packet size. For Ethernet, the optimal setting is 1500 while the optimal setting for Token Ring is 4160.

Option	Default	Values Allowed	Example	Description
IPX RETRY COUNT = # of retries	20	0 to 65535	IPX RETRY COUNT = 100	Tells IPX how many times it should attempt to resend a packet after it has been lost.
IPX SOCKETS = # of sockets	20	10 to 150	IPX SOCKETS = 40	On the workstation one IPX socket is used for each process that communicates with any other IPX device, such as LANSchool. Depending on the applications in use, this value may require that you increase it from the default.
MINIMUM SPX RETRIES = # of retries	20	0 to 255	MINIMUM SPX RETRIES = 60	Specifies how many times the workstation should attempt to establish a connection via SPX before giving up.*
SPX ABORT TIMEOUT = # of ticks	540	1 to 65535	SPX ABORT TIMEOUT = 1000	Determines how long SPX will wait without receiving a response before it terminates a connection. *Note:* 540 ticks is roughly 30 seconds.
SPX CONNECTIONS = # of connections	15	5 to 255	SPX CONNECTIONS = 15	Specifies the maximum number of SPX connections that can be used by the workstation at any one time.
SPX LISTEN TIMEOUT = # of ticks	108	1 to 65535	SPX LISTEN TIMEOUT = 15000	Specifies the amount of time that SPX will wait without receiving a response before it requests the connected node to acknowledge the connection is still valid. The request sent from the workstation is known as a "watchdog packet."

(continues)

Installation

Table 4.13 Continued.

Option	Default	Values Allowed	Example	Description
SPX VERIFY TIMEOUT = # of ticks	54	1 to 65535	SPX VERIFY TIMEOUT = 12000	Specifies the amount of time that SPX will wait before it sends a packet of information to the other connection that it is still on-line (known as being "alive").

* If you have an SPX application that is losing its connections from time to time, try increasing the MINIMUM SPX RETRIES.

TBMI2 Options

The options found in Table 4.14 are used in the NET.CFG file to affect how TBMI2 operates in a multitasking environment such as Windows. These options are placed under the section heading "TBMI2 Options."

Note

If you are running Windows in Enhanced mode on a 386 or better CPU, you should not run TBMI2.

Table 4.14 Available TBMI2 options to be used in the NET.CFG file.

Option	Default	Values Allowed	Description
DATA ECB COUNT = #	60	10 to 255	Specifies the number of DATA ECBs (Event Control Blocks) allocated to buffer packets for NetBIOS or IPX/SPX programs running in Windows. The maximum amount of memory that can be allocated to ECBs is 64K; therefore, since each data ECB requires 628 bytes of RAM, you would be hard pressed to use the maximum of 255 data ECBs. If 60 are not required on your station, you can try decreasing this value to 30 or 40 to salvage some valuable RAM.
ECB COUNT = #	20	10 TO 255	Specifies the number of non-data ECBs allocated. The maximum amount of memory that can be allocated to ECBs is 64K; therefore, since each ECB requires 52 bytes of RAM, in most cases, the maximum will be less than 255.

Option	Default	Values Allowed	Description
INT64 = *ON or OFF*	ON	ON or OFF	Similiar to the IPX INT64 setting, determines if IPX/SPX services can be accessed through interrupt 64.[1]
INT7A = *ON or OFF*	ON	ON or OFF	Similiar to the IPX INT7A setting, determines if IPX/SPX services can be accessed through interrupt 7A.[2]
USE MAX PACKETS			Tells TBMI2 to use the maximum packet size specified as the maximum IPX packet size.
USING WINDOWS 3.0			Tells TBMI2 it should use the TASKID program.

[1] *If an application was working with older versions of NetWare but will not work with your NetWare 3.11 or 3.12 server, try setting the INT64 parameter to OFF.*
[2] *If an application was working with older versions of NetWare but will not work with your NetWare 3.11 or 3.12 server, try setting the INT7A parameter to OFF.*

Loading the Workstation Files and Command-Line Options

Up to this point, everything covered has been a preparation for actually loading ODI/NETX or the DOS Requester. Depending on the method you have chosen, there will be slight differences within this section.

ODI/NETX

Loading the older ODI/NETX implementation of the workstation files is rather simple. Once the files have been installed, loading the files is as simple as 1, 2, 3, and 4. With your default drive and directory at the location of the ODI/NETX files, type:

1. **LSL**

2. **IPXODI**

3. **MLID** (replace with your NIC driver)

Tip
If you are using a Token Ring card, your workstation must be physically connected to the network cabling or the driver will not load.

4. **NETX** or **EMSNETX** or **XMSNETX**

After Step 4, a confirmation line should appear on the screen stating something similiar to `Attached To Server FS1`. If you do not see this confirmation line, there could be something wrong with your workstation or LAN. Refer to the heading "Resolving Problems with Users that Cannot Log In" in Chapter 29 for instructions on how to troubleshoot these problems.

The DOS Requester

If you went through the full DOS Requester installation procedure and allowed the INSTALL program to modify your AUTOEXEC.BAT and CONFIG.SYS files, you can reboot the workstation and it automatically loads all the necessary files to let you log into the server. If you didn't allow the INSTALL program to make the necessary adjustments, you must make the following changes manually.

First, in the CONFIG.SYS file, add the line `LASTDRIVE=Z` at the end of the file. Next, if you want the requester to load automatically when your PC boots, add the line `@CALL C:\NWCLIENT\STARTNET.BAT` at the beginning of the AUTOEXEC.BAT file.

Caution
Before you can load the DOS Requester properly, the workstation must be rebooted to make sure changes to the CONFIG.SYS are activated.

If you do *not* run the STARTNET.BAT file, it is still possible to access the network by loading the necessary components manually. To do so, you should:

1. Change to the directory where the Requester files are stored (type **CD \NWCLIENT** and press Enter).

2. Establish the language that you will be using by typing **SET NWLANGUAGE=XXXXXXXX** where *XXXXXXXX* is the supported language (for instance, **ENGLISH**) and press Enter.

3. Type **LSL** to load the Link Support Layer driver and press Enter.

4. Enter the name of the NIC driver (such as **TOKEN**) and press Enter.

5. Type **IPXODI** to load the IPX ODI driver and press Enter.

6. Type **VLM** to load the DOS Requester and establish a connection with the server and press Enter.

Tip
Other ODI drivers can be loaded into upper memory but you should never try to force the VLM.EXE file into the upper-memory region (for example, by using the DOS LOADHI command). VLM.EXE automatically loads itself into the best available memory area.

Once the requester (VLM.EXE) has been loaded, you should see a confirmation stating something like Attached To Server FS1. If you do not get a confirmation after loading VLM.EXE, there could be something wrong with your workstation or LAN. Refer to the heading "Resolving Problems with Users That Cannot Log In" in Chapter 29 for instructions on how to resolve these problems.

Advanced Loading Switches You Can Use with ODI/NETX and the DOS Requester

With the ODI files and the DOS Requester, there are several command-line "switches" you can use when loading the files for the first time or after they are already loaded; these switches are optional additions to the respective command lines.

Tables 4.15 through 4.18 provide listings of the switches that are available at the time of writing this book. As updated files becoming available, some switches may be removed and others may be added.

Table 4.15 Switches available for use with LSL.COM.		
Switch	**Example**	**Description**
/?	LSL /?	Displays the help screen and version information for LSL.COM.
/C=[path\]filename	LSL C:\NEW.TXT	Specifies a different configuration file to be used other than the default NET.CFG in the current directory.
/F	LSL /F	Forcibly unloads LSL.COM. Unlike the /U switch, /F unloads LSL.COM even if other TSRs have been loaded after it. This option should be used with caution, as it could cause errors that will force you to reboot.
/H	LSL /H	Displays the help screen and version information for LSL.COM.
/S	LSL /S	Provides statistical information on LSL.COM, such as that shown in Figure 4.5.
/U	LSL /U	Removes LSL.COM from memory after it has been loaded. You will not be able to use this option if any TSRs were loaded after LSL.COM.

Table 4.16 Switches available for use with IPXODI.COM.

Switch	Example	Description
/?	IPXODI /?	Displays the help screen and version information for IPXODI.COM.
/A	IPXODI /A	Forces IPXODI to load without the diagnostic responder and SPX portion of IPXODI reducing the memory requirement by 9K.
/C=[path\]FILENAME	IPXODI /C=C:\NEW.TXT	Allows you to specify a configuration file to be used other than the default NET.CFG in the current directory.
/D	IPXODI /D	Forces IPXODI to load without the diagnostic responder portion of IPXODI reducing the memory requirement by 3K.
/F	IPXODI /F	Forcibly unloads IPXODI from memory regardless of the TSRs that were loaded after it. This option should be used with caution as it could cause errors that will cause you to reboot.
/U	IPXODI /U	Cleanly unloads IPXODI from memory. You will not be able to use this option if TSRs were loaded after IPXODI.

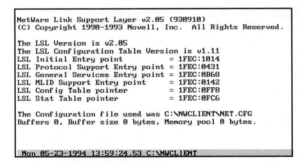

Fig. 4.5 Running LSL.COM with the /S statistics switch.

Table 4.17 Switches available for use with NET.EXE, EMSNETX.EXE, and XMSNETX.EXE. The old shell files used with the ODI/NETX implementation (EMSNETX or XMSNETX can be substituted for NETX throughout the table).

Switch	Example	Description
/?	NETX /?	Displays help screen and version information of NETX.EXE.
/C=[path\]FILENAME	NETX /C=C:\NEW.TXT	Allows you to specify a configuration file other than the default NET.CFG in the current directory to be used.
/F	NETX /F	Forcibly unloads NETX from memory regardless of the TSRs that were loaded after it. This option should be used with caution as it could cause errors that will cause you to reboot.
/PS=*XXXXXXXX*	NETX /PS=FS1	Specifies a preferred server location when loading. Replace *XXXXXXXX* with the name of a valid NetWare file server.
/U	NETX /U	Cleanly unloads NETX from memory. This option will not work if you have loaded any TSR after loading NETX.

Table 4.18 Switches available for use with VLM.EXE, the new DOS requester.

Switch	Example	Description
/?	VLM /?	Displays the help screen and version information for VLM.EXE.
/C=[path\]*filename*	VLM /C:\NEW.TXT	Enables you to specify a configuration file other than the default NET.CFG in the current directory to be used.
/D	VLM /D	Displays the VLM diagnotics screen as shown in Figures 4.6 and 4.7. You can use these diagnostic screens to determine what type of memory the Requester is using and what VLMs were loaded.
/M*x*	VLM /ME	Tells the Requester what type of memory you want to use. By default, VLM.EXE will try to use extended memory; if none is available, or it doesn't exist, VLM.EXE will try expanded memory. If no expanded memory is available, VLM.EXE will load into conventional memory. You can override this process by directing the Requester directly to the type of memory you want to use. Replace *x* with **X** for Extended, **E** for Expanded, or **C** for Conventional RAM.

(continues)

Table 4.18 Continued.		
Switch	**Example**	**Description**
/PS=*XXXXXXXX*	VLM /PS=FS1	Specifies a preferred server location when loading. Replace *XXXXXXXX* with the name of a valid NetWare file server.
/PT="*XXXXXXXX*"	VLM /PT="DJASYSTEMS"	Specifies the preferred tree to which you would like to attach in a NetWare 4.X environment.
/V*x*	VLM /V3	When the VLM loads, it is possible to control the amount of information that it provides to you. You have the following options for the value of *x*: **0**=Displays critical errors and copyright information only. **1**=Same as 0 plus warning messages. **2**=Same as 1 plus names of VLM modules that are loaded. **3**=Same as 2 plus configuration parameters. Figure 4.8 contains an example of VLM.EXE loading with the /V3 switch. **4**=Same as 3 plus diagnostic messages.

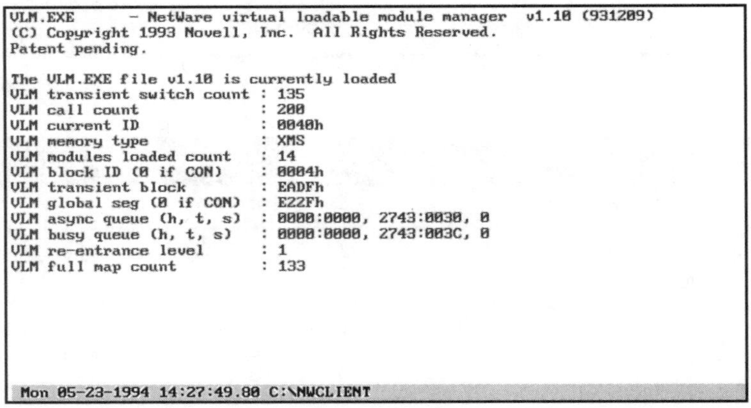

```
VLM.EXE      - NetWare virtual loadable module manager  v1.10 (931209)
(C) Copyright 1993 Novell, Inc.  All Rights Reserved.
Patent pending.

The VLM.EXE file v1.10 is currently loaded
VLM transient switch count : 135
VLM call count             : 200
VLM current ID             : 0040h
VLM memory type            : XMS
VLM modules loaded count   : 14
VLM block ID (0 if CON)    : 0004h
VLM transient block        : EADFh
VLM global seg (0 if CON)  : E22Fh
VLM async queue (h, t, s)  : 0000:0000, 2743:0030, 0
VLM busy queue (h, t, s)   : 0000:0000, 2743:003C, 0
VLM re-entrance level      : 1
VLM full map count         : 133



 Mon 05-23-1994 14:27:49.80 C:\NWCLIENT
```

Fig. 4.6 First half of VLM.EXE diagnostic screen.

```
VLM diagnostic information           Address       Memory Sizes (decimal)
NAME     ID   Flag Func Maps Call TSeg GSeg Low  High  TSize  GSize  SSize
-------- ---- ---- ---- ---- ---- ---- ---- ---- ----  -----  -----  -----
VLM      0001 A000 0005 0000 01BE 2743 08AF FFFF 0000   4912      0      0
CONN     0010 B000 0011 0000 003E E22F E2F3 FFFF FFFF   3136    384   6688
IPXNCP   0021 B000 000B 0000 0015 E30B E428 FFFF FFFF   4560   2928   1952
TRAN     0020 E000 000B 0001 0019 E30B E428 FFFF FFFF    285    183   1952
SECURITY 0061 A000 0005 0004 0003 EADF E4DF 0000 0000   4192      0   3280
NDS      0032 A000 0010 0018 0017 EADF E4DF 1060 0000   5952    896    992
BIND     0031 A000 0010 0006 0005 EADF E517 27A0 0000   2992    448    720
NWP      0030 A000 0011 0012 0004 EADF E533 3350 0000   2960   1824   1216
FIO      0041 A000 000B 0004 0003 EADF E5A5 3EE0 0000   6832  10176    400
GENERAL  0043 A000 000A 0018 0017 EADF E821 5990 0000   1744    624   1328
REDIR    0040 A000 0009 007B 006E EADF E848 6068 0000   9520   2400   1216
PRINT    0042 A000 000F 0019 0016 EADF E8DE 8590 0000   3936   2800   1520
NETX     0050 A000 0007 0029 0022 EADF E98D 94F0 0000   8992   4016   2112
NMR      0100 A000 0007 0009 0003 EADF EA88 B810 0000   1728    784   6128
AUTO     0060 A000 0006 0006 0003 EADF EAB9 BED0 0000   2256    592   1088
Total                                                  63712  27072
Maximum                                                 9520  10176   6688


 Mon 05-23-1994 14:09:13.44 C:\NWCLIENT
```

Fig. 4.7 Second half of VLM.EXE diagnostic screen.

```
 Mon 05-23-1994 14:13:52.63 C:\NWCLIENT vlm -v3
VLM.EXE       - NetWare virtual loadable module manager   v1.10 (931209)
(C) Copyright 1993 Novell, Inc.   All Rights Reserved.
Patent pending.
VLM NMR.VLM
VLM AUTO.VLM

The VLM.EXE file is pre-initializing the VLMs..............
The VLM.EXE file is using extended memory (XMS).
CONN.VLM      - NetWare connection table manager   v1.10 (931209)
IPXNCP.VLM    - NetWare IPX transport module  v1.10 (931209)
TRAN.VLM      - NetWare transport multiplexor module  v1.10 (931209)
SECURITY.VLM  - NetWare security enhancement module   v1.10 (931209)
NDS.VLM       - NetWare directory services protocol module   v1.10 (931209)
BIND.VLM      - NetWare bindery protocol module   v1.10 (931209)
NWP.VLM       - NetWare protocol multiplexor module   v1.10 (931209)
FIO.VLM       - NetWare file input-output module  v1.10 (931209)
GENERAL.VLM   - NetWare general purpose function module  v1.10 (931209)
REDIR.VLM     - NetWare DOS redirector module  v1.10 (931209)
PRINT.VLM     - NetWare printer redirection module  v1.10 (931209)
NETX.VLM      - NetWare workstation shell module  v4.10 (931209)
NMR.VLM       - NetWare management responder  v1.01 (930402)
AUTO.VLM      - NetWare auto-reconnect module  v1.10 (931209)
```

Fig. 4.8 Loading VLM.EXE so it displays detailed information while loading.

Chapter 5

Network Connection

NetWare file servers can provide a wide variety of resources to users on the LAN or WAN, ranging from printing capabilities and basic file sharing to in-depth and advanced database and communications systems. But before any of these services is available to the user, a connection must be established between the user's workstation and the file server.

In this section, we explore the options available to you for getting to these resources, and specifically:

- Checking a server's availability
- Logging into a file server
- Attaching to a file server
- Logging out of a file server

Locating a File Server

While most people logging into the network already know what server they are to log into, the time will come when either someone will forget the exact spelling of the server's name or you are on a LAN/WAN with multiple file servers and want to check if a server is up and running.

NetWare includes a utility called SLIST that provides a listing of all servers currently online and accessible. There are several ways to use SLIST, each of which are depicted below:

To view a listing of all file servers currently online, type:

```
SLIST
```

To view a listing of the domains on your LAN using the NetWare Naming Service, type:

```
SLIST /D
```

Tip

Wild cards can be used with the SLIST command to reduce the amount of output SLIST will provide. This is especially helpful on large LANs or WANs with multiple file servers. Using the * and ? wild cards, you can try to fine tune your search. For example, to search the LAN for all servers that begin with the letters PS, you could type **SLIST PS***.

Getting into the Server

After the server operating system has been installed, the network cabling has been set up, and the workstations are installed and configured, the next step is to establish a connection with the file server. You are not able to make use of the resources that the server has to offer until you either LOGIN or ATTACH to the server.

While attaching and logging into the server will both establish a connection, they serve different purposes. The purpose of logging in is to establish a connection with the server and run batch-like files, called *login scripts*, to configure your environment. Attaching to a server merely establishes a connection. Depending on your requirements, you may log in, attach, or both. Either way, there are several options available to you that are discussed in this section.

Logging in with LOGIN

Stored within the SYS:LOGIN and SYS:PUBLIC directories, LOGIN.EXE must be run to log into the file server. By using LOGIN, you not only establish a connection with the server, but, by default, you also will execute the server's login script and gain access to the server's resources. There are several methods to use with the LOGIN program, depending on your requirements. Following is a listing of the different options available to you:

Tip

If/When you update your LOGIN.EXE file with a newer version, always remember to copy it to the PUBLIC and LOGIN directories. Having two versions on the server can cause unpredictable results.

To log into a file server other than your default, use the following syntax:

```
LOGIN servername/username
```

To log into your default file server, use the following syntax:

```
LOGIN username
```

or

```
LOGIN servername/username
```

Note

In the above examples, you do not have to specify the servername or username from the command line if you don't want to. When left out, NetWare prompts you for them.

In addition to these commands, there are three switches that may prove useful when using the LOGIN program.

To clear the screen after entering your password, use this syntax:

```
LOGIN /c servername/username
```

To run a script file other than the system script when logging in, use this syntax:

```
LOGIN /s=path\scriptname servername/username
```

To run a script file when you are already logged into the file server, use this syntax:

```
LOGIN /na servername/username /s=path\scriptname
```

Tip

If you are logging into the server and getting a double mapping for the PUBLIC directory, it could be because the system login script *and* the default login script are being run. To prevent this, you can add a parameter to your system login script called NO_DEFAULT, but you must be running at least LOGIN.EXE version 3.70. To find out what version you are running, use the VERSION.EXE program stored in the PUBLIC directory.

Attaching to a Server with the ATTACH Command

Using the ATTACH command, you can access a file server and its resources—security permitting—without logging out of your current file server. Unlike the LOGIN command that runs a script file, ATTACH merely establishes the connection.

II

Environment Setup

To attach to a file server, use this syntax:

```
ATTACH servername/username
```

If you do not enter the servername and username on the command line, you will be prompted for them.

Connecting to a Server from within the Menus

Several of the NetWare menu utilities—such as SYSCON, FCONSOLE, and DSPACE—have a main menu option such as Change Current File Server or Change File Server. By selecting this menu option, you can see what servers to which you are currently attached *and* you can attach to other file servers. To do so:

1. Where available, select Change Current File Server or Change File Server.

2. Once selected, a window appears, showing you the servers that you are currently logged into. To attach to another server, press the Insert key and a listing of available servers is shown.

3. Cursor through the listing of servers and select the desired one by pressing the Enter key. When asked, type in your username and password.

Getting Out of the Server

Whether you want to change default file servers or you are leaving for the day, you must eventually break the connection between your workstation and the file server. There are a couple of methods that you can use to do so, as shown below.

Logging Out with LOGOUT

The LOGOUT command breaks the connection between your workstation and the file server(s) that you are logged into. Once the connection is broken, resources on that file server will not be accessible to you.

To log out of all file servers that you are logged into, use the following syntax:

```
LOGOUT
```

When you are logged into multiple servers at once, you can log out of only one by using:

```
LOGOUT servername
```

Shortcut
Wild cards can be used with the LOGOUT command. For example, assume you are logged into multiple servers called FS1, FS2, SERVA, and SERVB. If you want to log out of the FS1 and FS2 servers but remain connected to SERVA and SERVB, you could type **LOGOUT FS?** or **LOGOUT FS*.** In either method, you would be logged out of FS1 and FS2, but your connection to SERVA and SERVB would remain.

Disconnecting from a Server from within the Menus

Several of the NetWare menu utilities, such as SYSCON, FCONSOLE, or DSPACE, have a main menu option such as Change Current File Server or Change File Server. By selecting this menu option, you can see what servers you are currently attached to *and* you can log out from any of these servers *except* your default server. To do so:

1. Where available, select Change Current File Server or Change File Server.

2. Once selected, you are presented with a window showing you the servers that you are currently logged into. Select the server that you would like to log out from and press Delete.

Shortcut
From this listing, you can log out from several servers at once. Press the F5 key to select each one from which you would like to log out. Once the servers are all selected, press Delete.

II

Environment Setup

Chapter 6

Configuring the Server Default Setup

For some individuals, setting up users on the file server is a long and drawn out process. When the server only has a few users, configuring each ID on an individual basis is not too bad, but when there are numerous IDs to be set up, individual configuration is not always an option.

NetWare provides you with the option of setting up default configurations that pertain to all new users. By using default setups, the amount of time it takes you to get the users up and running can be drastically reduced. In this section, we look at using these defaults, and specifically:

■ Setting default account balances and restrictions

■ Setting default time restrictions

Note

These default parameters are not written in stone for each user ID. When required, these options can be changed on an individual basis within the user's personal configuration.

Setting Account Balance/Restrictions

Default account restrictions are established for a wide variety of reasons, such as setting password requirements or connection limitations. To view or change your server's default account restrictions, first log in to the file server as a SUPERVISOR or SUPERVISOR EQUIVALENT. Once in, access the PUBLIC directory and type **SYSCON**.

When SYSCON is loaded, you are presented with a menu entitled Available Topics. From this menu, you must select Supervisor Options, then Default Account Balance/Restrictions (see fig. 6.1).

This option establishes the default account restrictions that apply to all new users created on the file server. Any users currently set up on the server will *not* be affected by changes made within this area.

```
              Default Account Balance/Restrictions
Account has expiration date:              No
   Date account expires:
Limit Concurrent Connections:            Yes
   Maximum Connections:                  1
Create Home Directory for User:          Yes
Require Password:                        Yes
   Minimum Password Length:              5
Force Periodic Password Changes:         Yes
   Days Between Forced Changes:          40
   Limit Grace Logins:                   Yes
      Grace Logins Allowed:              1
Require Unique Passwords:                No
Account Balance:                         0
Allow Unlimited Credit:                  No
   Low Balance Limit:                    0
```

Fig. 6.1 The Default Account Balance/Restrictions for the file server.

Depending on your specific requirements, there are several items you may want to change from the default settings. Table 6.1 shows you what these settings are and what the acceptable values are.

Table 6.1 Account restrictions.

Setting	Acceptable Value	Description
Account has expiration date	Yes or No	Determines if the account eventually expires. When an account expires, NetWare does not delete the account; instead, it disables it to ensure no one can access the account until the supervisor reactivates the account. Unless there is some specific reason why you would want all new IDs to have an expiration date, leave the default setting at No.
Date account expires	01/01/1900 to 12/31/2155	When you answer Yes to the above, NetWare asks you to specify an account expiration date in this field.
Limit Concurrent Connections	Yes or No	Determines if you want to limit the number of stations a single user ID can be logged into the file server from at any given time.
Maximum Connections	1 to 250	When you answer Yes to the above, NetWare asks you to specify the maximum number of stations the ID can be logged into the file server from for any given time.

Setting	Acceptable Value	Description
Create Home Directory for User	Yes or No	If you answer Yes, NetWare prompts you for the name of the user's home directory when you create a new ID.
Require Password	Yes or No	When set to Yes, NetWare requires user IDs to have a password on the server.
Minimum Password Length	1 to 20	When Require Password is set to Yes, NetWare asks you for a minimum password length. By default, this value is set to 5.
Force Periodic Password Changes	Yes or No	When Require Password is set to Yes, NetWare asks you if you want to force the users to change their passwords from time to time.
Days Between Forced Changes	1 to 365	If Force Periodic Password Changes is set to Yes, you must then specify the number of days that can go by before the users must change their passwords.
Limit Grace Logins	Yes or No	If Force Periodic Password Changes is set to Yes, you must tell NetWare if you want to limit the number of grace logins. When the password expiration date is reached, the user can continue to log into the file server without changing their password if this value is set to No.
Grace Logins Allowed	1 to 200	Shows the number of times a user can log into the file server after their password has expired *without* changing it. Once the user has used all of their grace logins, and they have *not* changed the password, they cannot log into the file server until an ID with the proper security level over the ID—such as SUPERVISOR or SUPERVISOR EQUIVALENT, Account Manager, or Workgroup Manager—goes in and either increases the number of grace logins left *or* gives them a new password.
Require Unique Passwords	Yes or No	Specifies if users can reuse their passwords. When set to Yes, NetWare keeps track of the last eight passwords that were used for at least one day. The user can make use of any password that was used prior to one of these eight passwords.

II

Environment Setup

(continues)

Table 6.1 Continued.

Setting	Acceptable Value	Description
Account Balance	+ or - 99999999	If the file server is set up to use the accounting feature, this option specifies how many "credits" a user has when their account is first created.
Allow Unlimited Credit	Yes or No	If the file server is set up to use the accounting feature, this option specifies if an unlimited number of "credits" will be granted to new users.
Low Balance Limit	+ or - 99999999	If the file server is set up to use the accounting feature *and* unlimited credits are *not* allowed, this option specifies the minimum number of credits a user must still have for NetWare to continue servicing requests from the ID.

Caution

Even if Require Password is set to Yes, it does not guarantee that a user is required to have a password. If the number of grace logins is not restricted and you do not assign an initial password for the users, they can get away without having a password. If you want all users to require a password, set the Require Password option to Yes and either restrict the number of grace logins allowed or assign an initial password to the user ID.

Setting Time Restrictions

Default time restrictions specify when users can and cannot access the file server. To view or change your server's default time restrictions, first log into the file server as a SUPERVISOR or SUPERVISOR EQUIVALENT. Once in, access the PUBLIC directory and type **SYSCON**.

When SYSCON is loaded, you are presented with a menu entitled Available Topics. From this menu, you must select Supervisor Options, then Default Time Restrictions (see fig. 6.2).

On this screen, you see a box filled with asterisks (*) and row headings whose labels are based on the days of the week. Above each column of asterisks, the different times of the day are shown.

By default, users are allowed to log into the file server 24 hours a day, seven days a week. Depending on your environment, you may want to restrict the login times to certain days of the week or certain hours of the day.

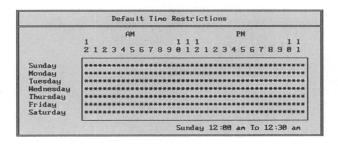

Fig. 6.2 The file server's default time restrictions that determine when users can and cannot log in.

To restrict the times a user can log into the file server, remove the asterisk (*) from the appropriate time spot by using the space bar or the Delete key. As an example, Figure 6.3 depicts a server with the default time restrictions adjusted so users cannot log in during the weekend or between the hours of midnight and 6:00 a.m. during the week.

Note

You cannot restrict the login times entirely. There must be at least one login time available.

Shortcut

When you want to remove large sections of text, you can do so by flagging the entire string of text instead of one character at a time by using the F5 key.

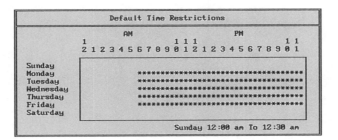

Fig. 6.3 Default time restrictions that do not allow users to log in on the weekends or between the hours of midnight and 6:00 a.m. during the week.

II

Environment Setup

Chapter 7

User IDs and Groups

When the file server is first installed, NetWare automatically creates two IDs (GUEST and SUPER-VISOR) and one group (EVERYONE). While these two IDs and the group provide you with a method of getting into the server, you will want additional IDs and groups that are specific to your installation. Using separate IDs and groups, you can restrict network resources on a per user or per group basis.

In this section, the following topics are discussed:

- Creating Groups

- Creating IDs with SYSCON

- Creating IDs with MAKEUSER

- Creating IDs with USERDEF

- Configuring Individual IDs

Groups

Groups are created on the NetWare file server to logically group individuals who require similar access or functionality. In this manner, rights and applications can be assigned to a group instead of on an individual basis. This not only reduces the amount of administration time required, but it also can improve the organizational structure on your server.

During installation, NetWare created the group EVERYONE on the file server. By default, all new users are automatically added to this group.

Creating and Viewing Groups

Using the SYSCON menu utility, you can create new groups or view the groups currently on the server by selecting the option Group Information from the Available Topics main menu of

SYSCON. After making your selection, you are presented with a window entitled Group Names that lists all of the groups currently set up on this server.

From the listing of groups, there are several tasks you can perform, such as creating a new group or deleting an existing one as you see in the following sections.

Creating a New Group

To create a new group:

1. Press the Insert key at the listing of Group Names.

2. Enter the name of the group you want to create.

> **Note**
>
> Group names can be a maximum of 47 characters.

After entering the new group's name, it is inserted into the listing of Group Names.

> **Note**
>
> You can delete a group from this screen by selecting the group name and then pressing Delete.

Viewing Detailed Information on a Group

After you have selected a group and chosen it by pressing the Enter key, you are presented with a new menu entitled Group Information (see fig. 7.1). Within this screen, there are several options you can use, as described below:

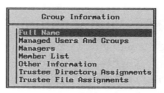

Fig. 7.1 Group Information screen that is presented after selecting a group name.

- *Full Name:* Enables you to specify the full name of this group, up to 127 characters. By using the full name, you can go into a little more depth to describe what the group is actually used for or by whom.

- *Managed Users And Groups:* Specifies the other users or groups this group manages. Refer to the heading "Operator and Manager Assignments" in Chapter 12, "Security Equivalences," for detailed information on what managers can do.

- *Managers:* Provides a listing of the users or groups that are managers of this group. Refer to the heading "Operator and Manager Assignments" in Chapter 12 for detailed information on what managers can do.

- *Member List:* Provides a listing of the users who are currently a member of this group. Refer to the heading "Adding and Deleting Users from Groups," later in this chapter for further information.

- *Other Information:* Tells you the group's bindery object ID number and if this group is assigned as a console operator. Refer to the heading "Operator and Manager Assignments," in Chapter 12 for detailed information on what console operators can do.

- *Trustee Directory Assignments:* Specifies which directories to which this group has access. Refer to Chapter 13, "Trustee Assignments and Rights," for detailed information on the various rights and how they are assigned.

- *Trustee File Assignments:* Specifies which files to which this group has access. Refer to Chapter 13, "Trustee Assignments and Rights," for detailed information on the various rights and how they are assigned.

Adding and Deleting Users from Groups

There are two ways to add or remove a user from a group listing: within the personal configuration of a user (refer to the heading "Groups Belonged To" later in the chapter), or within the Group Information option of SYSCON. To use the latter, first you must select the group with which you want to work.

From the Available Topics main menu of SYSCON, select Group Information and then select the group from the Group Names window. Next, you are presented with a window entitled Group Information; select the option Member List.

At this point, a listing of the users who are currently members of this group is shown. To remove a user from this listing, select the user name and press Delete. To add a user name, press the Insert key and select from the listing of users within the window Not Group Members.

Creating Users with SYSCON

Creating a user ID within SYSCON is a fairly simple process. First, you must login to the file server as the SUPERVISOR, SUPERVISOR EQUIVALENT, or WORKGROUP MANAGER.

While not necessarily the most efficient utility in NetWare for creating IDs, SYSCON is one of the most popular. After using it for some time, creating IDs will become almost second nature to you. Using this utility, you can create an ID by following the steps below:

1. From the Available Topics main menu of SYSCON, select User Information.

2. Next, you are presented with a window entitled User Names. The screen lists all IDs currently set up on the server. To add a new ID, press Insert and type the name of the new user's ID when prompted to do so.

> **Note**
>
> Login IDs must be between 1 and 47 characters. You *cannot* use any of the following characters within the name: = + * [ ] / \ | : ; . , < > ? or spaces.

3. If the setting "Create Home Directory for User" was set to Yes in the server's default account restrictions, you are now prompted for the `Path to Create User's Home Directory`. Insert the pathname of the desired user's home directory and then press Enter.

> **Note**
>
> By default, NetWare tries to create a home directory named after the first eight characters of the user's login name. You can change the name by backspacing over the directory name and typing another name.

> **Tip**
>
> Try to keep home directories all together. For example, a single directory, called HOME or USERS, could be created off the ROOT. Then, users' home directories could be created as subdirectories beneath the HOME or USERS directory.

Once your home directory has been created (when applicable), NetWare inserts the new user ID name into the listing of User Names presented on-screen. At this time, the ID is set up and ready to go *but*, before you allow the ID to be used, you should review the configuration to ensure there is nothing you want to adjust.

To view the user specific configuration, select the user ID and press Enter. You are presented with a screen entitled User Information (see fig. 7.2).

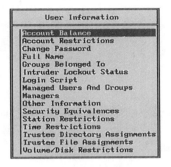

Fig. 7.2 User Information menu of SYSCON for configuring individual user IDs.

Reviewing And Changing User Specific Configurations

From the User Information menu presented after selecting an individual user ID from the listing of User Names in SYSCON, several options are available to you. While no additional configuration is *required*, you may want to step through each of the options to review the current settings or make any desired changes. For your reference, each of these options are discussed in the following sections.

Shortcut

Instead of working through each user one at a time, you can flag several users with F5 from the listing of User Names. Once flagged, pressing Enter enables you to edit some of the following items for all users who were flagged.

Account Balance

When accounting is installed on the file server, this option sets the number of credits (used to access server resources) available to the user and if they should have unlimited credits.

Account Restrictions

Upon selecting Account Restrictions, you are presented with a screenful of options. These options are mostly identical to those detailed in Chapter 6, Table 6.1, but here, there are two new options. For information regarding the other options, refer to Table 6.1.

■ *Account Disabled:* Specifies if an account has been disabled. When set to Yes, the account is not deleted, nor will any files owned by this ID be deleted, *but* no one will be able to login to the file server with this ID until the status is changed to No. The account can be set as disabled by anyone with the appropriate security *or* it will automatically switch to disabled if the ID has an expiration date that has been met.

■ *Allow User to Change Password:* Specifies if a user is able to change the password for their ID. This option is usually used only if there are IDs used by a group. Unless there is some specific reason why you do not want users to change their own passwords, leave this option as Yes.

Change Password

This option changes or assigns an initial password to the user ID. Once selected, you are prompted for the new password. After pressing Enter, you then must retype the password to ensure that you entered what you *think* you entered.

> **Note**
>
> The maximum password length is 127 characters.

Full Name

The Full Name field of a user ID is optional from NetWare's standpoint but can be very useful to the administrator. In some installations, user IDs are created randomly or are made up in such a way that it is not easy to distinguish who the person is, based on their ID. For example, some companies may set up a user's ID based on the first three letters of their last name and their HR payroll number. Using this field, you can include information such as the user's full name, department, or other criteria. Once set, this field can be called as a variable within the personal or system login scripts.

> **Note**
>
> The maximum length of the Full Name field is 127 characters.

Groups Belonged To

This option tells you what groups of which a user is a member. By default, all users are members of the group EVERYONE. To make the user a member of another group, press Enter on the Groups Belonged To option, then from the next window, press Insert to select additional groups.

> **Note**
>
> A user can belong to a maximum of 32 groups.

Intruder Lockout Status

When Intruder Lockout has been installed on the file server, this option shows you if the ID has been locked and from what station it was locked out. For detailed information on using the intruder lockout feature of NetWare, refer to the heading "Detecting Intruders" in Chapter 14, "Additional Security Measures."

Login Script

This option is used to view or change a user's login script. Refer to Chapter 8, "Login Scripts," to see how to create and modify a script.

Managed Users and Groups

This option is used to view or assign users and groups managed by this user. By pressing Enter on this option, you are shown a listing of the currently managed users and groups. To add an additional user or group to this listing, press Insert and select the users/groups from the Other Users And Groups screen you want this user to manage. For detailed information on the different types of users, refer to Chapter 12, "Security Equivalences."

Managers

This option specifies which users or groups are managers of this ID. By selecting this option, you are presented with a window showing you all the current workgroup managers. To add a manager, press Insert and select the users or groups from the Other Users And Groups screen you want to have managing this ID. For detailed information about what the different types of managers can do, refer to Chapter 12, "Security Equivalences."

> **Note**
>
> SYSCON will not allow you to add more than 32 managers.

Other Information

By selecting Other Information, you are presented with a small window that provides some basic information on this ID. Within this window, the following information is shown:

- *Last Login:* The last time this ID logged into the file server. If the ID has never been used, this value will be set to <Unknown>.

- *File Server Console Operator:* Tells you if this ID is set as a file server console operator. Refer to the heading "Operator and Manager Assignments" in Chapter 12 for detailed information on what Console Operators can do.

- *Disk Space In Use:* Shows you how much space this ID is using on the file server.

II

Environment Setup

■ *User ID:* The bindery object ID number for this user. The user's mail subdirectory is named based on this ID.

Tip

While the user IDs you create always have an eight-character ID number, the SUPERVISOR ID is always the number 1.

Security Equivalences

Once selected, a window entitled Security Equivalences is displayed, showing you the users and groups to which this ID is equivalent. To add an equivalence, press Insert and select a user or group from the listing of Other Users and Groups. For detailed information on how equivalencies work, refer to the heading "User and Group Security Equivalencies" in Chapter 12, "Security Equivalences."

Note

You cannot add more than 32 security equivalences for any given user.

Station Restrictions

When selected, a window called Allowed Login Addresses appears. When addresses are added to this listing, the user ID is only able to login from these addresses. By pressing the Insert key, you can specify the network and station address that you would like to restrict the user to.

Time Restrictions

This option enables you to view and change the times and days an ID can login to the file server. This option works in the same fashion the server's default time restrictions works, except here the option is specific to the user in question.

Trustee Directory Assignments

Trustee directory assignments specify the directories to which this specific user has access. Once selected, you are shown a window entitled Trustee Directory Assignments that displays the current settings. To add an additional assignment, press Insert and specify the desired directory and the associated rights. For information on how trustee assignments work, refer to Chapter 13, "Trustee Assignments and Rights."

Trustee File Assignments

Trustee file assignments specify what rights a user has to a specific file. Instead of granting rights to an entire directory, NetWare will let you pinpoint which files are accessible and how. Once selected, you are shown a window entitled Trustee File Assignments that displays the current settings. To add an additional assignment, press Insert and specify the desired files and the associated rights. For information on how trustee file assignments work, refer to Chapter 13, "Trustee Assignments and Rights."

Volume/Disk Restrictions

This option restricts the amount of disk space available to the user. To set a space restriction for this user, you should:

1. Select Volume/Disk Restrictions from the user's User Information window.

2. Next, select the volume on which you would like to impose the space restriction.

3. You are then presented with a window entitled User Volume/Disk Restrictions. Within this window, answer Yes to the question "Limit Volume Space?" and then on the next line, specify in kilobytes to what you would like to restrict this user.

> **Note**
>
> SYSCON can be used only to impose space restrictions on a per volume basis. If you want to set a space restriction for a single directory, use the DSPACE utility.

> **Tip**
>
> If you are going to set space restrictions for multiple users, you may want to look into the USERDEF utility. One of the options, Restrict Users, is much faster to use than SYSCON.

Creating Users with USERDEF

By using the USERDEF utility, multiple IDs can be created at one time by using a template—the template is used to tell USERDEF how you want the IDs to be set up. In addition to the creation of the actual user ID, you also can:

- Provide users with basic login scripts

- Copy print job configurations from other users

- Assign account and disk space restrictions

- Set up home directories

- Set up basic user security

To set up the user IDs, you must first login to the file server as a SUPERVISOR or SUPERVISOR EQUIVALENT. Once in, run the USERDEF utility, which is stored in the public directory. When USERDEF first loads, you are presented with a screen like the one shown in Figure 7.3.

Fig. 7.3 USERDEF's main menu.

From the main menu, the three options are:

- *Add Users*—actually creates the user IDs.

- *Edit/View Templates*—creates the different user templates.

- *Restrict User*—imposes disk space restrictions on user IDs that have already been created.

Creating USERDEF Templates

The first option most people choose from the USERDEF main menu is the Edit/View Templates option. While USERDEF comes configured with a default template, most people want to configure their own. You can create your own template by working through the following steps:

1. From the Available Options main menu of USERDEF, select Edit/View Templates, which then displays a listing of the currently available templates.

2. From the Templates window, press Insert to add a new template. Then, when prompted, type in the name of your new template—up to eight characters.

3. Next, you are presented with a window containing two options: Edit Login Script and Edit Parameters. First, select Edit Login Script.

4. The login script now shown is set up as the personal login script for each user created with the template. You can make additions to this area (refer to Chapter 8, "Login Scripts," for detailed information on the different login script commands and variables). Once you have finished with this screen, press Esc to return to the previous window.

Tip
The commands in this script are basic commands normally covered in your system login script. Therefore, if you already have a system login script on the server, you should delete this script.

Caution

If there is a system script and you leave this one intact, the result will be duplicate mappings to several areas such as the PUBLIC and DOS directories.

---

5. After editing or deleting the script, select Edit Parameters from the Template window.

6. You now are presented with a window entitled Parameters for Template (see fig. 7.4). On this screen, there are several options you can adjust, based on your specific requirements. For the most part, these options are similar to those found in the server's default account restrictions, but there are three unique to this menu, as shown below. If you want detailed info on the other options, refer to Chapter 6, "Configuring the Server Default Setup."

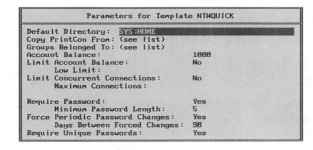

Fig. 7.4 Account restrictions that can be set for IDs created with USERDEF.

- *Default Directory:* Specifies the directory where the user's home subdirectory should be created. By default, this option is set to SYS: but you can change this to something off of the root directory, such as SYS:HOME. While you need to create this master directory before entering USERDEF, home directories should *not* be created off of the root.

Tip

If you do not want users to have a home directory, blank out this line.

Caution

Normally, if you have a directory called HOME off the root of the SYS: volume, you could refer to it as SYS:\HOME. If you use the backslash (\) in this option, your setup will not work; therefore, the directory HOME on the SYS: volume should be referred to as SYS:HOME.

■ *Copy PrintCon From:* Enables you to copy the PRINTCON.DAT printer database from an-other user's mail directory to each new user's mail subdirectory. As you see in Chapter 21, "Printing Management," you can set up printing to use a shared PRINTCON.DAT stored in the PUBLIC directory. Therefore, you may want to select NONE for this option.

Caution

If you are planning to use a shared PRINTCON.DAT, do not copy this file to every user's mail directory. When the file exists in both locations, and the user tries to print, NetWare will make use of the one in the mail directories. Therefore, any changes made to the shared PRINTCON.DAT will not be available to the user.

■ *Groups Belonged To:* This option specifies groups to which the IDs should be a member. To have all new users added to other groups besides the default group EVERYONE, press Insert on the Groups Belonged To screen and select the other groups from the listing provided.

Caution

In NetWare 3.11/3.12, a user cannot belong to more than 32 groups even though there can be more than 32 created on the server. By default, USERDEF will make all users members of the group EVERY-ONE, *but* it will also let you add 32 additional groups to this field, for a total of 33 groups. Even though it will not give you an error at this point, or when adding users, if you go into SYSCON and check group assignments, you will get an error. Do *not* add more than 31 groups if the user will remain as a member of the group EVERYONE.

---

7. Once you have set the desired options, press Esc until you return to the main menu entitled Available Options. When asked, confirm if you want to save the changes you made.

Creating Users Using Templates

Whether you have created your own templates or you are going to use the default template, cre-ating new user IDs is a cinch with USERDEF. To set up one or many user IDs, follow these steps:

1. From the USERDEF main menu, select Add Users and then from the listing of templates, select the template you want to use.

2. Next, the Users window will appear with a listing of the user IDs currently set up on the file server. To add a user, press the Insert key.

3. You will be asked to enter the Full Name of the ID. While you can enter anything in this field, words should be separated by a space. Avoid using extended ASCII characters.

> **Note**
>
> Even though the FULL NAME field within SYSCON will accept 1 to 127 characters, the FULL NAME field here only allows up to 32 characters.

4. When you press Enter after typing the full name, NetWare asks you for the user's Login Name—the ID the system uses. By default, USERDEF tries to use the first name, or first word entered as the Full Name. If the default is acceptable, press Enter. Otherwise, backspace over the default and create your own ID. When you are done, press Enter to record your changes.

> **Note**
>
> Even though SYSCON allows IDs up to 47 characters in length, USERDEF only allows you to enter an ID up to 32 characters long. No spaces are allowed!

5. After the Login Name is entered, you are returned to the Users window and you see the new ID was added to the listing. To the right of the ID, the word NEW signifies the addition. If you want to add more IDs, repeat steps 2 through 4; otherwise, proceed to step 6.

6. To create the user IDs, press Esc and you are prompted to `Create New Users Using Template?`, then to answer Yes or No. To create the IDs, answer Yes.

7. After answering Yes, USERDEF then creates each of the IDs on the file server. Once complete, a final screen appears, notifying you of any errors that occurred during the setup.

Creating Users with MAKEUSER

MAKEUSER is a powerful tool that enables you to create groups of users through the use of a scripting language. While MAKEUSER is a fairly basic menuing utility, writing the scripts can be a real challenge. The scripting language itself is not difficult, but you must exercise a great degree of care when writing the script. With the MAKEUSER USR scripts, layout is everything.

To create a script for yourself and the users, you must first login to the file server as a SUPERVISOR or a SUPERVISOR EQUIVALENT. Once in, run the program MAKEUSER.EXE from the PUBLIC directory. When MAKEUSER loads, you are presented with a screen like the one shown in Figure 7.5.

Creating MAKEUSER Script Files

To create your MAKEUSER script file, select Create New USR File from the Available Options menu. Once selected, you are presented with a blank screen where you can create your USR script.

II

Environment Setup

Fig. 7.5 The main menu of the MAKEUSER utility, listing the available options.

The script itself is written using keywords that tell NetWare exactly what you want to do. For a listing of these keywords and descriptions of what they can do, refer to Table 7.1. A sample script file is shown in Figure 7.6.

Table 7.1 Commands that can be used in the MAKEUSER USR file.		
Keyword	**Acceptable Values**	**Description**
#ACCOUNT_EXPIRATION	*month day year*	Sets the ID's expiration date. When not used, the account will never expire.
#ACCOUNTING	*balance, lowlimit*	Specifies the ID's accounting information.
#CLEAR		Starts a new setup of keywords within the same MAKEUSER USER file. Any commands prior to the #CLEAR command will have no affect on what follows.
#CONNECTIONS	*number*	Sets the maximum concurrent connections that are available to the ID. When not used, the maximum defaults to 250, whether the server supports 250 or not.
#CREATE	*username* [*;fullname*] [*;password*] [*;group*] [*;directory* [*rights*]]	Creates an ID on the file server. Replace *username* with the ID name, *fullname* with the user's full name, *password* with the user's password, *group* with the name of the group to which you want this user added, *directory* with the name of the directory to which you want to assign rights, and *rights* with the rights you want to assign. Multiple groups or directories can be specified by separating the group or directory names with commas. When rights are not specified, R and F will be granted by default.
#DELETE	*username*	Deletes a user ID. Multiple IDs can be deleted on the same line by separating the IDs by semi-colons (;). Also deletes the user's home directory *if* the #HOME_DIRECTORY command is included BEFORE the #DELETE command.
#GROUPS	*group*	Specifies groups of which the ID is a member. Multiple groups can be assigned by separating each one with a semicolon (;).

Keyword	Acceptable Values	Description
#HOME_DIRECTORY	*path*	Specifies the location of a home directory for an ID being created or deleted.
#LOGIN_SCRIPT	*path*	Specifies the login script file used as the personal script for each new ID.
#MAX_DISK_SPACE	*vol, number*	Specifies the space restriction imposed for each user, noted in blocks, not K. Multiple volume restrictions can be imposed by placing a semi-colon (;) between each set ·of variables.
#NO_HOME_DIRECTORY		Specifies when no home directory should be created for a user.
#PASSWORD_LENGTH	*length*	Specifies the minimum password length used on the server, between 1 and 20 characters. When not used, the minimum length is set to 5. #PASSWORD_REQUIRED must be entered before this command; otherwise, it will not work.
#PASSWORD_PERIOD	*days*	Specifies the password expiration period, between 1 and 365 days. When not used, the password never expires. #PASSWORD_REQUIRED must be entered before this command or it will not work.
#PASSWORD_REQUIRED		Specifies if a password is required. This command *must* be entered *before* the #PASSWORD_LENGTH, #PASSWORD_PERIOD, and #UNIQUE_PASSWORD commands for them to work.
#PURGE_USER_DIRECTORY		Deletes any subdirectories owned by an ID that you delete when using the #DELETE command.
#REM		Inserts remarks within the USR file. The leading # sign is not required.
#RESET		Same as #CLEAR.
#RESTRICTED_TIME	*day, start, end*	Specifies the time restrictions set for the user ID being created. Multiple blocks of time can be specified by replacing each block with a semi-colon (;).

II

Environment Setup

(continues)

Table 7.1 Continued.

Keyword	Acceptable Values	Description
#STATIONS	*network, station*	Sets the station restrictions for IDs you are creating. Replace *network* with the network number you are restricting and *station* with the workstation's physical address. You can specify multiple stations by separating the workstation physical addresses with semi-colons (;), or you can specify all stations by replacing the workstation address with the word ALL.
#UNIQUE_PASSWORD		Specifies if a unique password will be required.

```
                    Editing NTQUICK.USR

#REM This MAKEUSER script is being used as a demonstration for the
#REM readers of this book.
#REM Created June 12 1994
#NO_HOME_DIRECTORY
#STATIONS 01000283,ALL
#CONNECTIONS 2
#CREATE DJA19823; Doug Archell; newpassword; accounting,development;
#CREATE LAR44671; Larry Larrett; newpassword; development;
#CREATE ROG91029; Joanne Rogers; newpassword; accounting,development;
#CREATE STA66783; Craig Staples; newpassword; accounting,development;
#CREATE VAN12455; Michelle VanDeGeyn; newpassword; accounting,development;
#CREATE ARC44411; Bryan Archell; newpassword; accounting,development;
#CREATE MAL11223; Steven Male; newpassword; accounting,development;
#CREATE NOR11111; Brian Norris; newpassword; accounting,development;
#CREATE HOW18293; John Howell; newpassword; accounting,development;
#CREATE KUO23223; Peter Kuo; newpassword; accounting,development;
#CREATE KIA67133; George Kiang; newpassword; accounting,development;
```

Fig. 7.6 Sample MAKEUSER script file.

As you create your script, remember that formatting is everything. If you place the commands in the incorrect order, the script will not operate as it should. Below, several rules are listed; they must be followed when you are creating a script:

■ The #CLEAR command should be used to separate distinct areas of the script. Any commands used before the #CLEAR command will have *no* effect on those that come after.

■ To create or delete a home direcory, the #HOME_DIRECTORY command must appear before the #CREATE or #DELETE commands and must *not* be separated by the #CLEAR command.

■ If the #LOGIN_SCRIPT command is used, the login script file must be created before you attempt to execute the script.

■ To use the #PURGE_USER_DIRECTORY command, it must appear before the #DELETE command.

■ When using any of the password-related commands, the #PASSWORD_REQUIRED command must be included first before any of them will work.

When you are finished entering the script, you complete the process by following these steps:

1. Press Esc and confirm if you want to save your work.

2. At the `Enter the new USR file name:` prompt, type a file name up to eight characters in length.

Note

The script file is created within your current directory with the extension USR.

Running MAKEUSER Scripts

After you have created a MAKEUSER script, you can use it anytime. The actual execution of the script is achieved in one of two ways: from the MAKEUSER menu or from the command line. In either case, you should change your default directory to where the script is stored.

To run the script from the command line, use:

```
MAKEUSER scriptname
```

where *scriptname* is the name of the USR file.

To run the script using the MAKEUSER main menu, select Process USR file from the Available Options menu. Then type in the name of the USR file you want to run.

After executing the script, MAKEUSER displays a screen confirming the processes run and if there were any errors.

Deleting User IDs

There are two ways to delete an ID from the server: through the MAKEUSER scripts (refer to the previous heading "Creating Users with MAKEUSER" for further info), or with SYSCON. To delete an ID within SYSCON, select User Information from the Available Topics main menu, then from the listing of User Names, select the one you want to delete and press the Delete key. Confirm that you want to delete the ID.

Shortcut

You can delete multiple IDs at one time in SYSCON by flagging each one with F5.

Unforunately, since deleting IDs is so simple, there are a few points people overlook when deleting them. Specifically, you must determine what you want to do with the user's home directory—if it exists—and the mail directory.

The home directory can easily be removed from the command line using the DOS DEL command but you should *not* remove the mail directory in the same fashion. The mail directory is included as a parameter within the server's binderies and, therefore, you should let NetWare remove it. That is one minor flaw with SYSCON—it does not remove these mail directories on its own. To remove mail directories for deleted user IDs, you must use the BINDFIX utility included with NetWare. This utility is discussed in Chapter 28, "NetWare Utilities for Resolving Problems."

Renaming User IDs and Group Names

If you have created a user ID or group, and the name you chose is inappropriate, you can rename the object instead of re-creating it under the new name.

To rename a user ID:

1. Select User Information from the Available Topics main menu of SYSCON.

2. Select the ID you want to rename from the listing of User Names and press F3. When prompted, type in the new name.

> **Caution**
>
> Renaming the user ID has no effect on the name of the user's home directory. If your login scripts map the user's home directory using the LOGIN_NAME variable, you have to manually rename the directory or the user will get errors when logging in.

To rename a group:

1. Select Group Information from the Available Topics main menu of SYSCON.

2. Select the group you want to rename and press F3. When asked, type in the new name.

> **Caution**
>
> If you rename any groups, check in your system login script for references to the old name and make the necessary changes. Otherwise, users may not get all their mappings and environment settings during the login.

Chapter 8
Login Scripts

Login scripts provide a useful tool for connecting to the NetWare file server. While not necessarily a perfect comparison, login scripts can be considered detailed batch files that establish environment settings, drive mappings, and execute programs based on a wide variety of criteria. Essentially, the key benefit to using login scripts is that they can reduce the amount of work done each time a user logs in by automating these functions.

In this chapter, we take a closer look at login scripts, and specifically discuss:

- The different types of login scripts

- How to create a login script

- The different login script commands

- The different login script variables

- Using the commands and variables to produce a detailed script

Different Types of Login Scripts

For your NetWare file server, there are three different types of login scripts that can be used: SYSTEM, DEFAULT, and PERSONAL. Each script has its purpose and, depending on your requirements, you may use one or a combination of the three.

System Login Script

The system login script is the first script run when a user logs into the file server. This script sets variables and drive mappings that affect more than one person. When required, qualifiers are used to establish mappings or settings for a single user. This script is stored as an ASCII text file called NET$LOG.DAT within the PUBLIC directory of the SYS: volume.

> **Note**
>
> The system login script file is normally flagged Read Only Shareable. If you change the flagging for some reason, NetWare will switch it back to Read Only Shareable the next time you edit the file in SYSCON.

Default Login Script

When the file server is first installed, there are no system or personal login scripts. To establish basic drive mappings when the other scripts do not exist, NetWare uses a default login script. This script is part of the LOGIN.EXE program and cannot be edited or deleted.

> **Tip**
>
> If a user does not have a personal login script, NetWare runs the default script after the system script. This needlessly creates some duplicate mappings. To ensure that the default script does *not* run, either insert the command NO_DEFAULT in the system script *or* create an empty personal script for each user.

Personal Login Script

Personal login scripts pertain to a specific user. As the last script executed during the login process, the personal script establishes settings specific to the user in question. The personal script is stored within the user's mail subdirectory on the SYS: volume and is called LOGIN, or LOGIN.OS2 for OS/2 machines.

> **Note**
>
> To find out which mail directory belongs to a USER, check the Other Information screen within the user's personal information in SYSCON. When selected, SYSCON will give you the user's ID number. The user's mail subdirectory is named after this number as a subdirectory of the SYS:\MAIL directory.

> **Tip**
>
> If you ever accidentally delete a personal login script, don't worry. NetWare backs up the script whenever changes are made. To recover the old script, go to the user's mail directory and check for a file called LOGINBAK. If there, you can just rename it LOGIN to return the user's login script.

Creating and Editing Your Login Scripts

A login script can be short and simple or long and detailed. The contents of your scripts will differ from those used in other organizations, or even between the servers on your LAN depending on your requirements. In this section, we look specifically at how to create the script and the options available to you. First, there are a few rules that you should know:

- Only the SUPERVISOR or SUPERVISOR EQUIVALENT can edit the system login script from within the SYSCON utility.

- By default, users can edit their own system login scripts.

- An ACCOUNT MANAGER or WORKGROUP MANAGER can edit the system login scripts of any user he/she manages.

- Regular users *cannot* alter other users' login scripts.

Tip
If you do not want users to edit their own login scripts, change their trustee rights in their personal mail directories to only READ and FILESCAN.

Caution
SUPERVISOR and SUPERVISOR equivalent IDs may be the only ones that can edit the system script through the SYSCON utility, *but* if your security is not set up properly, others can do so from the command line. The system login script is stored as a file called NET$LOG.DAT in the public directory. If a user has sufficient rights in this directory, they can alter the system script using an ASCII file editor.

Since the default login script is a part of the LOGIN.EXE program, it cannot be changed, *but* you can change the system and personal login scripts. To change these scripts, first LOGIN to the file server with an ID that has the necessary rights; refer to the rules posted above. Once logged in, you can edit the scripts by following the steps noted below.

To edit the system login script:

1. From the Available Topics main menu, select Supervisor Options.

2. From the Supervisor Options menu, select System Login Script (see fig. 8.1).

3. Enter the desired script options; then press Esc and confirm that you want to save the script.

Environment Setup

```
          Supervisor Options
Default Account Balance/Restrictions
Default Time Restrictions
Edit System AUTOEXEC File
File Server Console Operators
Intruder Detection/Lockout
System Login Script
View File Server Error Log
Workgroup Managers
```

Fig. 8.1 Selecting the system login script option within SYSCON.

Tip
If you are editing a current system login script, you may get an error when trying to save it because some users may be in the middle of logging in, thus using the script. If this occurs, wait a few seconds and then try again to exit and save the script.

To edit a user's personal login script:

1. From the Available Topics main menu of SYSCON, select User Information, and then select the desired user.

2. From the listing of options in the User Information screen, select Login Script.

3. If a script does not exist for this user, a window entitled Login script does not exist pops up (see fig. 8.2). Within this window, the prompt Read Login Script From User: with the current user's name after the colon appears. If you want to create a new script, press Enter. If you want to use another user's script, type in that user's ID and press Enter.

```
      Login script does not exist
Read Login Script From User:  CNE19846
```

Fig. 8.2 Creating a personal login script.

4. Enter the new script, or the changes to the current script, and then press Esc and confirm that you want to save the new script.

Organizing the Login Script

When creating your script, careful consideration should be given as to how it is laid out. A script that is well thought out and organized is easier to expand and understand. As you write the script, break it into logical sections where you can group like commands. These section "headings" can be separated from the executable text by using the REM command. Below are five suggested headings that can be used for most system login scripts:

- REM This Section Is For DOS Environment Settings

- REM This Section Is For GLOBAL Drive Mappings

- REM This Section Is For Group-Specific Assignments

- REM This Section Is For User-Specific Assignments

- REM This Section Is For Printing Assignments

Commands that Can Be Used in the Login Script

Whichever script you are editing, if one previously existed, you can make any required changes. If the script is new, you see a blank screen in which to create the new script. To help you create your script, Table 8.1 details the various commands that can be used in the system or personal login scripts.

Table 8.1 NetWare LOGIN script commands.

Command	Example	Description
#	*#command*	Executes an external COM or EXE file. Replace *command* with the name of the COM or EXE file.
ATTACH	ATTACH *server/username*	Attaches to another file server.
BREAK	BREAK ON, BREAK OFF	Enables or disables the use of CTRL-BREAK to interrupt the system login script. This command should be placed near the beginning of the script.
COMSPEC	COMSPEC=*drive:\path\COMMAND.COM*	Tells DOS where it should look for the COMMAND.COM file. Replace *drive:\path* with the drive and path of the required COMMAND.COM file.
DISPLAY	DISPLAY *drive:\path\filename*	Displays the contents of an ASCII text file.
DOS BREAK	DOS BREAK ON DOS BREAK OFF	Specifies if you want the user to be able to issue a CTRL-BREAK command when a program is being executed from within the script. Unlike the BREAK command, DOS BREAK does not terminate the execution of the login script, only the program running at that time.
DOS VERIFY	DOS VERIFY ON DOS VERIFY OFF	Enables or disables DOS read-after-write verification.

II

Environment Setup

(continues)

Table 8.1 Continued.

Command	Example	Description
DOS SET	DOS SET *variable="value"*	Sets DOS environment variables from the login script. Refer to the heading "Variables that Can Be Used in the Login Script" later in this chapter for further info.
DRIVE	DRIVE *x:*	Tells NetWare what your default drive should be when the login script is complete. Replace *x:* with the desired drive letter.
EXIT	EXIT *"command"*	Halts the execution of the login script and executes the command specified within the quotes. If EXIT is used within the system login script, users' personal login scripts will not run. The *command* should be enclosed in double quotes.
FDISPLAY	FDISPLAY *drive:\path\filename*	Displays the contents of a text file and filters any formatting characters.
FIRE PHASERS	FIRE PHASERS *x* TIMES	Makes a phaser-type sound when logging in. Replace *x* with the number of times you want the phaser to sound.
GOTO	GOTO *label*	Jumps to another section of the login script. Replace *label* with the label name to which you want to jump. Refer to the heading "Using IF-THEN-ELSE Qualifiers in the Login Script" later in this chapter for further information.
IF-THEN-ELSE		Establishes conditional statements. Refer to the heading "Using IF-THEN-ELSE Qualifiers in the Login Script" later in this chapter for further information.
INCLUDE	INCLUDE *drive:\path\filename*	Executes additional login script commands stored within another ASCII text file. Replace *drive:\path* with the drive and path location of the file.
MACHINE NAME	MACHINE NAME = *"name"*	Changes the default MACHINE NAME setting during login. Replace *name* with the new machine name. Make sure the new machine name is enclosed in double quotes!
MAP	MAP *x:=server/volume:path*	Creates logical drive pointers to different areas of the NetWare server. Refer to the heading "Establishing Drive Mappings" later in this chapter for further information.

Command	Example	Description
MAP DISPLAY	MAP DISPLAY ON MAP DISPLAY OFF	Determines if NetWare displays the commands being executed from the login script.
MAP ERRORS	MAP ERRORS ON MAP ERRORS OFF	Determines if NetWare displays errors that result from the login script.
NO_DEFAULT		When used in the system login script, restricts the default script from running if there is no personal login script for the user.
PAUSE		Temporarily halts the execution of the login script until the user presses a key to continue.
PCCOMPATIBLE		Enables workstations with long machine names to use the EXIT script command.
REMARK	REMARK Script Created 01/01/94	Inserts comments that will not be executed during the login procedure. Instead of using REMARK, you also can use REM, ; or *.
SET		Same as DOS SET.
SHIFT	SHIFT 3	Shifts the position of the login command parameters. Refer to the heading "Advanced Options" later in this chapter for further information.
WAIT		Same as PAUSE.
WRITE	WRITE *"text"*	Writes text to the workstation's screen during login. Refer to the heading "Displaying Information" later in this chapter for further information.

II

Environment Setup

Variables that Can Be Used in the Login Script

NetWare login script variables provide a greater degree of control and functionality within the login script (see Table 8.2). The variables assist you in many ways, such as setting DOS environment variables, printing useful text on-screen, or creating conditional statements. Before using one of these variables, there are a few rules that you must know:

■ Unless specifically stated, script variables *must* be entered in CAPITAL letters; otherwise, they will not work.

■ When used within a pathname—as in a MAP command—or in a string of ASCII text, the variable must be preceded by a % sign.

■ When used in a qualifier statement—as in an IF-THEN-ELSE—the variable is *not* preceded by a % sign.

■ When used as the value in a SET command, if the variable is *not* enclosed in quotes, there is *no* preceding % sign. If the variable *is* enclosed in quotes, it must be preceded by a % sign.

Table 8.2 NetWare login script variables.

Variable	Description
AM_PM	Returns an AM or PM setting based on the current time.
ACCESS_SERVER	Determines if an Access Server is functional.
DAY	Returns a number between 1 and 31 based on the day of the month.
DAY_OF_WEEK	Returns the name of the current day—Monday, Tuesday....
ERROR_LEVEL	Returns an error level based on the last command.
FILE_SERVER	Returns the file server's name.
FULL_NAME	Returns the user's full name as assigned within SYSCON.
GREETING_TIME	Returns the generic time of day—Morning, Afternoon, or Evening.
HOUR	Returns a number between 1 and 12 based on the current hour of the day.
HOUR24	Returns a number between 00 and 23 based on the current hour of the day, in military time.
LOGIN_NAME	Returns the user's login name.
MACHINE or MACHINE NAME	Returns the long machine name set in the NET.CFG file.
MEMBER or NOT MEMBER	Checks if a user is a member of a group.
MINUTE	Returns a number between 00 and 59 based on the current minute.
MONTH	Returns a number between 1 and 12 based on the current month.
MONTH_NAME	Returns the name of the current month.
NDAY_OF_WEEK	Returns a number between 1 and 7 based on the current day of the week, where Monday is 1.
NETWORK_ADDRESS	Returns the network address of the cabling system.
OS	Returns the name of the operating system used on the workstation.
OS_VERSION	Returns the version number of the operating system used on the workstation—V.XX.

Variable	Description
PASSWORD_EXPIRES	Returns the number of days left before the user's password expires.
P_STATION	Returns the workstation's physical layer address—the node address.
SECOND	Returns a value between 00 and 59 based on the current second.
SHELL_TYPE	Returns the version number of the workstation's shell or requester.
SHORT_YEAR	Returns a number between 00 and 99 based on the current year—the year 1994 returns the value 94.
SMACHINE	Returns the short machine name setting from the workstation's NET.CFG file.
STATION	Returns a number identifying the workstation's connection number to the file server.
USER_ID	Returns the user's bindery object number. The result is the name of the user's mail subdirectory.
YEAR	Returns the current year—1995.
%1	Returns parameters specified after issuing the login command from the DOS prompt. Refer to the heading "Advanced Options" later in this chapter for further information.

Knowing the different commands and variables will help you to produce a script that is more than just functional. The following sections provide some helpful insight and tips you can use to help you organize your script and use these commands.

Setting and Using DOS Environment Variables

Along with the environment settings established within the workstation's configuration files, NetWare has several commands that can be used within the login script. While these settings can be used anywhere within the script, you should keep them together for organization.

The SET command can be used to establish DOS environment variables using NetWare script variables or values you directly assign. When used with the NetWare environment variables, the SET command is definitely enhanced. Using the SET command is fairly straightforward, but there are a few rules you must follow:

■ If a NetWare script variable is used as the value in a SET command, the script variable must be preceeded by a % sign *if* it is enclosed in quotes. If the variable is *not* enclosed in quotes, it does not require a preceeding % sign. For example:

```
SET NAME="%LOGIN_NAME"
```

or

```
SET NAME=LOGIN_NAME
```

■ When you are specifically assigning a value, this value *must* be enclosed in double quotes. For example, if you want to set a DOS environment variable called COMPANY as ABC, you enter the following within the script:

```
SET COMPANY="ABC"
```

Using Environment Settings Elsewhere in the Script

After a DOS environment setting is established with the SET command, it can be used elsewhere in the script, such as within a MAP command. When a DOS environment setting is used within the script, it must be enclosed between two angular brackets (< and >), and then preceded by a % sign. For example, assume you had the following command at the beginning of your script:

```
SET COMPANY="ACME"
```

Later in the script, you could use the DOS environment variable COMPANY. For example, you could map the J: drive to a directory named after the COMPANY environment variable by using the following login script command:

```
MAP J:=SYS:\%<COMPANY>
```

Establishing Drive Mappings

NetWare uses drive mappings as pointers to areas on the file server's disk drives. You use drive mappings to reduce the amount of work necessary to run an application or to locate files by changing directories.

Within the login scripts, drive mappings are created using the MAP command. With this command, there are three types of drive mappings you can create: standard drive mappings, search drive mappings, and drives "mapped to the root."

> **Note**
>
> Even though there is a program called MAP.EXE, MAP is also an internal script command. As such, you should *not* place a # before the command within the login scripts.

Standard Drive Mappings

A standard drive mapping creates a pointer to an area within the server's disk drive. To access files stored within the drive pointer, you must either reference the drive letter in your commands—such as F:\HOME> g:install—or you must make the drive letter your default drive.

There are two ways you can create a standard drive mapping:

```
MAP drive:=servername/volume:\directory
MAP *#:=servername/volume:\directory
```

Based on the syntax above, replace:

drive with the drive letter you want to assign, such as F, G, H....

with a number signifying the 1st, 2nd, 3rd... available network drive. When using this method, the number must be preceeded by an asterisk (*).

servername with the name of the file server to which you are mapping. This parameter is not required when mapping a drive to your default server. If the servername is left out, the *volume* name should *not* be preceded by a slash (/).

volume with the name of the volume on which the directory resides.

directory with the name of the directory to which you are mapping.

While both methods have the same effect, the manner in which they approach their tasks differs. As an example, assume your current drive mappings are:

DRIVE G:=DJASYSTEMS/SYS:\COMMON

DRIVE H:=DJASYSTEMS/SYS:\APPS

If you were to type **MAP F:=SYS:\HOME\DOUG**, your drive mappings would be changed to:

DRIVE F:=DJASYSTEMS/SYS:\HOME\DOUG

DRIVE G:=DJASYSTEMS/SYS:\COMMON

DRIVE H:=DJASYSTEMS/SYS:\APPS

But what if you didn't know that G: was the first drive mapped and you wanted to make sure the first available network drive was mapped to the user's home directory? You can achieve this effect by replacing the specified drive pointer—F: in the previous example—with *1. Therefore, typing **MAP *1:=SYS:\HOME\DOUG** would achieve the same effect.

The one thing to keep in mind when using the *# method is that, when used, it overwrites a drive mapping currently in the position the command is mapping to. For example, if there was already a drive mapping for F: to the HOME directory, typing **MAP *1:=SYS:\DATA** would change the drive mapping of F: from the HOME directory to DATA.

Mapping Search Drives

Search drive mappings are similar to the settings in the DOS PATH statement. Once the search drive is created, you can access files no matter to what your default drive is set. When search drives are created, drive letters are allocated in the reverse order of the alphabet, starting at Z: and working backwards.

There are two ways you can create a search drive mapping:

```
MAP search drive:=servername/volume:\directory
MAP INSERT search drive:=servername/volume:\directory
```

Based on the syntax above, replace:

search drive with the search drive's drive number, such as S1, S2, S3....

servername with the name of the file server to which you are mapping. This parameter is not required when mapping a drive to your default server. If the server name is left out, the *volume* name should *not* be preceded by a slash (/).

volume with the name of the volume on which the directory resides.

directory with the name of the directory to which you are mapping.

The main difference between the two commands is in how the mapping affects the rest of your search drives and the DOS PATH settings. When you use MAP INSERT, NetWare inserts the mapping into the desired path location. When you just use the MAP command, NetWare overwrites the path assignment stored in the position. For example, assume your current search drives are set as follows:

SEARCH1: = Z: [DJASYSTEMS\SYS: \PUBLIC]

SEARCH2: = Y: [DJASYSTEMS\SYS: \]

If you type **MAP INSERT S1:=SYS:\HOME**, your search drive's settings are adjusted as follows:

SEARCH1: = X: [DJASYSTEMS\SYS: \HOME]

SEARCH2: = Z: [DJASYSTEMS\SYS: \PUBLIC]

SEARCH3: = Y: [DJASYSTEMS\SYS: \]

Alternatively, if you typed **MAP S1:=SYS:\HOME**, your search drive's settings would be:

SEARCH1: = X: [DJASYSTEMS\SYS: \HOME]

SEARCH2: = Y: [DJASYSTEMS\SYS: \]

Using the MAP ROOT Command

With either of the MAP commands shown above, you can also use a feature known as "mapping to the root." When you "map to the root," you create a false root directory in your drive mapping. For example, if you mapped the F: drive to the directory HOME\JDOE, the user would have the following DOS prompt if they made the F: drive the default:

```
F:\HOME\JDOE>
```

With this prompt, the user could use the CD command to switch to HOME or another directory. When mapped to the ROOT, the user's F: drive prompt would appear as:

```
F:\>
```

To map a drive to the ROOT, insert the command ROOT directly after the word MAP in your mapping statements.

Using IF-THEN-ELSE Qualifiers in the Login Script

There are times when you want a section in your login script to run only if certain conditions are met. For these cases, NetWare offers a function known as IF-THEN-ELSE. This means that IF a certain condition has been met, THEN execute the following commands, ELSE (otherwise) run the next set of commands. There are three different ways that IF-THEN-ELSE commands are structured, as shown below:

```
IF condition THEN command

IF condition THEN
      command
END

IF condition THEN
      command
      ELSE
            command
END
```

In these examples, you replace *command* with the command(s) you want to run if the condition is met. The *condition* is the actual qualifier for these statements created with the various login script variables.

Using Conditions in the Login Script

There is a wide variety of conditions that can be used with your IF-THEN-ELSE qualifiers. Based on the IF-THEN-ELSE formats shown in the preceding section, you can create qualifiers with conditions such as the following:

```
IF LOGIN_NAME="JDOE" THEN WRITE "MEETING AT NOON"
```

In this example, the *condition* is LOGIN_NAME="JDOE" and the *command* is WRITE "MEETING AT NOON."

```
IF MEMBER OF "PRODUCTION" THEN
      MAP J:=SYS:\PROD\DATA
END
```

In this example, the *condition* is MEMBER OF "PRODUCTION" and the command is MAP J:=SYS:\PROD\DATA.

```
IF GREETING_TIME="MORNING" AND DAY_OF_WEEK="MONDAY" THEN
    WRITE "IT IS MONDAY MORNING!"
    WRITE "MAKE SURE YOU RUN THE VIRUS SCAN."
END
```

There are two conditions in this example. The first *condition* is GREETING_TIME="MORNING," the second *condition* is DAY_OF_WEEK="MONDAY," and the *commands* are the two WRITE statements.

Using Multiple Conditions

As shown in the third example, you can use more than one condition in your IF-THEN-ELSE qualifier. In these cases, multiple conditions are used to narrow the search even further.

When multiple conditions are used, they must be strung together to tell NetWare how to use them. There are several comparison statements to do this, and several ways to use them, as shown in Table 8.3.

Table 8.3 Statements used to compare conditions in login scripts.			
Comparison Statement	**Or**	**Or**	**Or**
EQUALS	=	IS	==
NOT EQUAL TO	!=	IS NOT	<>
LESS THAN	<		
GREATER THAN	>		
LESS THAN OR EQUAL TO	<=		
GREATER THAN OR EQUAL TO	>=		
AND	,		

Using the conditions shown in the above table, you can create some advanced qualifiers such as the following:

```
IF MEMBER OF "DEV" AND NDAY_OF_WEEK >="3" THEN
    WRITE "YOUR REPORTS ARE ALMOST DUE"
END

IF NETWORK_ADDRESS="00000001", HOUR24 IS GREATER THAN "13" THEN
    WRITE "REMINDER - THE RING IS BEING TAKEN DOWN"
    WRITE "FOR MAINTENANCE THIS EVENING."
END
```

Using GOTO Statements in the Login Script

Using qualifiers is one way to restrict what is executed during the login procedure. Another method is the GOTO statement. Similar in function to a DOS batch file's GOTO command, you use the NetWare GOTO script command when you want to interrupt the standard flow of the script by jumping to another area.

When you use it in conjunction with an IF-THEN statement, the GOTO statement is very simple to use. There are two lines that must be added to the script for each GOTO statement you want to include:

- GOTO *header*

- *header*:

> **Note**
>
> The header's name should only contain letters; no spaces or extended characters such as %, $, or @ should be used. If you try to use extended characters, you will get an error.

An example of a GOTO statement in action is:

```
IF MEMBER OF "DEV" THEN GOTO DEVELOPMENT
GOTO NEXT:
DEVELOPMENT:
WRITE "The developers' meeting is at 2:00pm.
PAUSE
GOTO NEXT
NEXT:
WRITE "THIS EXAMPLE IS OVER."
```

In this example, anyone who is a member of the group DEV jumps down to the heading DEVELOPMENT, where he sees an on-screen message about a meeting. After this, he sees the text THIS EXAMPLE IS OVER on-screen. All other users are sent directly to the heading NEXT.

> **Caution**
>
> Be careful when using the GOTO statement. Since it disrupts the flow of the login script, if you do not plan your script properly, important sections may be missed during the login.

Displaying Information

There are times when you want a line of text, or an entire file displayed when a user logs into the file server. To meet these demands, there are three login script commands at your disposal: WRITE, DISPLAY, and FDISPLAY.

II

Environment Setup

Using the WRITE Command to Display Information

WRITE is a basic login script command that enables you to display lines of text to the user during a login. The text you want displayed to the user is included between a set of double quotes, as in this example:

```
WRITE "Insert your text between these quotes!"
```

For added functionality, you can use the WRITE command with the NetWare script variables. There are two ways to do this. First, the entire string of text is enclosed in double quotes, including the variables, but the variables must be preceded by a % sign and be in capital letters, for example:

```
WRITE "The time is now %HOUR:%MINUTE:%SECOND."
```

The second method uses double quotes only around the written text. The variables are placed outside of the quotes without the % signs, but a semicolon (;) is placed before and after the variable, for example:

```
WRITE "The time is now ";HOUR:MINUTE:SECOND;" so don't be late!"
```

When choosing between the two methods, go with the first. It is easier to enter and there is less room for error.

Special Switches for Use with the WRITE Command. In addition to using the script variables to enhance your WRITE commands, there are four switches that can be used within the WRITE command. These switches, as shown in Table 8.4, are included directly in your WRITE command. For example, if you wanted the PC to beep in the middle of a WRITE command, add the following to your script:

```
WRITE "The PC will BEEP now \7 due to the backslash 7 switch."
```

Table 8.4 Switches that can be used with the WRITE command.

Switch	Description
\7	Makes the PC's speaker beep.
\"	Displays quotation marks.
\n	Forces a line feed. The n *must* be in lowercase.
\r	Forces a carriage return. The r *must* be in lowercase.

Using the DISPLAY Command to Display Information

When your requirements go beyond a simple line of text, you use the DISPLAY command to display an ASCII text file to the user during a login. DISPLAY is meant specifically to display straight text files that do not contain any special characters or printer codes. There are two methods to use the DISPLAY command. The first is:

```
DISPLAY servername/volume:\directory\filename
```

Based on the syntax above, replace:

servername with the name of the server on which the file resides. The server name is not mandatory when the file being displayed is on the default server. When left out, the *volume* name should *not* be preceded with a slash (/).

volume with the name of the volume on which the file resides.

directory with the full directory path where the file resides.

filename with the full file name, including extension.

The second method is similiar to the first, but you specify a drive letter instead of the server name and volume. Remember, you will not be able to specify a network drive letter with the DISPLAY command if the drive letter has not already been mapped in the login script.

Using the FDISPLAY Command to Display Information

Serving the same purpose as the DISPLAY command, FDISPLAY displays ASCII text files within the script. FDISPLAY differs in that it is capable of filtering some of the special character and printer codes that may be included in text files. There are two methods to use the FDISPLAY command; the first is:

```
FDISPLAY servername/volume:\directory\filename
```

Based on the syntax above, replace:

servername with the name of the server on which the file resides. The server name is *not* mandatory when the file resides on the default file server. When left out, the *volume* name should *not* be preceded by a slash (/).

volume with the name of the volume on which the file resides.

directory with the full directory path where the file resides.

filename with the full file name, including extension.

The second method is similiar to the first, but you specify a drive letter instead of the server name and volume. Remember, you will not be able to specify a network drive letter with the FDISPLAY command if the drive letter has not already been mapped in the login script. For example, if you wanted to display the file DATES.ANN that was stored in the directory DATA and the F: drive was mapped to the DATA directory, you could use either of the following commands in the login script:

```
FDISPLAY F:\DATA\DATES.ANN

FDISPLAY SYS:\DATA\DATES.ANN
```

Pausing Data as It Scrolls Down the Screen

When you use a command to display data on-screen during login, as in the WRITE, DISPLAY, or FDISPLAY commands, you want to make sure the user has a chance to read what you are displaying. NetWare has two login script commands, PAUSE and WAIT, for just this purpose. Like the DOS PAUSE command, these options stop the screen from scrolling and wait for the user to press any key to continue. An example of a script using a PAUSE or WAIT statement is:

```
WRITE "All employees should report to boardroom C for"
WRITE "a meeting at 2:30"
PAUSE
```

In this example, after the two WRITE commands are executed, the script prompts the user to press any key before it proceeds. Without the PAUSE or WAIT command, the text would likely scroll off the screen before it could be read.

Running External Programs from within the Script

There are instances when you want to run an external program from within the login script. Examples of such requirements are:

- Capturing to a print queue

- Running a virus scanner

- Exiting the script to a menu

For these cases, and others like them, there are two commands at your disposal, # and *EXIT*. The first command, #, runs a program from within the script when the script has not finished. When using the # command, you use one of the following formats:

```
#program name
#COMMAND /C command
```

In the first format, you replace the *program name* with the name of the EXE or COM program you want to execute. For example, assume you want to include CAPTURE statements within your script for each group; you use the # command as follows:

```
IF MEMBER OF "DEV" THEN
     #CAPTURE L=1 Q=PRINTQ1 TI=2
END

IF MEMBER OF "ACCOUNTING" THEN
     #CAPTURE L=1 Q=PRINTQ2 TI=2
END
```

These examples establish a printing capture to PRINTQ1 for users in the group DEV, and to PRINTQ2 for users in the group ACCOUNTING. After the CAPTURE commands run, the script continues.

You use the second format when you want to run a batch file or DOS internal command, such as DIR, from within the script. When you run one of these files, you also must run the DOS command processor for it to work. For example, assume you had a batch file, SCAN.BAT, to scan for viruses on the workstation. In this case, you use the following in your login script:

```
IF DAY_OF_WEEK="MONDAY" AND GREETING_TIME="MORNING" THEN
     WRITE "IT IS MONDAY MORNING, TIME TO SCAN FOR VIRUSES."
     #COMMAND /C Z:\PUBLIC\SCAN.BAT
END
```

This example runs the batch file SCAN.BAT stored in the PUBLIC directory every time a user logs into the server on Monday morning.

You use the EXIT command when you want to completely stop the login script's execution. The EXIT command can either be used on its own, or with another command to run a program or batch file. When used to exit the script and run an external batch file or program, the program name must be enclosed in double quotes. For example:

```
MAP F:=SYS:HOME\%LOGIN_NAME

IF LOGIN_NAME="BACKUP" THEN
     EXIT "BACKUP.BAT"
END

MAP G:=SYS:\COMMON
```

In this example, all users would first be given a drive mapping for the F: drive. Next, if the user's login name was BACKUP, the script's execution would be halted and the batch file BACKUP.BAT would be run. All other users would continue through the remainder of the script.

> **Caution**
>
> Using the EXIT command entirely halts the login script procedure. When used within the system login script, any users' personal scripts will *not* be run.

Advanced Options

In addition to the login script commands and variables already discussed in this section, there are a few more to consider. These options are considered advanced and are not used in most installations.

II

Environment Setup

Logging In with Additional Arguments

You might want your users to log in to a file server and specify additional arguments from the command line. Examples of such a situation are:

- When users use multiple printers or print queues

- When users use different configuration files

- When users occasionally require different mappings

When logging into the server, the standard command string is:

```
LOGIN servername/username
```

NetWare can include additional arguments after the username. Each argument must be separated by a single space and is assigned a percentage variable by NetWare, such as %1, % 2, ... Then, by using the SHIFT command, these arguments can be used within the login script.

To illustrate, assume the users occasionally use different databases, called DB3 and DB4, on the server. By default, the users are mapped to the DB3 directories and captured to print queue 1, but they were instructed that if they require the DB4 directory and print queue 2, to specify this on the command line as follows:

```
LOGIN servername/username DB4 PRINTQ2
```

Based on the text above, NetWare assigns the percentage variables as follows:

%0   servername

%1   username

%2   DB4

%3   PRINTQ2

To make use of these arguments, the following commands have to be added to the system login script:

```
LOOP:
      IF "%2"="DB4" THEN MAP I:=SYS:\APPS\DB4
      IF "%2"="PRINTQ_2" THEN #CAPTURE L=1 Q=PRINTQ_2 TI=2
SHIFT 1
      IF "%2" <> "" THEN GOTO LOOP
```

In the above text, the login process gets to the first line that asks if %2 is equal to DB4. As previously shown, it currently does, so NetWare makes the appropriate mapping. The second line then asks if %2 is equal to PRINTQ_2, which it currently does not, so NetWare skips this line. The 4th line, SHIFT 1, shifts the variables one place to the left. The process starts over, but this time, the word PRINTQ_2 is in the %2 spot, so NetWare captures to PRINTQ_2 as noted in line 3. After the queue is captured, the third line shifts the variables one space to the left again. Since there are no more variables, %2 is left blank. Line 5 breaks the loop by not sending the login process back to the LOOP label.

Manipulating Text

One little-known feature of login scripts is their ability to manipulate text from a DOS or NetWare environment variable. One reason for doing this is that you want to map a directory based on a NetWare script variable, but the script variable is greater than eight characters—the maximum filename size in DOS.

In these cases, there are two commands available to you: << and >>. The syntax for these commands is:

```
variable<<x
```

or

```
variable>>x
```

For these commands, you replace the *x* with the number of spaces you want the *variable* moved to the left << or the right >>.

As an example, assume there are several people on your LAN with IBM Token Ring cards. You know the unique vendor ID of the address is 10005A and the entire address is 12 bytes long. For these people, you want to create a drive mapping to a directory called SYS:\10005A.

If you use the P_STATION script variable on its own, you get errors since it reports a 12-byte address. So, to accomplish this task, add the following to your login script:

```
SET ADDR=P_STATION>>6
MAP J:=SYS:\%<ADDR>
```

The first line sets a DOS environment variable called STATIONDIR to the first six bytes of the twelve-byte station address and the second line maps a drive to a directory that was named after the first six bytes.

This concludes the review of the various commands and variables that you can use in the NetWare login scripts. Next, we examine NetWare's menuing system and how you can configure it for your specific requirements.

Chapter 9
Menus

In the initial days of computers, running applications required a lot of user legwork. Changing directories, running programs from the command line—it all takes time. With the popularity of LANs, it is almost mandatory to use some type of tool to automate these tasks. With LAN users ranging in experience from the novice to the expert, one cannot expect all users to follow complex commands to run an application.

Many people use menus to automate the various tasks. By doing so, complex scripts and commands can be launched simply by selecting a menu option. Novell has recognized this requirement and has licensed a menuing system from Saber Software Corporation for its NetWare operating system. In this section, we look at these menus, and specifically:

- Formatting the menu script

- Commands and variables that can be used in the menu

- Converting the older (pre-3.12) menus

Using and Creating Your Own Menus

As with most things related to computing, planning is a critical phase in the development of your menus. Before you even start to write your menus, you should sit down with pad and pencil and draw out how you want the menus to look.

Since the NetWare menus can have several different layers of submenus, it is important to first visualize how the finished product will look.

While you draw out the structuring of the menus, there are a few things you should keep in mind:

- *What do the users do at their desks?* By knowing what the users are doing on a day-to-day basis, you have a better understanding of what they require from the menus.

- *What applications do the users use?* Writing menus that do not include all the different applications in use can be pointless. Remember, the purpose of the menus is to make the user's life easier. Loading and unloading the menu to run an application that was not included in the menu does *not* do this.

- *Can you automate some of the more redundant tasks?* If there are tasks users must do on a regular basis, see if you can automate the task as a menu option. By automating these tasks, users will be able to perform their jobs more efficiently and the chances of typos are minimized.

- *How should the options be organized?* Menus should be structured in a well-organized format. If users need in-depth training to figure out how you designed the menus, then your work has been wasted. Remember, the goal of using menus is to reduce the amount of work.

Writing the Menu Script

The menu you are creating is a standard ASCII text file that contains some special commands. This text file can be created with the editor of your choice as long as the editor does not add any special formatting characters to the document. After you have written the menu, this file (referred to as the *SOURCE*) must then be compiled using a utility called MENUMAKE.

In the menu source file, there are some rules you must follow when entering the text.

- MENU commands are entered flush with the left margin. Each menu command must be followed by at least one ITEM line.

- ITEM commands follow the MENU commands and are indented one tab. Each ITEM command must be followed by at least one EXEC or LOAD command.

- EXEC or LOAD commands should be indented two tabs from the left margin.

- Remarks can be added to the menu as long as they are preceded by a semicolon (;).

- Menu source files should be named with an extension .SRC.

To illustrate these "rules," Figure 9.1 provides a sample login script.

```
;**********************************************************************
;*                                                                    *
;*                                                                    *
;* Ruling 9 Menu : MAIN.SRC                                           *
;* Created       : 21:16:00 08/16/94                                  *
;*                                                                    *
;**********************************************************************
;

;MAIN MENU
MENU 01,Main Menu
     ITEM Word Processing ...
         SHOW 10
     ITEM Utilities ...
         LOAD UTILS.DAT
     ITEM Printing Commands ...
         SHOW 20
     ITEM SHELL TO DOS
         EXEC DOS
     ITEM UNLOAD NMENU
         EXEC EXIT
     ITEM LOGOUT OF LAN
         EXEC LOGOUT
MENU 10, Wordprocessing
         ITEM Wordperfect
                 EXEC F:
                 EXEC CD H:\WP51
                 EXEC H:WP51
                 EXEC CD H:\
MENU 20, Printing Commands
         ITEM Capture To A Network Printer
GETR Enter The Print Q Number To Capture To:   {} 2,1, {}
             EXEC CAPTURE L=1 TI=2 Q=PRINTQ_
         ITEM Capture To A Local Printer
                 EXEC ENDCAP
```

Fig. 9.1 Sample NetWare menu script file.

The menu commands available to you have been summarized in Table 9.1. You can use these commands to create a powerful menuing system that can handle a wide range of tasks.

Caution
Unless noted otherwise, the parameters shown in the tables of this chapter should be entered in capital letters; otherwise, they may not work properly.

Table 9.1 Commands that can be used in your menu.		
Command	**Example**	**Description**
EXEC	EXEC H:\WP51.EXE	Tells NMENU the DOS commands you want executed.
GETO	GETO Enter The PrintQ Name: { } 10,PRINTQ1,{ }	Prompts the user for additional information on an optional basis.
GETP	GETP Enter The Name Of The File To Copy: { } 12,,{ }	Stores information entered by the user for use later.
GETR	GETR Enter The New Default Drive: { } 2,F,{:}	Prompts the user for additional information that is required.
ITEM	ITEM WordPerfect { BATCH }	Designates a menu entry.
LOAD	LOAD SUPPORT.DAT	Loads an additional menu from another script.
MENU	MENU 02, WORD-PROCESSING	Designates the name and start of the menu or submenu.
SHOW	SHOW 4	References a submenu within the same menu script.

Specifying Menus and Submenus

The MENU command names and identifies the beginning of the menu or submenu. When using this command, it must be entered into the script as:

```
MENU menu_number, menu_title
```

Based on the syntax above, replace:

menu_number with the number of the menu or submenu.

menu_title with the name of the menu or submenu.

Note

You can use up to 255 menu commands in one script.

Tip

The numbers assigned to each menu have no bearing on the order in which they appear in the finished product. The ordering of menus and options depends on how the ITEM commands are included. But, for the purpose of organization, it is better if groups of menus and submenus are structured neatly. Therefore, you may want to number your menu commands in increments of five or ten. This makes life easier should you need to add new options down the road.

Identifying Your Menu Options

The ITEM command signifies the different options within each menu or submenu. You can have a maximum of twelve ITEM commands per MENU command, and each ITEM command must be indented one tab from the left margin. When using the ITEM command, it is entered into the script as:

```
ITEM item title {parameters}
```

Based on the syntax above, replace:

item_title with the name or phrase you want to be used as the menu option up to a maximum of 40 characters in length.

parameters with one or more of the parameters shown in Table 9.2. When using multiple parameters, each one must be separated by a single space. When used, the parameter or group of parameters must be enclosed in curly brackets ({ }).

Table 9.2 Parameters that can be used with the ITEM command.

Command	Example	Description
BATCH	ITEM HARVARD GRAPHICS { BATCH }	Added to the end of the ITEM line to tell NMENU to remove the menu system from memory (temporarily) when executing a command. The BATCH parameter will save you 32K of RAM but slows down the reloading of the menus slightly.
CHDIR	ITEM LOTUS { CHDIR }	Added to the end of the ITEM line to tell NMENU to return to the previous default directory after the processing is completed.
PAUSE	ITEM DOS DIRECTORY LISTING { PAUSE }	When PAUSE is added to the end of the ITEM line, messages are left on-screen until the user presses a key.
SHOW	ITEM DOS COPY { SHOW }	By adding SHOW to the end of your ITEM line, NMENU displays the commands as they are executed.

Menu options are listed in the order in which the ITEM commands are shown. Starting with the first ITEM, each line will be labeled sequentially, beginning with the letter A.

> **Tip**
>
> To override the line assignments, you can insert your own using the carat (^) symbol. For example, if you want the letter S to be for spreadsheets, you can enter ITEM ^S SPREADSHEETS as the item name.

II

Environment Setup

Running DOS Commands and Script Commands from the Menu

The EXEC command executes a DOS command, or string of commands, following the ITEM command. There is no limit to the number of EXEC commands that can follow an ITEM command. When using the EXEC command, it is entered into the script as:

```
EXEC command
```

Based on the syntax above, replace:

command with the command(s) you want passed to DOS, up to a maximum of 250 characters. Since DOS will not accept commands of 250 characters on a single line, you can break up commands by using the + sign. An example is:

```
ITEM Capture To PrintQ1
    EXEC CAPTURE +
    L=1 Q=PRINTQ1 TI=2
```

If the above were added to a menu, selecting this item would successfully capture to PRINTQ1 with a time-out value of 2.

> **Note**
>
> When entering the command you want EXEC to execute, specify the drive letter and directory where it can be found if it is not in the path. NMENU does NOT recognize volume names.

In addition to executing standard DOS commands, there are a few script commands that can be used as shown in Table 9.3.

Table 9.3 Parameters that can be used with the EXEC command.

Parameter	Example	Description
CALL	EXEC CALL REPORT.BAT	Calls a batch file from within a batch file.
DOS	EXEC DOS	Lets the users jump to a DOS shell from within the menus. When they want to return to the menu, they must type EXIT from the DOS prompt.
EXIT	EXEC EXIT	Exits the menu program completely.
LOGOUT	EXEC LOGOUT	Exits from the menus and logs the user out of the network.

> **Tip**
>
> If you use the EXEC LOGOUT command in your menu file, selecting this option would produce the error Batch File Missing even though you would still be logged out. To get around this error, you could use the EXEC EXIT command with a batch file that would contain the LOGOUT command. To do so, first create a batch file called OUT.BAT in the LOGIN directory that contained the command LOGOUT. Then, add the following text to you menu file:
>
> ```
> ITEM LOGOUT OF SERVER
>     EXEC F:
>     EXEC CD\LOGIN
>     EXEC EXIT OUT.BAT
> ```
>
> Once added, and you have recompiled the menu source file, users can select this option and logout of the server without getting an error message.

> **Tip**
>
> If you want the users to get out of the menuing system completely, but remain logged into the server, make sure you add the EXEC EXIT command; otherwise, they cannot get out.

Getting Information from the User

The NetWare menus enable you to request information from the user that then can be passed onto an EXEC command by using one of three commands:

GETR—GETR requests mandatory information. The information gathered is added to the end of the following EXEC command.

GETO—GETO requests optional information. The information gathered here is added to the end of the following EXEC command.

GETP—GETP requests information that will be used in more complex EXEC commands from the user. There can be up to nine GETP commands after a single ITEM command. The information gathered from each GETP command is assigned a variable between %0 and %9. These variables then can be called into the following EXEC command.

Regardless of which parameter you use, the syntax for entering it in the script is as follows (the parameters shown below are explained in Table 9.4):

```
GETx prompt {prepend_text} length,prefill_text, {append_text}
```

II

Environment Setup

Table 9.4 GET parameters.	
Parameter	**Description**
prompt	The text displayed to the user.
{prepend_text}	The text entered before the user's text. Watch your spacing! Any spaces between the curly brackets will be used.
length	The maximum number of characters the user can enter—up to 255.
prefill_text	The text placed in the entry window by default. You can call DOS environment variables as the default by enclosing them in % signs (such as %SERVER%).
{append_text}	The text entered after the user's text. Watch your spacing! Any spaces between the curly brackets will be used.

Examples of acceptable GET*x* commands include:

```
GETO Enter the print queue number: {PRINTQ_} 2,, {}
GETR Enter the username to scan for: {} 47,%NAME%, {/a}
GETP Enter the file name: {} 12,, {}
```

Compiling the Menu Script

After you have completed the creation of the script file, you must compile it before it can be used. To compile the script you must use the MENUMAKE utility found in the PUBLIC directory. The proper syntax for using MENUMAKE is:

```
MENUMAKE menu_source_file
```

Based on the syntax above, replace:

menu_source_file with the name of the source file your created. By default, MENUMAKE expects the source file to have an extension of SRC. If you used a different extension, you must specify the full file name.

If there are no errors in your script, MENUMAKE converts your script and creates a new file called *XXXXXXXX*.DAT, where *XXXXXXX* is the name of your menu file. If there are errors, MENUMAKE tells you on which lines the errors have occurred, so you can resolve them.

Running the Menu

Once you have a finished menu (one that has been compiled without errors), there are a few more steps that must be completed before you actually run the menu.

First, you must determine where you want the menu file to be stored. The menu file should be placed in one of the search drives where users have at least Read and File Scan rights. Many people choose the PUBLIC directory for this purpose.

Next, you must create a directory somewhere on the server that will be used for temporary files. NMENU creates temporary files whenever the users access the menu or shell to DOS. Since you usually have a search drive pointing to the public directory, you can create the temporary directory as a subdirectory of PUBLIC.

> **Note**
>
> You must assign all users the rights RWCEMF in the temporary directory.

Finally, there are two environment variable settings you should add to the system login script:

> *SET S_FILE="%STATION"*: NMENU uses this variable for naming the temporary files.

> *SET S_FILEDIR="Z:\PUBLIC\TEMP\"*: This variable specifies where the temporary files should be stored. You should replace the directory name with the one you created. But you must ensure there is a backslash (\) at the end of the path!

When all is said and done, you should be able to login to the file server and type **NMENU** *menuname* from the command line to access your new menus (replace *menuname* with the name of your compiled menu).

> **Tip**
>
> You could add a command to the system login script to ensure that everyone uses the new menus automatically by adding the command EXIT "NMENU *menuname*" to the end of the script. Replace *menuname* with the name of your compiled script; also, remember, the quotes are needed when using the EXIT system login script command.

Converting Older NetWare Menus

If you upgraded from a previous version of NetWare, you may have been using the older menu system (MENU.EXE and MNU source menus). Instead of wasting time rewriting these scripts, you can convert them with the MENUCNVT utility. Once converted, they can be run in the same fashion as the newer menus.

Follow these steps to use an old menu:

1. Convert your old menu file by typing **MENUCNVT** *oldfile*.**mnu** *newfile*.**src** from the DOS prompt. MENUCNVT then converts your old script into the newer scripting language and creates a menu file with the extension SRC.

2. Compile the new menu source file by typing **MENUMAKE** *menuname*.**src**.

3. Run the newly compiled menu by typing **NMENU** *menuname*.

Changing the Colors of the Menu Utilities

Note

In NetWare V3.12, the COLORPAL utility cannot be used for changing the colors of your personal menus until an update is available from Novell. At the present time, COLORPAL is only used for changing the colors of the Novell utility (such as SYSCON and FCONSOLE) menus.

Anyone who has been using NetWare for a while is quite familiar with the menu utilities' standard blue screens. Well, if so much blue has got you down, all is not lost. To spice up your menus with a variety of colors, Novell has included a utility named COLORPAL. Using COLORPAL, you can revise the color palettes with a wide range of colors. Before you start making any changes, there are two things you should be aware of:

■ NetWare's default color schemes are stored in a file called IBM$RUN.OVL in the public directory. If COLORPAL is run from the PUBLIC directory, this overlay file is adjusted. To ensure that you still have the original file available (if things go astray), either back up this file or run COLORPAL from another directory first.

■ When run from another directory where IBM$RUN.OVL does not exist, COLORPAL creates the overlay file and flags it as a hidden file.

To change the colors of your utility menus, follow these steps:

1. From the DOS prompt, type COLORPAL. You are presented with a window entitled Defined Palettes that contains five default palettes.

2. Highlight the palette you want to edit and press Enter. If you want to create a new palette, just press the Ins key.

Tip

Palette 0 is used for the menu windows and palette 1 is used for the background (also called "wallpaper").

3. After selecting a palette, you are presented with a series of attributes you can adjust. For each attribute you select, NetWare presents you with a window of different colors to choose

from. As you make your selection, NetWare shows you what it will ultimately look like in the Current Palette window shown in the lower-left corner.

4. After you have made all the desired changes, press the Esc key until NetWare asks you if you want to save your changes. Answering Yes updates the overlay file and returns you to DOS.

Caution

Changing the color palette when there are workstations with monochrome monitors could cause problems for these users. Certain color schemes that may look great on the color screen may not even be readable on the monochrome. Should you run into this problem, you can prevent these stations from using the IBM$RUN.OVL file by setting the short machine name in the NET.CFG to CMPQ. Once set, these stations use the basic CMPQ$RUN.OVL.

II

Environment Setup

Chapter 10

Miscellaneous Commands for Environment Management

In NetWare, there are various utilities that can be used to manage the environment in which a user operates. Whether these changes are to a user's password, or how your drive pointers are set up, NetWare has a utility for it.

This chapter contains detailed information on various commands that play some role in the management of your NetWare environment but don't fit neatly into one of the other sections in this book.

In this chapter, we discuss numerous commands, and specifically:

- Changing passwords

- Checking who is logged into the server

- Sending and receiving messages

- Changing and viewing the date and time

- Reviewing information about your connection to the server

Changing Passwords

If your LAN is like most, users are required to have passwords on the file server. Although passwords protect the server from unauthorized access, they are easily forgotten. Should a user on your LAN forget their password, or if you want to change it for security reasons, you can use the SYSCON and SETPASS utilities.

Before changing a password, first consider whether you're authorized to do so. Your security level on the file server will determine whether you can change a certain ID's password. The following "rules" will help you determine whether you can change a password:

- *SUPERVISOR* or *SUPERVISOR EQUIVALENT* IDs can change *any* password on the server.

- IDs set up as *Account Managers* or *Workgroup Managers* can only change the IDs of those whom they manage.

- All other IDs can only change their own password.

> **Note**
>
> If the account restriction *Allow User To Change Password* has been set to No, regular users won't be able to change their password with any of these utilities. Instead, they must seek out someone with the appropriate access.

Changing a Password within SYSCON

With the help of the SYSCON menu utility, you can change your password, or the password of another user (depending on your security level), by following these steps:

1. From the Available Topics main menu of SYSCON, select User Information and then select the ID of the user whose password you want to change.

2. After selecting the user ID, you are presented with the User Information screen (this screen is specific to the user you selected). From this menu, select the option Change Password.

3. NetWare prompts you to enter a new password. When asked, retype the password to make sure you entered it correctly the first time.

> **Note**
>
> When a new password is created within SYSCON, it automatically expires when the user logs in. If you don't want the password to expire right away, you can select the Account Restrictions option for this user and change the date the password expires.

Changing a Password from the Command Line

The SETPASS command line utility enables you to change your password, or the password of a user ID you manage. The syntax is:

```
SETPASS [servername/][username]
```

Tip
After typing SETPASS, NetWare asks you to type in your current password before you can select a new one. If you don't have a password, just press Enter when asked.

Based on this syntax, replace:

servername with the name of the server the user ID resides on. You must be attached to this server before issuing the SETPASS command. You don't need this option if you're changing a password on your default server.

username with the name of the user ID for which you're changing the password. You don't need this option if you're changing your own password.

EXAMPLE 1: To change your password on your default server, type the following from the command line:

SETPASS

EXAMPLE 2: To change your password on the server that's not your default, NETWARE312, type the following from the command line:

SETPASS NETWARE312

EXAMPLE 3: One of the user IDs you manage, PETERVAN, on file server BILLING, requires a password reset. After attaching to the server, you can change the password by typing the following from the command line:

SETPASS BILLING/PETERVAN

Note
If you are changing your password, and you're attached to multiple file servers, NetWare asks if you want to Synchronize Your Password On Attached Servers. If you answer Yes, NetWare changes your current password on all attached servers to the new password you just entered.

Messages

Most people are familiar with e-mail and the many benefits of using it. Instead of sending letters or leaving voice mail messages, computer users are transmitting information in the form of an electronic message (e-mail). While there are various e-mail software packages on the market, the ability to send brief messages across the LAN is included with your NetWare server. Using the utilities we discuss in this section, you can send messages to one or more users or block them from being received on your workstation (almost like a "do not disturb" sign).

If you want detailed information on installing NetWare's Basic MHS system, used to send full-length messages or letters to other users, refer to the heading "Installing Basic MHS" in Appendix D, "Basic MHS and FirstMail."

Note

There are two types of message transmissions used in NetWare—*standard messages* and *broadcasts*. Standard messages are sent to one or more users or groups of your choice. Broadcast messages are sent to all attached nodes.

Sending Messages from the Workstation Command Line

NetWare provides a command line utility, called SEND, for sending messages to users across the LAN. SEND lets you send messages to one or more users on any file server you have access to. The SEND command uses the following format:

```
SEND "message" [TO] receiver(s)
```

Based on this syntax, replace:

message with the text you want transmitted. The message you are sending must be enclosed in double quotes.

receiver(s) with one or more of the items shown in Table 10.1.

Table 10.1 Receivers you can send messages to with the SEND command.		
Receiver	**Example**	**Description**
USER NAME	SEND "The Meeting Is At 2:00" JDOE	Sends a message to the user JDOE on the current server.
CONNECTION NUMBER	SEND "The Meeting At 2:00 Is Canceled" 12	Sends a message to the user logged into the server on connection number 12.
CONSOLE	SEND "Please do not DOWN the server yet!" CONSOLE	Sends a message to the file server console.
GROUPS	SEND "Expense reports are due today!!" ACCOUNTING	Sends a message to every user within the ACCOUNTING group.

Receiver	Example	Description
MULTIPLE USERS	SEND "The backups did not run last night" JDOE BJONES KSMITH	Sends a message to users JDOE, BJONES, and KSMITH.
A USER ON ANOTHER FILE SERVER FS1	SEND "The conference is canceled" FS1/JDOE	Sends a message to user JDOE on the file server.

Sending Messages and Broadcasts with FCONSOLE

Note

RIGHTS REQUIRED TO COMPLETE TASK: SUPERVISOR EQUIVALENT OR CONSOLE OPERATOR.

If you've used versions of NetWare prior to 3.X, you know FCONSOLE has lost a lot of the functionality it used to have. Even with the options that have gone astray, you can still use FCONSOLE to send messages on the LAN.

Using FCONSOLE, you can either broadcast a message to all users or send a message to certain individuals.

To broadcast a message to all users within FCONSOLE:

1. Select the Broadcast Console Message option from the Available Options main menu.

2. Type in the message you want to send, up to 55 characters.

To send a message to individual users within FCONSOLE:

1. Select Connection Information from the Available Options main menu.

2. From the listing of Current Connections, select the user to whom you want to send a message. Next, you are presented with a new window with two options—Other Information and Broadcast Console Message. By selecting the Broadcast Console Message Option, you can send a private message to the selected user up to 55 characters in length.

Note

Even though FCONSOLE gives you an option to "Broadcast Console Message" after selecting a specific connection, it's *not* a broadcast that is sent. When you select this option, you are actually sending a standard message, not a broadcast. This menu option was named incorrectly.

III

Environment Management

Sending Messages with SESSION

The SESSION menu utility probably provides the easiest method of sending short messages over the LAN/WAN. Using the menu interface, you can send messages to a group or a user by following the steps below:

1. Select the option User List or Group List from the Available Topics main menu based on whether you want to send a message to a user ID or a group.

2. If you chose the User List option, SESSION displays a listing of all users currently logged into the server. If you chose Group List, SESSION gives you a listing of all group names configured on the server. On either screen, select the user or group you want to send a message to.

3. SESSION presents a listing of Available Options. In this window, select Send Message and then type in your message up to 42 characters in length.

Shortcut

Instead of selecting a single user or group to send a message to, you can flag multiple objects by using the F5 key. Once you've flagged all the objects, press the Enter key and carry on with Step 3.

Broadcasting and Sending Messages from the Server's Console

The BROADCAST console command lets you send a message to one or more users logged into the server. Since this is a console command, you must be working directly on the file server, or you must be in control of the console through the RCONSOLE utility.

Note

The BROADCAST and SEND console commands operate in the same fashion. They are identical in every way except their names.

To send a message using BROADCAST, use the following syntax:

```
BROADCAST "message" [userid] [connection_number]
```

Based on this syntax, replace:

> *message* with the message you want to send.

> *userid* with the name of each ID to whom you want the message to be sent. If you want the message to go to every user/node attached to this server, don't specify any IDs.

connection_number with the connection number of the node to which you want to send the message. If you want the message to go to every user/node attached to this server, don't specify any connection number.

EXAMPLE 1: To send a message to all connections attached to the server, type the following from the console prompt:

BROADCAST "THIS IS THE FIRST TEST MESSAGE"

EXAMPLE 2: To send a message to the user on connection 4, type the following from the console prompt:

BROADCAST "PLEASE LOGOUT" 4

EXAMPLE 3: To send a message to the users JSTEVENS and SSMITH, type the following from the console prompt:

BROADCAST "THE MEETING IS CANCELED" JSTEVENS SSMITH

> **Note**
>
> You can enter a maximum of 249 characters at the console prompt, including the command and the message. While DOS won't display the messages entirely, Windows users can read the full message.

Disabling and Enabling the Receipt of Messages

Having the ability to send messages to users on the LAN can be a real time-saver, but for some people it can be a real pain. A user may be busy, or running a job on their PC that can't be disturbed. In these cases, receiving a message on the workstation wouldn't be acceptable.

To stop messages sent by other stations from appearing on your workstation, the syntax is:

    CASTOFF

To stop messages sent by other stations AND the console from appearing on your workstation, the syntax is:

    CASTOFF ALL

To allow messages to be received from other stations and the console, the syntax is:

    CASTON

> **Tip**
>
> There is a NET.CFG parameter called MESSAGE TIMEOUT you can use to set the amount of time a message will appear on your screen. Refer to Table 4.11 in Chapter 4, "Installing Workstations," for further information.

III

Environment Management

Checking to See What Program Versions Are Being Run

Someday, you may need or want to know what version of a program you are running. While this isn't a task you would need to run on a day-to-day basis, Novell sometimes releases updates or patches to existing programs, and then the version number might become a concern.

Viewing the Version Numbers of Executables

Novell provides you with the VERSION utility to help you determine what version of a program you have. This program is stored in the PUBLIC directory on the SYS volume and is capable of examining any of the NetWare EXE files to determine their version levels. To use VERSION, the syntax is:

```
VERSION filename.exe
```

Based on this syntax, replace:

filename.exe with the name of the EXE file you want to examine.

EXAMPLE: To determine the version of SYSCON you are running, type the following from the command line:

VERSION SYSCON

Checking Server and Workstation Driver Versions

You can check the versions of the file servers to which you are attached and some basic information on your workstation drivers with a NetWare command line utility called NVER. To use this utility, type **NVER** from the command line. When you use this command, you see a screen similar to the one in Figure 10.1.

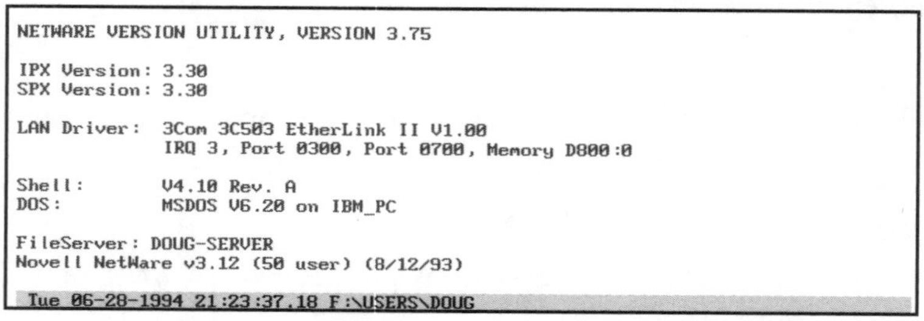

```
NETWARE VERSION UTILITY, VERSION 3.75

IPX Version: 3.30
SPX Version: 3.30

LAN Driver:  3Com 3C503 EtherLink II V1.00
             IRQ 3, Port 0300, Port 0700, Memory D000:0

Shell:       V4.10 Rev. A
DOS:         MSDOS V6.20 on IBM_PC

FileServer: DOUG-SERVER
Novell NetWare v3.12 (50 user) (8/12/93)

  Tue 06-28-1994 21:23:37,18 F:\USERS\DOUG
```

Fig. 10.1 Version information provided by the NVER command line utility.

Working with the Date and Time

On occasion, the date and time maintained on your server or workstation may be incorrect. To ensure the time is maintained properly and kept up to date (pun intended), the following options are available to you.

Synchronizing Your PC's Date and Time with the Server

The SYSTIME NetWare command line utility synchronizes the date and time of your PC with that of the file server. To synchronize the date and time of your PC, type the following from the command line:

SYSTIME

Tip
Unless you have configured your NET.CFG file *not* to synchronize your PC's date and time with the server, NetWare will do this automatically during a login.

Changing the Server's Date and Time

Note
RIGHTS REQUIRED TO COMPLETE TASK: SUPERVISOR EQUIVALENT OR CONSOLE OPERATOR.

You can change the date and time maintained by the file server using the FCONSOLE utility by following the steps below:

1. From the Available Options main menu of FCONSOLE, select Status.

2. You are then presented with a window entitled File Server Status. On this screen, adjust the values in the Server Date and Time fields to reflect your requirements (see fig. 10.2).

Fig. 10.2 Changing the date and time within the FCONSOLE menu utility.

Changing the Server's Date and Time from the Server Console

Using a command from the server's console, you can adjust the Date and Time maintained by the server by using the following syntax:

```
SET TIME [month/date/year] [hour:minute:second]
```

Replace the variables above with the appropriate settings. When changing the time, you should specify whether the time is AM or PM; otherwise, NetWare will assume AM (unless you use military time). For example, to set the date to February 6th and the time to 9:16 p.m., type:

SET TIME February 6 1994 9:16pm

Tip
You can check the current date and time on the file server by typing **SET TIME** or **TIME** from the console.

Checking Your Current Connection Information

At times, you may want to check your current status on the file server such as your security equivalences or maybe the servers that you are currently logged into. The WHOAMI command line utility provides you with information about "who you are" on the file server or LAN. To use WHOAMI, the syntax is:

```
WHOAMI [server] [option(s)]
```

Based on the syntax above, replace:

server with the name of the file server for which you want to check your connection information. If you do not specify a server name, WHOAMI provides you with the information for all servers to which you are currently attached.

option(s) with one or more of the options shown in Table 10.2.

Table 10.2 Switches that can be used with WHOAMI.	
Switch	**Description**
/A	Displays information gathered from all other options.
/C	Allows WHOAMI to scroll continuously. When not used, WHOAMI pauses after each full screen of text.
/G	Displays your group memberships on the specified file server.
/O	Displays supervisor object information and the objects (user and group) you manage.
/R	Displays your effective rights.
/S	Displays your user and group security equivalences.

Switch	Description
/SY	Displays basic system information such as the server you are logged into, your ID, NetWare version, and the time you logged in.
/W	Tells you if you are a Workgroup Manager.

EXAMPLE 1: To determine which file servers you are currently attached to, type the following from the command line:

WHOAMI

EXAMPLE 2: To determine which users and groups you are the security equivalent to, type the following from the command line:

WHOAMI /S

EXAMPLE 3: To determine if you are a Workgroup Manager on the file server FS1, type the following from the command line:

WHOAMI FS1 /S

Checking which Server Connections Are Active

At times, you may want to see who is currently logged into the file server. Some people like to see who is on-line before they send out a message, or maybe you want to know who is still using the server. In either case, there are several options available to you, some from the command line, and some from the console.

Reviewing Current Connections to the Server from the Command Line

USERLIST is a basic command line utility that provides you with a listing of all the users and nodes (such as print servers) logged into the file server, their connection number, and what time they initially logged in. Use USERLIST by using the following syntax:

```
USERLIST [server/][name] [/option(s)]
```

Based on the syntax above, replace:

server with the name of the file server you want to check. You must be attached to the file server and a forward slash must be placed at the end of the server name. If left out, USERLIST scans your default server.

name with the name of the user ID you're looking for. If left out, USERLIST displays *all* user IDs logged into the file server.

option(s) with one of the following options:

Address—displays the network and node address of each user.

Object—displays the object type for each connection.

Continuous—forces USERLIST to scroll continuously through the output without pause after each screen is full. This option can be used in conjunction with the other two (for instance, USERLIST /A /C).

EXAMPLE 1: To get a listing of all connections to your default file server, type the following from the command line:

USERLIST

EXAMPLE 2: To check if the user ID JHOWELL is logged into the server FMAS-1, when you are attached to FMAS-1, but it's not your default server, type the following from the command line:

USERLIST FMAS-1/JHOWELL

EXAMPLE 3: To view the network and workstation physical addresses for all connections to the MICJEN server, when you are attached to MICJEN, but it's not your default server, type the following from the command line:

USERLIST MICJEN/ /A

Tip
Wild cards can be used with the USERLIST command. For example, to scan the server for all users logged in who have IDs beginning with ABC, type **USERLIST ABC***.

Reviewing Current Connections with the FCONSOLE Menu Utility

Note
RIGHTS REQUIRED TO COMPLETE TASK: YOU MUST BE A SUPERVISOR EQUIVALENT OR CONSOLE OPERATOR TO COMPLETE STEP 3.

While a little more cumbersome than USERLIST, FCONSOLE can be used to find out what users and other nodes (for example, print servers) are logged into the file server by following these steps:

1. From the Available Options main menu of FCONSOLE, select Connection Information.

2. In the Current Connections window, cursor through the listing to view all users currently logged in and their connection numbers to the file server.

3. For additional information, press the Enter key on any user and select the Other Information option to view the login times and addresses of the user.

Reviewing Current Connections with SESSION

Like FCONSOLE, SESSION is a NetWare menu utility that can show you who and what is using your file server's connections. You can check the current file server connections with SESSION by following these steps:

1. Select User List from the Available Topics main menu of SESSION.

2. Next, you are presented with a window displaying the current users and their station numbers. You can scroll through this listing to view all of the current server connections. If you want further information, you can press Enter on any one of the connections and then, by selecting the Display User Information option, you can view the login times and addresses of the station.

Checking Server Connections from the Console

When working on the server console, you can use the MONITOR utility to check the current connections by following these steps:

1. From the Available Options main menu of MONITOR, select Connection Information. If MONITOR is not already loaded, you can load it from the server console by typing **LOAD MONITOR**.

2. In the Active Connections window, you can cursor through to view all the current server connections. For more detailed information, you can select a connection by pressing Enter where you then are presented with another screen that gives you information on the files in use by this connection, the address of the connection, and how many kilobytes have been read and written to the file server by this connection (see fig. 10.3).

Note

When scanning through the listing of active connections, you may come across one named NOT-LOGGED-IN. For further information on these types of connections and possible problems associated with them, refer to the heading "Not Logged In Clear Connections" in Chapter 29, "Miscellaneous Common Problems."

III

Environment Management

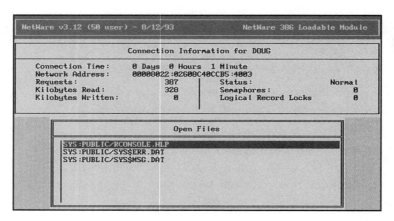

Fig. 10.3 Connection information displayed with the MONITOR console utility.

Chapter 11

Drive Mappings

Drive mappings are used in NetWare as pointers to areas on the file server's disk drives. By using drive mappings, you can reduce the amount of work necessary to run an application or to locate files by changing directories.

In this chapter, you learn how to do the following:

- Identify the different types of drive mappings

- Create drive mappings

- Delete drive mappings

- Change drive mappings

Types Of Drive Mappings

Before learning how to create or alter your drive mappings, you should first understand the three types of mappings used with NetWare:

- *Regular Drive Mapping:* A regular drive mapping uses a drive letter as a pointer to a volume and/or directory on the file server. The resources stored within the area to which you are mapping will only be accessible if the drive in question is your default drive or when you specify the drive letter in your command. For example, if your default drive is F: and you want to run a program called ABC.EXE stored on H:, you must either make H: your current drive or type **H:ABC** from the command line.

- *Search Drive Mapping:* The use of search drive mappings is similar to settings in the DOS PATH statement. Once the search drive is created, you can access files no matter what your default drive is set to. When search drives are created, drive letters are allocated in reverse alphabetical order, starting at Z. Once assigned, when you try to run a program from the command line, NetWare first checks your current directory for the program. If it is not there, it starts to look through each of the search drives in order until it finds the file.

■ *Fake Root Drive Mappings:* Fake root mappings are used in NetWare to restrict someone from changing the drive mapping to a higher directory. When you create the fake root, the drive letter may be assigned to a directory several layers beneath the root but the user will think the drive letter actually points to the root. For example, with a regular drive mapping, a user's F: prompt may show F:\HOME\ABC123>, but, if you were to create a fake root to the same directory, the user's F: prompt would be F:\>.

Working with Drive Mappings from the Command Line

MAP is a versatile command line utility used to view, create, change, or remove the drive mappings of your current session. In the following sections, we examine the MAP command and the various methods that it can be used.

> **Note**
>
> While MAP is a command line utility, it is also a basic login script command. When you are mapping drives in the login script, do not use the pound (#) command before the MAP command.

Viewing Your Current Drive Mappings

You may need to view a complete listing of all the drive mappings currently in effect for your connection. By typing **MAP** from the command line, you are presented with a screen similar to the one shown in Figure 11.1. Using the information provided from this screen, you can determine which drive letters are still left to map or from where to execute a program.

```
Drive   A:    maps to a local disk.
Drive   B:    maps to a local disk.
Drive   C:    maps to a local disk.
Drive   D:    maps to a local disk.
Drive   E:    maps to a local disk.
Drive   F: = DOUG-SERVER\SYS:  \USERS\DOUG
Drive   G: = DOUG-SERVER\SYS:  \COMMON
Drive   H: = DOUG-SERVER\SYS:APPS  \

SEARCH1:  = Z:. [DOUG-SERVER\SYS:  \PUBLIC]
SEARCH2:  = Y:. [DOUG-SERVER\SYS:  \APPS]
SEARCH3:  = X:. [DOUG-SERVER\SYS:  \SYSTEM]
SEARCH4:  = W:. [DOUG-SERVER\SYS:  \]
SEARCH5:  = C:\WINDOWS
SEARCH6:  = C:\WINDOWS\NLS
SEARCH7:  = C:\
SEARCH8:  = C:\DOS
SEARCH9:  = C:\NDW
SEARCH10: = C:\QEMM
SEARCH11: = C:\UTILITY
SEARCH12: = C:\QDC
SEARCH13: = C:\STACKER

Tue 06-28-1994 21:26:38.54 F:\USERS\DOUG
```

Fig. 11.1 A listing of the current drive mappings, created by entering **MAP** at the command line.

Shortcut

If you want to know what a single drive letter is mapped as, there is a faster way than typing **MAP** and scanning through the output. Type **MAP** *drive letter:* from the command line, and NetWare shows you how that single letter is mapped.

Creating Regular Drive Mappings

You can use the MAP command to create drive mappings. Depending on your requirements, you may use one method—or a combination of different methods—on a regular basis. The command below provides you with the syntax used for the basic MAP command:

```
MAP [root] drive:=[server/]volume:\directory
```

Based on the syntax above, replace:

drive with the drive letter you want to assign.

server with the name of the file server the directory resides on. When mapping to your default server, you don't have to include the server name, but when used, a forward slash (/) must be included after the server name.

volume with the name of the volume the directory resides on.

directory with the full directory path.

Note

The *ROOT* parameter is included only when you want to map a directory as a fake root.

EXAMPLE 1: To map the F: drive as a fake root to the HOME directory on your current file server (FS1), type either of the following:

MAP ROOT F:=SYS:\HOME

MAP ROOT F:=FS1/SYS:\HOME

EXAMPLE 2: To map the G: drive to the APPS directory on a server other than your default, type the following:

MAP G:=FS2/VOL1:\APPS

EXAMPLE 3: To insert a search drive mapping to the same location the J: drive is mapped to, type the following:

MAP INS S1:=J:

III

Environment Management

The NEXT Parameter

You also can use the NEXT parameter to create a drive mapping. When you use NEXT, NetWare maps the next available drive mapping to the specified path. The syntax for using the NEXT parameter is shown below (the other parameters shown below are described in the basic MAP command above):

```
MAP NEXT [server/]volume:\directory
```

To illustrate the use of this parameter, suppose you had the F: and G: drives currently mapped to different directories and you wanted to map the next available drive, H:, to the COMMON directory. To do so, type the following from the command line:

MAP NEXT FS1/SYS:\COMMON

Tip
The ROOT parameter can't be used in conjunction with the NEXT parameter.

Using Drive Numbers Instead of Letters

In the first method, you were shown that a drive mapping was created by specifying a drive letter to which to map. Instead of using letters, NetWare also lets you use drive numbers. To use a drive number, instead of a drive letter, the syntax is as follows:

```
MAP [root] *number:=[server/]volume:\directory
```

The parameters are the same as those used with the Basic Map Command except for the replacement of the *DRIVE* parameter with the *NUMBER* parameter. To use this method, you must tell NetWare which drive number you want to map. The drive number is dependent on what your first network drive is set to (refer to the heading "Configuring and Customizing Your NET.CFG File" in Chapter 4, "Installing Workstations"). Based on the first network drive, NetWare starts counting from the bottom and working up. For example, if your first network drive is F:, NetWare will assign the number 1 to F:, 2 to G:, 3 to H: and so on.

To illustrate, assume you want your 3rd drive letter mapped to the APPS directory on the SYS volume. Type the following from the command line:

MAP *3:=SYS:\APPS

Creating Search Drive Mappings

As noted earlier, you can create search drive mappings that are used in a similiar fashion to that of the drives or directories in the DOS PATH statement. By doing so, you can access the files or data stored within the directory that a search drive is mapped to no matter what your default drive is. The following MAP command syntax shows you how to create a search drive mapping:

```
MAP [root] [ins] search#:=[server/]volume:\directory
```

Based on this syntax, replace:

search# with the search drive number you want assigned to the directory.

server with the name of the file server the directory resides on. When mapping to your default server, you don't have to include the *server* name. But, if you are creating a mapping to another server, the server's name must be included followed by a forward slash (/).

volume with the name of the volume the directory resides on.

directory with the full directory path.

From the command above, there are two parameters included (when needed) as shown below:

root: This parameter is only included when you want to map a directory as a fake root.

ins: This parameter is included when you want the search mapping to be inserted into the current path. By inserting, you won't overwrite the currently established mappings.

EXAMPLE 1: To map the first search drive to the public directory on your SYS: volume, type the following:

MAP S1:=SYS:\PUBLIC

EXAMPLE 2: To have the APPS directory as the first available search drive when there are already three search drives set up, type the following:

MAP INS S1:=SYS:\APPS

EXAMPLE 3: To map the next available search drive to the COMMON directory when you don't know how many search drives are currently set up, type the following:

MAP S16:=SYS:\COMMON

> **Note**
>
> In this example, NetWare checks what the last search drive mapping is and then makes this search drive the next available number. For example, if the last search drive number is 7, the COMMON directory will be set up as search drive 8.

III

Environment Management

Removing Drive Mappings

With the MAP command, two parameters can be used interchangeably to delete a current drive mapping, *DEL* and *REM*. To remove a current mapping, type the following from the command line:

```
MAP DEL drive
```

Based on the syntax above, replace:

drive with the letter or number of the drive you want to remove:

EXAMPLE 1: To delete drive G, type either of the following from the command line:

MAP DEL G:

MAP REM *2:

> **Note**
>
> The second example assumes your first network drive is F: (which would be assigned the number 1 by NetWare).

EXAMPLE 2: To delete the third search drive mapping, type either of the following from the command line (assume the third search drive is set up as drive X):

MAP REM S3:

MAP DEL X:

> **Note**
>
> With the second example, NetWare first tells you the drive has been set up as a search drive, and then you have to confirm if you want the drive deleted before NetWare proceeds.

Working with Drive Mappings Using the SESSION Menu Utility

SESSION can be used to view, create, modify, or delete the drive mappings for your current connection. By typing **SESSION** from the command line, you are presented with a menu you can use to make the desired changes (see fig. 11.2).

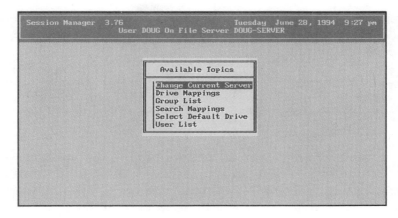

Fig 11.2 The main menu of SESSION.

The two options from this menu used when working with drive mappings are Search Mappings and Drive Mappings.

Viewing Your Current Drive Mappings

To use the SESSION utility to view your current drive mappings, select Drive Mappings (for regular drive mappings) or Search Mappings (for search drive mappings) from the Available Topics main menu of SESSION. Once selected, SESSION provides you with a window like the one shown in Figure 11.3, displaying your current mappings.

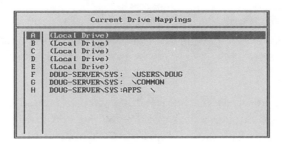

Fig. 11.3 Current drive mappings as displayed with the SESSION utility.

Creating New Drive Mappings

To use the SESSION utility to create a drive mapping, select Drive Mappings (for regular drive mappings) or Search Mappings (for search drive mappings) from the Available Topics main menu of SESSION. You are then presented with a window showing your current mappings. To create a new mapping:

1. Press Insert to add a new mapping. If you're creating a regular mapping, SESSION asks for a drive letter. If you are creating a search drive mapping, SESSION asks for the search drive number.

2. After specifying the drive letter or search drive number, SESSION asks you for the path in a Select Directory window (see fig. 11.4). If you know the full path to the directory, type it in here; otherwise, press Insert.

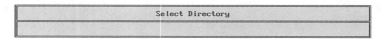

Fig. 11.4 Entering the desired path to map a drive to.

3. If you have manually typed the path for the drive mapping, you now can press Enter and SESSION creates the drive mapping for you. But, if you pressed Insert, SESSION presents a listing of file servers (and local drives when creating a search drive) from which you can choose (see fig. 11.5). At this point, select the server/drive for which you want to create the mapping.

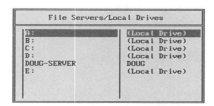

Fig. 11.5 Selecting the server or drive you want to create a drive mapping to with SESSION.

> **Note**
>
> If you want to create a mapping to an unattached server, press Insert again to view a listing of Other Servers. From this screen, select the desired server and enter your login ID and password as prompted.

4. Once you have selected the server (or local drive when creating a search drive) to which you want to map, SESSION displays a listing of the volumes and then the directories you can map to. As you work through these listings, SESSION updates the Select Directory window with each selection (see fig. 11.6). When the desired path is shown in the Select Directory window, press Esc to return to this window; then press Enter to complete the mapping.

Changing Your Current Drive Mappings

To use the SESSION utility to change drive mappings, first select Drive Mappings or Search Mappings from the Available Topics main menu of SESSION. Next, a window appears, showing your current mappings. To change a drive mapping, highlight the desired drive letter or search drive number and press the F3 key. SESSION displays the Select Directory window. At this point, you can make the desired changes manually or you can press the Insert key and repeat steps 3 and 4 shown in the previous heading.

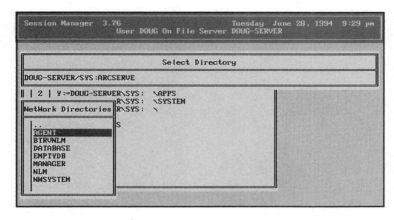

Fig. 11.6 Selecting the server and directory to which you want to map, by working through the SESSION windows.

Deleting Drive Mappings

To use the SESSION utility to delete drive mappings, first select Drive Mappings or Search Mappings from the Available Topics main menu of SESSION. Next, a window appears showing your current mappings. To delete a drive mapping, select the desired drive letter or search drive number and press the Delete key. When asked, confirm if you want SESSION to delete the mapping.

Chapter 12

Security Equivalences

Depending on the size of the LAN and the number of users accessing each file server, managing the system resources can be a fairly involved assignment. To alleviate the administrator from some of the more mundane tasks, NetWare has a feature known as security equivalences. This feature minimizes the work necessary when granting rights to users on the file server. By doing so, the administrator's job is made easier, thereby freeing the administrator to perform other tasks.

In this chapter, we explore this feature of NetWare, and specifically:

■ Assigning user and group equivalences

■ The different types of managers and operators that can be set up on the server

■ The tasks each type of manager and operator can perform

■ Granting the various manager and operator statuses to certain users and groups

User and Group Security Equivalences

The first aspect of security equivalences we look at pertains to users and groups. In NetWare, you have three choices when assigning rights:

■ Assign rights for the different resources to each individual user,

■ Make users equivalent to other users, or

■ Create groups and assign users to the groups

If you have been working with NetWare for a while, you already know the first option really is not a viable solution. Even for a small server with only a few users, assigning all the necessary rights to the different resources can be a very time-consuming process. This leaves you, therefore, with the latter two options.

Creating group and/or user equivalences minimizes the amount of work necessary to create a secure environment. With user equivalences, you can grant rights to one user ID and then make other IDs the equivalent of this ID. When you do so, other users have access to the same resources without your having to directly assign each one.

Group equivalences operate in a fashion similar to user equivalences. Instead of granting rights for a resource to a specific user ID, you can assign these rights to a group you create on the file server. Once you have assigned rights to a group, you then can add users to the group's membership list. By doing so, all users who are members of the group then inherit the rights granted to that group.

Before we go on to assigning security equivalences, there are two points you should be aware of:

■ When one user is made the equivalent of another, the second user inherits only the rights directly assigned to the first user. For example, if user A is made the equivalent of user B and user B already is the security equivalent to user C, user A only gains the rights assigned to user B and is not granted any of the rights directly assigned to user C.

■ When you make a user the security equivalent of another, this user has access to the other user's home and mail directories.

Granting User Equivalences

Note

RIGHTS REQUIRED TO COMPLETE TASK: SUPERVISOR AND USER ACCOUNT MANAGERS/WORKGROUP MANAGERS THAT HAVE BEEN ASSIGNED AS THE MANAGER OVER THE SELECTED ID.

Follow these steps to set up one user as equivalent to another:

1. From the Available Topics main menu of SYSCON, select User Information and then, from the listing of user names, select the user ID to whom you want to grant the equivalency.

2. After selecting the user name, you are presented with another window entitled User Information. From this window, select the option Security Equivalences to view the users and groups to which this ID is already equivalent.

3. To make this ID equivalent to another ID or group, press the Insert key and select one or more IDs from the listing of Other Users And Groups. After you select the IDs, SYSCON updates the listing provided in the Security Equivalences window.

Granting Group Equivalences (Memberships)

> **Note**
>
> RIGHTS REQUIRED TO COMPLETE TASK: SUPERVISOR OR USER ACCOUNT MANAGERS AND WORKGROUP MANAGERS THAT HAVE BEEN ASSIGNED AS MANAGERS OVER THE SELECTED ID.

Setting up a user ID as a member of a group can be done in two different ways. The method you choose depends on how many IDs you plan to add to the group's member list. For one or more users, either method will do. But, if you plan on adding multiple IDs to the group's member list, you should use Method 2.

Method 1: Adding IDs to the Group's Member List within the Personal User Information
Follow these steps to set up a user ID as a security equivalent to a group (also known as *group membership*):

1. From the Available Topics main menu of SYSCON, select User Information and then, from the listing of user names, select the user ID to which you want to grant the equivalency.

2. After selecting the user name, you are presented with another window entitled User Information. From this window, select the option Groups Belonged To to view the groups of which this ID is already a member.

3. To make this ID a member of another group, press the Insert key and select one or more groups from the listing of Groups Not Belonged To. After selecting the group(s), SYSCON updates the listing provided in the Groups Belonged To window.

> **Note**
>
> A user ID can have a maximum of 32 security equivalences.

Method 2: Adding Multiple IDs to a Group's Member List within the Individual Group's Configuration
Follow these steps to set up one or more user IDs as security equivalents to a group (also known as *group membership*):

1. From the Available Topics main menu of SYSCON, select Group Information and then, from the listing of Group Names, select the group to which you want to add the users.

2. After selecting the group, you are presented with another window entitled Group Information. From this window, select the option Member List to view the user IDs that are already members of this group.

3. To add one or more IDs to the group's member list, press the Insert key and select one or more IDs from the listing of Not Group Members. After you select the ID(s), SYSCON updates the listing provided in the Group Members window.

Operator and Manager Assignments

Managing a file server can be a very time-consuming task, especially when there are lots of users, each demanding a small portion of your time. To help you manage the server and the associated resources, NetWare provides several security assignments known as operators or managers. An operator/manager assists the SUPERVISOR to administrate the server without having to grant the SUPERVISOR status. As you may already know, granting an ID SUPERVISOR EQUIVALENCE gives the ID full access to everything on the server, without exceptions. Instead, by setting up users or groups with a certain operator/manager status, you can pass on some of the management responsibilities for a specific area of the server.

A listing of the different operator and manager assignments can be found in Table 12.1, along with a description of each.

Note

Except for SUPERVISOR EQUIVALENCE, all other operators and managers can be assigned to a user ID or a group. SUPERVISOR EQUIVALENCE can be granted only to a user ID.

Table 12.1 NetWare security assignments.

Assignment	Description
SUPERVISOR	The SUPERVISOR ID is the highest security level that can be granted to the NetWare file server. With a SUPERVISOR ID, full rights are granted to all files, directories, and features of NetWare.
SUPERVISOR EQUIVALENT	An ID set up as a SUPERVISOR EQUIVALENT has full access to the server and can do all the things the SUPERVISOR ID can. Any references to the SUPERVISOR ID also apply to all IDs with SUPERVISOR EQUIVALENCE. DESIGNATION CAN BE GRANTED ONLY BY ANOTHER SUPERVISOR EQUIVALENT.
CONSOLE OPERATOR	An ID granted the Console Operator status by the SUPERVISOR can make use of some additional features in FCONSOLE, such as sending messages and disabling/enabling logins. DESIGNATION CAN BE GRANTED ONLY BY A SUPERVISOR EQUIVALENT.
WORKGROUP MANAGER	Workgroup Managers are created on the file server to allow one or more users to create IDs and manage the restrictions of the users they manage. DESIGNATION CAN BE GRANTED ONLY BY A SUPERVISOR EQUIVALENT.

IV

Assignment	Description
USER ACCOUNT MANAGER	A User Account Manager can be created on the file server to assist the SUPERVISOR with managing the users on the file server. Unlike a Workgroup Manager, the User Account Manager cannot create any new users. DESIGNATION CAN BE GRANTED ONLY BY A SUPERVISOR EQUIVALENT, WORKGROUP MANAGER, OR A USER ACCOUNT MANAGER.
PRINT SERVER OPERATOR	Print Server Operators are users who have additional privileges to the operation of the assigned print servers over other users on the server. By assigning a user as a PRINT SERVER OPERATOR, those with SUPERVISOR status can pass on some management and troubleshooting responsibilities, thereby alleviating themselves of some of their duties. DESIGNATION CAN BE GRANTED ONLY BY A SUPERVISOR EQUIVALENT.
PRINT QUEUE OPERATOR	Print Queue Operators take on some of the printing management responsibilities, thereby freeing those with SUPERVISOR status to work on other tasks. DESIGNATION CAN BE GRANTED ONLY BY A SUPERVISOR EQUIVALENT.

Tasks that Operators and Managers Can Do

Knowing the different types of operators and managers is one thing; knowing what each can do is another. It is important that you fully understand what rights are associated with each of the designations *before* you grant them to users on your server. Granting excessive rights to users may not only be unnecessary but it also could cause you a lot of grief during a security audit.

Below, each of the manager and operator types is shown with detailed information on what a user or group can accomplish with this designation.

SUPERVISOR and SUPERVISOR EQUIVALENT

The SUPERVISOR and SUPERVISOR EQUIVALENT IDs have full rights to all the resources on the file server. With SUPERVISOR status, a user can create, modify, or delete any ID, print server, print queue, file, or directory on the server.

User Account Manager

The following tasks can be completed by a user or group with the User Account Manager status:

> **Note**
>
> These tasks are only applicable on IDs the User Account Manager is configured to manage. For IDs not managed by the User Account Manager, the rights available are no more than a regular user's.

- Change user account balance
- Change user account restrictions
- Change a user's or group's full name

- Change a user's password

- Change group memberships

- Change a user's login script

- Assign User Account Manager status

- Assign security equivalences

- Set station restrictions

- Set time restrictions

- Grant trustee directory and file assignments (only if the account manager has the necessary trustee rights)

- Delete a user

Workgroup Manager

The Workgroup Manager has all the rights the User Account Manager has, plus the ability to create new user IDs.

Console Operator

The following tasks can be completed by a user or group that has been granted the Console Operator status:

- Broadcast a console message with FCONSOLE

- Change server date and time with FCONSOLE

- Enable or disable logins to the file server

- Enable or disable transaction tracking

Print Queue Operator

The following tasks can be completed by a user or group with the Print Queue Operator status:

- Change the configuration of any job within the print queue

- Delete any job from the print queue

- Place a print job on hold or change the time it prints

- Change the order jobs are to be printed

- Change the print queue status

> **Note**
>
> Only the SUPERVISOR or SUPERVISOR EQUIVALENT can create or delete a print queue.

Print Server Operator

The following tasks can be completed by a user or group with the Print Server Operator status:

- Take down the print server

- Allow the print server to service another file server

- Set printer notifications

- Send commands to the printer

- Add or remove queues serviced by a printer

- Change the priority of queues being serviced by a printer

- Change the forms being used by a printer

> **Note**
>
> Only the SUPERVISOR or SUPERVISOR EQUIVALENT can create or delete a print server.

Granting Operator and Manager Status

When you are enlisting others to assist you with managing the file server or LAN, you may want to increase their security levels to one of the operator or manager designations previously discussed. Using the instructions shown in this section, you can grant the appropriate designation for any of the users or groups on the server.

Setting Up a User Account Manager

> **Note**
>
> RIGHTS REQUIRED TO COMPLETE TASK: YOU MUST BE A SUPERVISOR EQUIVALENT TO GRANT THIS DESIGNATION TO ANY USER. WORKGROUP MANAGERS AND USER ACCOUNT MANAGERS CAN GRANT THIS DESIGNATION TO ANY USER THEY MANAGE.

Creating a User Account Manager is a little different than setting up the other operator and manager designations. With the other designations, you can go to one location and add any user or group to the designations listing. But, with the User Account Manager status, the options you choose depend on whether you are assigning this designation to a group or to a user. Follow these steps to assign this designation with SYSCON:

1. From the Available Topics main menu of SYSCON, select User Information (if assigning this status to a user) or Group Information (if assigning this status to a group), and then select, from the listing provided, the user or group to which you want to grant this designation.

2. After selecting the user or group, you are presented with a window containing several options specific to the object in question. Regardless of whether or not you chose User Information or Group Information, you should select the option Managed Users And Groups.

3. If this object is not already set up as a User Account Manager, the window now presented to you (Managed Users And Groups) is empty. To add a user or group to this listing, press the Insert key and select one or more users or groups from the listing of Other Users And Groups. Once you have added a user or group ID to the listing of Managed Users And Groups, this object is automatically granted the User Account Manager designation over the IDs and groups shown in this window.

Setting Up a Workgroup Manager

> **Note**
>
> RIGHTS REQUIRED TO COMPLETE TASK: SUPERVISOR EQUIVALENT.

Follow these steps to grant Workgroup Manager status to a user or group:

1. From the Available Topics main menu of SYSCON, select Supervisor Options and then Workgroup Managers.

2. After you select Workgroup Managers, you are presented with a window showing all the users and groups that have been set up as workgroup managers so far. To add a new user or group, press the Insert key and make your selection from the Other Users And Groups window (see fig. 12.1).

> **Note**
>
> RIGHTS REQUIRED TO COMPLETE TASK: SUPERVISOR EQUIVALENT.

The Console Operator status can be granted to a user or group by following these steps:

1. From the Available Topics main menu of SYSCON, select Supervisor Options and then File Server Console Operators.

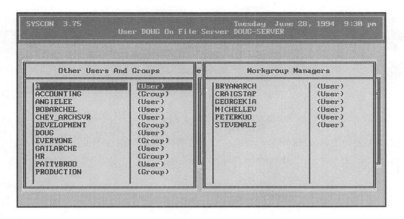

Fig. 12.1 Granting Workgroup Manager status with SYSCON.

2. After selecting File Server Console Operators, you are presented with a window showing all the users and groups that have been set up as Console Operators so far. To add a new user or group, press the Insert key and make your selection from the Other Users And Groups window.

Setting Up a PRINT SERVER OPERATOR

Note

RIGHTS REQUIRED TO COMPLETE TASK: SUPERVISOR EQUIVALENT.

Follow these steps to grant a user or group the PRINT SERVER OPERATOR status:

1. From the Available Options main menu of PCONSOLE, select Print Server Information and then, from the Print Servers window, select the print server to which you want to assign an operator.

2. After selecting the desired print server, you are presented with a new window entitled Print Server Information. From this window, select Print Server Operators to view a listing of the current PRINT SERVER OPERATORS. To add a new user or group, press the Insert key and make your selection from the Print Server Operator Candidates window.

Note

Users or groups set up as PRINT SERVER OPERATORs only have the extra privileges associated with the designation for the individual print servers for which they are set up as operators.

Setting Up a Print Queue Operator

Note

RIGHTS REQUIRED TO COMPLETE TASK: SUPERVISOR EQUIVALENT.

Follow these steps to grant a user or group the PRINT QUEUE OPERATOR status:

1. From the Available Options main menu of PCONSOLE, select Print Queue Information and then select, from the Print Queues window, the print queue to which you want to assign an operator.

2. After selecting the desired print queue, you are presented with a new window entitled Print Queue Information. From this window select Queue Operators to view a listing of the current queues operators. To add a new user or group, press the Insert key and make your selection from the Queue Operator Candidates window.

Note

Users or groups set up as PRINT QUEUE OPERATORs only have the extra privileges associated with the designation for the individual print queues for which they are set up as operators.

Chapter 13

Trustee Assignments and Rights

Trustee rights really are the bread and butter of NetWare's security. Using trustee assignments and rights, you can take control of the server's file and directory resources by restricting who can perform which tasks.

In this chapter, we discuss trustee rights in detail, and specifically:

- What trustee rights are

- Assigning trustee rights

- Revoking trustee rights

- Viewing trustee rights

- The Inherited Rights Mask and how it affects a user's effective rights

What Trustee Rights Are

To answer the question that was suggested in the title of this section, simply put, trustee rights are the entire foundation of NetWare security. Trustee rights are attributes granted to a user or group object that permit that object to perform a certain task (as in reading a file). Using these rights, you can grant or remove access to files and directories on the NetWare file server.

Before discussing how to assign or revoke these rights, you must first understand what each of the rights are and how they operate.

In NetWare 3.12, there are eight different trustee rights that can be assigned to a user or group. While these rights can be applied to a directory or file, the manner in which they function differs between the two. Found in Table 13.1, a listing of each of the 3.12 trustee rights is shown along with a brief description of their effects on a directory or a file.

Table 13.1 Trustee rights and how they affect directory and file access.

Trustee Right	Effect on a Directory	Effect on a File
Supervisory	Grants full rights to the directory and all subdirectories regardless of the other rights granted and the Inherited Rights Mask (IRM).	Grants full rights to all files in the current directory and those within every subdirectory.
Read	Enables users to open files in a directory and read the contents of the file or execute the program.	Enables users to open a file and read the contents or execute the program even if the Read right has not been granted at the directory level.
Write	Enables users to open and write to any files in the directory.	Enables a user to open and write to a file even if the Write right has not been granted at the directory level.
Create	Enables users to create files and subdirectories within the current directory.	Enables a user to salvage a file if it has been deleted by accident.
Erase	Enables users to delete a directory, its file and its subdirectories.	Enables a user to delete a file even if the Erase right has not been granted at the directory level.
Modify	Enables a user to modify any file or subdirectory's name or attributes.	Enables a user to modify a file's name or attributes even if the Modify right has not been granted at the directory level.
FileScan	Enables the user to see the files and subdirectories.	Enables a user to see the file even if the File Scan right has not been granted at the directory level.
Access Control	Enables users to modify the IRM and trustee assignments for the directory. With this right, the user can grant any of the rights for this directory to another group or user *except* the Supervisory right.	Enables the user to modify the IRM and trustee assignments for the file. With this right, the user can grant any of the rights for this file to another group or user *except* the Supervisory right.

Along with the rights outlined in the table above, there are several rules or, rather, guidelines, you should be aware of regarding the operation of these rights. Failure to understand these guidelines can result in an inadequate security structure that could pose a potential security risk for your file server or organization.

■ The Supervisory right grants a user *full* access to the directory or file it was assigned to regardless of the other rights that have been assigned. For example, if a user is granted the

Read and Supervisory rights to a directory, all the other rights also will be available even though you did not grant them, thanks to the Supervisory right.

- Once granted to a directory, the Supervisory right *cannot* be blocked or revoked from any of the tree's subdirectories.

- If the Supervisory right is granted to a user or group for the ROOT directory, all group members will have *full* access to *every* directory and file on that volume.

- The Access Control right enables the user or group with this access to grant *any* trustee right to *any* user or group on the server. This can create problems for you as these rights can be assigned without your knowledge. In many cases, this right is only assigned to a user for their home directory.

- Rights assigned to files *always* overrule the rights assigned at the directory level.

- Unless you specifically assign trustee rights to the files, users will have the same rights to these files that they received from their directory assignments.

How Rights Are Acquired

There are four ways a user can receive trustee assignments to a directory or file:

Through group memberships: Any file or directory trustee assignments set for a group are granted automatically to all members of that group.

Through direct trustee assignments: File and directory trustee assignments can be granted specifically to a certain user ID.

Through security equivalences: When a user ID is configured as the security equivalent to another, it receives all the file and directory trustee assignments granted directly to the other ID.

Through inheritance: Unless blocked by the Inherited Rights Mask (described later in this chapter), trustee rights granted to one directory on the server filter down through the subdirectories of this directory.

When these rights have all been blended together, we have what is known as the user's *effective rights*. The effective rights are the rights that can actually be executed by the user in question. Even though a user may be assigned certain rights to a directory, these rights can be blocked by using the IRM. Essentially then, a user's *effective* rights are:

```
DIRECT ASSIGNMENTS + GROUP ASSIGNMENTS/SECURITY EQUIVALENCES + INHERITED RIGHTS -
RIGHTS REVOKED BY THE IRM = EFFECTIVE RIGHTS
```

To illustrate these rules, assume you have a file server called FS1 with one volume, SYS:. From the ROOT of this volume, there are five subdirectories, LOGIN, PUBLIC, SYSTEM, MAIL, and APPS.

In addition to these directories, there are two other directories, 123 and WORD, that are subdirectories of APPS. This directory structure is shown below.

```
FS1/SYS:
        LOGIN
        PUBLIC
        SYSTEM
        MAIL
        APPS
                123
                WORD
```

On this server, a user ID called JDOE has been granted R F trustee rights to the APPS directory. A group also has been created called SUPPORT, of which JDOE is a member, that has been granted R M F rights to the APPS directory. In addition, the supervisor has made the ID JDOE a security equivalent to the user MVANDEGEYN that was granted the C right to the ROOT directory.

On the server, the supervisor wants to make sure no one can Create or Erase any files stored within the APPS directory or any of its subdirectories, so an Inherited Rights Mask of S R W M F A was created for the APPS directory.

Note	
The rights noted in the IRM are the maximum rights a user can inherit from a parent directory. They do not grant the rights to the user.	

Table 13.2 below has been provided to show you how these rights actually come together. To explain how this table works:

- JDOE's effective rights in the ROOT directory is C because the ID is the equivalent of another ID with this right.

- JDOE's effective rights to the LOGIN directory is C because this right was inherited from the parent directory, the ROOT.

- JDOE's effective rights to the APPS directory are R M F. Even though JDOE could inherit the C right from the parent directory (the root), this right was blocked by the IRM.

- JDOE's effective rights to the 123 and WORD directories are R M F because these rights were inherited from the parent directory, APPS.

Directory	Direct Rights	Equivalence Rights	Inheritance	IRM	Effective Rights
SYS:\		C			C
SYS:\LOGIN			C (from the root)		C
SYS:\APPS	R F	R M F	C (from the root)	S R W M F A	R M F
SYS:\APPS\123			R M F		R M F
SYS:\APPS\WORD			R M F		R M F

Table 13.2 Trustee assignments that are accessible to the JDOE user ID.

Rights Required to Complete Common Tasks

Knowing each of the trustee assignments is one thing; knowing what trustee assignments are needed is another. While it is impossible to tell you what rights are required for every software package on the market, here are a few guidelines to assist you in setting up the trustee rights on your server:

■ When installing an application on your server, always check through the application's instructions for information on the trustee requirements. You do not want to grant excessive rights, nor do you want to grant insufficient rights. Granting insufficient trustee rights could result in the application's not working at all or with intermittent errors.

■ NetWare assigns different trustee rights as a default to some of the directories on your server. Unless there is some unique reason why you must change these rights, don't. The default trustee assignments established by NetWare are:

> *LOGIN directory:* Read, File Scan (assigned to the group EVERYONE)
>
> *PUBLIC directory:* Read, File Scan (assigned to the group EVERYONE)
>
> *MAIL directory:* Create (assigned to the group EVERYONE)
>
> *MAIL (subdirectories):* Read, Write, Create, Erase, Modify, and File Scan rights are granted to each user for their personal mail subdirectory.
>
> *SYSTEM directory:* NONE
>
> *ROOT directory:* NONE
>
> *USER's HOME directory:* Read, Write, Create, Erase, Modify, File Scan and Access Control rights are granted to each user for their personal home directory (when created).

Further to these basic guidelines, at times you may create directories to which you only want to grant a certain function. For example, you have a directory where you only want users to be able to see what files are there without copying them or altering them in any fashion. To assist you, Table 13.3 provides a listing of some of the more common tasks and the trustee rights that are required to complete the task.

Table 13.3 Trustee rights required to complete common tasks.	
Task	**Minimum Rights Required**
Change Trustee Assignments	A
Change the Inherited Rights Mask	A
Change Directory Attributes	M
Change File Attributes	F M
Create and Write to an Open File	C W
Delete a File	E
Rename a Directory or File	M
Write to a Closed File	W
Read from a Closed File	R
Copy File from a Directory	R F
Copy File or Directory into Directory	C
Create a Directory	C
Delete a Subdirectory	E
See a File	F
See a Directory	R or F

Viewing Trustee Assignments

Using the instructions contained in this section, you can check the trustee assignments to files and/or directories on the server. Each of the utilities discussed in this section has its own pros and cons to using it but, for the most part, people will usually use the utility with which they feel most comfortable.

Reviewing a User's or Group's Trustee Assignments with SYSCON

Note

RIGHTS REQUIRED TO COMPLETE TASK: YOU MUST BE A SUPERVISOR EQUIVALENT TO VIEW THE TRUSTEE ASSIGNMENTS FOR ANY USER ON THE SERVER. OTHERWISE, USER ACCOUNT MANAGERS AND WORKGROUP MANAGERS CAN VIEW THE TRUSTEE ASSIGNMENTS OF ANY USERS OR GROUPS THEY MANAGE. ALL OTHER USERS CAN ONLY VIEW THEIR PERSONAL TRUSTEE ASSIGNMENTS.

With the SYSCON utility, you can review user or group trustee assignments to the files and directories stored on the server by following these steps:

1. From the Available Topics main menu of SYSCON, select User Information (if you want to view trustee rights for a user) or Group Information (if you want to view trustee rights for a group). From the screen that is presented to you next, select the User ID or Group with which you want to work.

2. After you select the user or group to work with, you are presented with an additional window with several options specific to the object in question. While these two windows will differ, two options are common to both: Trustee Directory Assignments and Trustee File Assignments. If you want to view the object's directory assignments, select Trustee Directory Assignments; otherwise, choose the latter for file assignments. After making your selection, you are presented with a window showing you the current trustee assignments for this object.

Reviewing Trustee Assignments and Rights with FILER

FILER, NetWare's file management menu utility, views your rights to directories and files on the server as well as checking which users or groups are trustees of the different directories and files. Unlike SYSCON, that displays trustee assignment information for individual users and groups, FILER reviews trustee information on a per file or per directory basis. When a directory or file is selected, FILER shows you all of the trustees to the directory or file and their rights.

The instructions included within the following headings assist you in acquiring the desired information.

Checking Your Rights and Trustees to the Current Directory

You can check your rights or the trustees of your current directory by following these steps:

1. From the Available Topics main menu of FILER, select Current Directory Information.

2. Next, you are presented with a screen detailing the Directory Information for the current directory. There are several options on this screen, but to view the rights, there are only three that you must concern yourself with as follow:

Current Effective Rights: This option displays your current rights to the directory and is for viewing only. You cannot directly modify the values in this field.

Inherited Rights Mask: This option shows you the maximum rights that can be inherited from the root directory. Refer to the next section on Inherited Rights for a full description.

Trustees: By selecting this option, a listing of the current trustees and their rights is shown.

Viewing the Trustees and Your Rights to a File

To view rights to a file and the file's trustees, first make sure you are in the same directory as the file. You can do this either by using the DOS CD command or through FILER by using the Select Current Directory option from the main menu. Once in the appropriate directory, you can view the file information by following these steps:

1. From the Available Topics main menu of FILER, select Directory Contents and then the file you want to view.

2. After you select the file, you are presented with a window entitled File Options. From this window, you can either select Who has rights here, to view the trustees and their rights to the file, or you can select View/Set File Information.

3. If you chose the latter, you are presented with another window that provides detailed information on the file. From this screen, the only options you should concern yourself with are Inherited Rights Mask, Trustees, and Current Effective Rights. For descriptions of these three options, refer to Step 2 in the previous heading, "Checking Your Rights and Trustees to the Current Directory."

Viewing another Directory's Trustees and Your Rights to the Directory

With FILER, you also can view the rights and trustees to a directory even when it is not your current directory. To do so, follow the steps outlined above, but instead of selecting a file, select a subdirectory.

Reviewing Trustee Rights and Assignments from the Command Line

Previously in this chapter, you saw how you could view the trustee assignments to a directory or file using SYSCON or FILER, two of NetWare's menuing utilities. In addition to these utilities, there are several others that can be used from the command line to perform the same tasks. Within the following sections, we explore each of these utilities and how they can be used to their fullest potential.

Checking Trustee Assignments for Directories and Files with TLIST

TLIST is a NetWare command line utility that lets you view the user or group trustee assignments for a directory or file. To use the TLIST command, the syntax is:

```
TLIST [path][filename] [/user] [/groups]
```

Based on the syntax above, replace:

path with the path of the directory for which you want to view the trustee assignments.

filename with the name of the file for which you want to view the trustee assignments.

In addition to these two parameters, the two switches, */user* and */groups*, also can be used to isolate your search. Use:

/user to only view the USER trustees

/groups to only view the GROUP trustees.

EXAMPLE 1: To view all trustees to the current directory, type the following from the command line:

TLIST

EXAMPLE 2: To only view the user trustees to the APPS directory on the SYS: volume, type the following from the command line:

TLIST SYS:APPS /USER

EXAMPLE 3: To view the group trustees to the file ET.EXE, type the following from the command line:

TLIST ET.EXE /GROUPS

Tip

Wild cards can be used with the TLIST command. For example, to view all user trustees to files in the current directory with the extension ERR, type **TLIST *.ERR /USER** from the command line.

Checking Your Personal Rights to a Directory or File with RIGHTS

The RIGHTS command can be used to view your effective rights to a file or directory. To use this command, the syntax is:

```
RIGHTS [path] [filename]
```

Based on the syntax above, replace:

path with the path of the directory to which you want to view your rights.

filename with the name of the file to which you want to view your rights.

EXAMPLE 1: To check your rights in the current directory, type the following from the command line:

RIGHTS

EXAMPLE 2: To check your rights to the file ABC.EXE in the current directory, type the following from the command line:

RIGHTS ABC.EXE

EXAMPLE 3: To check your rights in the PUBLIC directory when your current directory is LOGIN, type the following from the command line:

RIGHTS SYS:\PUBLIC

EXAMPLE 4: To check your rights to the directory mapped to your J: drive, type the following from the command line:

RIGHTS J:

> **Note**
>
> Wild cards *cannot* be used with the RIGHTS command.

Checking Your Rights on the Entire Server with WHOAMI

Few people use WHOAMI to view their rights because they don't know what it can really do for them. Traditionally used by users to view their login information, the WHOAMI utility also can be used to view your rights on the file server. After typing **WHOAMI /R** from the command line, you are presented with a screen similar to the one shown in Figure 13.1.

WHOAMI is so good because it shows you all your rights on the *entire* file server in one neat and concise screen. As shown in the figure above, WHOAMI gives you a breakdown of the file server volumes and directories to inform you of the rights you have. Even though WHOAMI does not display every directory on the server, you can determine what your rights are to *any* directory from this screen by following the rules of inheritance.

Previously, you saw that rights assigned in one directory flow down the directory tree unless they are blocked by the IRM. With this rule in mind, you can determine what rights you have for a directory from this screen, even if the directory is not shown. For example, Figure 13.1 shows you that the user has the Read and File Scan rights to the PUBLIC directory. Even though there are no subdirectories of PUBLIC shown, you know you have the same rights for any of the subdirectories thanks to inheritance.

For information on other uses of the WHOAMI utility, see Table 10.2 in Chapter 10, "Miscellaneous Commands for Environment Management."

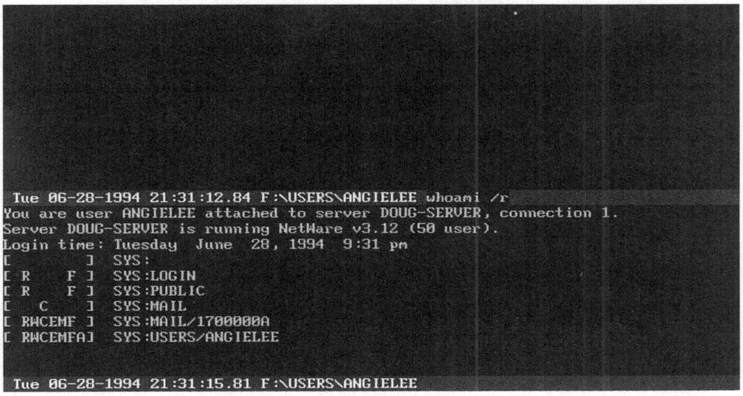

```
Tue 06-28-1994 21:31:12.84 F:\USERS\ANGIELEE whoami /r
You are user ANGIELEE attached to server DOUG-SERVER, connection 1.
Server DOUG-SERVER is running NetWare v3.12 (50 user).
Login time: Tuesday  June  28, 1994  9:31 pm
[      ]  SYS:
[ R    F ]  SYS:LOGIN
[ R    F ]  SYS:PUBLIC
[   C  ]  SYS:MAIL
[ RWCEMF ]  SYS:MAIL/1700000A
[ RWCEMFA]  SYS:USERS/ANGIELEE

Tue 06-28-1994 21:31:15.81 F:\USERS\ANGIELEE
```

Fig. 13.1 Viewing your rights with the WHOAMI utility.

Checking Your Effective Rights to Directories with LISTDIR

While normally used as a utility to view the directory structures on the server, the LISTDIR utility also can be used to see what your effective rights are to a directory.

To use the LISTDIR command, the syntax is:

    LISTDIR *[path]* [/E] [/S] [/R]

Based on the syntax above, replace:

path with the name of the directory or the path to the subdirectory, directory, or volume to which you want to check your rights. If you do not include the path, LISTDIR reviews the subdirectories of the current directory.

Note

The /S parameter is included when you want LISTDIR to scan through all the subdirectories of the noted path, /E is used to view the effective rights and /R is used to view the inherited rights.

EXAMPLE 1: To check your effective rights for the directories contained within your current directory, type the following from the command line:

LISTDIR /E

EXAMPLE 2: To check your effective rights to every directory on the SYS: volume, including all subdirectories, type the following from the command line:

LISTDIR SYS:\ /E /S

Tip
Wild cards can be used with the LISTDIR command. For example, to view your effective rights to all directories that begin with the letter D within the current directory, type **LISTDIR D* /E**.

Checking Your Effective Rights to a File or Directory with NDIR

NDIR is NetWare's most powerful command line file management utility. While it is not normally used for this task, you can use NDIR to view your effective rights to file or directory on the server. To use the NDIR command, the syntax is:

```
NDIR [path] /RIGHTS [/SUB]
```

Based on the syntax above, replace:

path with the name of the directory or file for which you want to view your effective rights to.

Note
Include the switch /SUB when you want NDIR to scan all subdirectories of the noted path.

EXAMPLE: To view your effective rights to all files in the directory PUBLIC that is stored off the root of the SYS: volume, and all its subdirectories, type the following from the command line:

NDIR SYS:\PUBLIC /RIGHTS /SUB

Tip
Wild cards can be used with the NDIR command. For example, to view your effective rights to all files with the extension EXE within the current directory, type **NDIR *.EXE /RIGHTS**.

Working with Trustee Rights and Assignments

With the appropriate security level on the server, you can take complete control of the rights any user or group has. In this section, we examine the various utilities that can be used to grant, revoke, or modify trustee assignments and how to use them to their potential.

Using SYSCON to Grant, Revoke, and Modify Trustee Assignments

> **Note**
>
> RIGHTS REQUIRED TO COMPLETE TASK: YOU MUST BE A SUPERVISOR EQUIVALENT TO CHANGE THE RIGHTS OF ANY USER ON THE SYSTEM. OTHERWISE, IF YOU ARE A USER ACCOUNT MANAGER OR WORKGROUP MANAGER, YOU CAN MODIFY THE RIGHTS OF YOUR MANAGED USERS AS LONG AS YOU HAVE THE ACCESS CONTROL OR SUPERVISORY TRUSTEE RIGHT TO THE DIRECTORY OR FILE IN QUESTION.

The SYSCON menu utility can be used to grant or revoke trustee assignments on a per user or per group basis. Before you can actually grant or revoke these rights, there are a few steps that you must follow as shown below:

1. From the Available Topics main menu of SYSCON, select User Information (if you want to grant/remove trustee rights from a user) or Group Information (if you want to grant/remove trustee rights from a group). From the screen that is presented to you next, select the User ID or Group that you want to work with.

2. After selecting the user or group to work with, you are presented with an additional window with several options specific to the object in question. While these two windows will differ, there are two options common to both: Trustee Directory Assignments and Trustee File Assignments. If you want to set a directory assignment, select Trustee Directory Assignments; otherwise, choose the latter for file assignments.

3. With either option that you choose, you are then presented with a window showing you the assignments currently set up for this object. From this window, you either can add a new trustee assignment, delete a current trustee assignment, or modify a current trustee assignment.

Adding a Trustee Assignment

From the window presented in Step 3 above, you can add a Trustee Assignment by following these steps:

1. Tell SYSCON the path of the directory to which you are setting the trustee assignment by pressing the Insert key and then entering the full directory path. In this window, you either can enter the path manually, or you can press the Insert key again to have SYSCON assist you in finding the appropriate directory within the server and its volumes.

2. After you have entered the full path, press the Enter key to have NetWare add this directory to the listing of trustee assignments for the object. If you are adding a trustee assignment for a file, you are asked to enter the name of the file before completing the assignment. As in Step 1, you can press the Insert key to view a listing of all available files (see fig. 13.2).

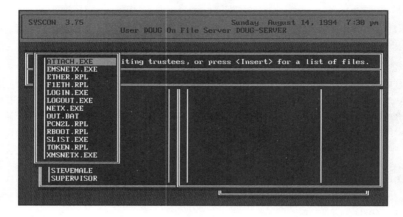

Fig. 13.2 Adding a trustee file assignment using the SYSCON utility.

Tip
By default, NetWare automatically grants the Read and File Scan assignments to every new trustee.

Note

Wild cards cannot be used with SYSCON for trustee file assignments, but they can be used with the GRANT command. Also, if a trustee file assignment is granted to a user or group, and the file is then deleted, the trustee assignment is automatically removed from the server.

Modifying a Trustee Assignment

From the window presented in Step 3 (see "Using SYSCON To Grant, Revoke, And Modify Trustee Assignments"), you can modify a current trustee assignment to grant additional rights or remove some of the current rights by following these steps:

1. Select the trustee assignment you want to modify by highlighting it and then pressing Enter.

Shortcut
If you want to work with several assignments that should all be set to the same rights, you can flag each one with the F5 key before hitting Enter. In situations like this, changes made in Step 2 below affect all assignments that were flagged.

2. After you select the trustee assignment, you are presented with a window entitled Trustee Rights Granted which lists all of the currently assigned rights. To remove a right, highlight the right and press Delete; otherwise, press the Insert key to select from the listing of Trustee Rights Not Granted.

Deleting a Trustee Assignment

From the window presented in Step 3 (see "Using SYSCON To Grant, Revoke, and Modify Trustee Assignments"), you can delete a current trustee assignment by highlighting the desired option and pressing the Delete key.

Using FILER to Grant, Revoke, and Modify Trustee Assignments

Note
RIGHTS REQUIRED TO COMPLETE TASK: YOU MUST BE A SUPERVISOR EQUIVALENT OR HAVE THE ACCESS CONTROL OR SUPERVISORY TRUSTEE RIGHT TO THE DIRECTORY OR FILE FROM WHICH YOU WILL BE GRANTING/REVOKING RIGHTS.

Previously, you saw how you could use the SYSCON menu utility to grant trustee rights within a user or group ID. While this approach is fine when you are only granting trustee assignments to a few users, if you must create assignments for a large number of users at a time, then you should consider using FILER. Unlike SYSCON, that grants assignments per user or per group, FILER creates these assignments on a per file or per directory basis by following the instructions in the following sections.

Modifying Trustee Rights to the Current Directory

You can modify the trustee rights for the current directory by following these steps:

1. From the Available Topics main menu of FILER, select Current Directory Information.

2. Next, you are presented with a screen detailing the Directory Information for the current directory. There are several options on this screen, but to modify the trustee assignments, select the Trustees option to view the current directory trustees (see fig. 13.3). With the trustee listing on-screen, you have three choices:

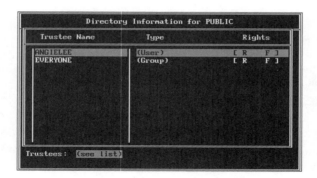

Fig. 13.3 Trustee assignments to the current directory shown with FILER.

To remove a trustee: Highlight the trustee you want to remove and press Delete. When asked, confirm whether or not you want to remove the trustee.

To add a trustee: To add a trustee, press the Insert key and select a user or group from the listing provided. You can add multiple users or groups at one time by flagging each one with the F5 key.

> **Note**
>
> By default, all new trustees are granted the Read and File Scan rights.

To modify a trustee's rights: To modify a trustee's rights to the directory, select the trustee and press Enter. When presented with the listing of trustee rights, press the Insert key to add additional rights or highlight the rights you want to remove and press Delete.

Modifying Trustee Rights to a File

To modify a trustee's rights to a file, first make sure you are in the same directory as the file. You can do this either by using the DOS CD command or through FILER by using the Select Current Directory option from the main menu. Once in the appropriate directory, you can modify the trustee information by following these steps:

1. From the Available Topics main menu of FILER, select Directory Contents and then the file to which you want to modify the rights.

2. After selecting the file, you are presented with a window entitled File Options. From this window, by selecting View/Set File Information, you are then presented with a window showing you the current trustees to this file.

> **Note**
>
> If this window is empty, it does *not* mean no one can access the file. The screen only shows you users and groups that have been directly assigned rights to the file. When a user does not have a direct trustee assignment to a file, they inherit the directory rights for the file in question.

3. From the listing of trustees, there are three options available to you: remove a trustee, add a trustee, or modify a current trustee. Refer to Step 2 under the heading "Modifying Trustee Rights to the Current Directory" for instructions on how to proceed.

Modifying Trustee Rights to another Directory

With FILER, you also can modify the rights and trustees to a directory even when it is not your current directory. To do so, follow the steps outlined above but, instead of selecting a file, select a subdirectory.

Granting and Revoking Rights from the Command Line

Previously you saw how you could use NetWare's menuing utilities to grant or revoke trustee assignments. While they serve the purpose, most of these tasks can be completed a lot faster by using some basic command-line utilities. In this section, we explore each of the command line utilities you can use to grant and/or revoke trustee assignments from users and groups.

Giving Trustee Rights with GRANT

> **Note**
>
> RIGHTS REQUIRED TO COMPELTE TASK: YOU MUST BE A SUPERVISOR EQUIVALENT OR HAVE THE ACCESS CONTROL OR SUPERVISORY TRUSTEE RIGHT TO THE DIRECTORY OR FILE TO WHICH YOU WANT TO GRANT ACCESS.

The GRANT command is used to grant specific rights to a user or group for directories and files. To use the GRANT command, the syntax is:

```
GRANT rights [FOR] [path] TO [USER ¦ GROUP] object_name
```

Based on the syntax above, replace:

> *rights* with a listing of the rights you want to grant. You must use the short form for the right (as in R is for Read) and when granting multiple rights, each right must be separated by a space. The rights that can be granted, and their short forms, are as follows:

Right	Short Form
SUPERVISORY	S
READ	R
WRITE	W
CREATE	C
ERASE	E
MODIFY	M
FILE SCAN	F
ACCESS CONTROL	A
NONE	N
ALL RIGHTS	ALL

Note

For descriptions of these rights, refer to Table 13.1 earlier in this chapter.

path with the name of the directory or file to which you are granting rights.

object_name with the name of the user or group to which you are granting rights.

The other parameters not mentioned above are:

USER: specifies that the object_name is a user and not a group. This parameter only has to be included when you have users and groups that have the same name.

GROUP: specifies that the object_name is a group and not a user. This parameter only has to be included when you have users and groups that have the same name.

EXAMPLE 1: To grant all rights for the current directory to the group FLEX, type the following from the command line:

GRANT ALL TO FLEX

EXAMPLE 2: To grant the Erase and Modify right for the directory DCDATA to the user LLARRETT, when DCDATA is not your current directory, type the following from the command line:

GRANT E M FOR SYS:\DCDATA TO LLARRETT

EXAMPLE 3: To grant all rights for the file SHELL.MJV stored in the PUBLIC\DATA directory to the user BNORRIS, type the following from the command line:

GRANT ALL FOR SYS:\PUBLIC\DATA\SHELL.MJV TO BNORRIS

EXAMPLE 4: To grant the Access Control right for the directory mapped to your T: drive to the group FINLEY, when there also is a user called FINLEY, type the following from the command line:

GRANT A FOR T: TO GROUP FINLEY

Tip
Wild cards can be used with the GRANT command. For example, to grant the rights Read and File Scan for all subdirectories of the current directory to the group UOTENGIN, type **GRANT R F FOR *. TO EVERYONE**.

Tip
Even though GRANT is meant for use in granting rights, you also can use it when you want to revoke all rights to the directory by using the N "right." For example, to revoke all rights to the current directory from the user ABC1234, type **GRANT N TO ABC1234**.

Removing Trustee Assignments with REMOVE

Note
RIGHTS REQUIRED TO COMPELTE TASK: YOU MUST BE A SUPERVISOR EQUIVALENT OR HAVE THE ACCESS CONTROL OR SUPERVISORY TRUSTEE RIGHT TO THE DIRECTORY OR FILE FROM WHICH YOU WANT TO REMOVE A TRUSTEE.

The REMOVE command line utility removes a user or group trustee assignment from a file or directory. Unlike the REVOKE command that only removes specified rights for a trustee, REMOVE removes the entire trustee assignment to the directory or file. To use the REMOVE command, the syntax is:

```
REMOVE [USER ¦ GROUP] object_name [FROM] [path] [/option(s)]
```

Based on the syntax above, replace:

object_name with the name of the user or group you are removing as a trustee.

path with the name of the directory or file from which you are removing the trustee.

/option(s) with SUB to remove the named trustee from all subdirectories or F to remove the named trustee from the files.

The other parameters not mentioned above are:

USER: specifies that the object_name is a user and not a group. This parameter only has to be included when you have users and groups that have the same name.

GROUP: specifies that the object_name is a group and not a user. This parameter only has to be included when you have users and groups that have the same name.

EXAMPLE 1: To remove the group ACCOUNTING from the trustee listing of the current directory, type the following from the command line:

REMOVE ACCOUNTING

EXAMPLE 2: To remove the user JDOE from the trustee listing of the current directory and all of its subdirectories, type the following from the command line:

REMOVE JDOE /SUB

EXAMPLE 3: To remove the user MVANDEGEYN as a trustee to the file NOV28.TXT from the APPS directory, when APPS is not the current directory, type the following from the command line:

REMOVE MVANDEGEYN FROM SYS:\APPS\NOV28.TXT

EXAMPLE 4: To remove the group TESTER as a trustee to the directory that is mapped to your K: drive when there is also a user ID called TESTER, type the following from the command line:

REMOVE GROUP TESTER FROM K:

Tip

Wild cards can be used with the REMOVE command. For example, to remove JDOE as a trustee for all files in the current directory with the extension TXT, type **REMOVE JDOE FROM *.TXT**.

Revoking Trustee Rights with REVOKE

Note

RIGHTS REQUIRED TO COMPELTE TASK: YOU MUST BE A SUPERVISOR EQUIVALENT OR HAVE THE ACCESS CONTROL OR SUPERVISORY TRUSTEE RIGHT TO THE DIRECTORY OR FILE FROM WHICH YOU WANT TO REVOKE A TRUSTEE RIGHT.

The REVOKE command is used to revoke specific rights from a user's or group's trustee assignments to a directory or file. To use the REVOKE command, the syntax is:

```
REVOKE rights [FOR] [path] FROM [USER ¦ GROUP ] object_name [/option(s)]
```

Based on the syntax above, replace:

rights with a listing of the rights you want to revoke. You must use the short form for the right (for example, R is for Read) and when revoking multiple rights, each right must be separated by a space. The rights that can be revoked, and their short form are as follows:

Right	Short Form
SUPERVISORY	S
READ	R
WRITE	W
CREATE	C
ERASE	E
MODIFY	M
FILE SCAN	F
ACCESS CONTROL	A
ALL RIGHTS	ALL

Note

For descriptions of these rights, refer to Table 13.1 earlier in this chapter.

path with the name of the directory or file from which you are revoking rights.

object_name with the name of the user or group from which you are revoking rights.

/option(s) with SUB to remove the named trustee from all subdirectories or F to remove the named trustee from the files.

The other parameters not mentioned above are:

USER: specifies that the object_name is a user and not a group. This parameter only has to be included when you have users and groups that have the same name.

GROUP: specifies that the object_name is a group and not a user. This parameter only has to be included when you have users and groups that have the same name.

EXAMPLE 1: To revoke the rights Read and Write from the user CSTAPLES in the current directory, type the following from the command line:

REVOKE R W FROM CSTAPLES

EXAMPLE 2: To revoke all rights to the file DATATD.SRC stored in the DATA directory on the SYS volume from the group HR, type the following from the command line:

REVOKE ALL FOR SYS:\DATA\DATATD.SRC FROM HR

EXAMPLE 3: To revoke the rights Read, Write, and Create from all subdirectories of the current directory from the group SUPPORT when there also is a user ID called SUPPORT, type the following from the command line:

REVOKE R W C FROM GROUP SUPPORT /SUB

EXAMPLE 4: To revoke all rights from the user A-LEE for the directory mapped to your S: drive, type the following from the command line:

REVOKE ALL FOR S: FROM A-LEE

Tip

Wild cards can be used with the REVOKE command. For example, to revoke the rights Create and Erase from the user DDARBY for all subdirectories of the current directory, type **REVOKE C E FOR *. FROM DDARBY**.

The Inherited Rights Mask (IRM)

The Inherited Rights Mask is a powerful feature of the NetWare security system. Earlier in this chapter, you saw how there were four ways users attain trustee rights, and one of these ways was through inheritance from a parent directory. With the IRM, you can set the maximum rights any user or group can inherit from a parent directory.

Before explaining how to set or review the IRM on your server, there are a few guidelines/rules you must know:

- The IRM set for a directory determines which rights can be inherited from the parent directory.

- The IRM set for a file determines which rights can be inherited from the current directory's rights. Remember, when a direct trustee assignment has *not* been set for a file, the user inherits the rights from the current directory.

- The IRM *cannot* be used to restrict the SUPERVISORY right. Once this right has been granted,
  it filters down through the entire directory tree.

- Only users with SUPERVISOR equivalence or the ACCESS CONTROL or SUPERVISORY trustee right can alter the IRM for a directory or file.

Tip

While we will be covering how to create and modify your IRM in the following sections, it is *not* recommended that you use the Inherited Rights Mask on your server. It can be very difficult to manage and any of the functions it provides can easily be duplicated by using Trustee Assignments.

Setting and Viewing the IRM with FILER

Note

RIGHTS REQUIRED TO COMPLETE TASK: YOU MUST BE A SUPERVISOR EQUIVALENT OR HAVE THE ACCESS CONTROL OR SUPERVISORY TRUSTEE RIGHT TO THE DIRECTORY OR FILE FOR WHICH YOU ARE CHANGING THE IRM.

When you use the NetWare file management utility FILER, you can view and modify the IRM settings for a directory or file by following the steps outlined in the following sections.

For the Current Directory

You can modify the IRM for the current directory by following these steps:

1. From the Available Topics main menu of FILER, select Current Directory Information.

2. Next, you are presented with a screen detailing the Directory Information for the current directory. The second option from the bottom, Inherited Rights Mask, shows you the rights currently being allowed.

3. If you want to make changes to the IRM, after selecting Inherited Rights Mask, you are presented with a screen called Inherited Rights (see fig. 13.4). From this screen, you can press the Insert key to add any rights not in the listing or highlight the rights you want to remove and press Delete.

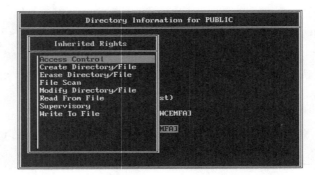

Fig. 13.4 The inherited rights mask for the current directory shown with the FILER utility.

For a File

To modify the IRM for a file, first make sure you are in the same directory as the file. You can do this by either using the DOS CD command or through FILER by using the Select Current Directory option from the main menu. Once in the appropriate directory, you can modify the IRM by following these steps:

1. From the Available Topics main menu of FILER, select Directory Contents and then the file to which you want to modify the IRM.

2. After selecting the file, you are presented with a window entitled File Options. From this window, by selecting View/Set File Information, you are then presented with a window showing you the current IRM for this file.

3. If you want to make changes to the IRM, after selecting Inherited Rights Mask, you are presented with a screen called Inherited Rights. From this screen, you can press the Insert key to add any rights not in the listing or highlight the rights you want to remove and press Delete.

For Directories other than the Current Directory

With FILER, you also can modify the IRM to a directory even when it is not your current directory. To do so, follow the steps outlined above but, instead of selecting a file, select a subdirectory.

Setting and Viewing the IRM from the Command Line

Note

RIGHTS REQUIRED TO COMPLETE TASK: YOU MUST BE A SUPERVISOR EQUIVALENT OR HAVE THE ACCESS CONTROL OR SUPERVISORY TRUSTEE RIGHT TO THE DIRECTORY OR FILE FOR WHICH YOU ARE CHANGING THE IRM.

The ALLOW command specifies which rights can be inherited by a user or group to a directory or file. To use the ALLOW command, type the following from the command line:

```
ALLOW [path] [TO INHERIT] [rights]
```

Based on the syntax above, replace:

> *path* with the name of the directory or file to which you are allowing rights. You *must* specify a directory or file, even when using ALLOW on the current directory.

Tip

Instead of typing the full path, ALLOW accepts the DOS identifiers such as "." for the current directory, ".." for the parent directory, and so on.

> *rights* with a listing of the rights you want to allow. You must use the short form for the right (such as R is for Read) and when including several rights in the same command each right must be separated by a space. The rights that can be allowed, and their short form are listed below:

Right	Short Form
SUPERVISORY	S
READ	R
WRITE	W
CREATE	C
ERASE	E
MODIFY	M
FILE SCAN	F
ACCESS CONTROL	A
NO RIGHTS	N
ALL RIGHTS	ALL

> **Note**
>
> For descriptions of these rights, refer to Table 13.1 earlier in this chapter.

EXAMPLE 1: To only allow the rights Read, File Scan, and Modify to be inherited in the DEVELOP directory on the SYS: volume, type the following from the command line:

ALLOW SYS:\DEVELOP R F M

EXAMPLE 2: To only allow the Create right for the file DATRUN.EXE in the current directory, type the following from the command line:

ALLOW DATRUN.EXE C

> **Tip**
>
> To view the IRM for the current directory's files and subdirectories, type **ALLOW** by itself.

> **Tip**
>
> Wildcards can be used with the ALLOW command. For example, to allow the Read and File Scan rights to be inherited for all files in the current directory with the extension EXE, type **ALLOW *.EXE R F**.

Viewing a Directory's IRM with LISTDIR

While normally used as a utility to view the directory structures on the server, the LISTDIR utility also can be used to see what the Inherited Rights Mask is for a directory.

To use the LISTDIR command, type the following from the command line:

```
LISTDIR [path] /R [/S]
```

Based on the syntax above, replace:

path with the name of the directory or the path to the subdirectory, directory, or volume to which you want to view the IRM.

> **Note**
>
> The /S parameter is included when you want to view the IRM for all subdirectories of the noted path.

EXAMPLE 1: To view the IRM for all directories off the root of the SYS: volume, type the following from the command line:

LISTDIR SYS:\ /R

EXAMPLE 2: To view the IRM for every directory and subdirectory starting at the root of the SYS: volume, type the following from the command line:

LISTDIR SYS:\ /R /S

Tip

Wild cards can be used with the LISTDIR command. For example, to view the IRM to all directories that begin with the letters DA within the current directory, type **LISTDIR DA* /RIGHTS**.

Viewing a File or Directory's IRM with NDIR

NDIR is NetWare's most powerful command line file management utility. While it is not normally used for this task, you can use NDIR to view the IRM for a file or directory on the server. To use the NDIR command, the syntax is:

```
NDIR [path] /RIGHTS [/SUB]
```

Based on the syntax above, replace:

path with the name of the directory or file for which you want to view the IRM.

Note

Include the /SUB switch when you want NDIR to scan through all subdirectories of the noted path.

EXAMPLE 1: To view the IRM for all files, directories, and their subdirectories in the current directory, type the following from the command line:

NDIR /SUB

EXAMPLE 2: To view the IRM for all files that begin with the letter A that are stored in the PROD\DATA directory off the root of VOL1:, type the following from the command line:

NDIR VOL1:\PROD\DATA\A*.* /RIGHTS

Tip

Wild cards can be used with the NDIR command. For example, to view the IRM for all files with the extension COM within the current directory, type **NDIR *.COM /RIGHTS**.

Chapter 14

Additional Security Measures

Previous chapters in this section told you how you could protect your LAN by using security equivalancies and trustee rights. In addition to these NetWare features, there are several others that will help you protect the server and the data it maintains.

In this chapter, we review some of the additional security measures you can put into place, and specifically:

- Detecting and preventing intruders

- Checking for security "holes"

- Viewing security violations

- Securing the server console

Detecting Intruders

To protect your server against unauthorized login attempts, NetWare has a feature called Intruder Lockout Detection. Essentially, this feature monitors each ID logging into the server to see if the password was entered incorrectly. Based on the configuration you have set, NetWare will lock out an account for a period of time after a password has been entered incorrectly a certain number of times. Once an account has been locked out, no one can use it until a SUPERVISOR EQUIVALENT re-enables the account or the lockout time expires.

Tip
If you have locked out your SUPERVISOR ID on the server and you do not have any other IDs that are SUPERVISOR EQUIVALENTs, you can clear the Intruder Lockout Status by typing ENABLE LOGIN at the file server console prompt. This *only* clears the Intruder Lockout Status for the SUPERVISOR ID.

Caution	
Since ENABLE LOGIN clears the Intruder Lockout Status on the SUPERVISOR ID, it is extremely important that the server console is secured. Refer to the heading "Protecting the File Server Console" later in this chapter.	

Configuring Intruder Lockout Status

Note	
REQUIRED RIGHTS TO COMPLETE TASK: SUPERVISOR EQUIVALENT	

Intruder Lockout Status can be configured on the file server by following these steps:

1. From the Available Topics main menu of SYSCON, select Supervisor Options and then Intruder Detection/Lockout.

2. At this point, SYSCON displays a window showing you the current configuration of the Intruder Lockout feature. There are several options on this screen, each of which is explained below:

    Detect Intruders: To enable Intruder Detection on the server, select Yes.

    Incorrect Login Attempts: Specifies how many times someone can try to log in to the server with an invalid password. The range for this setting is between 1 and 10000 attempts.

    Bad Login Count Retention Time: Tells NetWare how long you want it to remember a password was entered incorrectly. Once the password has been entered correctly, NetWare resets its counter. The maximum setting for this option is 40 days, 23 hours, and 59 minutes.

    Lock Account After Detection: To have the account locked out after the settings above have been reached, set this option to Yes. When set to No, NetWare will not lock out the account but will log the condition on the server's console and in the file server error log called SYS$LOG.ERR in the SYSTEM directory.

    Length Of Account Lockout: Tells NetWare for how long you want the account locked out. The maximum setting for this option is 40 days, 23 hours, and 59 minutes.

Resetting and Viewing Locked-Out IDs

Note	
REQUIRED RIGHTS TO COMPLETE TASK: SUPERVISOR EQUIVALENT	

You can reset IDs that were locked out by the Intruder Lockout Detection system or view information about when the ID was locked out by following these steps:

1. From the Available Topics main menu of SYSCON, select User Information and then, from the listing of user names, the user ID you want to reset.

2. After selecting the ID, you are presented with the User Information window that is specific to the user in question. From this screen, you should select Intruder Lockout Status, where you are then presented with a screen similar to the one shown in Figure 14.1. Following the figure below, a description of each of the options is provided.

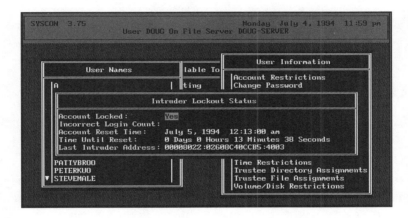

Fig. 14.1 SYSCON information screen showing the intruder lockout status for a user.

Account Locked: When the account has been locked out, this option is set to Yes. To reset the ID, change this option to No.

Incorrect Login Count: This field shows you the number of incorrect login attempts made for the ID in question.

Account Reset Time: This field tells you the time the Intruder Lockout Status will automatically be cleared (when the ID is already locked out), or the time the invalid login retention time will be cleared.

Time Until Reset: Countdown time showing you how long it will be before the account is automatically reset.

Last Intruder Address: Shows the network and workstation address of the user who locked out the account. When the account is not yet locked, this field shows you the address of the user who entered the password incorrectly.

Tip

If a user calls you stating they are getting "Access Denied" errors when logging in, you can use the information here to determine if they are entering their password incorrectly. While watching the Incorrect Login Count field, ask the user to try and log into the server. If the value in this field increments, they are entering the wrong password.

Note

When an account is locked out, NetWare makes a note of this in the server's error log. For further information, refer to the heading "Viewing NetWare Warnings Regarding Security Issues" later in this chapter.

Protecting the File Server Console

In almost any LAN, the most important node is the file server itself. As the focal point of the LAN where users can store and retrieve their data, the server is also the focal point of someone trying to retrieve this data for their personal gain.

Previous chapters in this section showed you how to restrict access to the server and protect the data contained on its disks, but this does not help you protect the server itself. Thankfully, there are a few things you can do to protect the server, as shown in the following sections.

Physically Protecting the File Server

Physically restricting access to the server plays a very important role in your overall security plan. By ensuring that only authorized personnel have physical access to the server, you can minimize the chance that someone can gain access to your corporate data. There are several methods for physically restricting access you can pursue, as shown below:

- *Keep the server in a locked, secure room:* Some people feel that placing the server behind a locked door is all the security they need, but in many cases, this theory is flawed. In most offices, dropped ceilings are used so cabling and plumbing can be run through the space between the ceiling and the floor above. While dropped ceilings may serve their purpose, they also can create a potential security "hole." If your server is behind a locked door, make sure the room's walls run from the floor right up to the floor above, and not just to the dropped ceiling. When the walls only extend to the dropped ceiling, an intruder can remove a few tiles from the ceiling and climb over the wall in less than a minute, thereby making that expensive lock worthless.

IV

Security Management

- *Lock the file server to the desk or cabinet:* There are several devices on the market that allow you to lock the server down to an object such as a cabinet or desk. This acts as a barrier to someone trying to walk away with the server.

- *Lock the server's case:* Almost every computer these days comes with a locking case. By using the lock on the case, you can restrict someone from trying to open the server and removing the drives.

Preventing Changes from the Console

NetWare has a console command called SECURE CONSOLE that implements additional security measures for the file server. By typing **SECURE CONSOLE** from the console prompt, the following security measures are put into place:

> ### Note
>
> SECURE CONSOLE does not prevent someone from "cracking" into the server from a workstation. It is only meant to restrict changes from the console itself.

- *Unauthorized Module Loading:* SECURE CONSOLE prevents someone from loading modules from a location other than the current path. Under normal circumstances, NetWare allows you to load a module from any location on the server's local drives or volumes. In cases like this, a user could create an NLM to access server data or alter bindery information and then load it from the server's floppy drives or a directory on the server to which they have access.

- *Removal Of DOS:* Instead of running an unauthorized NLM, an intruder can DOWN the file server and, using disk editor utilities, access data from anywhere on the server's disk. To protect the server from this, the SECURE CONSOLE command automatically removes DOS from memory. Once DOS is removed, if the server is brought DOWN, it must be rebooted and cannot be returned to the DOS prompt. For the best protection, this option should be used with a power-on password for the server itself.

- *Server Date And Time:* Many of the accounting and account restrictions depend on the server's date or time for their enforcement (such as account expiration dates and password expiration dates). With the SECURE CONSOLE command, changes to the date and time maintained by the server are restricted to the FCONSOLE utility. You, or an intruder, will *not* be able to make these changes from the console.

- *The NetWare Debugger:* Using the NetWare debugger, an intruder could find out critical information about the server or even reset it. Once the SECURE CONSOLE command is issued, access to the debugger is removed.

> **Note**
>
> Once the SECURE CONSOLE command has been issued, the only way to remove it is to reboot the file server.

Locking the File Server Console

The MONITOR utility provides you with an option to restrict access to any console command until the appropriate password has been entered. Using MONITOR, you can lock the console by following these steps:

1. Select Lock File Server Console from the Available Options main menu of MONITOR. If MONITOR is not loaded, you can load it from the server prompt by typing **LOAD MONITOR**.

2. At this point, NetWare asks you to enter a password that will be used to lock the console. Once the password is entered, the console will be locked. NetWare does *not* ask you to re-enter it to make sure you typed what you *think* you typed.

> **Tip**
>
> If you forget the password you entered to lock the console, you also can use the password for the SUPERVI-SOR ID to unlock the console.

Finding Potential Security "Holes"

> **Note**
>
> REQUIRED RIGHTS TO COMPLETE TASK: SUPERVISOR EQUIVALENT

To check your server's bindery files for potential security "holes," NetWare comes equipped with a utility called SECURITY that is maintained in the SYSTEM directory. Using this utility, you can check your server for any of the following potential problems:

- Disabled accounts
- Expired accounts
- Objects without a full name assigned
- Number of users managed by object

- Number of groups managed by object

- Accounts that have not been used for more than three weeks

- Users or print servers that do not require passwords

- IDs that do not require unique passwords

- IDs with password expiration dates that are greater than sixty days

- IDs that can use passwords of fewer than five characters

- IDs without passwords assigned

- Users that are SUPERVISOR EQUIVALENTs

- Users that are SUPERVISOR EQUIVALENTs and are managed by another user or group

- IDs without login scripts

- Objects with excessive rights directories

According to SECURITY, the maximum rights should be:

Directory	Rights
SYS:\SYSTEM	NO RIGHTS
SYS:\MAIL	CREATE
SYS:\LOGIN	READ and FILE SCAN
SYS:\PUBLIC	READ and FILE SCAN
SYS:\	NO RIGHTS

Note

When SECURITY checks an ID to see if it has a login script, it does so by scanning the ID's personal mail directory for a file named LOGIN. If this file exists, SECURITY assumes the ID does have a login script. Unfortunately, if you create a login script for an ID and then delete it in SYSCON, the LOGIN file is *not* removed. Instead, SYSCON only takes all the data out of the LOGIN file, leaving it with a record length of zero. If this empty file exists, SECURITY assumes the ID has a login script.

You can run a security check on your server by typing **SECURITY** from the command line. By default, SECURITY writes all the information to the screen, but by using the DOS REDIRECTOR you can reroute the information provided by security to a file (as in **SECURITY > SECURE.RPT**).

Unfortunately, you cannot modify the items SECURITY checks for, nor are there any special command line parameters that can be used except for the /C switch that tells SECURITY to display its information continuously instead of pausing after each screen.

Tip

When you redirect the output to a file (such as SECURITY > REPORT.RPT), your workstation might appear to hang. What actually could be happening is that the security output has paused and is waiting for you to press any key for the next screen. If this happens to you, try incorporating the /C switch for continuous mode (such as typing **SECURITY /C > REPORT.RPT**).

Viewing NetWare Warnings Regarding Security Issues

In addition to the reporting generated by the SECURITY program, NetWare also keeps track of security violations and certain changes to the operating environment in the SYS$LOG.ERR error log file stored in the SYS:\SYSTEM directory. This file is a standard ASCII text file that can be viewed from the command line (access permitting) or from SYSCON by selecting Supervisor Options from the main menu and then View Server Error Log.

Besides server errors that occur, you can find notes in this log regarding the following points:

- Accounts that have been locked out
- Access granted or refused to the console from the RCONSOLE utility
- Changes to the date and time maintained by the server
- Changes to the status of NetWare's TTS
- Open and close requests made to the bindery
- Removal of station connections to the server

Tip

If security violations and errors are not being added to the error log, check the attribute flagging of the file SYS$LOG.ERR. It must be flagged as Read-Write. When flagged as Read-Only, NetWare cannot add information to this file.

Network Packet Signing

To protect your LAN from unauthorized stations trying to access the server, NetWare 3.12 comes with a feature known as Packet Signing. Essentially, this means that NetWare can be configured to check each packet it receives to ensure it is coming from a valid client. Any unauthorized packets received are discarded. There are two parts to configuring packet signing on your LAN—the *server side* and the *workstation side*.

To configure packet signing on the file server, add the following command to the server's STARTUP.NCF file:

```
SET NCP PACKET SIGNATURE OPTION = X
```

Based on the syntax above, replace *X* with one of the following:

0	Do not perform packet signing
1	Use packet signing if required by the client
2	Use packet signing if the client can, but do not require packet signing from clients who do not support it
3	Require packet signing for all communications

To configure packet signing at the workstation, add the following command to the DOS RE-QUESTER section of your NET.CFG file (refer to Chapter 4, "Installing Workstations," for further info on the NET.CFG file):

```
SIGNATURE LEVEL = X
```

Based on the syntax above, replace *X* with one of the following parameters:

0	Do not use packet signatures
1	Use packet signatures when requested
2	Use packet signatures if the server can sign packets
3	Require packet signing

Chapter 15

File and Directory Attributes

The previous chapter, "Additional Security Measures," showed various ways you could implement a secure environment for your servers and LAN. To further enhance the tasks shown previously, there are attributes that can be used for the files and directories on the server. Attributes are used to determine how a directory or file operates and what a user can and cannot do with them.

In this chapter, we review the different file and directory attributes, and specifically:

- What each of the attributes are
- How to view what attributes are set
- How to modify a file's or directory's attributes

What Attributes Are Available

In NetWare 3.12, there are several attributes used to determine what can actually be done with a directory or file. Using these attributes, you can tell NetWare if a file should be protected from updates—or even from deletion.

Found within the following two headings, each of the attributes is shown and a brief description is provided for each one. The actual attributes available to you depend on whether you are working with a file or a directory.

File Attributes

File attributes tell NetWare how a file should and should not be used. Found in Table 15.1, the different file attributes are discussed and a description is provided with each one along with its abbreviated form.

Note
The abbreviated form is used by NetWare when viewing or modifying a file's attributes.

Table 15.1 File attributes.		
Attribute	**Abbreviation**	**Description**
ARCHIVE	A	Determines whether or not a file has been changed and is usually used by backup software or certain copying commands such as XCOPY. When you run a backup, most software examines the file's attributes, looking for the ARCHIVE bit. When found, the software knows the file has been changed since the last backup and then makes another backup and removes the bit. The ARCHIVE bit is not set again for the file until it is updated in some fashion.
COPY INHIBIT	CI	Restricts which files can be copied from the network. For example, you may want to flag licensed software stored on the file server with the COPY INHIBIT attribute. *Note:* THIS ATTRIBUTE ONLY WORKS FOR MACINTOSH USERS.
DELETE INHIBIT	DI	Prevents users who have the ERASE or SUPERVISORY right from being able to delete a file. While this attribute prevents a file from being deleted, it still can be updated or changed.
EXECUTE ONLY	X	Restricts users from copying EXE or COM files. While this attribute prevents a user from copying a file with the DOS copying commands, the file can still be copied with NCOPY. *Note:* ONCE SET, THIS ATTRIBUTE CANNOT BE REMOVED AND YOU MAY ENCOUNTER PROBLEMS WHEN TRYING TO BACK UP THE FILE.
HIDDEN	H	Makes a file "invisible" to a user so it cannot be deleted, viewed in a directory listing, or copied. While this attribute prevents a file from appearing in the standard DOS DIR command, it does not stop NetWare's NDIR and FILER utilities from showing you the file.
PURGE	P	NetWare has a feature known as SALVAGE that can be used to recover a file that has just been deleted. By using the PURGE attribute, you are telling NetWare that, if this file is deleted, you do *not* want it to be available for recovery.
READ AUDIT	RA	This attribute is supposed to be used for auditing who reads a file but as of the time of writing, setting this attribute for a file does not do anything.
READ ONLY	RO	Files flagged as READ ONLY can be viewed, copied, and executed but they *cannot* be deleted or edited. When the READ ONLY attribute is set, NetWare also sets the RENAME INHIBIT and DELETE INHIBIT attributes for the file(s) in question.
READ WRITE	RW	The READ-WRITE attribute is the standard flagging that permits the user to alter, copy, or delete the file at their discretion (trustee rights permitting).
RENAME INHIBIT	RI	Restricts a user from changing the name of a file no matter what their trustee rights are to the file.

Attribute	Abbreviation	Description
SHAREABLE	S	Makes files accessible to more than one user at a time. You should exercise some caution before setting this attribute on database files. Some database applications require that its files should *not* be flagged as being SHAREABLE as it handles the sharing of the file on its own.
SYSTEM	SY	This attribute is used by the operating system for certain key files (such as the bindery files).
TRANSACTIONAL	T	Used in conjunction with NetWare's Transaction Tracking System to ensure any updates to a file are made in their entirety. Should a critical error occur before the update is completed, NetWare will backout any partial changes. For full use of this attribute, the application you are using must be "TTS AWARE."
WRITE AUDIT	WA	This attribute is supposed to be used for auditing who writes to a file but as of the time of writing, setting this attribute for a file does not do anything.

Directory Attributes

Directory attributes tell NetWare how a directory should and should not be used. Found in Table 15.2, the different directory attributes are discussed and a description is provided with each one along with its abbreviated form.

> **Note**
>
> While some of these attributes appear to be similar to those used with files, the manner in which they work may vary.

Table 15.2 Directory attributes.

Attribute	Abbreviation	Description
DELETE INHIBIT	DI	Prevents users who have the ERASE or SUPERVISORY right from being able to delete a directory. When this attribute is set for a directory, you still can delete files within the directory but you cannot remove the directory itself.
HIDDEN	H	Makes a directory "invisible" to a user. While this attribute prevents a directory from appearing in the standard DOS DIR command, it does not stop NetWare's NDIR and FILER utilities from showing you the file. *Note:* WHEN THE DIRECTORY IS FLAGGED AS HIDDEN, YOU CAN STILL MAP A DRIVE TO IT OR CHANGE DIRECTORIES TO IT IF YOU KNOW ITS FULL NAME.

V

File and Directory Management

(continues)

Table 15.2 Continued.		
Attribute	**Abbreviation**	**Description**
PURGE	P	NetWare has a feature known as SALVAGE that can be used to recover a file that has just been deleted. By using the PURGE attribute, you are telling NetWare that, if any files in the directory are deleted, you do NOT want them to be available for recovery.
RENAME INHIBIT	RI	Restricts a user from changing the name of a directory no matter what their trustee rights are to the directory.
SYSTEM	SY	This attribute can used by the operating system for directories used specifically by the operating system.

Viewing and Modifying Attributes

Note

RIGHTS REQUIRED TO COMPLETE TASK: YOU MUST HAVE THE MODIFY OR SUPERVISORY TRUSTEE RIGHTS TO CHANGE A DIRECTORY'S OR FILE'S ATTRIBUTES.

There are three NetWare utilities that can be used to view or modify the attributes of directories and files on the server—FLAG, FLAGDIR, and FILER. In the following sections, we discuss each of these utilities and how they can be used to their fullest.

Changing and Viewing File Attributes from the Command Line

The FLAG command is used to view or modify a file's attributes. To use the FLAG command, the syntax is:

```
FLAG [path] [option] [+¦-] [attribute(s)] [/C]
```

Based on the syntax above, replace:

path with the name and location of the file for which you want to change or view the attributes.

option with ALL for all rights or N to flag the file as being "NORMAL." When flagging a file as NORMAL, you are removing all the current attributes and setting the file's attributes as READ-WRITE.

Note

The + and - signs only are included when you want to add or delete attributes from a file without disrupting the rest of the file's attributes. Adding the /C switch to the end of your command tells NetWare to scroll continuously. When viewing or modifying the attributes for a large number of files, without the /C switch, NetWare pauses after every screen, asking you to press any key when ready.

attributes with a listing of the attributes you want to add or remove. You must use the short form for the attribute (such as RW for READ-WRITE) and when adding or removing multiple attributes, each attribute can be separated by a space but a space is not required. The attributes that can be used, and their short form, are as follows:

Attribute	Short Form
ARCHIVE	A
COPY INHIBIT	CI
DELETE INHIBIT	DI
EXECUTE ONLY	X
HIDDEN	H
PURGE	P
READ AUDIT	RA
READ ONLY	RO
READ-WRITE	RW
RENAME INHIBIT	RI
SHAREABLE	S
SYSTEM	SY
TRANSACTIONAL	T
WRITE AUDIT	WA

V

File and Directory Management

Tip

Typing FLAG on its own shows you the attributes of each file stored in the current directory.

EXAMPLE 1: To view the attributes for the file DCPART.DAT, type the following from the command line:

FLAG DCPART.DAT

EXAMPLE 2: To view the attributes of the files in the directory mapped to your Z: drive, type the following from the command line:

FLAG Z:

EXAMPLE 3: To change the attributes for the file ABC.EXE in the current directory to Read-Write and Shareable, type the following from the command line:

FLAG ABC.EXE RWS

EXAMPLE 4: To add the Shareable attribute to the file DATA.DTA without altering its current attributes, type the following from the command line:

FLAG DATA.DTA + S

EXAMPLE 5: To flag all files in the current directory and each subdirectory as READ-ONLY, type the following from the command line:

FLAG *.* RO SUB

EXAMPLE 6: To set all attributes for the file TEST.TXT that is stored in the DEVELOP directory off the root of the SYS volume, type the following from the command line:

FLAG SYS:\DEVELOP\TEST.TXT ALL

Tip
Wildcards can be used with the FLAG command. For example, to flag all files with the extension EXE in the current directory as EXECUTE ONLY, type **FLAG *.EXE X** from the command line.

Changing and Viewing Directory Attributes from the Command Line

The FLAGDIR command is used to view or modify a directory's attributes. To use the FLAGDIR command, the syntax is:

```
FLAGDIR [path] [attribute(s)]
```

Based on the syntax above, replace:

path with the name and location of the directory for which you want to change or view the attributes.

attributes with a listing of the attributes you want to add or remove. You either can use the short form for the attribute (for example, P is for PURGE) or the attribute's full name. The attributes that can be used, and their short form, are as follows:

Attribute	Short Form
DELETE INHIBIT	DI
HIDDEN	H
PURGE	P
RENAME INHIBIT	RI
SYSTEM	SY

EXAMPLE 1: To view the attributes for your current directory, type the following from the command line:

FLAGDIR

EXAMPLE 2: To set the attributes for the directory EVALS to RENAME INHIBIT and HIDDEN, type the following from the command line:

FLAGDIR EVALS RI H

EXAMPLE 3: To set the attributes for the directory DATA that is off the root directory of the SYS volume to DELETE INHIBIT, type the following from the command line:

FLAGDIR SYS:\DATA DI

Tip
Wildcards can be used with the FLAGDIR command. For example, to change the attributes for each subdirectory that begins with USER to RENAME INHIBIT, type **FLAG USER* RI**.

Working with the FILER Menu Utility, you can modify or view the attributes to a directory or a file by following the steps outlined in the following sections.

V

File and Directory
Management

Modifying or Viewing the Current Directory's Attributes

You can modify the attributes of the current directory by following these steps:

1. From the Available Topics main menu of FILER, select Current Directory Information.

2. Next, you are presented with a screen detailing the Directory Information for the current directory. From this screen, select the option Directory Attributes where you are then shown a window of the attributes currently set for this directory, called Current Attributes.

3. If you want to remove one or more attributes, highlight the desired attribute and press the Delete key; otherwise, you can press the Insert key to add additional attributes to the directory (see fig. 15.1).

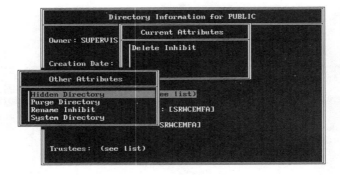

Fig. 15.1 Changing the attributes of the current directory using the FILER menu utility.

Shortcut
When adding or removing attributes, you can use the F5 key to mark multiple entries at once.

Modifying or Viewing a File's Attributes

To modify the attributes of a file, first make sure you are in the same directory as the file. You can do this either by using the DOS CD command or through FILER by using the Select Current Directory option from the main menu. Once in the appropriate directory, you can modify the attributes by following these steps:

1. From the Available Topics main menu of FILER, select Directory Contents and then the file for which you want to modify the attributes.

2. After selecting the file, you are presented with a window entitled File Options. From this window, by selecting View/Set File Information, you are then presented with another window with detailed information on this file. The first option, Attributes, shows you the attributes currently set for this file (see fig. 15.2).

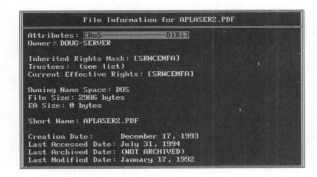

```
                File Information for APLASER2.PDF

 Attributes: [RoS                      DiRi]
 Owner : DOUG-SERVER

 Inherited Rights Mask: [SRWCEMFA]
 Trustees:  (see list)
 Current Effective Rights: [SRWCEMFA]

 Owning Name Space: DOS
 File Size: 2986 bytes
 EA Size: 0 bytes

 Short Name: APLASER2.PDF

 Creation Date:        December 17, 1993
 Last Accessed Date: July 31, 1994
 Last Archived Date: (NOT ARCHIVED)
 Last Modified Date: January 17, 1992
```

Fig. 15.2 File information shown with the FILER menu utility.

3. You can modify the file's current attributes by selecting the Attributes option and pressing the Insert key to select another attribute, or you can press the Delete key to remove one of the attributes already set.

Modifying the Attributes of another Directory

With FILER, you also can modify the attributes of a directory even when it is not your current directory. To do so, follow the steps outlined above but instead of selecting a file, however, select a subdirectory.

Chapter 16

Viewing, Copying, Deleting, and Modifying

If you are a DOS user, you are familiar with the basic COPY or XCOPY commands. While these utilities are fine for your workstations, NetWare is a bit more complex than DOS. With all of the different attributes and security settings, NetWare includes several utilities that help you manage your file and directory structures while maintaining the NetWare attributes. Unlike the NetWare utilities, the standard DOS commands are not "NetWare aware." For example, the DOS COPY has no idea what a server or a volume is.

In this section, we discuss the different utilities included with NetWare for file and directory management and specifically:

- Using the NDIR command-line utility for listing files and directories
- Copying files and directories with NCOPY
- Reviewing directory structures
- Renaming directories
- Setting search patterns for executables
- Using the FILER file management utility

Directory and File Listings from the Command Line

The NDIR command is a powerful tool provided with NetWare. It enables you to view any directory on the server (rights permitting) for different files or subdirectories of your choosing. Using one of the many options provided with this command, you can retrieve entire directory listings or you can narrow your search down to one or two files with certain characteristics. To use the NDIR command, follow this syntax:

```
NDIR [path] [/option(s)]
```

Based on the preceding syntax, replace:

path with the name of the directory you want to examine or the file for which you want to search.

*/option(s)_* with one or more of the options that are discussed in the following sections.

NDIR Formatting Options

NDIR provides you with several formatting options that determine how NDIR provides its information to you. Found in Table 16.1, a listing of each of the options is shown along with a description of each.

Table 16.1 Formatting options you can use with NDIR.	
Option	**Description**
/DATES	Show last archived, last accessed, and created dates.
/LONG	Show long machine name of file (such as OS/2, MAC).
/MAC	Show MAC file and directory names (a maximum of 31 characters).
/RIGHTS	Show effective and inherited rights for directories and files.

EXAMPLE: To search the current directory for all files and display the date the files were created, the last date they were archived, and the last date they were accessed, type the following from the command line:

NDIR /DATES

Note

You only can use one of these options per NDIR command.

NDIR Sorting Options

To organize the information provided by NDIR, there are several options you can use to determine how the information should be sorted (see Table 16.2). When used as shown, these options sort the output in numeric or alphabetical order (depending on whether the data is alpha or numeric). You can tell NDIR to provide the information in reverse order by preceding one of the options in Table 16.2 with a /REV switch.

Option	Description
/SORT ACcess	Sort by last accessed date.
/SORT ARchive	Sort by last archived date.
/SORT CReate	Sort by creation date.
/SORT OWner	Sort by owner name.
/SORT UPdate	Sort by last modified date.
/SORT SIze	Sort by size.

Table 16.2 Sorting options you can use with NDIR.

EXAMPLE 1: To search the directory mapped to the G: drive for all files and have output sorted in alphabetical order based on the file owner's name, type the following from the command line:

NDIR G: /SORT OW

EXAMPLE 2: To search the current directory for all files and sort the output from the largest to smallest sized file, type the following from the command line:

NDIR /REV /SORT SI

NDIR Attribute Options

Using NDIR, you can search for files with specific attributes by using one or more of the options shown in Table 16.3. You also can search for files that do *not* have one of the attributes set by preceding the appropriate option with a /NOT switch. For detailed information on each of the different attributes, please refer to Chapter 15, "File And Directory Attributes."

Option	Description
/A	Show files with Archive attribute.
/CI	Show files with Copy Inhibit attribute.
/DI	Show files with Delete Inhibit attribute.

Table 16.3 Attribute options you can use with NDIR.

(continues)

V

File and Directory
Management

Table 16.3 Continued.	
Option	**Description**
/H	Show files with Hidden attribute.
/I	Show indexed files.
/P	Show files with Purge attribute.
/RA	Show files with Read-Audit attribute.
/RI	Show files with Rename Inhibit attribute.
/RO	Show files with Read-Only attribute.
/S	Show files with Shareable attribute.
/SY	Show files with System attribute.
/T	Show files with Transactional attribute.
/WA	Show files with Write Audit attribute.
/X	Show files with Execute-Only attribute.

EXAMPLE 1: To search the directory DEVELOP off the root directory of the SYS: volume for all files that have the Read-Only attribute, type the following from the command line:

NDIR SYS:\DEVELOP /RO

EXAMPLE 2: To search the directory mapped to the S: drive for all files that do not have the Purge attribute set, type the following from the command line:

NDIR P: /NOT /P

Qualifiers that Can Be Used with NDIR

The final method you can use to narrow down your search with the NDIR command is to use one of the qualifiers shown in Table 16.4. In this table, each of the available qualifiers is shown along with the variables that they can be used with. With each of these qualifiers and variables, you either can use the entire word or just the letters shown in **bold text** (for example, Greater than or **GR**). You also can search for files or directories for the opposite of the qualifiers shown by inserting a /NOT after the variable. For your reference, each of the variables are described below:

Owner: The owner is the person that created the directory or file.

Size: The size of the directory or file in bytes.

Updated: The last date the file was updated.

Created: The date the directory or file was first created.

Accessed: The date the file was last accessed.

Archived: The last time the file was backed up, or the last time the archive bit was removed.

Note

When searching for a qualifier whose value is a date, the date should be entered as MM-DD-YY (as in **NDIR / Archived Equal to 12-31-93**).

Table 16.4 Qualifiers you can use with NDIR and the associated variables.

Qualifiers	Variables
EQual to	**OW**ner, **SI**ze, **UP**dated, **CR**eated, **AC**cessed, **AR**chived
GReater than	**SI**ze
LEss than	**SI**ze
BEFore	**UP**dated, **CR**eated, **AC**cessed, **AR**chived
AFTer	**UP**dated, **CR**eated, **AC**cessed, **AR**chived

In addition to the qualifiers shown previously that can be used, there are three other restrictions that can be added to your NDIR command. They are used on their own and are shown as follows:

Option	Description
/FO	Displays files only.
/DO	Displays directories only.
/SUB	Displays current directory's subdirectories and all subsequent subdirectories.

EXAMPLE 1: To view a listing of all files in the current directory that are owned by the user MICHVANDE, type the following from the command line:

NDIR /OWNER EQUAL TO MICHVANDE

EXAMPLE 2: To view a listing of the files in the G: drive that are 2,000 bytes or more, type the following from the command line:

NDIR G: /SI GR 2000

EXAMPLE 3: To search the DATA directory off the root of the SYS: volume for all files that were not updated after February 6, 1994, type the following from the command line:

NDIR SYS:\DATA /UP NOT AFT 02-06-94

EXAMPLE 4: To look for the file ABC.TXT in the current directory tree, type the following from the command line:

NDIR ABC.TXT /SUB

Tip
Wild cards can be used with the NDIR command. For example, to search for all files in the current directory with the first three letters ABC, type **NDIR ABC*.***.

Using NDIR with Multiple Options

As you have seen so far, NDIR can be a very powerful tool when searching for files or directories on the server. To enhance each of these options further, NDIR also supports multiple options on the same command line. The only thing you must remember when using multiple options is that a forward slash must precede the first element within the option listing. Following are two examples to get you on your way to using NDIR to its fullest potential:

EXAMPLE 1: To scan the current directory for all files that begin with the letter A, that are owned by the user ALEE, and are flagged as Read-Only, type the following from the command line:

NDIR A* /OW EQ ALEE /RO

EXAMPLE 2: To scan the current directory and all subdirectories for files owned by JDOE that were created after January 1, 1994 and greater than 10,000 bytes in size, type the following from the command line:

NDIR *.* /OW EQ JDOE /CR GR 01-01-94 /SI GR 10,000

Using LISTDIR to View Directory Tree Information

The LISTDIR command is used to examine directories and subdirectories for the following criteria:

- Viewing the directory structure
- Viewing the creation dates for each subdirectory

- Viewing the IRM for each subdirectory

- Viewing the effective rights for each subdirectory

To use the LISTDIR command, follow this syntax:

```
LISTDIR [path] [/option(s)]
```

Based on the preceding syntax, replace:

path with the name of the directory or the path to the subdirectory, directory, or volume you want to examine.

/option(s) with one or more of the abbreviations for the options found in Table 16.5.

Table 16.5 Options that can be used with the LISTDIR command.		
Option	**Abbreviation**	**Description**
All	A	Combines all the other options into one output.
Date	D	Views the creation date and time of the subdirectory(s). This option is the same as Time.
Effective Rights	E	Views your effective rights to the subdirectory(s).
Inherited Rights	I	Views the Inherited Rights Mask for the subdirectory(s). This option is the same as Rights.
Rights	R	Views the Inherited Rights Mask for the subdirectory(s). This option is the same as Inherited Rights.
Subdirectories	S	Views the directory's subdirectories and all subsequent subdirectories.
Time	T	Views the creation date and time of the subdirectory(s). This option is the same as Date.

Note

When using multiple options, a forward slash (/) must precede each option; otherwise, you get an error.

EXAMPLE 1: To view a listing of all subdirectories of the current directory, type the following from the command line:

LISTDIR

EXAMPLE 2: To view your effective rights to all subdirectories of the current directory and their creation dates, type the following from the command line:

LISTDIR /E /D

EXAMPLE 3: To view the entire directory tree beneath your current directory, type the following from the command line:

LISTDIR /S

EXAMPLE 4: To view a listing of the subdirectories of the directory mapped to the K: drive and the Inherited Rights Mask of each, type the following from the command line:

LISTDIR K: /S /R

Tip

Wild cards can be used with the LISTDIR command. For example, to view a listing of directories and their subdirectories that begin with the letters AB, type **LISTDIR AB* /S**.

Copying Directories and Files from the Command Line

The NCOPY command-line utility is provided with NetWare to enable you to copy one or more files or directories. While there are a couple of DOS commands (such as COPY and XCOPY) that also let you copy one or more files at a time, NCOPY has the following advantages over these commands:

- NCOPY maintains the NetWare file attributes

- NCOPY copies sparse files

- NCOPY is faster than the DOS commands as it communicates with the server's operating system in a more efficient manner

To use the NCOPY command, follow this syntax:

```
NCOPY [path1]filename1 [path2][filename2] [/option(s)]
```

Based on the syntax above, replace:

path1 with the full directory path of the file(s) you want to copy.

filename1 with the name of the file(s) you want to copy.

path2 with the name of the directory, or the path to the subdirectory, directory, or volume to which you want to copy the file.

filename2 with the new file name if you are renaming the file(s) when you copy.

/option(s) with one or more of the abbreviations for the options found in Table 16.6.

Table 16.6 Options that can be used with the NCOPY command.

Option	Abbreviation	Description
Archive	A	Copies files that have the archive bit set. The archive bit on the source file is not to be removed.
Clear Archive Bit	M	Copies files that have the archive bit set. NCOPY removes the bit from the source file after copying.
Copy	C	Copies files without preserving the NetWare attributes or name space information. Also known as a "DOS Copy."
Empty Subdirectories	E	Copies empty subdirectories. Only valid when used in conjunction with the Subdirectories option.
Force Sparse Files	F	Forces NCOPY to copy sparse files.
Inform	I	Notifies you when a file's attributes or name space information cannot be copied because the destination does not support them (such as trying to copy a Macintosh file to a volume that does not support Macintosh name spaces).
Subdirectories	S	Copies all subdirectories of the current directory.
Verify	V	Verifies that the file was copied properly.

Note

When using multiple options, a forward slash (/) must precede each option; otherwise, you get an error.

EXAMPLE 1: To copy the file NETWARE.DRV in the current directory to the directory mapped to the H: drive, type the following from the command line:

NCOPY NETWARE.DRV H:

EXAMPLE 2: To copy all files in the current directory, and its subdirectories, to the directory WRITING off the root directory of the SYS: volume, type the following from the command line:

NCOPY *.* SYS:\WRITING /S /E

V

File and Directory
Management

EXAMPLE 3: To copy the file ALEE.DOC on the G: drive to the I: drive and verify that it was copied properly, type the following from the command line:

NCOPY G:ALEE.DOC I: /V

Tip
NCOPY supports wild cards. For example, to copy all files that begin with the letter S in the current directory to the U: drive, type **NCOPY S*.* U:**.

Renaming Directories from the Command Line

Note
RIGHTS REQUIRED TO COMPLETE TASK: YOU MUST HAVE THE MODIFY OR SUPERVISORY TRUSTEE RIGHT TO THE DIRECTORY TO RENAME ONE OF ITS SUBDIRECTORIES.

The RENDIR command is provided with NetWare to enable you to easily rename a directory. To use the RENDIR command, use the following syntax:

```
RENDIR [path] [new_name]
```

Based on the preceding syntax, replace:

path with the name of the directory or the path to the subdirectory, directory, or volume you want to rename.

new_name with the new name of the directory.

EXAMPLE 1: To rename the directory TEST that is a subdirectory of your current directory to PROD, type the following from the command line:

RENDIR TEST PROD

EXAMPLE 2: To rename the directory APPS that is a directory off the root of the SYS: volume to APPLIC, type the following from the command line:

RENDIR SYS:\APPS APPLIC

> **Note**
>
> When you change a directory name, the associated trustee assignments are adjusted automatically. For example, if you rename the directory APPLIC where you have directly assigned trustees to APPS, you do not have to reassign the trustee rights to the APPS directory. They are automatically changed to the new directory name.

Changing File Search Patterns

Some programs require other programs or data files to operate. Depending on how these programs are written, they may look for the necessary files within a specific volume or directory. A perfect example of such a program is NetWare's CAPTURE utility. By default, CAPTURE looks for print job information, stored in the PRINTCON.DAT file, in a user's personal mail directory.

By using the SMODE utility, you can override the standard searching method of the program by setting a "search mode" for the EXE or COM program. By doing so, you are actually changing where the program will look for its supplementary files. You can use SMODE by following this syntax:

```
SMODE [path] [mode_option]
```

Based on the preceding syntax, replace:

path with the name of the file or the full path to the file, including the file name, for which you want to view or change the search mode.

mode_option with one of the search mode options shown within Table 16.7.

Table 16.7 Search mode options.	
Mode	**Description**
0	Use the mode specified within the workstation NET.CFG file. Refer to Chapter 4, "Installing Workstations," for further information on the NET.CFG file.
1	If the program is designed to search a specific directory, it should search only that directory; otherwise, it scans the default directory and then each of the search drives.
2	The program should only search the default directory.
3	If the program is designed to search a specific directory, it should search only that directory; otherwise, if the program opens the data file as Read-Only, it scans the default directory and then each of the search drives.

(continues)

V

File and Directory
Management

Mode	Description
Table 16.7 Continued.	
4	Mode number not used.
5	The program should search the default directory and then all search drives regardless of the location specified within the program.
6	Mode number not used.
7	If the program opens the data file as Read-Only, it should scan the default directory and then each of the search drives.

Tip

You can view the search mode of all files in the current directory by typing **SMODE**, to another directory by typing **SMODE directory** without a search mode number, or a file by typing **SMODE filename** without a search mode number.

EXAMPLE 1: To change the search mode for the file CAPTURE.EXE in the current directory to 5, type the following from the command line:

SMODE CAPTURE.EXE 5

EXAMPLE 2: To change the search mode of the file VIEW.EXE in the DATA directory off the root of the SYS: volume to 7, type the following from the command line:

SMODE SYS:\DATA\VIEW.EXE 7

EXAMPLE 3: To view the search mode of all files in the current directory, type the following from the command line:

SMODE

Tip

Wild cards can be used with the SMODE command. For example, to change the search mode for all files in the current directory that begin with the letter A to 2, type **SMODE A*.* 2**.

FILER—NetWare's Most Complete File Management Utility

If you have been reading through the entire book so far, you already know that FILER is *the* key file management utility for NetWare 3.X. Using FILER, you can take complete control of your NetWare server's files and directories all through the convenient menu interface. In this section, we explore many of the options available to you with FILER and how you can manage your data with FILER.

Establishing FILER Settings

When you first start the FILER menu utility, there are several assumptions it makes regarding the types of files it looks for and how it handles some of your requests. In most cases, these default settings are just fine, but you may want to make a few adjustments depending on what you are doing. For instance, if you are looking for a specific file, you may want to tell FILER about a certain search pattern.

You can make any needed adjustments by selecting Set Filer Options from the Available Topics main menu of FILER. After making your selection, you are presented with a window like the one shown in Figure 16.1. From this screen, you can make any changes necessary. For your convenience, each of these options is described as follows:

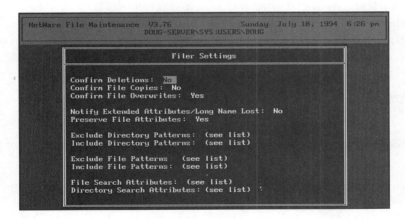

Fig. 16.1 FILER options settings used to customize your current FILER session.

Confirm Deletions: When deleting more than one file at once, FILER only asks you to confirm the first file deletion. If you want to be prompted before deleting each file, change this option to Yes.

Confirm File Copies: If you are copying multiple files, set this option to Yes if you want FILER to prompt you to confirm the copying before each file.

Confirm File Overwrites: By default, if you are copying one file over another, FILER prompts you to confirm that you want to overwrite the current file. If you do not want to be prompted, change this option to No.

Notify Extended Attributes/Long Name Lost: When copying files that have extended attributes (such as OS/2 and MAC files), the attributes and long names may be lost. By default, FILER does not notify you for every file whose attributes are lost. If you want to be notified, change this option to Yes. This option works in conjunction with the Preserve File Attributes option.

Preserve File Attributes: When copying files that have extended attributes (such as OS/2 and MAC files), by default, FILER preserves the extended attributes and long names of the files. If you do not want these attributes preserved, change this option to No.

Exclude Directory Patterns: With this option, you can tell FILER what types of directories you do not want FILER to show you. By selecting this option, you are presented with a window of the current patterns that are excluded. A new search pattern can be added by pressing the Insert key and entering the pattern in the window provided. Wild cards *can* be used with this pattern (for example, to exclude all directories that begin with a P, enter the pattern P*).

Include Directory Patterns: By default, FILER shows you all directories on the server (rights permitting). If you want to narrow your search, you can tell FILER which files you want to see by selecting this option. Once selected, a window appears, showing you the current pattern that is shown, which is * (all directories by default). You can add a new search pattern by pressing the Insert key and entering your pattern in the window provided. (To view only the directories that begin with the letters AB, enter the pattern AB*.)

Exclude File Patterns: Same as Exclude Directory Patterns option except this option is used for files.

Include File Patterns: Same as Include Directory Patterns option except this option is used for files.

File Search Attributes: By default, FILER does not display any files that are flagged with the Hidden or System attributes. To view files with these flaggings, you must select this option and then press the Insert key when presented with the Search File Attributes window. After pressing Insert, you are presented with an additional window showing the Hidden and System attribute. By selecting these options and adding them to the Search File Attributes window, FILER shows the files in question.

Directory Search Attributes: Same as File Search Attributes except this option pertains to directories.

Managing a Single Directory or File

There are several management tasks you can perform using the FILER utility. Before you can work with a single directory or file, you must first select Directory Contents from the Available Topics main menu of FILER. After selecting this option, FILER presents you with a listing of the files and directories contained within the current directory (see fig. 16.2).

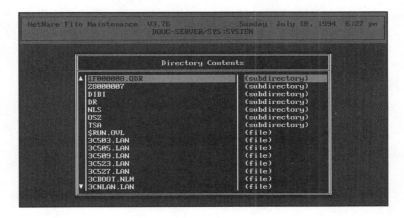

Fig. 16.2 FILER directory contents screen.

Tip

If the file or directory is not in your current directory, you can change your current directory within FILER by selecting the Select Current Directory option from the main menu, by pressing F2 from within the Directory Contents window, or by selecting Parent or Root from the Directory Contents window.

After skimming through the Directory Contents window and placing your cursor on the desired directory or file, there are several options available to you as shown in the following sections.

Deleting a Directory or File

To delete a directory or file, highlight it and press the Delete key. If you are deleting a file, when asked, confirm that you want to delete the file. But, if you are deleting a directory, FILER presents you with a window entitled Delete Subdirectory Options that contains two options—Delete Entire Subdirectory Structure and Delete Subdirectory's Files Only. If you want to delete the entire directory structure, including the files stored within each subdirectory, select the first option; otherwise, choose the latter. When asked, confirm that you want FILER to proceed with the deletion.

Renaming a Directory or File

To rename a directory or file, highlight it and press the F3 key. When asked, enter the new name for the object.

Copying a Directory or File

To copy a file, highlight it and press the Enter key. Next, you are presented with the File Options window. From this screen, select the first option, Copy File, and enter the location to which you want to copy the file into the Destination Directory window that is presented next. After entering the location, FILER asks you for the Destination File Name (see fig. 16.3). By default, it wants to copy the file to the new location with the same name, but, if you want to change the name of the copied file, enter the new name in the window provided.

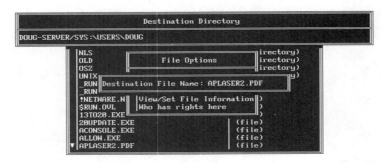

Fig. 16.3 Copying a file with the FILER menu utility.

If you want to copy a directory, highlight the directory name and press the Enter key. FILER then presents you with a new window entitled Subdirectory Options. From this screen, there are two options that you can use to copy the directory—Copy Subdirectory's Files and Copy Subdirectory's Structure. The first option only copies the files within the selected directory while the latter makes an exact copy of the directory including any subdirectories it may contain. Regardless of the option you choose, enter the location to which you want to copy in the Copy Directory To: window.

Moving a Directory or File

To move a file, highlight it and press the Enter key. Next, you are presented with the File Options window. From this screen, select the second option, Move File, and enter the location to which you want to move the file into the Destination Directory window that is presented next. After entering the location, FILER asks you for the Destination File Name. By default, it wants to move the file to the new location with the same name, but, if you want to change the name of the moved file, enter the new name in the window provided.

If you want to move a directory, highlight the directory name and press Enter. Next, from the window of Subdirectory Options, select Move Subdirectory's Structure. At this point, FILER asks you for the Destination Directory to which you want to move the selected directory. After entering the location, FILER asks one last question, New Name. If you want to maintain the same name for the directory, press Enter; otherwise, you can enter a new name for the directory.

> **Caution**
>
> When you move a directory or file, you are removing it from the source location.

Viewing a File

To view a file, highlight it and press the Enter key. Next, you are presented with the File Options window. From this screen, select the View File option, and a new window appears, showing you the contents of the selected file.

Viewing/Changing Additional Information Maintained for Directories and Files

To view some of the additional information NetWare maintains for a directory or file, highlight the object and press the Enter key. From the options screen that appears next, select View/Set File Information (for files) or View/Set Directory Information (for directories) (see fig. 16.4), and a new window appears, showing you the information NetWare maintains. On this screen, there are several options pertaining to the selected file or directory, each of which is explained in the following list:

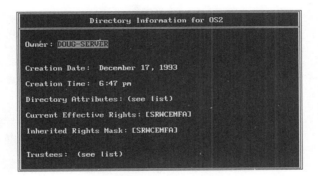

Fig. 16.4 Directory information window shown in FILER.

The available options for files are:

Attributes: This option shows you the different file attributes for the selected file. By selecting this option, you can remove any of these attributes or add new ones.

Owner: This option shows you the name of the ID that owns the selected file. To change the file's owner, select this option and then select an ID from the Known Users window.

Inherited Rights Mask: This option shows you the Inherited Rights Mask for the selected file. You can modify this field by selecting it and making the desired changes from the Inherited Rights window.

Trustees: By selecting this option, you can view all the trustees that have been directly assigned rights to the selected file.

Current Effective Rights: For viewing purposes only, this field shows you your effective rights to the selected file.

Owning Name Space: This option shows the type of name space this file uses; it is for viewing only.

File Size: This option shows the size of the file and is for viewing only.

EA Size: When the selected file uses Extended Attributes (as in OS/2 and MAC files), this option shows you how much space is used to maintain the extended attributes of the file. This option is for viewing only.

Short Name: This option shows you the Short Name (the DOS name) of the file. This option is for viewing only.

Long Name: This option is only available when a file that supports extended length names (such as Macintosh files) has been selected. When shown, you can select this option to view the full name of the file. This option is for viewing only.

Creation Date: This option gives the date the file was first created or copied into the directory. You can change the creation date by selecting this option and entering a new date.

Last Accessed Date: This option shows you the last day the file was viewed, edited, or executed. You can change the last accessed date by selecting this option and entering a new date.

Last Archived Date: The last archived date shows you the date the file was last backed up and is for viewing only.

Last Modified Date: The last modified date shows you the last time this file was changed in any way. You can change the date by selecting the option and entering a new date.

When a directory was selected, there will not be as many options available to you, but the ones that are shown (refer to fig. 16.4) operate in the same fashion as those explained previously for files.

Viewing Directory or File Trustees

You can view the trustees of a directory or file by selecting the object and pressing Enter. From the next window of options, select Who Has Rights Here, and a new window appears, showing the trustees. For detailed information on Trustees, refer to Chapter 13, "Trustee Assignments and Rights."

Managing Multiple Directories and Files

Instead of working with a single directory or file at a time, FILER enables you to work with two or more within a given directory. Before you can proceed, you must first tell FILER which directories or files you want to work with. From the Directory Contents window, there are two methods for selecting multiple objects:

■ You can tag several objects by highlighting each one that you want to work with and pressing the F5 key.

■ By pressing the F6 key, you can tell FILER to tag all directories or files that conform to a certain pattern. For example, to tag all files with the extension TXT, press the F6 key and when presented with the Mark Pattern window, enter ***.TXT.**

Tip

If you tagged multiple objects, you can use the F7 key if you want to untag all of them, or you can use the F8 key to untag certain objects based on a certain pattern.

After you have tagged all the directories or files with which you want to work, you can perform any of the tasks shown in the following sections.

Note

You cannot perform any of the following tasks on both directories and files at the same time.

Deleting Multiple Directories and Files

After tagging the directories or files, you can delete all of them at once by pressing the Delete key. When asked, confirm that you want FILER to proceed with the deletion.

Renaming Multiple Files

After tagging the files, you can rename several of them at once by pressing the F3 key. Once you have pressed F3, FILER asks you to enter the Original Name Pattern and then the Rename Pattern. For example, if you tagged multiple files and want to rename all files with the extension TXT to the extension OLD, you would press F3, then enter ***.TXT** when asked for the Original Name Pattern and ***.OLD** when asked for the Rename Pattern.

Note

You cannot rename multiple directories at once.

Copying Multiple Directories and Files

After tagging multiple directories or files, you can copy them all at once by pressing the Enter key and then selecting Copy Marked Files (for files) or Copy Subdirectory's Files or Copy Subdirectory's Structure (for directories) from the Multiple Operations window. When asked, enter the path to the location to which you want to copy the directories or files.

Changing/Viewing Additional Information Maintained for the Directories or Files

NetWare maintains a wide variety of information for a directory or file such as the file's attributes, creation date, last accessed date, and owner. To make changes to any additional information maintained for the tagged directories and files, you can press the Enter key and select the appropriate option from the listing of Multiple File Operations (see fig. 16.5) or Multiple Subdirectory Operations (see fig. 16.6).

Fig. 16.5 Muliple operations menu presented after selecting multiple files.

Fig. 16.6 Muliple operations menu presented after selecting multiple directories.

Updating Workstation Files

One of the most difficult tasks of managing a LAN is controlling the files stored on the workstations' hard drives. With periodic updates to workstation drivers and other locally stored utilities, keeping each workstation up to the most current version can be a job all in itself.

To help you in this task, NetWare comes equipped with a program called WSUPDATE. Using WSUPDATE, you can update any of the programs stored on your LAN's workstations.

When NetWare is first installed, WSUPDATE is placed in the SYSTEM directory. Because users do not have access to this directory, before you can use WSUPDATE, you must first place it in a directory that is accessible to all of the users. Once accessible to the users, you can use WSUPDATE by following this syntax:

```
WSUPDATE [/F=config_file] [Source_Path] [DestinationDrive:Filename] [/option(s)]
```

Based on the preceding syntax, replace:

config_file with the name of the configuration file that will contain all the commands. When you want to update multiple files, it is easier to use a config file than to issue multiple WSUPDATE commands. The config file is a standard ASCII text file that contains the Source_Path, DestinationDrive:Filename, and option(s) parameters as you would enter them from the command line. If you are using the /F= option, it must be the only option used.

Source_Path with the full path leading to the current file including the file name you are updating.

DestinationDrive:Filename with the full path leading to the file you will be updating, including the file name. Alternately, you can replace DestinationDrive with ALL (to search all valid drives including network mappings) or ALL_LOCAL to search all local drives (such as A, B, C...).

/option(s) with one of the WSUPDATE options shown in Table 16.8.

Table 16.8 Options that can be used with WSUPDATE.

Option	Description
/C	Copy over the older file.
/R	Rename the older file.
/S	Scan through all subdirectories.
/O	Update Read-Only files.
/L=LogName	Create a log of the updates that were made. Replace LogName with the name of the log file you want to create.
/N	Create the file if it does not exist.
/V=drive	Update the CONFIG.SYS file with the command LASTDRIVE=Z (for NetWare Requester). Replace drive with the drive letter of the boot drive if it is not C:.

EXAMPLE 1: To update the NETX file on the workstation when you don't know in which directory it is stored on the workstation, type the following WSUPDATE command:

WSUPDATE SYS:\PUBLIC\UPDATES\NETX.EXE ALL_LOCAL:NETX.EXE /S

EXAMPLE 2: To update a series of files on the workstation, use a configuration file by using the following WSUPDATE command:

WSUPDATE /F=UPDATE.CFG

EXAMPLE 3: To update the LSL.COM and NETX.EXE files stored on the workstation and are flagged as Read-Only, you could create a configuration file that contains the following commands:

SYS:\PUBLIC\UPDATES\LSL.COM C:LSL.COM /O

SYS:\PUBLIC\UPDATES\NETX.EXE C:NETX.EXE /O

EXAMPLE 4: To update the IPXODI.COM program on the workstation and maintain a log of all workstations that were updated, use the following WSUPDATE command:

WSUPDATE SYS:\PUBLIC\UPDATES\IPXODI.COM ALL_LOCAL:IPXODI /S / L=SYS:\PUBLIC\UPDATES\UPDATE.LOG

Tip
Using the external program execution command (#) in the system login script with WSUPDATE is a good way of ensuring that everyone gets the necessary updates when they log in.

Chapter 17

Volume Space Information and Restrictions

So far within this section, you read about the different directory and file attributes and how you can maneuver through and manipulate the server's directory structuring. To complete the discussion on file and directory management, we must look at how the disk space is being used.

Whether you are a LAN Administrator or an end-user, the time will come when you need to know how much space is available to you. Or, if you are the administrator, you may want to restrict the amount of space available to your users. In this chapter, we discuss the different utilities available to you for space management, and specifically:

■ Checking how much space is available on the server

■ Checking the amount of space available to a specific user

■ Restricting disk space to a user

■ Restricting the size of a directory

Viewing Available Space

NetWare includes several utilities to help you determine the amount of free space available on the volume or within a specific directory. Shown within the following sections, each of these utilities is discussed, along with the required steps for getting the information you need.

Checking the Amount of Space on a Volume with VOLINFO

VOLINFO is a NetWare menu utility that provides you with the space information for all the volumes on a server. By typing VOLINFO from the command line, you are presented with a screen showing you statistics for each of the volumes (up to six volumes per screen) and a menu of Available Options (see fig. 17.1). From this screen, you can see what the capacity is for the maximum disk space and directory entries as well as how much of the volume's capacity is being used.

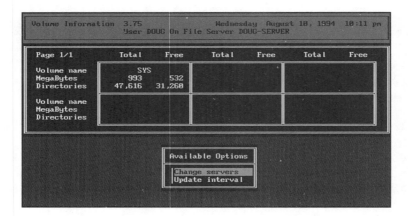

Fig. 17.1 The VOLINFO utility used to examine the amount of space on a volume.

Using the Available Options menu, you can select one of two options, Change Servers or Update Interval. The first option lets you attach to another server to view that server's volume statistics while the latter changes the interval that VOLINFO scans the server to see how much space is left.

Checking Volume Space Information from the Command Line with CHKVOL

CHKVOL is a NetWare command line utility that provides you with detailed information on how the space is being used and what is available to you on the file server's volumes. To use CHKVOL, type the following from the command line:

```
CHKVOL [path] /C
```

Based on the syntax above, replace:

> *path* with the volume name you want to check or the pointer to that volume (such as a drive letter mapped to the volume).

Note

The /C option forces NetWare to scroll the information continuously instead of pausing after each screen. /C only works if the path has been specified.

After issuing the CHKVOL command, the volume information is scanned and the following information is displayed (see fig. 17.2):

```
Wed 08-10-1994 22:11:41.48 F:\SYSTEM chkvol

Statistics for fixed volume DOUG-SERVER/SYS:

Total volume space:                    1,017,488  K Bytes
Space used by files:                     471,976  K Bytes
Space in use by deleted files:            94,592  K Bytes
Space available from deleted files:       94,592  K Bytes
Space remaining on volume:               545,512  K Bytes
Space available to DOUG:                 545,512  K Bytes

Wed 08-10-1994 22:11:43.13 F:\SYSTEM
```

Fig. 17.2 Volume space information as shown with the CHKVOL utility.

- The name of the server and the volume being reviewed

- The total space capacity of the volume

- The amount of space in use by files

- The amount of space being used by deleted files (files that have not yet been purged from the system)

- The amount of space available from deleted files

- The amount of free space left on the volume

- The amount of free space left available for you (unless your account has been restricted to a certain amount of space, this value will be the same as the amount of free space on the volume).

EXAMPLE 1: To check the volume information for the volume mapped to your default drive, type the following from the command line:

> **CHKVOL**

EXAMPLE 2: To check the volume information for the volume mapped to the G: drive, type the following from the command line:

> **CHKVOL G:**

EXAMPLE 3: To check the volume information for the VOL1 volume that is not mapped to your current drive, type the following from the command line:

> **CHKVOL VOL1:**

Tip

Wild cards can be used with the CHKVOL command. For example, to view the volume information for all volumes on the default server, type **CHKVOL *** or, to check all volumes for all servers you are attached to, type **CHKVOL */***. Alternately, you can tell NetWare to display information for all volumes you have drive mappings to by typing **CHKVOL ?**.

V

File and Directory Management

Checking Directory Space Information from the Command Line with CHKDIR

CHKDIR is a NetWare command line utility that provides you with space information for a directory such as your restrictions to the directory and how much space is being used by that directory (including all of its files and subdirectories). To use CHKDIR, type the following from the command line:

```
CHKDIR [path]
```

Based on the syntax above, replace:

> *path* with the directory name you want to check or the pointer to that directory (such as a drive letter mapped to the directory).

After issuing the CHKDIR command, the following information is shown:

- The server, volume, and directory name being scanned

- The maximum disk capacity for the volume

- The amount of space in use on that volume and directory

- The amount of space available to you on the volume and directory

EXAMPLE 1: To check the amount of space in use for the current directory and all of its subdirectories, type the following from the command line:

> **CHKDIR**

EXAMPLE 2: To check the amount of space in use for the directory mapped to the G: drive, type the following from the command line:

> **CHKDIR G:**

EXAMPLE 3: To check the amount of space in use within the DATA directory stored directly off of the root of the SYS: volume, when there is no drive mapping to the directory, type the following from the command line:

> **CHKDIR SYS:\DATA**

Checking How Much Disk Space a User Is Taking on the Server

Previous examples of checking the server disk space utilization did not differentiate between the different users on the server. The values provided from these utilities only tell you how much space is free or being used, not what a specific user is utilizing.

If you need to determine how much space a specific user is using, there are a few options available to you as shown below.

Determining Space Consumption with SYSCON

You can determine how much space a certain user is utilizing on the server by following the steps below:

1. From the SYSCON Available Topics main menu, select User Information and then, from the listing of User Names, the desired user ID.

2. After selecting the user ID, you are presented with another window, entitled User Information, that is specific to the selected user. To determine how much space the user is using, select Volume/Disk Restrictions and then, from the listing of available volumes, select the volume you want to view. SYSCON then presents you with another window that tells you how much space is in use.

Determining Space Consumption with USERDEF

You can determine how much space a certain user is utilizing on the server by following these steps:

1. From the Available Options main menu of USERDEF, select Restrict User and then, from the Users On Server window, the desired user ID.

2. After selecting the user ID, you are presented with a listing of the available volumes. From this screen, once you select a volume, USERDEF presents you with an additional window detailing the amount of space being used on the volume by the selected user.

Determining Space Consumption by a User from the Command Line

SYSCON and USERDEF both show you the amount of space a user is using on the entire volume, but the need may arise for you to determine how much space is in use by a user within a certain directory structure. Using the NDIR command line utility with the OW (owner) switch, you can determine how much space is used on the entire volume or within a certain directory structure. For example, to determine how much space is in use by the user JDOE within the current directory structure, use the following syntax:

```
NDIR /OW=JDOE /SUB
```

Once you issue the command above, NDIR scans all the files in the current directory and each subdirectory to see which ones are owned by JDOE. After NDIR completes the scan, it displays on-screen the information it has found. At the very end of the report, NDIR tells you the total space used by JDOE.

For further information on the NDIR command, refer to Chapter 16, "Viewing, Copying, Deleting, and Modifying."

V

File and Directory Management

> **Note**
>
> It is not recommended that you use NDIR for checking space utilization for the entire volume. It can take a considerable amount of time, depending on the size of the volume.

Setting and Reviewing Disk Space Restrictions

> **Note**
>
> RIGHTS REQUIRED TO COMPLETE TASK: YOU MUST BE A SUPERVISOR EQUIVALENT TO IMPOSE OR REVOKE A SPACE RESTRICTION.

As the LAN Administrator, you occasionally may want to restrict the amount of space available to a user within a directory or the entire volume. Or, maybe you are an end-user who wants to check what your space restrictions are before you try copying some files or installing a new utility.

To assist you in these tasks, NetWare includes several utilities that can be used to modify and review the disk space restrictions as shown in the following sections.

> **Caution**
>
> Don't be too stingy with the space. When a user sends a print job to the NetWare queues, a temporary copy of the file is made in the print queue directory on the SYS: volume. If you restrict the space too much, they may not be able to print their data. For example, if you set a space restriction on the SYS: volume to 1M, the user cannot print any job that is greater than 1M, or the amount of space they still have available based on any other files they have stored on the directory.

DSPACE, NetWare's Disk Space Management Utility

DSPACE has been included with NetWare for some time now as the main utility for restricting disk space on the server, yet many people don't even know about it. Using this utility, you can restrict the maximum space available to a user on a volume, *or* you also can set the maximum size a directory can be.

Setting Volume Space Restrictions

You can impose a volume space restriction for a user ID with DSPACE. Once set, the user can use as much space as they like, up to the restricted value, in any directory on the volume to which they have sufficient security access. The volume space restriction can be set by following these steps:

1. From the Available Options main menu of DSPACE, select User Restrictions and then, from the Users on Server window that is presented to you, the desired ID.

2. After selecting an ID, DSPACE presents you with a window of the volumes currently available on the server. From this screen, you should select the volume on which you want to impose the restriction.

3. Once a volume has been selected, the User Disk Space Limitation Information screen appears; it contains five fields, each of which is explained below (see fig. 17.3):

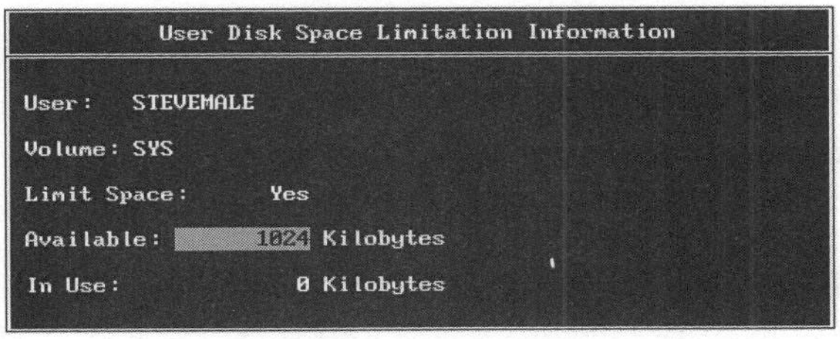

```
╔══════════════════════════════════════════════════════╗
║        User Disk Space Limitation Information         ║
╠══════════════════════════════════════════════════════╣
║                                                       ║
║   User :   STEVEMALE                                  ║
║                                                       ║
║   Volume : SYS                                        ║
║                                                       ║
║   Limit Space:        Yes                             ║
║                                                       ║
║   Available:      1024 Kilobytes                      ║
║                                                       ║
║   In Use:            0 Kilobytes                      ║
║                                                       ║
╚══════════════════════════════════════════════════════╝
```

Fig. 17.3 Disk space restriction screen as shown in DSPACE.

User: For viewing purposes only, this field tells you the name of the ID on which you are imposing the restriction.

Volume: For viewing purposes only, this field tells you the volume on which you are imposing the restriction.

Limit Space: Set to No by default, you can change this field to Yes if you want to impose a space restriction on the volume for the selected user.

Available: After selecting Yes, this field lets you set the maximum space that should be made available to the selected user.

In Use: For viewing purposes only, this field tells you how much space is in use on the volume for the selected user.

Setting Directory Size Limitations

Occasionally, you may have a directory on your server that you want to restrict to a certain size. There are various reasons for doing so, but the key advantage is that you can take control of your server and how the directory strucures are being used. In many instances, an administrator will refrain from setting individual space restrictions on the server in favor of restricting the size of the directories.

By restricting the size of the directory, instead of the total space a user can access on the server, you are increasing the amount of freedom the users have, and you reduce the amount of work required on your part. For example, you may have a database directory on your server that ten people access. If you do not want the directory to grow beyond 100M, you could set a space restriction for the directory itself. But, if you wanted to set the restrictions on a per user basis, how will you, as the LAN Administrator, know exactly how much each user needs? The answer is most probably, you won't. Chances are, some users may only use a couple of megabytes while others may use ten or fifteen; this is far too difficult to judge.

Using DSPACE, you can restrict the maximum size of a directory by following these steps:

1. From the Available Options main menu, select Directory Restrictions and then enter the directory name within the window provided next. If you do not know the name of the directory, you can press the Insert key and select from the listing of NetWork Directories presented.

2. After selecting the desired directory, DSPACE presents you with the Directory Disk Space Limitation Information window that contains four fields, each of which is explained below:

   Path Space Limit: For viewing purposes only, this field tells you what the minimum size is for subdirectories of the current directory. If a space restriction has been imposed on a directory above the current directory, that limit is shown here.

   Limit Space: Set to No by default, you can impose a restriction on the selected directory by changing this field to Yes.

   Directory Space Limit: Using this field, you can set the maximum space that can be used within the selected directory.

   Currently Available: For viewing purposes only, this field tells you how much space is still available based on what is currently being used, and the space limit imposed from the previous field.

Restricting Volume Space Availability with SYSCON

Using the SYSCON menu utility, you can restrict the amount of space available to a user by following the steps below:

1. From the Available Topics main menu of SYSCON, select User Information and then, from the listing of User Names, the desired user ID.

2. After selecting the desired ID, you are presented with a window entitled User Information that contains configuration information specific to the ID in question. From this screen, you should select Volume/Disk Restrictions and then, from the listing of available volumes, the volume on which you want to impose the restriction.

3. Once you have selected the desired volume, SYSCON presents you with a window entitled User Volume/Disk Restrictions that contains three fields, each of which is explained below:

Limit Volume Space: By default, this field is set to No. If you want to impose a space restriction for this user on the selected volume, change this setting to Yes.

Volume Space Limit: After selecting Yes, you can enter the number of kilobytes to which you want to restrict this user.

Volume Space In Use: For viewing purposes only, this field tells you how much space the user currently has in use on the volume.

Restricting Volume Space Availability with USERDEF

Normally used when creating users, USERDEF also can be used to impose space restrictions for a volume on the server by following the steps below:

1. From the Available Options main menu of USERDEF, select Restrict User and, from the Users On Server window, the desired user ID.

2. After selecting the user ID, USERDEF presents you with a window showing the available volumes on the server. At this point, you must select the volume on which you want to impose the restriction.

3. Once a volume has been selected, USERDEF presents you with a window entitled User Disk Space Limitation Information that contains five fields, each of which is explained below:

   User: For viewing purposes only, this field tells you the name of the ID on which you are imposing the restriction.

   Volume: For viewing purposes only, this field tells you the volume on which you are imposing the restriction.

   Limit Space: Set to No by default, you can change this field to Yes if you want to impose a space restriction on the volume for the selected user.

   Available: After selecting Yes, this field lets you set the maximum space that should be made available to the selected user.

   In Use: For viewing purposes only, this field tells you how much space is in use on the volume for the selected user.

Chapter 18

Creating Printing Services

Currently, there are various hardware- and software-based products on the market that offer print server-type functions, but for the most part, they all have one thing in common: they all interface with NetWare's printing services in some fashion or another. While it is not possible to discuss each of these products, in this chapter we examine NetWare's own print services and specifically:

- Creating a print server

- Creating print queues

- Configuring a print server

- Configuring print servers to service multiple file servers

Creating the Print Server

Taking into account all the parts involved with printing, the print server is probably the most critical component of all. As the printing "control center," it is the print server's responsibility to send jobs from the queues to the printer and to manage how the printers interact with NetWare.

Using the PCONSOLE utility, you can create your print server by following these steps:

1. When you select Print Server Information from the Available Options main menu of PCONSOLE, NetWare displays the Print Servers window that shows all the print servers currently installed on the file server.

2. A new print server can be created by pressing the Insert key and entering the desired name at the New Print Server Name: prompt.

Note

The print server name can be a maximum of 47 characters. NetWare interprets any spaces you enter in the print server name as underscores (_).

After these two short steps, you then have a NetWare print server set up and ready to be configured. While the configuration process may seem a little long and drawn out the first time you do it, after a while it becomes second nature to you.

Providing Additional Print Server Information

While not essential to the operation of the print server, there are several options available to you once the print server has been created. By selecting Print Server Information from the main menu of PCONSOLE and then selecting the desired print server from the Print Servers window, these options are made available to you (see fig. 18.1). Each of these options is discussed under the following headings and your use of them really depends on what your specific requirements are.

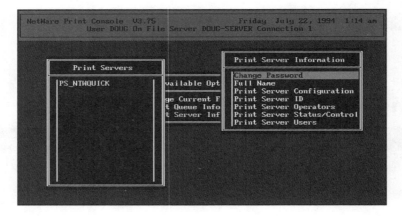

Fig. 18.1 Options available to you from within PCONSOLE to provide additional information about the print server.

Setting a Print Server Password

A password can be assigned for the print server to ensure that only authorized personnel can load the actual print server configuration in question. When a password is not used, an intruder could load the print server on a workstation equipped with a printer and have the jobs diverted to their own printer.

You can set a new password, or change an existing one, by selecting Change Password from the Print Server Information window and entering the password. When asked, reenter the password to confirm that you entered what you think you entered.

Tip
You can remove a password from the print server by selecting Change Password and then just pressing the Enter key when asked for 'the new password.

Note

The maximum size of the print server password is 127 characters.

Setting a Print Server's Full Name

While not necessary for the purpose of configuration, a full name can be set for the print server. The print server's full name can be used to provide distinguishing information, such as its location or purpose. To set a full name for the print server, select Full Name from the Print Server Information window and enter the name at the prompt provided.

Note

The maximum size of the print server's full name is 62 characters.

Creating Print Server Operators to Manage the Print Server

Print server operators can be created for each print server to help the LAN administrator with the day-to-day management duties. You can create a print server operator by selecting Print Server Operators from the Print Server Information screen and then pressing the Insert key at the Print Server Operators window to select the desired operators from the listing of Print Server Operator Candidates.

For detailed information on what print server operators can do, refer to the heading "Tasks that Managers and Operators Can Do" in Chapter 12, "Security Equivalences."

Note

By default, the SUPERVISOR ID is a operator for every print server.

VI

Network Printing

> **Tip**
>
> If you are going to have several people who will be Print Server Operators, you can use SYSCON to create a group called PRINT-SERVER-OPERATORS. Once created, you then can assign this group as an operator instead of assigning individual IDs. This is especially useful when the same users will be operators for multiple print servers.

Determining Who Can and Cannot Use the Print Server

When a print server is created, by default, NetWare enables any user that is a member of the group EVERYONE to access the services provided. Depending on your specific requirements, the occasion may arise that you must restrict access to the print server to a single user or a select group of users. One such example is a print server created on the network that will be used for confidential information such as that produced by the Human Resources department.

Within PCONSOLE, you can restrict who can and cannot use the print server by selecting the Print Server Users option from the Print Server Information window. After you select this option, NetWare provides you with a listing of all the users and groups that are currently allowed to use the print server. You can remove a user from this listing by highlighting the user ID and pressing the Delete key, or you can add a new user to this listing by pressing the Insert key and selecting the desired user ID or group from the listing of Print Server User Candidates.

> **Caution**
>
> Because NetWare assigns the group EVERYONE as a print server user, if you want to restrict access to the print server for a select group of users, you must remove the EVERYONE group as a print server user; otherwise, all members of this group (usually all users on the server) will have access to the print server's resources.

Configuring the Print Server

Once a print server has been set up on the file server, it can be configured at any time by selecting Print Server Information from the main menu of PCONSOLE and then selecting the desired print server from the Print Servers window. After the print server has been selected, NetWare displays the Print Server Information window. When you select Print Server Configuration, NetWare presents yet another menu that provides you with several options for configuring the print server (see fig. 18.2). While it is not mandatory to use each option, for your reference, each one is discussed in the following sections.

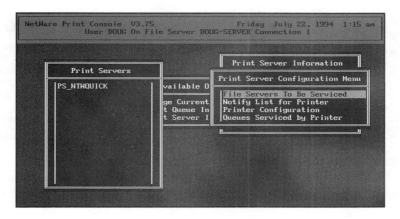

Fig. 18.2 Options available within PCONSOLE to configure a print server.

Determining which File Servers Should Be Serviced by the Print Server

NetWare's printing facilities offer you the capability of configuring a print server to service multiple file servers. By doing so, you can reduce the amount of configuration and equipment needed to service all your clients. When you select the option File Servers To Be Serviced from the Print Server Configuration menu, NetWare provides a window showing you the file servers this print server is configured to service. To add another server to this listing, press the Insert key and select the desired server from the listing of available servers. For detailed information on configuring your multi-server printing, refer to the heading "Printing in a Multi-Server Environment" later in this chapter.

> **Note**
>
> The NetWare print server can service a maximum of eight file servers.

Creating Notify Listings

While unfortunate, the time will come when some type of problem arises with your NetWare printing. To ensure the fastest response time to these failures, the print server can be configured so that printer errors are reported to a select group of users. By sending a message across the LAN, the print server notifies the selected users of various printer-related problems. You can create this listing by following these steps:

> **Note**
>
> This option is not available until a printer has been created on the print server.

VI

Network Printing

> **Note**
>
> The notify list is specific to the selected printer. If you have multiple printers on your print server for which you would like to set up notification, you must repeat the following steps for each configured printer.

1. Select Notify List for Printer from the Print Server Configuration Menu window and then, from the window of Defined Printers, the printer for which you want to create the listing.

2. After you select the printer, a window showing the current users to be notified appears. You can add a user or group to this listing by pressing the Insert key and selecting an ID from the Notify Candidates window.

> **Shortcut**
>
> You can add multiple users or groups at one time by highlighting each one and flagging them with the F5 key prior to pressing Enter.

3. Once an object (user or group) has been selected, NetWare presents one final window entitled Notify Intervals with two options—First and Next. The First option specifies how many seconds must go by before the first warning message is sent, while the Next parameter tells NetWare how often to repeat the error message until the problem is resolved.

> **Caution**
>
> Do not set these values too low. It can be rather annoying to receive a message on your PC every 30 seconds telling you the printer is out of service when it has only run out of paper.

Creating and Configuring Printers

Even though the print server has already been created, one of the most vital components is still missing—the printers. Using PCONSOLE, you can create printer assignments that can then be used to service the print queues on the server. You can create printers for your print server by following these steps:

1. When you select Printer Configuration from the Print Server Configuration Menu window, PCONSOLE presents you with a window entitled Configured Printers that lists all of the printers currently set up for the print server.

2. To create a printer, you must first select one of the openings available from the Configured Printers window (numbered 0 through 15). After making your selection, PCONSOLE presents you with a screen like the one shown in Figure 18.3. For your reference, each of the options shown on this screen is noted below.

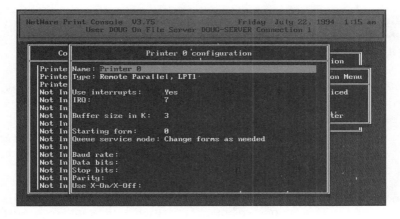

Fig. 18.3 Printer configuration screen of PCONSOLE.

> **Note**
>
> You can configure a maximum of 16 printers per print server, of which only five can be connected directly to the file server.

Name: The name field can be used to assign a name to the printer that appears on the print server console. Ideally, you should choose something descriptive. For example, the name field could be used to specify the make/model of a printer or the printer's location. The name field accepts a maximum of 47 characters.

Type: This field specifies the type of connection used for this printer. By selecting this option, NetWare displays a window with the following connection types you can use:

- *Local Parallel/Serial*—Used for a printer physically connected to the print server.

- *Remote Parallel/Serial*—Used for a printer physically connected to one of the workstations on the network.

- *Remote Other/Unknown*—Used with remote printers equipped with network cards (such as HP's JetDirect card).

> **Caution**
>
> Do not use the Remote Other/Unknown option unless you are specifically told to in the documentation of your remote printing hardware.

- *Defined Elsewhere*—Used only when you are configuring printing for a multi-server environment. Selecting this option tells NetWare the printer configuration has been defined on another file server. For detailed information on configuring multi-server printing services, refer to the heading "Printing in a Multi-Server Environment" later in this chapter.

Use interrupts: Interrupts tell the CPU a specific task must be completed. During the installation of your file server hardware, you most probably had to configure the interrupts used for the server hardware such as the printer ports, disk controllers, and so on. If you want to use interrupts for the printer, answer Yes in this field; otherwise, you can answer No and use the "polled" process. Polled is slower but does not require the use of a dedicated IRQ, which can be a valuable asset in the server!

IRQ: When you answer Yes to Use interrupts, you must then specify the interrupt you want used for the printer. This option must match up with the interrupt you configured when installing the workstation or file server hardware.

Buffer size in K: Specifies the amount of memory available for the printer's buffer. For most installations, the default value of 3K is sufficient.

Tip
If your printer stops and starts while printing a job, increasing the buffer size may resolve the problem.

Starting form: Specifies the form loaded in the printer when the print server first initializes. By default, NetWare assigns form 0 for this field but you can change it to any form you have created with the PRINTDEF utility. Refer to Chapter 21, "Printing Management," for information on creating forms.

Queue service mode: Tells NetWare how you want the printer to service requests that require different form types. By selecting this field, you are presented with the four options shown below:

- *Change forms as needed*: The printer prints all jobs as received. When a job arrives that requires a different form, the printer is paused and a request for a form change appears on the printer status console.

- *Minimize form changes across queues*: The printer prints all jobs in the highest priority queues that require the mounted form and then scans other queues with jobs that require the mounted form. Once these jobs have been cleared, the printer pauses and a request for a form change appears on the printer status console.

- *Minimize form changes within queues*: The printer prints all jobs in the highest priority queues that require the mounted form and it then processes the remaining print jobs.

■ *Service only currently mounted form*: The printer only services jobs that require the currently mounted form.

Baud rate: Used for serial printers only, this field determines how fast data can be transmitted to the printer. Refer to your printer and server documentation to determine the fastest acceptable baud rate.

Data bits: Used for serial printers only, this field specifies the number of bits used to form a character (between five and eight bits). Refer to your printer documentation to determine the number of bits that should be used.

Stop bits: Used for serial printers only, this field specifies the number of stop bits required for your printer. Refer to your printer documentation to determine the number of stop bits that should be used.

Parity: Used for serial printers only, this field specifies the parity required for your printer. Refer to your printer documentation to determine the number of stop bits that should be used.

Use X-On/X-Off: Used for serial printers only, this field specifies whether or not you want to use the X-ON/X-OFF transmission method. Refer to your printer documentation to determine whether or not your printer supports this type of transmission.

3. After you have made all the appropriate settings for the printer, save your configuration by pressing the Esc key and confirming that you want to save these changes.

Viewing or Setting Queues Serviced by a Printer

Probably the last step you take to configure your print server is to assign print queues to each of the defined printers. By assigning a queue to a printer, you are authorizing the print server to send any jobs it receives for that queue to the selected printer. You can assign a print queue to a printer by following these steps:

> **Note**
>
> These steps assume that you have already created the printers and queues on your server.

1. Select Queues Serviced by Printer from the Print Server Configuration Menu window and then select the desired printer from the listing of Defined Printers.

2. Once you have selected a printer, NetWare displays a listing of the print queues that have already been set up for this printer. You can add a new print queue to this listing by pressing the Insert key and then selecting a queue from the listing of Available Queues.

VI

Network Printing

3. After selecting the queue, the last step to adding the queue to the printer's listing is to specify the queue's priority. The priority is a numerical-based value, 1 being the highest, that tells NetWare how you want to service the printers. Jobs placed in queues with the highest priority are printed before jobs in any other queue.

Creating Print Queues

Note

RIGHTS REQUIRED TO COMPLETE TASK: YOU MUST BE A SUPERVISOR EQUIVALENT TO CREATE A PRINT QUEUE.

Print Queues are used as a type of holding area for print jobs. When a user on the file server requests a file or screen to be printed, the print job is first sent to the print queue to which it is captured. The job then remains in the print queue until such time that a printer is available to accept the job for printing.

You can create a print queue on the file server by following these steps:

1. From the Available Options main menu of PCONSOLE, select Print Queue Information to view the Print Queues window that lists all the queues currently configured.

2. To create a new queue, press the Insert key and enter the desired queue name at the New Print Queue Name: prompt.

Note

The print queue name can be a maximum of 47 characters.

After these two short steps, you have a fully operational print queue at your disposal. To ensure the queue that you created operates to your requirements, the following sections provide you with the detailed information you need to configure the queues you created.

Configuring Print Queues

After the print queue has been created, there are a few options available to you that can be used to customize how the queue operates. By selecting the desired print queue from the Print Queues window, a new window entitled Print Queue Information (see fig. 18.4) appears with options specific to the queue. For your reference, each of these options is discussed in the following sections.

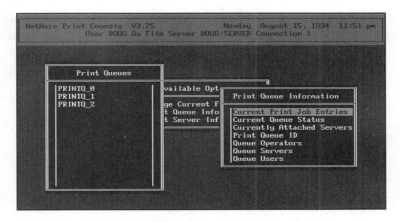

Fig. 18.4 The Print Queue Information window shown within PCONSOLE.

Current Print Job Entries

Selecting this option displays a listing of all the jobs currently in the queue. Refer to the heading "Viewing and Manipulating Jobs in the Print Queue" in Chapter 21, "Printing Management," for further information.

Current Queue Status

The Current Queue Status option displays some basic information on the queue, such as the number of jobs currently in the queue and whether users can submit jobs to the queue. For further information on this option, refer to the heading "Viewing and Changing the Status of a Print Queue" in Chapter 21, "Printing Management."

Currently Attached Servers

The information provided by selecting this option is for viewing purposes only and displays the names of the print servers currently servicing this queue.

Print Queue ID

When NetWare creates a print queue, it is assigned a unique number and a subdirectory of the SYSTEM directory is then created, based on this unique number, with an extension QDR. For example, if NetWare assigns the number 09000009 as the queue ID, a directory called 09000009.QDR is created in the SYSTEM directory. Within this directory, NetWare stores two hidden files that provide configuration information of the queue, and any print jobs that are sent to the queue. As the jobs are printed, NetWare deletes them from the queue directory.

By selecting this option, you can view the unique number assigned to the selected queue.

> **Note**
>
> Because NetWare stores print jobs as files in the print queue directory, if the file server goes down when there are still jobs in the queue, these jobs will still be available for printing when the server is brought back up.

Creating Print Queue Operators to Manage a Queue

Print queue operators can be assigned for each print queue to help the LAN administrator with the day-to-day management duties. You can assign a print queue operator by selecting Print Queue Operators from the Print Queue Information screen and then pressing the Insert key to select the desired operators from the listing of Queue Operator Candidates.

For detailed information on what print queue operators can do, please refer to the heading "Tasks that Operators and Managers Can Do" in Chapter 12, "Security Equivalences."

> **Note**
>
> By default, the SUPERVISOR ID is an operator for every print queue.

Determining Who Can and Cannot Use a Print Queue

When a print queue is created, by default, NetWare enables any user who is a member of the group EVERYONE to submit jobs to it. Depending on your specific requirements, the occasion may arise when you must restrict access to a print queue to a single user or a select group of users. Within PCONSOLE, you can restrict who can and cannot use a print queue by selecting the Queue Users option from the Print Queue Information window. After selecting this option, NetWare provides you with a listing of all the users and groups currently allowed to use the print queue. You can remove a user or group from this listing by highlighting the ID and pressing the Delete key, or, you can add a new user or group to this listing by pressing the Insert key and selecting the desired user ID or group from the listing of Queue User Candidates (see fig. 18.5).

> **Caution**
>
> Because NetWare assigns the group EVERYONE as a queue user, if you want to restrict access to the print queue for a select group of users, you must remove the EVERYONE group as a print queue user; otherwise, all members of this group (usually all users on the server) are able to submit jobs to the queue.

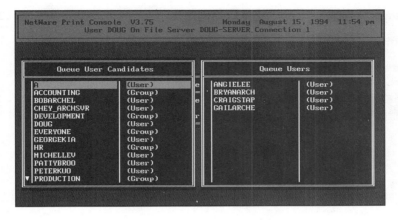

Fig. 18.5 Using PCONSOLE to allow additional users to use a print queue.

Printing in a Multi-Server Environment

> **Note**
>
> In this section, two terms are used when describing how to configure your muli-server printing—"home" file server and "serviced" file server. The main print server configuration is stored on the "home" file server. The print server configuration on the "serviced" file server is merely an extension of the printing services from the home server and only contains a very basic print server configuration used to assign the queues on the serviced file server to printers.

One aspect of printing with NetWare that tends to confuse some people is printing in a multi-server environment. When there is more than one file server on the network, you have the option of creating a print server that services queues from multiple file servers. By doing so, you can minimize the amount of configuration required to get the printing services up and running while reducing the amount of hardware required.

Before you even start to configure your multi-server printing services, document how it will all be set up. Many of the problems people encounter with their multi-server printing can be attributed to improper configuration. By documenting how the printing is set up beforehand, you minimize the chance of errors due to configuration. Your documentation should contain the following information:

- The proposed name of the print server

- The name of the "home" file server

- The names of the "serviced" file servers

- The print queues that are set up on each file server

- The quantity and types of printers that will be used

- The queues that will be serviced by each printer

> **Note**
>
> A single print server can service a maximum of eight file servers and 16 printers, so plan your printing services accordingly.

Once you have documented your proposed printing services, you can begin the configuration by following these five basic steps:

> **Note**
>
> For the sake of not repeating information already provided, the following steps assume you have already created a print server on your "home" file server. If you have not done so already, please refer to the headings "Creating the Print Server" and "Creating Print Queues," earlier in this chapter.

1. Within the print server configuration on the "home" file server, add the names of the file servers you want to be serviced by this print server using the File Servers To Be Serviced option of the selected print servers configuration. Refer to the heading "Determing which File Servers Should Be Serviced by the Print Server" earlier in this chapter for detailed information on how to do this.

2. Create the desired print queues on the "serviced" file servers. Refer to the heading "Creating Print Queues" earlier in this chapter for detailed information on how to do this.

3. Create the print server on the "serviced" file server. When asked for the name of the print server, you must enter the exact name of the print server you configured on the "home" file server. Refer to the heading "Creating the Print Server" earlier in this chapter for detailed information on how to do this.

4. Create the printers on the "serviced" file server for the print server. When creating the printer, you should select the same printer number as the one you chose in the print server configuration on the "home" file server. When you enter the printer configuration on the "serviced" file server, there are two fields you have to concern yourself with (refer to the heading "Creating and Configuring Printers" earlier in this chapter for detailed information on how to do this).

   Name: While you can enter anything you want in this field, you should enter the same name you chose within the printer configuration on the "home" server.

Type: In this field, you should select the Defined Elsewhere option as the print configuration is defined on the "home" server.

5. Assign print queues to the printers within the print server configuration maintained on the "serviced" file server. Refer to the heading "Viewing or Setting Queues Serviced by a Printer" earlier in this chapter for detailed information on how to do this.

After completing these steps, your multi-server printing is ready to go. To see how you can initialize your printing services, refer to Chapter 19, "Initializing Printing Services."

Chapter 19

Initializing Printing Services

Once you have configured your NetWare print server, you must decide if you will be running the print server on a dedicated PC or as a process on the file server. Both methods are acceptable, but there are a few pros and cons for each one.

In this section, we discuss some of the problems associated with each type of print server and more specifically:

- Configuring a dedicated print server
- Configuring a non-dedicated print server
- Configuring and initializing remote printers

Setting Up Your Dedicated Print Server

Running the print server on a dedicated PC alleviates any potential performance problems at the file server that can be caused by printing. Since a dedicated PC is being used, no additional memory or CPU time is required from the file server. While the performance of the file server is not affected as much, overall printing services will be slower since print jobs sent from a workstation must first travel to the file server, then to the dedicated print server on the network. In most cases, the slightly reduced performance is not a problem, but the associated cost is.

When running the print server on a dedicated PC, you must be willing to spend the money on a PC that does nothing but sit there, waiting to print jobs. To soften the financial blow, you can try using an older 286 PC as the workstation, but, if your printing is too slow, you may have to upgrade the workstation to at least a 386.

Setting up the dedicated print server is a fairly simple task compared to the other steps involved in configuring your printing services. The steps required to install your dedicated print server are discussed in the following headings.

Step 1: Setting Up the Workstation

The first step is to set up a PC on the network that is used as the dedicated print server. At a minimum, the PC should be a 286, but a 386 is preferred. For this stage, think of the PC as any other workstation on the network. Therefore, you must install a network card in the PC with all the appropriate drivers and the workstation shells or DOS requester. Before proceeding past this stage, test your installation by logging into the file server from this PC. If you cannot login to the server, double-check your installation. For detailed information on installing and configuring the workstation, refer to Chapter 4, "Installing Workstations."

Step 2: Editing the Workstation's NET.CFG File.

Once you have set up the PC and made sure you can access the file server from it, there are a couple of modifications that should be made to the NET.CFG file. Using a basic ASCII DOS editor (such as EDIT), add the following line to the NET.CFG file:

```
SPX CONNECTIONS=60
```

The next modification to the NET.CFG file is strictly voluntary. When initializing the print server, PSERVER.EXE needs to know on which file server the print server has been created. To make sure PSERVER looks for the appropriate file server, you either can specify the server name when loading PSERVER or you can use the Preferred Server statement in the NET.CFG file. By using the Preferred Server statement, the workstation establishes a connection with the desired file server when it is first turned on.

If you do not specify a file server name in the PSERVER load line, it checks the file server to which the workstation has been attached. Using a basic ASCII DOS editor (for example, EDIT) add the following line to the NET.CFG file (replace *file_server_name* with the name of the desired file server):

```
PREFERRED SERVER = file_server_name
```

Step 3: Making the Necessary Files Accessible

In addition to the workstation shell or the DOS Requester files, there are five files that must be accessible from the dedicated workstation:

PSERVER.EXE
IBM$RUN.OVL
SYS$ERR.DAT
SYS$MSG.DAT
SYS$HELP.DAT

These files are located in the PUBLIC directory of the file server and either can be copied to the local drives of the workstation or to another directory on the file server.

Tip

Keeping the files in a directory on the server makes your life much easier when performing upgrades, especially when there are multiple dedicated print servers. Instead of going to each dedicated workstation and upgrading multiple files, when on the server, you can upgrade the files from a single location.

Tip

If you are going to keep the files on the server, create a subdirectory in the LOGIN directory to store them. Since the LOGIN directory is the only directory accessible without actually logging into the server, this reduces the steps needed to run the PSERVER.EXE program. Instead of having to log in to the file server each time you load the print server, you can run the PSERVER.EXE program right after loading the workstation shell or DOS requester.

Step 4: Loading the Print Server

Once you have completed the first three steps, the only step left is to actually load the print server software. You can do so by using the following syntax from the directory where the print server files have been installed:

Note

If the print server files were installed on the file server in a directory other than the LOGIN directory or a subdirectory of LOGIN, you have to login to the file server before proceeding.

```
PSERVER [fileserver/]printserver
```

Based on the preceding syntax, replace:

fileserver with the name of the file server on which the print server configuration resides. The fileserver name is not needed in a single-server environment or when the Preferred Server setting was used appropriately (refer to Step 2 above).

printserver with the name of the print server you want to load.

EXAMPLE 1: To load the print server PS1 when the Preferred Server option has been set in the NET.CFG file, type the following:

PSERVER PS1

VI

EXAMPLE 2: To load the print server PS2 that was configured on the ACCOUNTING file server when the Preferred Server option has not been used, type the following from the command line:

PSERVER ACCOUNTING/PS2

Shortcut
You can add the PSERVER command to the workstation's AUTOEXEC.BAT file to have the print server load automatically when the workstation is turned on.

Setting Up Your Print Server as a Process on the File Server

Running the print server as a file server process is probably the easiest method available. When you use the PSERVER.NLM module, all print server functions are run directly on the file server console. Like any other modules, PSERVER.NLM can be loaded and unloaded at any time. Since the print server is run as a process directly on the file server, printing services can be faster than printing with a dedicated print server.

Caution
Before choosing this method, you first should determine if your file server can handle the additional load. If your server is already running at or near capacity, this method may actually result in slower performance for your printing services and may reduce the performance of the other file server functions.

Loading the print server as a process on the file server can be completed in one simple task. When you use the following syntax, NetWare loads the print server and begins servicing the printing requests:

```
LOAD PSERVER printserver_name [poll=XX] [delay=YY]
```

Based on the preceding syntax, replace:

printserver_name with the name of the print server you are loading.

poll=XX with the number of seconds you want PSERVER to check the queues for jobs (such as poll=5). This setting is optional and when left out, PSERVER checks the print queues every fifteen seconds for jobs waiting to be printed.

delay=YY with the number of seconds you want used to delay printing to the parallel port. In some cases, printing to the parallel port on a 486 or pentium computer can result in the print job being corrupted. If this happens to you, try using this option (such as delay=10).

EXAMPLE: To load the print server PS1 and have it check the print queues for jobs every five seconds, type the following from the command line:

LOAD PSERVER PS1 POLL=5

Tip
To ensure the print server loads whenever the server is first booted, you can add the command to the server's AUTOEXEC.NCF file stored in the SYSTEM directory.

Setting Up Remote Printers

Once the print server has been brought on-line, it is then time to initialize any printers attached to a LAN workstation that services network print queues. Using a utility called RPRINTER at the workstation, a printer that is physically connected to the workstation can then service these queues.

There are two methods for using the RPRINTER utility—as a menuing system or from the command line. Either method will do, but most people choose the command line method since it allows you to automate the process by inserting the command in the workstation's AUTOEXEC.BAT file.

Files Required by RPRINTER

Before discussing the two methods that are available to you, there is a little bit of preparation that must be done. To run the RPRINTER utility, there are six files that must be accessible from the workstation:

RPRINTER.EXE
RPRINTER.HLP
IBM$RUN.OVL
SYS$ERR.DAT
SYS$MSG.DAT
SYS$HELP.DAT

These files are located in the PUBLIC directory of the file server and can either be copied to the local drives of the workstation or to another directory on the file server.

VI

Network Printing

Tip

Keeping the files in a directory on the server makes your life much easier when performing upgrades, especially when there are multiple stations using RPRINTER. Instead of going to each dedicated workstation and upgrading multiple files, when on the server, you can upgrade the files in a single location.

Tip

If you are going to keep the files on the server, create a subdirectory within the LOGIN directory to store them. Since the LOGIN directory is the only directory that is accessible without actually logging into the server, this reduces the steps needed to run the RPRINTER.EXE program. Instead of having to log into the file server each time you want to initialize a remote printer, you can run the RPRINTER.EXE program right after loading the workstation shell or DOS requester.

Initializing a Remote Printer from a Menu

With the necessary files available from the workstation, you can use RPRINTER as a menu utility by following these steps:

Note

You cannot load or unload a remote printer from within Windows. These tasks must be completed before you enter Windows or after exiting Windows.

---

1. After typing RPRINTER from the command line, a menu entitled Available Print Servers appears that lists all the print servers currently on-line. From this listing, select the desired print server.

2. Once the print server has been selected, a listing of remote printers that have not been loaded elsewhere is shown. These printers are those whose type have been configured in PCONSOLE as being Remote. From this listing, once you select the desired printer, RPRINTER initializes the connection between your workstation and the print server.

Tip

In some instances, you may want to load a printer in "polled" mode. By doing so, you are telling the printing facilities you want to ignore the configured interrupt settings. When using the menuing method, you can load printers in "polled" mode by typing **RPRINTER -P** from the command line instead of **RPRINTER**.

Initializing a Remote Printer from the Command Line

Using RPRINTER from the command line provides the user with increased functionality over the menuing method. Unlike the menuing method that can only be used to initialize a remote printer, from the command line, RPRINTER can be used to complete any of the following tasks:

- Initialize a remote printer

- Uninstall a remote printer

- Review the remote printer configuration and status

You can complete any of the tasks shown above by using the following syntax:

```
RPRINTER [print_server_name printer_number] [-R] [-S] [-P]
```

Based on the syntax above, replace:

print_server_name with the name of the print server.

printer_number with the printer number assigned in PCONSOLE.

The last three options are used as follows:

- The -R switch removes the specified remote printer.

- The -S switch displays the status of the specified remote printer.

- The -P switch loads the specified printer in "polled" mode, thereby ignoring the configured interrupts.

> **Note**
>
> You cannot load or unload a remote printer from within Windows. These tasks must be completed before you enter Windows or after exiting Windows.

EXAMPLE 1: To initialize remote printer number 5 from the PS1 print server at your workstation, type the following from the command line:

RPRINTER PS1 5

EXAMPLE 2: To initialize the remote printer number 2 from print server PSNTWQUICK and ignore the established interrupt settings, type the following from the command line:

RPRINTER PSNTWQUICK 2 -P

VI

Network Printing

EXAMPLE 3: To remove printer number 3 of print server PS2 from your workstation, thereby removing it from active service, type the following from the command line:

RPRINTER PS2 3 -R

Tip

Instead of specifying the print server name and printer number when unloading a remote printer (for instance, RPRINTER PS1 0 -R), type **RPRINTER -R** to remove the printer that was loaded last.

Tip

To automate the loading of the remote printer software, some people load the RPRINTER command within the workstation's AUTOEXEC.BAT file. While this works fine for some installations, others may find that when the workstation is warm booted, the RPRINTER software does not load properly. If you are having problems reloading RPRINTER when you warm boot your PC, try adding an RPRINTER command with the -R switch prior to the load line. For example, if your AUTOEXEC.BAT file currently has a line to load a remote printer such as:

```
RPRINTER PSNTWQUICK 0
```

Try editing your AUTOEXEC.BAT to include the RPRINTER command with the -R switch prior to this line such as:

```
RPRINTER PSNTWQUICK 0 -R
RPRINTER PSNTWQUICK 0
```

Chapter 20

Sending Print Jobs

NetWare's printing facilities provide you with a great deal of functionality when you want to send a simple print screen or a file to be printed. Using one of NetWare's printing commands, you can customize how the job is sent and how the printer handles it.

In this section, we discuss the different commands involved with printing to a network printer and specifically:

- Using the CAPTURE command to attach to print queues
- Using the NPRINT command to print files to a network printer
- Submitting jobs directly to a print queue from PCONSOLE

Connecting Your Workstation to a Print Queue

One of the key files involved in printing on a LAN is the CAPTURE utility. Unlike the NPRINT utility whose basic function is to send jobs to a print queue, CAPTURE is used to perform one of three tasks:

- To enable nonnetwork-aware applications to print jobs to a network printer
- To save data, such as screen captures, to a file
- To print screens to a network printer

To use CAPTURE, use the following syntax:

    CAPTURE [option(s)]

Based on the preceding syntax, replace:

option(s) with one or more of the options found in Table 20.1

Tip

Instead of using the CAPTURE command with multiple variables on a regular basis, you can create print jobs with PRINTCON that group these commands into a single "job." Once created, you would then only have to use the *Job* parameter with CAPTURE. For further information on print jobs, refer to the heading "Working with Print Job Configurations" in Chapter 21, "Printing Management."

Table 20.1 Parameters that can be used with the CAPTURE command.

Parameter	Abbr.	Example	Description
AUTOENDCAP	AU	CAPTURE AU	When used, NetWare does not complete your print request until you exit from the application you are using.
BANNER=*text*	B=*text*	CAPTURE B= CONFIDENTIAL	Specifies up to 12 characters you want printed on the lower half of your banner page.
COPIES=#	C=#	CAPTURE C=2	Specifies how many copies you want of each job that is sent, up to a maximum of 255 copies.
CREATE=*file*	CR=*file*	CAPTURE CR=F:\USERS\ CSTAPLES\SCREEN.TXT	Instead of sending output to the print queue, CAPTURE can redirect the information to a file. You must have sufficient trustee rights to create the file in the directory specified.
FORM=#	F=#	CAPTURE F=12	Specifies a form you created with the PRINTDEF utility. By using forms, you can distinguish between different types or sizes of paper that should be loaded into the printer. You can either specify the form name or number with this option.

Parameter	Abbr.	Example	Description
FORMFEED	FF	CAPTURE FF	Tells NetWare that a form feed (page eject) command should be issued to the printer after the job is completed. Most applications do this normally, thus, using this option may cause NetWare to print a blank page after every print job.
JOB=*job_name*	J=*job_name*	CAPTURE J=STATEMENTS	Specifies a print job config file you created with PRINTCON that should be used. Print job config files contain the same type of information you would issue with the CAPTURE command. Using a print job config file reduces the amount of work needed to issue a CAPTURE command because you would not have to enter all the other variables at the command line.
LOCAL=#	L=#	CAPTURE L=2	Specifies which printer port you want captured (LPT1=1, LPT2=2, LPT3=3). By capturing different ports, you can be captured to multiple queues at the same time.
KEEP	K	CAPTURE K	Under normal situations, if your PC is disconnected from the network while sending a print job (such as during a power failure), NetWare discards the partial print job. Using the Keep parameter, you can instruct NetWare to print whatever it receives, even if it is a partial job. This parameter is mostly used when issuing a print request that could take a long time.
NAME=*name*	NAM=*name*	CAPTURE NAM=BRYANKENT	Specifies the name that should be printed in the upper half of the banner sheet, up to 12 characters. When left out, NetWare uses the ID of the user sending the job as the name.

VI

Network Printing

(continues)

Table 20.1 Continued.

Parameter	Abbr.	Example	Description
NOAUTOENDCAP	NA	CAPTURE NA	Tells NetWare not to send the print job to the queue when exiting or entering an application. When used, NetWare does not complete the print request until the user types ENDCAP at the workstation. This parameter is usually required when printing to PostScript printers.
NOBANNER	NB	CAPTURE NB	Tells NetWare you do not want a banner page to be printed before the job.
NOFORMFEED	NFF	CAPTURE NFF	Tells NetWare you do not want a form feed (page eject) command sent after the print job. This parameter is usually required when printing to PostScript printers.
NONOTIFY	NNOTI	CAPTURE NNOTI	Tells NetWare you do not want to be notified when your print job has completed. This option is only needed if you are using a print job that has the notification enabled.
NOTABS	NT	CAPTURE NT	Tells NetWare you do not want it to replace the tab characters with spaces. Generally, you use this parameter when printing to PostScript printers or if you are having problems printing graphics jobs.
NOTIFY	NOTI	CAPTURE NOTI	When you use this parameter with your CAPTURE statement, you are requesting NetWare to send you a message after your print job has completed.
QUEUE=*print_queue*	Q=*print_queue*	CAPTURE Q=PRINTQ1	Tells NetWare which print queue to which you want to print.

Parameter	Abbr.	Example	Description
SERVER=*server_name*	S=*server_name*	CAPTURE S=FS1	Tells NetWare which file server to which you want to print.
SHOW	SH	CAPTURE SH	Forces CAPTURE to show you your current capture settings.
TABS=#	T=#	CAPTURE T=10	Tells NetWare the number of spaces you want CAPTURE to substitute for each TAB character found within the print job. The default value is 8 and the acceptable range is between 1 and 18.
TIMEOUT=*seconds*	TI=*seconds*	CAPTURE TI=60	Specifies how long NetWare should wait before closing the print request from the time the print request is actually made. If you are having problems with jobs not being sent in their entirety, try increasing the timeout from the default of five seconds. The acceptable range for the timeout field is from 0 to 1000; 0 disables the timeout.

EXAMPLE 1: To capture the workstation to the PRINTQ0 queue on the default server with a timeout value of two seconds without a banner, type the following from the command line:

CAPTURE Q=PRINTQ0 TI=2 NB

EXAMPLE 2: To capture the workstation to the ACCOUNTING print queue on file server FS1 with a timeout value of 25 seconds with no banner, and no formfeed, type the following from the command line:

CAPTURE Q=ACCOUNTING S=FS1 TI=25 NB NFF

Tip
To ensure that users can print when they log into the file server, add the CAPTURE command with the associated options to one of the login scripts using the # login script command.

VI

Network Printing

Tip
If you have not captured to a print queue and there are no printers attached to the workstation, the workstation may hang if the user attempts to print a screen. To alleviate this problem, add the command LOCAL PRINTERS=0 to the NET.CFG file.

Stopping the Capturing Process

NetWare comes equipped with a utility known as ENDCAP that is used to end the capturing of a workstation to a print queue. You generally use ENDCAP in one of two situations:

■ When you want to stop capturing to all print queues

■ If you used the NOAUTOENDCAP parameter with CAPTURE or your timeout value was too high, using ENDCAP closes your print job immediately. Once closed, the next available printer is able to service it

To use ENDCAP, follow this syntax:

```
ENDCAP [option(s)]
```

Based on the preceding syntax, replace:

option(s) with one of the options noted in Table 20.2.

Table 20.2 Options that can be used with the ENDCAP utility.

Option	Abbr.	Example	Description
Local=#	L=#	ENDCAP L=1	Ends the capture of a specific LPT port.
ALL		ENDCAP ALL	Ends the capturing of all LPT ports.
Cancel	C	ENDCAP C	Ends the capturing of LPT1 and discards all data sent to the port without printing it.
CancelLocal=#	CL=#	ENDCAP CL=2	Ends the capturing of a specific LPT port and discards all data sent to the port without printing it.

Printing Files from the Command Line

The NPRINT command is used when you want to print a DOS ASCII file or a file that has been properly formatted by an application for your printer to a NetWare print queue. You can use NPRINT by following this syntax:

```
NPRINT path [option(s)]
```

Based on the preceding syntax, replace:

path with the directory path of the file to which you want to print, including the file name.

option(s) with one or more of the options shown in Table 20.3. If no options are specified, NPRINT uses the default print configuration specified in PRINTCON.

Tip

Instead of using the NPRINT command with multiple variables on a regular basis, you can create print jobs with PRINTCON that group these commands into a single "job." Once created, you would then only have to use the Job parameter with NPRINT.

Tip

You can print multiple files from the single command by separating each file name with a comma.

Table 20.3 Parameters that can be used with the NPRINT command.

Parameter	Abbr.	Example	Description
BANNER=*text*	B=*text*	NPRINT TEST.PAG Q=PRINTQ1 B=RUSH-DELIVER	Specifies up to 12 characters you want printed on the lower half of your banner page.
COPIES=#	C=#	NPRINT FILE.PRN C=14 Q=PRINTQ1	Specifies how many copies you want of each job that is sent, up to a maximum of 999 copies.
DELETE	D	NPRINT CONFIDENT.DOC D	Deletes the file you are printing as soon as the print job is sent to the queue.

VI

Network Printing

(continues)

Table 20.3 Continued.

Parameter	Abbr.	Example	Description
FORM=#	F=#	NPRINT WORK.FLO F=21	Specifies a specific form you created with the PRINTDEF utility. By using forms, you can distinguish between different types or sizes of paper that should be loaded into the printer. You can either specify the form name or the form number with this option.
FORMFEED	FF	NPRINT ASSIGN.DOC FF	Tells NetWare a form feed (page eject) command should be issued to the printer after the job is completed.
JOB=#	J=#	NPRINT RAISES.WP5 J=HR Q=HRQ1	Specifies a print job config file you created with PRINTCON that should be used. Print job config files contain the same type of information you would issue with NPRINT from the command line. Using a print job config file reduces the amount of work needed to issue an NPRINT command because you would not have to enter all the other variables at the command line.
NAME=*name*	NAM=*name*	NPRINT PERSONAL.DOC S=FS1 NAM=BRYANKENT	Specifies the name that should be printed in the upper half of the banner sheet, up to 12 characters. When left out, NetWare uses the ID of the user sending the job as the name.
NOBANNER	NB	NPRINT SAMPLE.TXT NB	Tells NetWare you do not want a banner page to be printed before the job.
NOFORMFEED	NFF	NPRINT SAMPLE2.TXT NFF	Tells NetWare you do not want a form feed (page eject) command sent after the print job. This parameter is usually required when printing to PostScript printers.

Parameter	Abbr.	Example	Description
NONOTIFY	NNOTI	NPRINT YASQY.001 NNOTI	Tells NetWare you do not want to be notified when your print job has completed. This option is only needed if you are using a print job that has the notification enabled.
NOTABS	NT	NPRINT NTWQUICK.DJA NT	Tells NetWare you do not want to replace the tab characters with spaces. Generally, you use this parameter when printing to PostScript printers or if you are having problems printing graphics jobs.
NOTIFY	NOTI	NPRINT NEWFILE.PRN NOTI	Requests NetWare to send you a message after your print job has completed.
PRINTSERVER= *print_server_name*	PS= *print_server_name*	NPRINT MOVE.PRN PS=EBO-1	Specifies the print server to which you want to send the print job.
QUEUE=*print_queue*	Q=*print_queue*	NPRINT CHAPT2.DOC Q=PRINTQ3	Tells NetWare the print queue to which you want to print.
SERVER=*file_server*	S=*file_server*	NPRINT FILENAME.TXT S=FS2	Tells NetWare the file server to which you want to print.
TABS=#	T=#	NPRINT TESTPG.HG T=1	Tells NetWare the number of spaces you want NPRINT to substitute for each TAB character found within the print job. The default value is 8 and the acceptable range is between 1 and 18.

EXAMPLE 1: To print the file SUPPORT.TXT to the PRINTQ0 queue on the FS1 file server with a banner called DELIVER, type the following from the command line:

NPRINT SUPPORT.TXT Q=PRINTQ0 S=FS1 B=DELIVER

EXAMPLE 2: To print two copies each of the files TEST1.TXT and TEST2.TXT to the PRINTQ1 queue on the default file server, type the following from the command line:

NPRINT TEST1.TXT,TEST2.TXT Q=PRINTQ1 C=2

VI

Network Printing

EXAMPLE 3: To print the file SALARY.TXT located in the SYS:\DATA directory to the HR print queue without a banner, type the following from the command line:

NPRINT SYS:\DATA\SALARY.TXT Q=HR NB

Tip
Wild cards can be used with the NPRINT utility. For example, to print all files in the current directory with the extension TXT to the ACCOUNTING queue, type **NPRINT *.TXT Q=ACCOUNTING** from the command line.

Printing Files from within PCONSOLE

Note
RIGHTS REQUIRED TO COMPLETE TASK: YOU MUST BE IN THE PRINT QUEUE'S LISTING OF "QUEUE US-ERS;" OTHERWISE, YOU CANNOT SUBMIT A JOB TO THE QUEUE, REGARDLESS OF WHETHER OR NOT YOU ARE A SUPERVISOR EQUIVALENT OR PRINT QUEUE OPERATOR.

Previous discussions showed you how to print a file from the command line. One usually over-looked feature is the ability to print a file right from within the PCONSOLE utility. In most cases, printing a file is achieved from within a third-party application or by using the NPRINT utility from the command line. Using the PCONSOLE utility, you can insert a job directly into a print queue by following these steps:

1. From the Available Options main menu of PCONSOLE, select Print Queue Information and then the desired print queue from the Print Queues window.

2. After selecting the desired queue, PCONSOLE displays a new window entitled Print Queue Information that provides options specific to the selected queue. From this screen, you can select Current Print Job Entries which displays all the jobs currently in the queue.

3. While viewing the screen of current queue jobs, you can add a new job directly to the queue by pressing the Insert key and specifying the location of the file you want to print in the Select Directory to Print From window. After specifying the directory and pressing En-ter, PCONSOLE displays a window entitled Available Files that lists all the files in the direc-tory (see fig. 20.1). From this screen, highlight the file you want to print and press the Enter key.

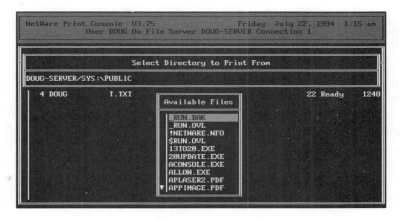

Fig. 20.1 Adding a new job to the print queue from within PCONSOLE.

Shortcut

Instead of submitting a single file, you can flag multiple files to be added to the queue by scrolling through the listing and pressing the F5 key on each of the files before pressing Enter. Alternatively, you can flag multiple files at once by pressing F6 and using a Tag Filter. A Tag Filter tells NetWare you want it to flag multiple files based on certain criteria. For example, if you create a Tag Filter for *.TXT, NetWare automatically tags all files with the extension TXT.

---

4. After selecting the file, a new window appears, showing you all the print job configurations currently available on the server. At this point, you should select the job configuration you want to use.

5. The final step to submitting the job involves a window entitled New Print Job to be Submitted that enables you to customize how you want this job to be handled. After making the changes and pressing the Esc key, you are asked to confirm that you want PCONSOLE to save the job. Once saved, it is submitted into the queue and printed as soon as a printer is available.

VI

Network Printing

Chapter 21

Printing Management

When some people configure their network printing, they do so at a very basic level. The print server is configured and brought on-line so the users can get their documents from their PC to a printer. While this is all well and good for some, others want to take a little more control over what is being printed and how.

One of the nice things about NetWare's printing facilities is that there are several tools available to you to "personalize" your printing services as well as manage them. In this section, we discuss printing management and specifically:

- Using and modifying printing devices
- Creating form types
- Creating and using print jobs
- Managing print queues
- Managing the print server and network printers

Defining Your Printing Resources

> **Note**
>
> RIGHTS REQUIRED TO COMPLETE TASK: YOU MUST BE A SUPERVISOR EQUIVALENT TO CREATE OR EDIT FORMS AND PRINTING DEVICES.

Depending on the size of your LAN and your organization, printing can be a very complex facility. While some companies may only use one type of printer and standard plain paper to print with, others may have a variety of printers and paper they use. To keep all this information organized and available to the user, NetWare includes a utility known as PRINTDEF.

When you use PRINTDEF, you can create a database of information regarding the different types of paper and the printers you use. Once created, you then can take advantage of some of the options available with the other NetWare printing commands such as those listed below:

- The PRINTCON utility uses the PRINTDEF database when configuring print jobs for information regarding the different types of forms and printer functions that are available.

- The FORMS options of the CAPTURE and NPRINT utilities rely on the PRINTDEF database for information regarding the different types of forms that have been created.

- The JOB options of the CAPTURE and NPRINT utilities rely on the jobs created in the PRINTCON utility that, in turn, relies on the PRINTDEF databases.

- The PCONSOLE utility relies on the PRINTDEF databases to determine how printing requests should be handled and for information regarding the types of forms and printer functions that are available.

Creating a Database of Printer Types

At any given time, there are probably more makes and models of printers than you could possibly imagine. While they all serve the same purpose, to print your documents, the manner in which they complete their tasks will vary between makes and even between models.

To ensure that you can use all your printers to their full potential, you can create a database of printer device information that can be used to view or modify the functions the printer can complete. Under the following headings, you see how you can load, view, and modify your printer's device files.

Loading a New Printing Device

Before you can view or modify a printer device file, you must first import one into the printing database stored in file form as NET$PRN.DAT in the PUBLIC directory. Printing device files are known as PDF files, due to their extension, and can be found on the configuration disks supplied by your printer manufacturer or, if you're lucky, Novell may have one available for your specific printer. Alternately, if you do not have a PDF file available, you even can create your own!

> **Note**
>
> The PDF files supplied by Novell are placed in the PUBLIC directory during the installation of your file server.

Loading a Device with a PDF File. If you have the printer's PDF file, whether it was supplied by Novell or you have it on a diskette, you can load it into the printer device database by following these steps:

1. From the PrintDef Options main menu of PRINTDEF, select Print Devices and then Import Print Device from the Print Device Options menu.

2. After selecting the import option, PRINTDEF presents you with the prompt Source Directory where you then must specify where the PDF file can be found (see fig. 21.1). At this point, the steps you take depend on where the PDF file is stored:

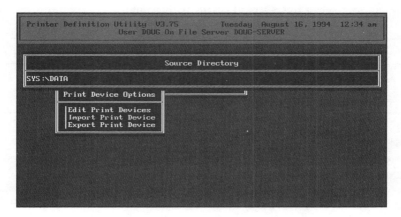

Fig. 21.1 Importing a print device definition with PRINTDEF.

- If the PDF file is stored in the current directory, just press the Enter key.

- If the PDF file is stored in another directory, but on the current file server, backspace over the directory name (but not the server and volume name) and enter the appropriate directory name. For example, if your current directory is DATA and your current file server is FS1, the Source Directory prompt displays, by default, FS1/SYS:\DATA. If your PDF file is stored in the PUBLIC directory, backspace over DATA and type in PUBLIC so the window shows FS1/SYS:\PUBLIC. Once the Source Directory prompt displays the appropriate location, press the Enter key to continue.

- If the PDF file is stored on a local disk drive, backspace over the text placed by default in the Source Directory prompt, press Insert and then select the local drive letter. After specifying the drive letter, PRINTDEF then asks you for the appropriate directory name. Once the Source Directory prompt displays the appropriate location, press Esc until it is the current window and then press the Enter key.

- If the PDF file is stored on another file server, backspace over the text placed by default in the Source Directory prompt, press Insert and then select, from the listing provided, a server to which you are attached. If you want to import the file from a server that you are not attached to, press the Insert key again to select another file server on the network. You then need to provide PRINTDEF with your ID and password for the other file server as required. After specifying the server, PRINTDEF then

VI

Network Printing

asks you for the appropriate volume and directory name. Once the Source Directory prompt displays the appropriate location, press Esc until it is the current window and then press the Enter key.

3. Once the appropriate directory has been selected, PRINTDEF checks the directory for all available PDF files and the results are displayed in a window entitled Available .PDFs. From this window, select the desired PDF file by highlighting it and pressing Enter.

Shortcut
You can add multiple PDF files at one time by flagging each one with the F5 key before pressing Enter to select the files.

Creating a New Device. If you have a printer for which Novell has not provided a PDF file and you do not have the configuration disks provided by the manufacturer, you can create a new device by following the steps below:

1. From the PrintDef Options main menu of PRINTDEF, select Print Devices and then Edit Print Devices from the Print Device Options window.

2. After selecting the Edit option, PRINTDEF provides you with a window entitled Defined Print Devices. You can create a new print device by pressing the Insert key and entering the new device name in the window provided (up to a maximum of 32 characters).

Editing Currently Loaded Printing Devices

When you use PRINTDEF, you can edit any of the currently loaded printing devices to alter the manner in which they operate. By changing or adding new escape sequences, you can take better control of how your printer operates.

You can edit a print device by following the steps below:

1. From the PrintDef Options main menu of PRINTDEF, select Print Devices and then Edit Print Devices from the Print Device Options window.

2. After selecting Print Device Options, a window entitled Defined Print Devices appears, listing all the printer devices currently defined on the server. You can edit any of these devices by highlighting the device name and pressing the Enter key.

3. Once the device has been selected, a new menu entitled Edit Device Options appears; it contains two options:

   Device Modes: This option views or creates new modes for the selected printer. In basic terms, a mode is a grouping of printer escape sequences that tell the printer what you want it to do. For example, you could create a device mode called *condensed* that would first reset the printer and then provide it with all the necessary information to print your text in a condensed format.

Note
The device modes created are used when configuring print jobs with the PRINTCON utility.

Tip
Using device modes is an excellent way of printing documents in certain fonts. While Windows-based applications usually enable you to pick from a variety of fonts, DOS-based applications can be very limiting. By creating different modes for the desired fonts, you can use these modes in the different print job configurations to acheive the desired effect.

Device Functions: This option views or creates new functions for the selected printer. By creating a new function, you are assigning a name to a series of "escape sequences" used to control how the printer performs certain tasks. While this may sound similar to a Device Mode, an easy way to distinguish between the two is that a Device Mode can be made up of one or more functions. For example, in the description of the Device Modes, you saw that you can create a device mode that would reset the printer and then print in condensed format. In this case, the Mode is made up of two functions, a reset function and a condensed function.

Note
Refer to your printer documentation to review the exact escape sequences it can accept.

VI

Network Printing

4. By selecting Device Mode, you are presented with a window showing you all the modes for the current device (see fig. 21.2). You can view the functions of each mode by highlighting the mode and pressing the Enter key or you can add a new mode by pressing the Insert key and specifying the new mode name, up to 32 characters. To add a function to the mode, select the mode by highlighting it and pressing Enter, then press the Insert key to select a function currently defined for the device.

5. By selecting Device Functions, you are presented with a window showing you all the functions for the current device. You can add a new function by pressing the Insert Key and entering the function name (up to 32 characters) and the desired escape sequence. Once the function has been created, it cannot be utilized until added to one of the device's modes (refer to Step 4).

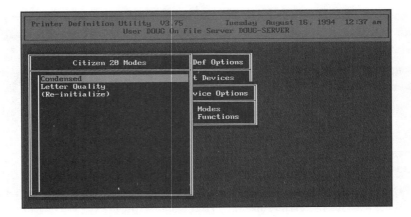

Fig. 21.2 Reviewing the device modes of a selected printer device using the PRINTDEF utility.

Exporting a Printing Device to a File

Since PRINTDEF uses a single database file (NET$PRN.DAT) to store your printer database, it also provides you with a method of extracting device information to a PDF file that then can be imported into another file server's database. The device you extract into a PDF file maintains all the modifications you have made to its modes and functions.

> **Note**
>
> If you created your own printer device, this is the only way you can use the information on another server unless you want to recreate it from scratch.

You can extract this information to a file by following these steps:

1. From the PrintDef Options main menu of PRINTDEF, select Print Devices and then Export Print Device from the Print Device Options menu.

2. After you select the export option, PRINTDEF presents you with a window entitled Defined Print Devices that contains a listing of all print devices currently configured on the server. From this listing, select the device you want to export and press the Enter key.

> **Note**
>
> You can only export one print device at a time.

3. Once you have selected the device, a prompt entitled Destination Directory appears where you must then specify where the PDF file should be created. At this point, the steps you take depend on where you want the file to be created:

- If you want the PDF file to be created in the current directory, just press the Enter key.

- If you want the PDF file to be created in another directory, but on the current file server, backspace over the directory name (but not the server and volume name) and enter the appropriate directory name. For example, if your current directory is DATA and your current file server is FS1, the Destination Directory prompt displays, by default, FS1/SYS:\DATA. If you want to create the PDF file in the PUBLIC directory, backspace over DATA and type in PUBLIC so the window shows FS1/SYS:\PUBLIC. Once the Destination Directory prompt displays the appropriate locations, press the Enter key to continue.

- If you want the PDF file to be created on a local disk drive, backspace over the text placed by default in the Destination Directory prompt, press Insert and then select the local drive letter. After specifying the drive letter, PRINTDEF then asks you for the appropriate directory name. Once the Destination Directory prompt displays the appropriate location, press Esc until it is the current window and then press the Enter key.

- If you want the PDF file to be created on another file server, backspace over the text placed by default in the Destination Directory prompt, press the Insert key and then, from the listing provided, select one of the servers to which you are attached. To create the file on a server you are not attached to, press the Insert key again to select another file server on the network. You then must provide PRINTDEF with your ID and password for the other file server as required. After specifying the server, PRINTDEF asks you for the appropriate volume and directory name. Once the Destination Directory prompt displays the appropriate location, press Esc until it is the current window and then press the Enter key.

4. Once the appropriate directory has been selected, PRINTDEF asks you to specify the name of the file you want it to create in a window entitled Export File Name. The name you specify must be a maximum of eight characters without an extension. After you enter the file name and pressing the Enter key, PRINTDEF then creates the named file in the specified directory.

Creating Form Types

When you are printing documents, the time will most probably come when you want to use a different type of paper. With NetWare you have two choices—you either can send your print job as normal and rush to the printer to change the paper in time, or you can tell NetWare which type of paper you want to use.

Using the PRINTDEF utility, you can create different codes that will be associated with the various types of paper you use. When a print server is configured, or first brought on-line, the SUPERVISOR or print server operator can tell PCONSOLE what type of paper is loaded in the printer using these form codes. If you use these when sending a print request, NetWare's printing facilities ask you to mount the correct type of paper in the printer when a different form is currently in use.

You can create a variety of forms by following the steps below:

1. From the PrintDef Options main menu of PRINTDEF, select Forms to view the forms currently in use on your server. You can create a new form by pressing the Insert key.

2. After you press Insert, NetWare provides you with a new window entitled Form Definition. This window contains four fields you use to define your required form type (see fig. 21.3). These fields are:

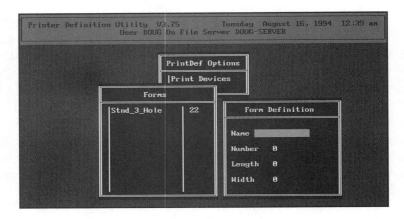

Fig. 21.3 Creating forms with the PRINTDEF utility.

Name: Specifies the name you want associated with your form type. You can enter up to twelve characters that help you remember what the form is for. For example, if you are creating a form type for 8 1/2-x-11, three-hole-punched paper, use a form name of Stnd_3_Hole.

> **Note**
>
> The first letter of your form name must be an alpha character.

Number: Similar in function to the Name field, the Number distinguishes the form you are creating from all other form types on the server. The form number must be between 0 and 255 and it must be unique on the server.

> **Tip**
>
> When numbering your forms, you may want to assign certain ranges for the different types of forms. For example, forms 0 through 20 could be for different types of statement paper, and forms 21 through 40 for different types of letterhead.

Length: The Length field specifies how many lines can be printed per page. The value must be between 1 and 255 and is for your reference only. Your printer and application software ultimately determine how many lines can be printed per page.

Width: The Width field specifies how many columns can be printed per line. The value must be between 1 and 99 and is for your reference only. Your printer and application software ultimately determine how many columns can be printed per line.

3. After you have entered all the required information, you can save your changes by pressing Esc and then confirming that you want to save your form. At this point, PRINTDEF returns you to the forms window where you then see your newly created form added to the listing. From here, you can either create another form (refer to Step 2) or you can leave PRINTDEF by pressing Esc twice and confirming that you want to leave PRINTDEF.

4. If you created any new forms, and you are exiting from PRINTDEF, you have to confirm if you want PRINTDEF to save your changes.

> **Note**
>
> When you save your new form types, PRINTDEF updates the NET$PRN.DAT file stored in the PUBLIC directory.

Working with Print Job Configurations

There are so many things for users and administrators to remember regarding NetWare that life can seem difficult, especially with respect to printing. It is at times like this a utility such as PRINTCON can really come to good use.

If you are familiar with the NPRINT or CAPTURE commands, you already know there are numerous parameters available for each. Instead of having to remember each of these parameters, and to make your printing services more streamlined, you can use the PRINTCON utility to create print "jobs." In basic terms, a print job is a type of configuration file that defines a variety of parameters. In the case of NPRINT and CAPTURE, the print job configuration can group the different parameters into the single configuration file. Instead of specifying several parameters when using NPRINT and CAPTURE, you can use a single parameter, JOB, to specify the print job you create.

Creating and Editing Print Job Configurations

When you use the PRINTCON utility, you can create or edit your own customized print jobs by following the steps below:

VI

Network Printing

1. From the Available Options main menu of PRINTCON, select Edit Print Job Configurations.

2. After selecting the edit option, PRINTCON displays a window entitled Print Job Configurations that lists all the print jobs currently configured on the server. To edit one of the print jobs listed in this window, highlight the job and press the Enter key. Otherwise, you can create a new print job by pressing the Insert key and specifying the new job name in the window provided.

3. Whether you selected a current print job configuration or you created a new one, PRINTCON presents you with another window providing the configuration information for the selected job (see fig. 21.4). This window contains several parameters, each of which is explained below:

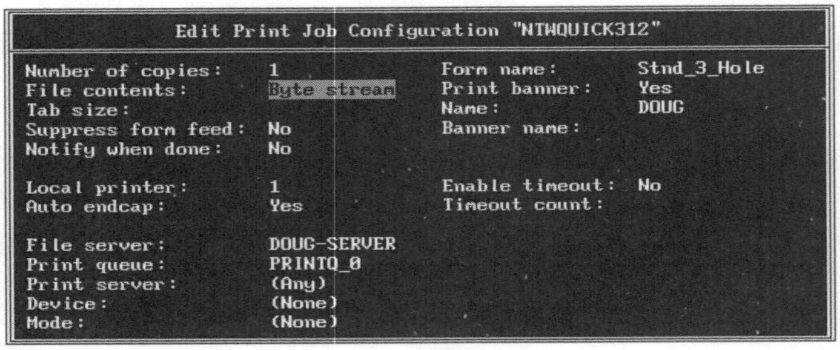

Fig. 21.4 Print job configuration window shown in PRINTCON.

Number of copies: This field can be adjusted to change the number of copies that are printed from the selected job.

File contents: With this option, you can specify how you want NetWare to handle the print job. By selecting Byte stream, formatting is handled by the application, while selecting Text tells NetWare you want tabs to be converted to spaces.

Tab size: When Text is selected for the File contents option, you can use this option to specify how many spaces should be allocated per tab character.

Suppress form feed: When set to No, NetWare sends a form feed command to the printer after the job is complete; otherwise, a setting of Yes restricts NetWare from sending the form feed.

Notify when done: If set to Yes, NetWare sends a message to the user that sent the job confirming the printing is complete.

Local printer: This field specifies which printer port should be used for the capture command. Acceptable values are 1 (for LPT1), 2 (for LPT2), or 3 (for LPT3).

Auto endcap: This field specifies whether or not the job should be printed when you exit from a program (Yes) or until the ENDCAP command is issued (No).

File server: This field specifies which file server the print job should be sent to.

Print queue: This field specifies which print queue the job should be sent to. You can select any print queue that is currently available on the file server you selected.

Print server: This field specifies which print server the job should be sent to. By selecting this field, you can either select a specific print server or the option "Any." When "Any" is selected, the print job is printed by any print server that services the selected queue.

Device: This field specifies the printer device that you want to handle the print job that was configured in the PRINTDEF utility. By selecting this field, you can either select a specific print device or the option "None." When "None" is selected, there is no special formatting performed on the job. For further information on creating printer devices, refer to the heading "Loading a New Printing Device" earlier in this chapter.

Mode: This field specifies the printer mode you want used for this print job that was configured in the PRINTDEF utility. By selecting this field, you can either select a specific printer mode or the option "None." When "None" is selected, the job is printed "as is." For further information on creating printer modes, refer to the heading "Editing Currently Loaded Printing Devices" earlier in this chapter.

Form name: This option specifies which form should be used for printing this job. You can change the desired form by selecting this option and scrolling through the listing of forms that were set up with the PRINTDEF utility. For further information on creating forms, refer to the heading "Creating Form Types" earlier in this chapter.

Print banner: When set to Yes, NetWare prints a banner page before the print job; otherwise, a setting of No restricts NetWare from creating a banner page.

Name: This option specifies the name that appears on the banner page. By default, this name is set to the name of the user ID creating the job, but it can be changed by selecting the option and entering up to twelve characters.

Tip
If several users will make use of this print job, leave the Name field blank. By leaving this field blank, the name field on the banner page is set to the ID of the user sending the job each time.

Banner name: This field specifies what you want printed on the banner page. When left blank, the name of the file being printed is used each time. The banner name field can be changed by selecting the option and entering up to twelve characters.

VI

Network Printing

Enable timeout: This field specifies whether or not you want a timeout value to be used for your print job. When a timeout value is used, your job is automatically printed after the specified time has elapsed. If you do not use a timeout value, after sending your print job, you must use the ENDCAP command before it can be printed.

Timeout count: When Enable timeout is set to Yes, you then can use this field to specify how many seconds must pass before your job will be printed.

Tip

The default value of five seconds is usually more than sufficient for most print jobs. The exception is when you are printing large graphics files or from certain database applications. If you are noticing your print job is being broken up onto several pages, try increasing the timeout value to see if it improves your output.

---

4. After you have edited the various fields to suit your needs, you can exit from this menu by pressing the Esc key and confirming if you want to save your changes. After confirming your intentions, PRINTCON returns you to the Print Job Configurations window. From this point, you can either create another print job, or if you are done, you can save your newly created jobs by pressing the Esc key twice and then confirming that you want to save your new jobs.

Specifying a Default Print Job Configuration

When users are printing on the LAN with the NPRINT or CAPTURE commands, they usually have to specify a variety of parameters, such as the server they want to print to and the queue they want to use. Instead of burdening the users with these chores, you can set a default print job configuration that is used when the additional parameters are not specified with NPRINT or CAPTURE. For example, if you set a print job called REGULAR that specifies the queue PRINTQ1 and the server FS1 as the default, a user could print a file with NPRINT by merely typing **NPRINT** *filename* without having to use the additional NPRINT parameters.

You can specify which print job you want used as the default by following the steps below:

Note

If you have only created one print job configuration, NetWare automatically makes it the default.

---

1. From the Available Options main menu of PRINTCON, select the option Select Default Print Job Configuration.

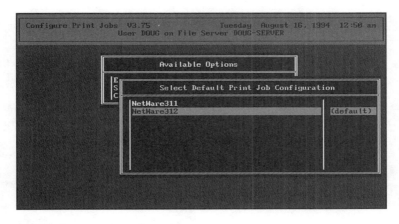

Fig. 21.5 Selecting a default print job configuration.

2. Next, from the the window provided, highlight the job you want to set as the default and press the Enter key (see fig. 21.5).

3. After selecting a new print job as the default, you can save your changes by pressing the Esc key twice to exit PRINTCON and, when asked, confirm if you want to save your changes.

Using Individual Print Job Databases or Shared Databases

One of the benefits to the PRINTCON utility is that it can be used by any user on the server. There are no special rights or security assignments that must be granted to a user's ID before he or she can create their own database of print job configurations.

When a user accesses PRINTCON and creates one or more print jobs, a new file, called PRINTCON.DAT, is created. By default, this file is stored in the personal mail directory of the user that created it. Once created, the user can then edit or use any of the print jobs contained within this file. While this provides a certain degree of flexibility by allowing users to have their own print job databases, it doesn't make life easier when trying to manage a network.

Since PRINTCON saves its database file within the user's mail directory, it is not accessible to any other user on the server. Therefore, each user would have to create their own print jobs, most of which would be identical to those of other users. Luckily, there are a few ways around this dilemma. With NetWare, you can either copy the database files into all users' mail directories or you can share one common database.

Copying Database Files to Individual Users

Note

RIGHTS REQUIRED TO COMPLETE TASK: YOU MUST BE A SUPERVISOR EQUIVALENT TO COPY THE PRINTCON.DAT FILE TO ANY USER ON THE SERVER. OTHERWISE, IF YOU ARE A USER OR WORKGROUP ACCOUNT MANAGER, YOU CAN COPY YOUR PRINTCON.DAT FILE TO ANY USER THAT YOU MANAGE.

VI

Network Printing

Using the PRINTCON utility, you can copy the PRINTCON.DAT database files to other users by following the steps below:

1. From the Available Options main menu of PRINTCON, select Copy Print Job Configurations.

2. From the Source User prompt, enter the name of the user from whom you want to copy the PRINTCON.DAT file, then press Enter. Next, enter the name of the user to whom you want to copy the PRINTCON.DAT file and press Enter.

> **Note**
>
> This method is *not* recommended. It is tedious and cumbersome to maintain. Unless you have some specific reason why you must choose this route, you are better off using the single database method.

Sharing a Single Database File among All Users

After you have created your master PRINTCON.DAT file that contains all the required print jobs, you can make this file accessible to everyone on the server by copying it from your personal mail directory into the PUBLIC directory. Once it has been copied, you then have to make one slight modification.

Using the SMODE command, you should change the search mode of the CAPTURE, NPRINT, PRINTCON, PRINTDEF, and ENDCAP files to 5. Once changed, print requests then make use of the PRINTCON.DAT file you copied into the PUBLIC directory.

> **Tip**
>
> You can find out what your personal mail directory is called by selecting User Information from the SYSCON main menu and then selecting your ID. Next, select the option Other Information from the window provided. Your personal mail directory is named after the value shown in the User ID: field and is a subdirectory of the MAIL directory on the SYS volume.
>
> The SUPERVISOR ID's mail subdirectory is always the number 1.

Using the Print Jobs You Have Created

Once your print jobs have been created, it's time to start making use of them. Using the NPRINT and CAPTURE utilities, you can utilitize your print jobs through the use of the JOB parameter.

EXAMPLE 1: To use the CAPTURE command with the parameters you specified in a print job called REGULAR, type the following from the command line:

CAPTURE J=REGULAR

EXAMPLE 2: To capture your workstation's printing ports using the parameters you specified in a print job called DEFJOB, which you set as your default print job, type the following from the command line:

CAPTURE

EXAMPLE 3: To print a file called DISPLAY.TXT in the current directory using the parameters you specified in a print job called SUPPORT, type the following from the command line:

NPRINT DISPLAY.TXT J=SUPPORT

EXAMPLE 4: To print a file called PAYROLL.FIL in the current directory using the parameters you specified in a print job called DEFJOB you set as your default job, type the following from the command line:

NPRINT PAYROLL.FIL

> **Note**
>
> In examples 2 and 4 you did not have to use the "J" parameter since the job you were using was set up as your default print job.

Managing Print Queues

When the print server is up and running, on occasion, you will have to spend some time managing outstanding print jobs and the queues themselves. Using the PCONSOLE utility, you can perform a variety of tasks such as:

- Viewing the jobs currently in a queue
- Deleting print jobs that are not needed
- Modifying the configuration parameters of print queue entries
- Restricting access to the queue

In the following sections, you learn to perform these tasks in detail.

VI

Network Printing

Viewing and Manipulating Jobs in the Print Queue

Note

RIGHTS REQUIRED TO COMPLETE TASK: ANY USER CAN MODIFY OR DELETE THEIR OWN PRINT JOBS BUT THEY CAN ONLY VIEW THE PRINT JOBS OF OTHER USERS. ONLY A SUPERVISOR EQUIVALENT OR THE PRINT QUEUE OPERATOR CAN MODIFY OR DELETE ANY JOB IN THE QUEUE WHETHER IT IS THEIRS OR NOT.

When you use the PCONSOLE utility, you can examine a print queue to determine which jobs are still waiting to be printed and, security permitting, you also can modify a variety of parameters for each print job by following the steps below:

1. From the Available Options main menu of PCONSOLE, select Print Queue Information and then select the desired queue from the listing provided.

2. After selecting the print queue, PCONSOLE displays a window entitled Print Queue Information that provides a variety of options that are specific to the queue in question. From this window, you can view the jobs currently in the queue by selecting the Current Print Job Entries option (see fig 21.6).

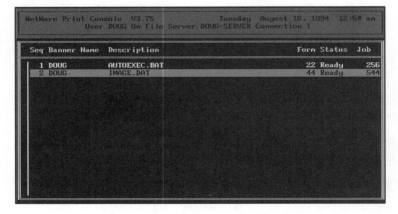

Fig. 21.6 Print jobs waiting in the queue as shown with PCONSOLE.

Note

The Current Print Job Entries window can only display 250 jobs at any given time but there is no limit to the number of jobs that can actually be waiting in the queue.

3. Once the window listing the current print jobs is shown, there are two main things you can do. If you want to delete one of the jobs in the queue, highlight the entry and press the

Delete key or, to view additional information on the print job, highlight the job and press Enter.

Shortcut
If you want to delete multiple jobs at once, you either can flag each job with the F5 key or you can flag a series of jobs based on a pattern in their description field with the F6 key. For example, if you have 100 print jobs and you want to delete all jobs whose description begins with the letter T, press F6 and then enter T* as the Mark Pattern and press Enter. Then, to remove the files from the queue, press Delete and confirm your request.

4. If you selected one of the print jobs, PCONSOLE provides you with a window entitled Print Queue Entry Information that is full of parameters specific to the selected job. Some of these are for viewing only; others can be modified (see fig. 21.7). For your reference, each of these parameters is listed below:

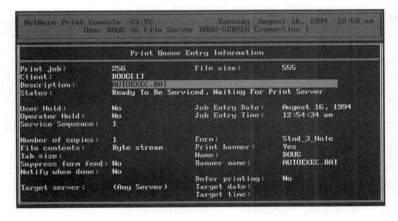

Fig. 21.7 Viewing a print queue entry's configuration parameters using PCONSOLE.

File size: For viewing only, this field tells you the size of the file.

Client: For viewing purposes only, this field tells you the user ID and connection number that submitted the job.

Description: This field provides additional information about the job. While this option is usually set to the name of the file being printed, you can adjust this field as required. The information in this field is printed on the banner page. The maximum size for this field is 49 characters.

Status: For viewing purposes only, this field tells you the status of the job (such as waiting for print server, waiting for target execution date/time, on hold, or currently being printed).

User Hold: With this field, the user that sent the job, the Queue Operator, or a SUPER-VISOR EQUIVALENT can place the job on hold. When placed on hold, the printer servicing the queue does not print the job until the hold is removed.

Operator Hold: Same as User Hold except only the Queue Operator or a SUPERVISOR EQUIVALENT can use this field.

Service Sequence: This field specifies in which order the jobs are to be printed. Usually, this option is used when there are numerous jobs in the queue and an important job must be printed out ASAP. Only the Queue Operator or a SUPERVISOR EQUIVALENT can change the service sequence.

Number of copies: This field can be adjusted to change the number of copies printed from the selected job.

File contents: With this option, you can specify how you want NetWare to handle the print job. By selecting Byte stream, formatting is handled by the application, while selecting Text tells NetWare you want tabs to be converted to spaces.

Tab size: When Text is selecting for the File contents option, this option specifies how many spaces should be allocated per tab character.

Suppress form feed: When set to No, NetWare sends a form feed command to the printer after the job is complete; otherwise, a setting of Yes restricts NetWare from sending the form feed.

Notify when done: If set to Yes, NetWare sends a message to the user that sent the job confirming the printing is complete.

Target server: If there are multiple print servers configured to service the selected queue, selecting this option specifies which server should handle the print job.

Job Entry Date: For viewing purposes only, this field tells you the date the print job was submitted into the queue.

Job Entry Time: For viewing purposes only, this field tells you the time the print job was submitted into the queue.

Form: This option specifies which form should be used for printing this job. You can change the desired form by selecting this option and scrolling through the listing of forms that were set up with the PRINTDEF utility.

Print banner: When set to Yes, NetWare prints a banner page before the print job; otherwise, a setting of No restricts NetWare from creating a banner page.

Name: This option specifies the name that appears on the banner page. By default, this name is set to the name of the user ID that set the job, but it can be changed by selecting the option and entering up to twelve characters.

Banner name: By default, the banner name is the name of the file being printed. The name can be changed by selecting the option and entering up to twelve characters.

Defer printing: By default, NetWare prints the job as soon as a printer is available, but you can defer printing to a later date if you choose by setting this field to Yes.

Target Date: When you set Defer printing to Yes, this field specifies the date you want the print job to be released to a printer.

Target time: When you set Defer printing to Yes, this field specifies the time you want the print job to be released to a printer.

Viewing and Changing the Status of a Print Queue

As a Print Queue Operator or a SUPERVISOR EQUIVALENT user, you can use PCONSOLE to view and modify the status of a print queue. By doing so, you can restrict whether or not users can add jobs to the queue or even if servers should be allowed to print jobs in the queue.

When you use PCONSOLE, you can view or modify the queue's status by following these steps:

1. From the Available Options main menu of PCONSOLE, select Print Queue Information and then the desired print queue from the listing provided.

2. After you select the queue, PCONSOLE provides you with another screen entitled Print Queue Information that provides options specific to the selected queue. By selecting the option Current Queue Status, an additional window appears with the following fields:

Number of entries in queue: This field is for viewing only and shows how many jobs are currently in the queue.

Number of servers attached: This field is for viewing only and shows how many print servers are currently on-line and servicing this queue.

Users can place entries in queue: By default, this field is set to Yes to allow users to add new print jobs to the queue. You can restrict all users from adding new jobs by changing this field to No.

Servers can service entries in queue: By default, this field is set to Yes to allow print servers to print the jobs within the queue. You can stop jobs within the queue from being printed by changing this field to No.

New servers can attach to queue: By default, this field is set to Yes to enable print servers currently not on-line to attach to the queue when they are initialized. You can stop any new print servers from attaching to this queue by changing this field to No.

Managing Printers and the Print Server with PCONSOLE

Note

RIGHTS REQUIRED TO COMPLETE TASK: YOU MUST BE A PRINT SERVER OPERATOR TO MODIFY THE OPER-ATING STATUS OF THE PRINT SERVER OR A NETWORK PRINTER. IF YOU ARE A SUPERVISOR EQUIVALENT BUT NOT A PRINT SERVER OPERATOR, YOU MUST ADD YOURSELF TO THE LISTING OF PRINT SERVER OP-ERATORS; OTHERWISE, YOU CAN ONLY VIEW, NOT MODIFY, THE STATUS.

In addition to configuring printers and the print server, PCONSOLE plays a critical role in the management of your printers and the print server itself. With PCONSOLE, you can monitor and even change the status of the print server and its printers. While some of these options are similar to those shown earlier for configuring the print server, there is one key difference: changes made here are temporary. Anything you change within the Print Server Status/Control option only remains in effect until the print server is rebooted.

When your print server is up and running, you can access PCONSOLE's management facilities by following these steps:

1. From the Available Options main menu of PCONSOLE, select the option Print Server Infor-mation and then the desired print server from the listing provided.

2. After selecting the print server, PCONSOLE presents you with a window entitled Print Server Information that provides options specific to this print server. You can access the management facilities of PCONSOLE by selecting the option Print Server Status/Control.

Note

The Print Server Status/Control option is available only if the print server is on-line.

Once you select the Print Server Status/Control option, PCONSOLE presents you with a menu like the one in Figure 21.8. Using this menu, you can perform any of the tasks shown in the following sections.

Adding or Removing File Servers from the Serviced Listing

When you are printing in a multi-server environment where the print server has been configured to service multiple file servers, you can modify which servers are currently being serviced. By selecting the option File Servers Being Serviced, you can add a server to this listing by pressing Insert, or remove a server by pressing Delete.

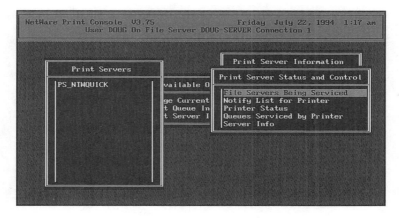

Fig. 21.8 PCONSOLE's Print Server Status and Control menu, used to manage a print server currently on-line.

Note

To be effective, this task must be completed on the "home" file server (where the print server's master configuration resides).

Tip

When the print server is servicing multiple file servers, if a file server other than the "home" server goes down, the print server continues to function but does not service queues from this file server. Once the server is back on-line, the print server does not automatically service its queues. Instead of rebooting the print server to reset it, you can select the File Servers Being Serviced option and re-insert the file server into the listing. By doing so, the print server then begins servicing its queues again.

Adding Users to a Printer's Notification Listing

The option Notify List for Printer is identical in function to the same option within the print server's configuration with one difference: changes made here are only in effect until the print server is reset. For information on how these options work, you can refer to the heading "Creating Notify Listings" in Chapter 18, "Creating Printing Services."

Viewing and Modifying a Printer's Status

By selecting the option Printer Status and then the desired printer, PCONSOLE provides you with a screen similiar to the one shown in Figure 21.9. From this screen, you can determine what, if any, job is being printed as well as modify the status of this printer.

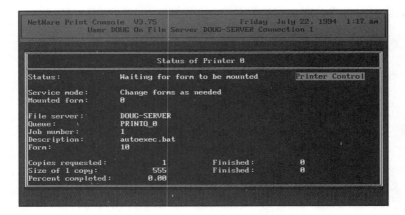

Fig. 21.9 Print status screen of PCONSOLE.

The status window provides you with several fields, most of which are for viewing only and provide you with information on which job is being printed. Of these fields, there are three that require a bit of explanation.

- *Status:* For viewing purposes only, this field tells you if the printer has been connected to the print server, if it is printing a job, or if it has been stopped or paused.

- *Service mode:* If you are a print server operator, you can modify the printer's service mode that determines how it handles jobs that require a form other than the mounted one. To access this field, press the down cursor and then press Enter.

- *Mounted form:* This field informs you about the form type that is currently mounted in the printer. If you are a print server operator, you can scroll down to this field and by pressing the Enter key, you can select any of the available form types.

Aside from these fields, if you are a print server operator, you notice your cursor is highlighting the words Printer Control in the upper right hand corner. When you press the Enter key, a pulldown menu appears with several options, each of which is described below:

- *Abort print job:* When you select this option, you force the printer to abandon the job currently being printed. Once abandoned, the job is deleted from the queue.

- *Form Feed:* This option forces the printer to eject one page.

- *Mark top of form:* When you select this option, the printer prints a line of asterisks (*) across the page.

Tip
Marking the top of the form can help you line up your printer paper when you use continuous form paper.

- *Pause printer:* When you select this option, the job currently being printed is placed on hold and printing does not restart until you select the option Start printer.

- *Rewind printer:* This option moves back or jumps forward within the print job currently being printed.

Tip
The Rewind printer option is especially useful when a printer has jammed on a large job. Instead of reprinting the job from the beginning, you can Rewind the print job to the point where it jammed.

- *Start printer:* Selecting this option restarts the printer after is has been paused or stopped.

- *Stop printer:* Selecting this option places the printer in an idle state; it is unable to accept jobs until the Start printer option is selected. If it was in the midst of printing a job, the job is returned to the print queue.

Viewing and Modifying the Queues Serviced by a Printer

When you use PCONSOLE, you can change the queues a printer services while the print server is up and running. Instead of changing the basic configuration of the server and then resetting the server, queues can be added or removed from the printer's listing of serviced queues by selecting the option Queues Serviced by Printer.

After you select this option and the desired printer, PCONSOLE provides you with a listing of the queues currently being serviced. From this screen, there are several tasks that you can perform:

- If you want to remove a queue from the listing, highlight the desired queue and press the Delete key.

- If you want to modify the priority of the queue, highlight the queue and after pressing Enter, enter the new priority, 1 being the highest.

- If you want to add a queue to the listing of serviced queues, press the Insert key and select a queue from the listing of available queues.

Note
If you are a SUPERVISOR EQUIVALENT, you can add any queue on the file server to this listing, but, if you are only a Print Server Operator, you only can add queues that have already been configured to service this print server.

VI

Network Printing

Downing the Print Server

Whether you need to bring the print server down for maintenance or you made changes to the basic configuration (such as adding a new printer), the time will come when you must reboot the print server. If you select the Server Info option, you are presented with a screen like the one shown in Figure 21.10. From this screen, you can down the print server by selecting the option Current server status and selecting one of the following options:

- *Down:* Selecting this option forces the print server down immediately whether it is in the middle of printing jobs or not.

- *Going down after current jobs:* This option sends a down request to the print server informing it that it should complete the jobs currently being printed and then shut down. Unless you must bring the print server down in an emergency, this is the option you should use.

- *Running:* Selecting this option returns you to the previous menu and does not bring down the print server.

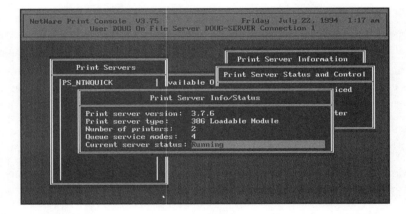

Fig. 21.10 Print Server Information/Status screen used to bring down the server.

Managing Printers and Print Servers with the PSC Command Line Utility

While most people choose the PCONSOLE menu utility to manage their network printers and print servers, NetWare provides you with a utility called PSC that can be used from the command line. Instead of having to work through the various menus of PCONSOLE, PSC can be used in a quicker and more efficient manner.

You can use the PSC command by following this syntax:

```
PSC [PS=print_server_name] [P=printer_number] [options]
```

Based on the syntax above, replace:

print_server_name with the name of the print server.

printer_number with the printer number as defined in PCONSOLE.

options with one or more of the options shown in Table 21.1.

Table 21.1 Options that can be used with the PSC command.		
Option	**Abbr.**	**Description**
Abort	AB	Aborts the job currently printing on the specified printer. The job is deleted and the printer will begin servicing the next job.
CancelDown	CD	If the "Going down after current job" option was selected to down the print server in PCONSOLE, you can cancel the request with this option.
FormFeed	FF	Forces the specified printer to eject one page.
Keep	K	Used in conjunction with the Stop parameter to force NetWare to keep the print job. When not used, the Stop parameter deletes the job from the queue.
Mark	M	Forces the printer to print a line of asterisks across the paper. The main purpose for this option is to assist you with aligning the printer.
Mount Form=#	MOF=#	Tells NetWare you have mounted a new form in the printer. When using this option, replace the # sign with the number of the mounted form.
Pause	PAU	Temporarily stops the printer from servicing jobs. The printer will not start servicing jobs again until the Start option is used.
Private	PRI	Used with remote printers, this option allows a user to temporarily restrict other network users from printing to a printer attached to their workstation.
Shared	SH	When the Private flag was used for a network printer, this option returns the printer to the service of the print server.
Start	STAR	Restarts a printer after is has been stopped or paused.
Status	STAT	Displays the status of the network printers. If you do not specify the Printer option in the command line (P=*printer_number*), PSC displays the status of all printers on the selected print server.
Stop	STO	Stops the printer from servicing print jobs. If the printer is in the middle of a job, the job is deleted unless the Keep option is also used.

VI

Network Printing

EXAMPLE 1: To restrict a remote printer (number 0) attached to your workstation from accepting print requests from the print server PS1, type the following at the command line:

PSC PS=PS1 P=0 PRI

EXAMPLE 2: To pause network printer 4 on print server PS2, type the following at the command line:

PSC PS=PS2 P=4 PAU

EXAMPLE 3: To mount form 6 on printer 0 which services the ACCOUNTING print server, type the following at the command line:

PSC PS=ACCOUNT P=0 MO=6

Tip
To make life easier for yourself and your users, create batch files to use the PSC commands.

Tip
Instead of typing the print server name and printer number every time, create a DOS environment variable for PSC by typing the following from the command line, adding it to your AUTOEXEC.BAT file or to your login script: **SET PSC=PS*print_server_name* P*printer_number***. Replace *print_server_name* and *printer_number* accordingly.

Chapter 22

Console Commands

From the file server console, there are various commands that can be used for a wide variety of administration and configuration tasks. Using these commands, you can alter how your server operates on its own and within a multi-server environment.

In this chapter, we explore each of these commands and how they can be used.

ABORT REMIRROR

If your NetWare server is currently remirroring the partitions on your server, you can stop the process by typing **ABORT REMIRROR *partition_number*** from the file server prompt. If you do not know the correct partition number, you can use the MIRROR STATUS command to review a listing of your NetWare partitions.

ADD NAME SPACE

One of the nice features of NetWare is that it can support various name spaces on a volume. A *name space* is essentially the ability to store the additional information of a file used by some operating systems. For example, while DOS only stores very basic information about a file with an eight-character file name (plus a three-character extension), Macintosh computers maintain extended attributes for a file and allow larger file names.

After loading the required NLMs for the name space you will be using, you can add name space support to a volume by typing **ADD NAME SPACE *name volume***. Within this command, replace *name* with the name of the name space you are adding and *volume* with the name of the volume to which you are adding the name space.

BIND and UNBIND

When you have loaded the drivers for a NIC in the server, you must inform NetWare which protocol you want to use with the card. When you use the BIND command, NetWare establishes a logical attachment between the protocol and the NIC, thus establishing the communications between the server and the network. Refer to the heading "Binding a Protocol to the Network Interface Card" in Chapter 3, "Installing the File Server," for detailed information on using the BIND command.

If you want to prevent the NIC from transmitting and receiving information from the network, or if you need to update the NIC's driver while the server is up and running, the first thing you must do is break the connection between the card and the protocol. This simple task can be achieved by typing **UNBIND *protocol NIC***, replacing *protocol* with the name of the protocol you want to remove and *NIC* with the name you assigned to the NIC or the NIC's driver name.

BROADCAST

From the server's console, you can send a message to a single user or a group of users with the BROADCAST command. For detailed information on using the BROADCAST command, refer to the heading "Broadcasting and Sending Messages from the Server's Console" in Chapter 10, "Miscellaneous Commands for Environment Management."

CLEAR STATION

At times, you may want to remove an inactive connection (that is, NOT-LOGGED-IN) or a user connection from the file server. To do so, you can use the CLEAR STATION command at the file server console prompt. Before you can proceed, you must know the connection number of the station you want to remove. From the console, this information can be gathered by selecting the Connection Information option from the main menu of MONITOR.NLM. After you know the connection number, type **CLEAR STATION *station#***. Replace *station#* with the number of the connection in question.

Caution	
If you use the CLEAR STATION command on a workstation that is in the middle of updating a file, there is a chance the file being updated could be corrupted.	

CLS and OFF

You can clear the file server's console display and return the prompt to the upper-left corner by typing **CLS** or **OFF** from the file server prompt.

CONFIG

When your server is up and running, you may want to check which NICs are in use and how they are configured. When you use the CONFIG command, NetWare examines the server and displays a screen that contains a wide variety of information pertaining to your NICs (see fig. 22.1).

```
DOUG-SERVER:config
File server name: DOUG-SERVER
IPX internal network number: 00000050

3Com 3C503 EtherLink II
    Version 4.00     September 1, 1992
        Hardware setting: I/O Port 300h to 30Fh and 700h to 70Fh, Memory CC000h to
CFFFFh, Interrupt 3h
        Node address: 02608C3F0AE0
        Frame type: ETHERNET_802.2
        No board name defined
        LAN protocol: IPX network 00008022

3Com 3C503 EtherLink II
    Version 4.00     September 1, 1992
        Hardware setting: I/O Port 300h to 30Fh and 700h to 70Fh, Memory CC000h to
CFFFFh, Interrupt 3h
        Node address: 02608C3F0AE0
        Frame type: ETHERNET_SNAP
        No board name defined
        LAN protocol: IPX network 00010000
DOUG-SERVER:
```

Fig. 22.1 Network Interface Card information is provided at the server's console when you use the CONFIG command.

DISABLE LOGIN

You can prevent anyone new from logging into the file server simply by typing **DISABLE LOGIN** from the file server console. Once disabled, no new users can log into the file server until the ENABLE LOGIN command is issued.

> **Note**
>
> When you disable logins to the server, users currently logged in continue to function normally.

DISABLE TTS and ENABLE TTS

NetWare has a feature known as the Transaction Tracking System (TTS) that is used to protect the integrity of the data on the server. When you use TTS, NetWare ensures that if the server is brought down or "crashes," partially completed transactions are backed out, returning the files to their original state. TTS is essentially an "all or nothing" type of facility.

When you type **DISABLE TTS** from the file server prompt, you can force NetWare to disable all its transaction tracking facilities so you can test an application you may be developing for use with TTS. When your testing is completed, type **ENABLE TTS** to restart the transaction tracking.

Caution	
You should not leave TTS disabled for extended periods of time because NetWare uses it to ensure the integrity of its own database files (that is, the binderies).	

DISPLAY NETWORKS

When you installed the file server, there were at least two network numbers you had to supply: the IPX internal network number and the network number used by the NIC. When you type **DISPLAY NETWORKS** from the file server console, NetWare provides you with a listing of all the network numbers it knows about. This listing provides you with all the IPX internal network numbers and NIC network numbers in use, as well as the "hop count," which tells you how many routers must be traversed to reach the network in question.

DISPLAY SERVERS

Servers of all types (file servers, print servers, database servers, and so on) advertise their presence on the network to allow other servers or nodes to make use of their services. From the file server prompt, type **DISPLAY SERVERS** to have NetWare provide you with a listing of all the servers it currently knows about. This listing gives you each server's name, the total number of servers, and the server's "hop count," which tells you how many routers must be traversed to reach the server in question.

Note	
If you are looking for a specific server in the listing provided by DISPLAY SERVERS and it cannot be found, the SYS: volume of the server in question may not be mounted.	

DOWN and EXIT

If you ever need to take down the file server for maintenance, you should never simply turn it off. When the server is up and running, NetWare has numerous files open that must be closed properly to ensure their integrity.

When you type **DOWN** from the file server prompt, NetWare begins its shutdown sequence to ensure everything is closed properly. While the server is shutting down, NetWare first checks for any user connections that have files open. If any files are open, you can send a message to each of the users connected to the server requesting that they log out (the preferred method), or you can instruct DOWN to proceed with the shutdown process and close any files that are open.

Once the server has been shut down, you can reboot the server, or you can type **EXIT** to return to the DOS prompt.

Note
If you have used the REMOVE DOS command to remove DOS from the server's memory, typing **EXIT** forces the server to reboot. If you have used the SECURE CONSOLE command, you cannot use EXIT. Your only recourse then is to reboot the server.

ENABLE LOGIN

You can allow new users to log into the file server by typing **ENABLE LOGIN** from the file server prompt. This command is used to reverse the effects of the DISABLE LOGIN command.

Tip
If you have triggered the Intruder Lockout status on the SUPERVISOR ID, you can use the ENABLE LOGIN command to unlock the account. This only works for the SUPERVISOR ID.

LIST DEVICES

When you type **LIST DEVICES** from the file server prompt, NetWare provides you with a listing of the hard disk and CD-ROM devices currently accessible on the server. This listing provides you with information such as the device number, the device name, and the manufacturer's code.

LOAD and UNLOAD

You can load or unload any NLM utility or driver by typing **LOAD** *filename* or **UNLOAD** *filename*, replacing *filename* with the name of the NLM or driver you want to load or unload.

For detailed information on:

- *Loading disk drivers*, refer to the heading "Activating the File Server's Hard Disks" in Chapter 3, "Installing the File Server."

- *Loading NIC drivers*, refer to the heading "Activating the Server Network Interface Cards" in Chapter 3, "Installing the File Server."

MEMORY

When you type **MEMORY** from the file server prompt, NetWare checks the server and informs you of the total amount of memory installed in the file server. The value provided is not the amount of free memory; for this information, you must use the MONITOR.NLM utility.

MIRROR STATUS

Sometimes, when your server's disk drives have been mirrored, a problem arises that causes them to be unmirrored. Even though an error message appears on-screen, if it is not seen in time, it could scroll off the display. Unless you check your server error logs on a regular basis, you could be unaware that the drives had been unmirrored.

When you type **MIRROR STATUS** from the file server prompt, NetWare reviews the mirroring status of each NetWare partition and provides you with a master listing. This listing gives you the number of each partition and informs you of the status of the partion as defined below:

Status	Description
Being remirrored	The partition is currently being remirrored. When remirroring, the percentage of remirroring completed is shown.
Fully syncronized	The partitions are fully mirrored and functioning properly.
Not mirrored	The partition in question is not mirrored.
Out of syncronization	A critical error may have occured with the mirrored partition that places the integrity of the data at risk. As such, the partition has been unmirrored. Refer to Chapter 27, "Disk Problems," for information on resolving mirroring problems.

MODULES

When you type **MODULES** from the file server prompt, NetWare provides you with a listing of all of the NLMs, disk drivers, and utilities currently loaded on the file server. With this listing, you can review the name of all modules and their version and revision numbers.

MOUNT and DISMOUNT

When you installed and configured your NetWare file server, you created volumes to store the various directories and files for your applications. Even though you created the volumes, they are not accessible unless they are mounted at the server's console. When you type **MOUNT** *volume_name* from the console prompt, NetWare checks the server for the named volume and then makes it accessible to all users with the appropriate security rights.

Shortcut
When there are multiple volumes on the server, you can mount all of them at once by typing **MOUNT ALL**.

If a volume is mounted and you want to change its configuration (that is, its name) or perform some maintenance tasks (that is, VREPAIR), you must deactivate the volume by typing **DISMOUNT** *volume_name* from the file server prompt.

NAME

When you type **NAME** at the file server console, NetWare provides you with the name of the server you are working on. This option is a throw-back to versions of NetWare prior to version 3.12 where the console prompt was only a colon. In NetWare 3.12, by default, the console prompt is the server name, so this command is rarely required.

PROTOCOL

You can check which protocols are loaded and in use on the file server by typing **PROTOCOL** at the file server console. This command tells you the names of the protocols, the frame types, and the protocol IDs.

REGISTER MEMORY

When your server hardware uses the ISA bus technology, you must inform NetWare of the amount of memory that you have installed above 16M using the REGISTER MEMORY command. To use REGISTER MEMORY, follow this syntax:

```
REGISTER MEMORY starting_address length
```

Based on the preceding syntax, replace:

starting_address with the starting hexadecimal memory address of where the memory above the 16M limit begins (usually 1000000). Refer to Appendix C, "Hexadecimal Memory Conversion Table," for a listing of the various M hexadecimal values.

length with the hexadecimal value for the number of megabytes that have been installed in the server above the 16M boundary. Refer to Appendix C, "Hexadecimal Memory Conversion Table," for a listing of the various M hexadecimal values.

EXAMPLE: When you have installed a total of 32M of RAM in the server, type the following from the file server prompt:

REGISTER MEMORY 1000000 1000000

Tip

The REGISTER MEMORY command can be added to the server's AUTOEXEC.NCF file to ensure that it executes whenever the server is rebooted.

Caution

If you have installed more than 16M of RAM and the server has adapter boards that use DMA, you may have a conflict that could cause the server to abend. Check with the vendors of your adapter cards to see if they have updated drivers that prevent this problem.

REMIRROR PARTITION

If your NetWare partitions are mirrored and a critical error occurs on one of the devices, NetWare may unmirror the partitions. Once unmirrored, the faulty partition can be removed from the server and repaired. When the partition is reinstalled in the server, NetWare then goes through a process to remirror the partitions so they are in sync with each other.

Normally, NetWare initiates a remirroring process, if needed, when the server is first brought on-line. With removable disks systems that can be removed when the server is up, you have to initiate this process manually by typing **REMIRROR PARTITION** from the file server prompt.

REMOVE DOS

When you type **REMOVE DOS** at the server console, NetWare removes DOS from the server's memory. By doing so, the server's local hard disk and floppy drives are not accessible from the server's console. If the server is brought down, when you type **EXIT**, NetWare reboots the server instead of returning you to the DOS prompt.

RESET ROUTER

In the multi-server network, servers of all types (for example, file servers, database servers, and print servers), broadcast their presence to the rest of the network. By doing so, they inform the other servers and nodes that they are able to transmit or receive requests.

When these broadcast transmissions are received by the NetWare file server, a table is built in the server's memory that is used when the server's OS must determine how to get a transmission from one point or another. Unfortunately, at times, this table may be out of date. Since the broadcast transmissions only occur every 60 seconds, if a server goes down or comes on-line before the next broadcast, the server's routing table will be temporarily inaccurate. Thus, to force the NetWare server to update its routing tables immediately, type **RESET ROUTER** from the file server prompt.

SCAN FOR NEW DEVICES and LIST NEW DEVICES

With the advent of CD-ROM and removable disk systems, in some systems it is possible to add an additional device while the server is up and running. Previous technology required you to bring the server down before adding the device.

When you type **SCAN FOR NEW DEVICES** from the file server prompt, NetWare checks its disk channels for any devices that were attached since the server was brought on-line. You then can type **LIST DEVICES** at the server prompt to see the updated listing.

SEARCH

When your server is first brought on-line, NetWare looks in the server's SYSTEM directory when loading an NLM or other module by default. When you use the SEARCH command, you can provide NetWare with a listing of additional locations to look at when a module is being loaded.

By doing so, NLMs can be placed in locations other than the SYSTEM directory and loaded at the console without having to use the full path each time you want to load the module. Essentially, the SEARCH command is similar in function to the DOS PATH statement. You can use the SEARCH command in one of four ways:

- SEARCH: When you type **SEARCH** from the console prompt, NetWare provides you with a listing of the locations currently in its search path.

- SEARCH ADD *path:* To add an additional location to the server's search path, use this command, replacing *path* with the full path to the location (for example, SEARCH ADD SYS:\PUBLIC). This method adds the search location to the end of the listing.

- SEARCH ADD *search# path:* When you use this command, you can insert a location within the current search path by replacing *search#* with the desired search path number and *path* with the full path to the location. For example, if you currently have three locations in the server's search path and you type **SEARCH ADD 1 SYS:\NEWNLMS**, NetWare checks the NEWNLMS directory before any other location when loading any new modules.

- SEARCH DEL *search#:* When you use this command, you can remove a location from the server's search path by replacing *search#* with the search location number you want removed. You can get a listing of all the search path numbers by merely typing **SEARCH** from the file server prompt.

SECURE CONSOLE

One "feature" of NetWare is the ability to create search paths at the console for loading NLMs from various locations and to access the server's local hard disk. Unfortunately, these "features" can also act as security holes for your server. If an intruder were to gain access to the file server's console, they can load NLMs or other modules from anywhere on the server, which can be used to crack passwords or gain unauthorized access to your server's data.

To protect yourself from these possible intrusions, type **SECURE CONSOLE** from the file server prompt. Once this command is issued, you cannot load any NLMs from locations other than the current search path nor can you access the server's local drive. If the server is brought down after SECURE CONSOLE is used, the server must be rebooted—you are unable to use the EXIT command to return to the DOS prompt.

SEND

From the server's console, you can send a message to a single user or a group of users with the SEND command. For detailed information on using the SEND command, refer to "Broadcasting and Sending Messages from the Server's Console" in Chapter 10, "Miscellaneous Commands for Environment Management."

SET

NetWare provides you with numerous parameters that can be used to configure and, to a certain degree, optimize your server. Through the use of the SET command, you can review or change these parameters and how they operate.

To view the current settings of a parameter, you have two choices:

■ From the console prompt, type **SET** and press Enter. A screen similiar to the one shown in Figure 22.2 appears. Once this screen appears, you can select the desired section number to review all the parameters in that section.

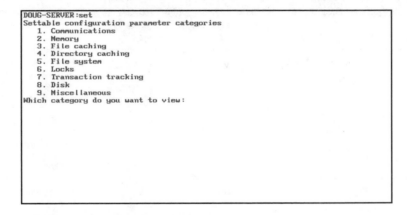

```
DOUG-SERVER:set
Settable configuration parameter categories
     1. Communications
     2. Memory
     3. File caching
     4. Directory caching
     5. File system
     6. Locks
     7. Transaction tracking
     8. Disk
     9. Miscellaneous
Which category do you want to view:
```

Fig. 22.2 The menu presented by NetWare after typing SET.

■ From the console prompt, type **SET *parameter***, replacing *parameter* with the parameter you want to view without a defining variable. For example, to check what the parameter Cache Buffer Size is set to, type **SET CACHE BUFFER SIZE** from the server prompt.

The actual method you use to set these parameters varies depending on the parameter itself. Some parameters can only be set within the STARTUP.NCF file; others can be set directly from the command line or the AUTOEXEC.NCF file. Either way, the syntax for using the parameters is

```
SET parameter = variable
```

Based on the syntax above, replace *parameter* with one of the parameters and *variable* with an acceptable variable for the parameter as noted in Tables 22.1 through 22.9.

In the nine tables that follow, the parameters are shown and separated into their appropriate sections. Within the tables, you not only find the correct parameter name but also its default value, the acceptable range, a description of the parameter, and notes on whether it can be loaded in the STARTUP.NCF file or the AUTOEXEC.NCF file.

Note

Any parameters used in the STARTUP.NCF file don't take effect until the server is rebooted.

Tip

Any setting that can be used in the AUTOEXEC.NCF file also can be used from the console command line.

Table 22.1 Communications parameters that can be adjusted on the file server.

Parameter	Default	Acceptable Range	AUTOEXEC. NCF	STARTUP. NCF	Description
CONSOLE DISPLAY WATCHDOG LOGOUTS	OFF	ON or OFF	YES	NO	Periodically, NetWare sends out a "watchdog" packet that determines if a station is still active. You can set this parameter to ON if you want the server to display an alert when the workstation does not respond to the watchdog packet.
ENABLE PACKET BURST STATISTICS SCREEN	OFF	ON or OFF	YES	NO	Set the parameter to ON to display the NetWare packet bursting statistics screen. The screen itself is of little use to the user as, at the time of writing, Novell considers the data in the screen to be proprietary, so a full description of the output is not available.
NEW PACKET RECEIVE BUFFER WAIT TIME	0.1s	0.1s to 20 sec	YES	NO	Determines the amount of time that must pass before NetWare allocates an additional packet receive buffer on the server. With the default setting, NetWare allocates a new receive buffer almost as soon as it is requested. You may want to increase this parameter slightly because, if your network is having communications problems, NetWare may unnecessarily allocate new packet receive buffers.

Parameter	Default	Acceptable Range	AUTOEXEC. NCF	STARTUP. NCF	Description
MAXIMUM PHYSICAL RECEIVE PACKET SIZE	4202	618 to 24682	NO	YES	Sets the maximum packet size that the server is capable of accepting. You should set this parameter to the maximum packet size that can be used by any NIC on the network.
MAXIMUM PACKET RECEIVE BUFFERS	400	50 to 2000	YES	YES	Specifies the maximum packet receive buffers that can be allocated by the file server. You have to increase this value if/when the server's receive buffer usage is equal to the maximum. A single packet receive buffer uses roughly 1K of RAM. You can view the number of receive buffers currently in use from the main screen of the MONITOR.NLM.
REPLY TO GET NEAREST SERVER	ON	ON or OFF	YES	YES	When a workstation first loads the network drivers, it issues a "Get Nearest Server" request on the network. When a server receives this request, it sends an acknowledgment to the workstation and a connection is then established. If you do not want the server to respond to these requests, set this parameter to OFF. If you set this parameter to OFF in a single-server environment, no one can log in.
MINIMUM PACKET RECEIVE BUFFERS	100	10 to 1000	NO	YES	Determines the minimum number of packet receive buffers that should be allocated to the server. After your server has been up for a few weeks, check MONITOR.NLM to see what your current receive buffer usage is. If it is significantly higher than the minimum, increase this parameter. A single packet receive buffer uses roughly 1K of RAM.

VII

Console Management

(continues)

Table 22.1 Continued.

Parameter	Default	Acceptable Range	AUTOEXEC. NCF	STARTUP. NCF	Description
NUMBER OF WATCHDOG PACKETS	10	5 to 100	YES	NO	Periodically, NetWare sends out a "watchdog" packet to a workstation to determine if it is still active. Using this parameter, NetWare determines how many times it sends out a watchdog packet without receiving a response before it assumes that the station is no longer active and clears the connection.
DELAY BETWEEN WATCHDOG PACKETS	59.3s	9.9s to 10min 26.2s	YES	NO	Determines the amount of time NetWare waits before sending additional watchdog packets to a workstation.
DELAY BEFORE FIRST WATCHDOG PACKET	4min 56.6s	15.7s to 20min 52.3s	YES	NO	Specifies the amount of time a workstation can go without issuing any requests to the server before NetWare sends out the first watchdog packet.
ENABLE IPX CHECKSUMS	1	0 to 2	YES	NO	NetWare has the capability of performing a checksum on a packet to determine if the packet has been corrupted while traveling from the workstation to the server. With this parameter, you can specify how NetWare handles checksums: 0=Do not use checksums, 1=Use checksums only when the workstation is capable, 2=Require checksums from all workstations.
ALLOW LIP	ON	ON or OFF	YES	NO	In previous versions of NetWare, packets that had to pass through a router to reach the source or destination defaults to a 576-byte packet size. Using LIP (Large Internet Packet),

Parameter	Default	Acceptable Range	AUTOEXEC. NCF	STARTUP. NCF	Description
					NetWare negotiates with the station sending the packet to determine the maximum packet size that can be used instead of defaulting to 576 bytes. Unfortunately, this does not guarantee a larger packet size as your routers may not support a larger packet size.
NCP PACKET SIGNATURE OPTION	1	0 to 3	YES	YES	To ensure the highest degree of security for communications between the server and a work-station, NetWare can use a feature known as NCP packe packet signing. The purpose of packet signing is to ensure that a station cannot "pretend" to be another station and intercept its packets. There are four possible settings: 0=Do not use packet signatures, 1=Use packet signatures requested by the workstation, 2=Use packet signatures if supported by the work-station, 3=Require packet signatures from all stations.

Table 22.2 Memory parameters that can be adjusted on the file server.

Parameter	Default	Acceptable Range	AUTOEXEC. NCF	STARTUP. NCF	Description
CACHE BUFFER SIZE	4096	4096 to 16384	NO	YES	Sets the size of the file server's cache buffers. For optimal performance, this value should be set equal to the volume's block size. Note that this value cannot exceed the volume block size.

(continues)

Table 22.2 Continued.

Parameter	Default	Acceptable Range	AUTOEXEC. NCF	STARTUP. NCF	Description
MAXIMUM ALLOC SHORT TERM MEMORY	8388608	50000 to 33554432	YES	YES	One of NetWare's memory pools, ALLOC Short Term, is used to supply memory to NLMs on a short-term basis. This setting specifies the maximum size of this pool.
AUTO REGISTER MEMORY ABOVE 16 MEGABYTES	ON	ON or OFF	NO	YES	This parameter must be set to ON when you are using an EISA server that is equipped with more than 16M of RAM. If you are using adapter cards in the server that require DMA, change this setting to OFF.

Table 22.3 File-caching parameters that can be adjusted on the file server.

Parameter	Default	Acceptable Range	AUTOEXEC. NCF	STARTUP. NCF	Description
READ AHEAD ENABLED	ON	ON or OFF	YES	NO	When a workstation is issuing read requests to the server, NetWare may assume the station wants to read an entire file. Instead of waiting for each request from the station, when this setting is enabled, NetWare attempts to cache the entire file into memory, thereby improving the access time for the station.
READ AHEAD LRU SITTING TIME THRESHOLD	10s	0s to 1h	YES	NO	Determines how fast the server's file cache is being used up. If an LRU cache block is in memory for less than the amount of time specified by this command, NetWare does not proceed with the next read ahead cache request.

Console Management

Parameter	Default	Acceptable Range	AUTOEXEC. NCF	STARTUP. NCF	Description
MAXIMUM CONCURRENT DISK CACHE WRITES	50	10 to 1000	YES	NO	NetWare uses a parameter known as dirty cache buffers that are used to determine how many requests are outstanding for access to the disk drive that can be viewed from the main screen of MONITOR.NLM. When the dirty cache buffers are consistently high, you can increase the number of concurrent cache writes that are the number of writes NetWare performs with a single pass of the disk heads across the disk. Care should taken when in-creasing this value as it reduces the amount of time NetWare has for read-ing information for the disk.
DIRTY DISK CACHE DELAY TIME	3.3s	0.1s to 10s	YES	NO	When a dirty disk cache block is full, NetWare writes the information to disk as soon as possible, but a block that is only partially filled is held in anticipation that it will be filled soon. Use this parameter to specify how long NetWare waits before writing a partially filled block to disk.
MINIMUM FILE CACHE REPORT THRESHOLD	20	0 to 1000	YES	NO	When NetWare starts to run low on file cache blocks, it issues a warning to the file server console. With this parameter, you can specify how many blocks can be remaining before NetWare issues this warning.
RESERVED BUFFERS BELOW 16 MEG	16	8 to 300	NO	YES	Specifies how many file cache buffers are reserved below the 16M boundary for drivers that cannot access memory above 16M.

(continues)

Table 22.3 Continued.

Parameter	Default	Acceptable Range	AUTOEXEC. NCF	STARTUP. NCF	Description
MINIMUM FILE CACHE BUFFERS	20	20 to 1000	YES	NO	When your NetWare server is first brought on-line, the required amount of memory is allocated to the various memory pools and any memory left over is used for the server's file cache buffers. As the other pools require memory, NetWare takes memory away from the file cache buffers and grants it as needed. Use this setting to tell NetWare the minimum number of file cache buffers it must maintain. a single file cache buffer is equal in size to the Cache Buffer ize parameter noted earlier.

Table 22.4 Directory-caching parameters that can be adjusted on the file server.

Parameter	Default	Acceptable Range	AUTOEXEC. NCF	STARTUP. NCF	Description
DIRTY DIRECTORY CACHE DELAY TIME	0.5s	0s to 10s	YES	NO	NetWare uses directory cache buffers to store information about a directory in memory. By doing so, read or write requests to a directory can be sped up as the server searches the memory for the necessary information before looking to the disk. When one of these directory cache buffers is written to in memory, NetWare must write this information to disk at some point or another. Use this parameter to specify the amount of time that must go by before writing a directory cache buffer to disk. Increasing this value can improve performance slightly but also could increase the chance of corruption in your directory tables.

Parameter	Default	Acceptable Range	AUTOEXEC. NCF	STARTUP. NCF	Description
MAXIMUM CONCURRENT DIRECTORY CACHE WRITES	10	5 to 50	YES	NO	Specifies the maximum number of directory cache writes that can be written to the disk within a single pass of the drive's heads across the disk. Care should be taken when increasing this value as it reduces the amount of time NetWare has available for reading information for the disk.
DIRECTORY CACHE ALLOCATION WAIT TIME	2.2s	0.5s to 2min	YES	NO	Used by NetWare when all directory cache buffers are in use to determine how long it must wait before allocating a new buffer. Increasing this value can improve performance as directory cache buffers will be allocated as needed more quickly.
DIRECTORY CACHE BUFFER NONREFER-ENCED DELAY	5.5s	1s to 5min	YES	NO	Determines the amount of time that can go by without a directory cache buffer being used before it is rewritten.
MAXIMUM DIRECTORY CACHE BUFFERS	500	20 to 4000	YES	NO	Determines the maximum number of buffers that can be allocated for caching directory information. If your current directory cache buffer usage, which can be viewed from the main screen of MONITOR.NLM, is equal to or near the maximum, increase this parameter to avoid any potential problems. When maxed out, the server will respond slowly to directory searches.
MINIMUM DIRECTORY CACHE BUFFERS	20	10 to 2000	YES	NO	Determines the minimum number of buffers that can be allocated for caching. For optimal performance, if your current directory cache buffer usage (viewable from the main screen of MONITOR.NLM) is significantly greater, increase the minimum number of directory cache buffers.

Table 22.5 File-system parameters that can be adjusted on the file server.

Parameter	Default	Acceptable Range	AUTOEXEC. NCF	STARTUP. NCF	Description
MAXIMUM PERCENT OF VOLUME SPACE ALLOWED FOR EXTENDED ATTRIBUTES	10	5 to 50	YES	NO	When you are using multiple name spaces for a volume (for example, OS/2 or Mac), NetWare uses this setting to determine the maximum amount of space that can be used on the volume for storing information on a file or directory's extended attributes.
MAXIMUM EXTENDED ATTRIBUTES PER FILE OR PATH	8	4 to 512	YES	NO	When you are using multiple name spaces for a volume, NetWare uses this parameter to determine the maximum number of extended attributes that can be used for each directory or file.
MAXIMUM PERCENT OF VOLUME USED BY DIRECTORY	13	5 to 50	YES	NO	Specifies the maximum percentage of a volume that can be used by a single directory.
IMMEDIATE PURGE OF DELETED FILES	OFF	ON or OFF	YES	NO	When a file is deleted on the server, NetWare can maintain the file in a hidden format that allows the user to recover the file if it was deleted by accident. As space is required on the volume, NetWare automatically purges some of these deleted files to make room. Using this setting, you can instruct NetWare that you do not want any deleted file maintained in a salvageable format and to purge them immediately.
MAXIMUM SUBDIRECTORY TREE DEPTH	25	10 to 100	NO	YES	Specifies the maximum number of levels that there can be within a single directory tree.

Parameter	Default	Acceptable Range	AUTOEXEC. NCF	STARTUP. NCF	Description
VOLUME LOW WARN ALL USERS	ON	ON or OFF	YES	NO	Instructs NetWare whether or not you want a warning message to be sent out to all users when space is running low. This warning is issued when the VOLUME LOW WARNING value is reached and continues until the VOLUME LOW WARNING RESET THRESHOLD value is achieved.
VOLUME LOW WARNING RESET THRESHOLD	256	0 to 100000	YES	NO	When the parameter is set to YES, this parameter specifies the number of blocks of free space that must be cleared up before the warnings stop. To determine the actual amount of space that must be cleared, multiply the number of blocks you set here by the block size that you set for the volume during installation.
VOLUME LOW WARNING THRESHOLD	256	0 to 100000	YES	NO	When the VOLUME LOW WARN ALL USERS parameter is set to YES, this parameter determines the minimum amount of space that can be left on a volume before the first warning is issued. Because this parameter is specified in blocks, to determine the actual amount of space that must remain, multiply this setting by the block size that you set for the volume during installation.
TURBO FAT RE-USE WAIT TIME	5min 29.6s	0.3s to 1h 5min 54.6s	YES	NO	NetWare has a feature known as the "turbo fat" that is a listing of all the blocks used by a large file. When one of these files is opened, NetWare uses a buffer to cache the file's "turbo fat" entry. This parameter specifies the amount of time that must pass after a file is closed before the buffer can be freed up.

(continues)

Table 22.5 Continued.

Parameter	Default	Acceptable Range	AUTOEXEC. NCF	STARTUP. NCF	Description
MINIMUM FILE DELETE WAIT TIME	1min 5.9s	0s to 7 days	YES	NO	When a file is deleted on the server, NetWare can maintain the file in a hidden format that enables the user to recover the file if it was deleted by accident. As space is required on the volume, NetWare automatically purges some of these deleted files to make room. Specifies the minimum amount of time NetWare must maintain this file in a salvageable format before it can be purged from the system whether space is low or not.
FILE DELETE WAIT TIME	5min 29.6s	0s to 7 days	YES	NO	Specifies how much time must pass before a file is flagged as being purgeable. Should the volume start to run low on space, NetWare first removes the purgeable files to alleviate the space problem before it starts to purge other salvageable files. This parameter does not guarantee that the file remains on the system for any set period of time.
NCP FILE COMMIT	ON	ON or OFF	YES	NO	Specifies whether an application can force all outstanding NCP file write requests to disk. Do not change this value unless specifically instructed to do so by Novell or the application's vendor.

Table 22.6 Lock parameters that can be adjusted on the file server.

Parameter	Default	Acceptable Range	AUTOEXEC. NCF	STARTUP. NCF	Description
MAXIMUM RECORD LOCKS PER CONNEC-TION	500	10 to 10000	YES	NO	Specifies the maximum number of record locks that can be used by a single-user connection.
MAXIMUM FILE LOCKS PER CONNEC-TION	250	10 to 1000	YES	NO	Specifies the maximum number of files that can be opened and locked by a single-user.
MAXIMUM RECORD LOCKS	20000	100 to 200000	YES	NO	Specifies the maximum number of record locks acceptable on the server at any given time.
MAXIMUM FILE LOCKS	10000	100 to 100000	YES	NO	Specifies the maximum number of files that can be opened and locked on the server at any given time.

Table 22.7 Transaction-tracking parameters that can be adjusted on the file server.

Parameter	Default	Acceptable Range	AUTOEXEC. NCF	STARTUP. NCF	Description
AUTO TTS BACKOUT FLAG	OFF	ON or OFF	NO	YES	NetWare has a feature known as Transaction Tracking that backs out requests that were not completed in their entirety (for example, during a server failure). After a server crashes and is brought back on-line, NetWare asks if you want any incomplete transactions to be backed out. The server doesn't finish booting until you answer this question. If you want NetWare to assume that you always want these transactions to be backed out, you can answer Yes.

(continues)

Table 22.7 Continued.

Parameter	Default	Acceptable Range	AUTOEXEC. NCF	STARTUP. NCF	Description
TTS ABORT DUMP FLAG	OFF	ON or OFF	YES	NO	Specifies if you want NetWare to write the data that it is backing out using TTS to a file called TTS$LOG.ERR at the root of the SYS volume.
MAXIMUM TRANS-ACTIONS	10000	100 to 10000	YES	NO	Specifies the maximum number of transactions that can occur on the file server at any given time.
TTS UNWRITTEN CACHE WAIT TIME	1min 5.9s	11s to 10min 59.1s	YES	NO	Specifies the maximum amount of time that TTS can prevent a cache buffer from being written to disk.
TTS BACKOUT FILE TRUNCATION WAIT TIME	59min 19.2s	1min 5.9s to 1 day 2 h 21min 51.3s	YES	NO	At times, the backout file maintained by the Transaction Tracking System can exceed what is actually required. Use this parameter to specify the amount of time that must pass before TTS can truncate the size of the overly large file.

Table 22.8 Disk parameters that can be adjusted on the file server.

Parameter	Default	Acceptable Range	AUTOEXEC. NCF	STARTUP. NCF	Description
ENABLE DISK READ AFTER WRITE VERIFY	ON	ON or OFF	YES	YES	Tells NetWare if you want it to perform software read-after-write verification for the disk. Most of the latest disk drives and controllers handle this task on the hardware level, which is much faster. If your disk or controller can handle this task, you can set this para-meter to OFF, but you should check your disk/controller documentation first.

Parameter	Default	Acceptable Range	AUTOEXEC. NCF	STARTUP. NCF	Description
CONCURRENT REMIRROR REQUESTS	4	2 to 30	NO	YES	Specifies the maximum number of remirror requests that can be issued at any one time when the server is trying to recover from a disk failure.

Table 22.9 Miscellaneous parameters that can be adjusted on the file server.

Parameter	Default	Acceptable Range	AUTOEXEC. NCF	STARTUP. NCF	Description
MAXIMUM OUTSTANDING NCP SEARCHES	51	10 to 1000	YES	NO	Specifies the maximum number of NCP searches that can be issued by a single connection at any one time.
ALLOW UNENCRYPTED PASSWORDS	OFF	ON or OFF	YES	NO	With NetWare 3.X, passwords are encrypted to ensure that someone with the correct tools, such as a protocol analyzer, cannot monitor the network cabling and intercept a user's password. Previous versions of NetWare could not perform this type of encryption during a login. To accommodate these older systems, you can set this parameter to YES. Alternatively, you can update the LOGIN and ATTACH programs on the older (2.X) servers which then allow them to encrypt passwords.
NEW SERVICE PROCESS WAIT TIME	2.2s	0.3s to 20s	YES	NO	In NetWare, a service process is a type of buffer that determines how many requests can be processed at any one time. When you use this parameter, you can specify the amount of time that must pass before NetWare allocates an additional service process.

(continues)

Table 22.9 Continued.

Parameter	Default	Acceptable Range	AUTOEXEC. NCF	STARTUP. NCF	Description
PSEUDO PREEMPTION TIME	2000	1000 to 10000	YES	NO	Specifies the amount of time an NLM can control the server's processor before it must relinquish control to another task. Using this parameter, NetWare can restrict an NLM from monopolizing the server's CPU.
DISPLAY SPURIOUS INTERRUPT ALERTS	ON	ON or OFF	YES	YES	While usually related to a faulty driver, a spurious interrupt error may appear on the server when one of your hardware devices is being overloaded. When you use this parameter, you can enable or disable these messages from appearing on the console.
DISPLAY LOST INTERRUPT ALERTS	ON	ON or OFF	YES	YES	When a request is inter-rupted before NetWare can respond, the problem is said to be a "lost interrupt request." This problem is usually caused by a faulty device driver or an over-loaded component. When you use this parameter, you can enable or disable the displaying of these errors to the console.
DISPLAY DISK DEVICE ALERTS	OFF	ON or OFF	YES	YES	Instructs NetWare to display a message on the server console whenever a change occurs with the disk status (for example, when a drive is mounted or dismounted or when an error is encountered).
DISPLAY RELINQUISH CONTROL ALERTS	OFF	ON or OFF	YES	YES	Instructs NetWare to display an error message on a console when an NLM does not relinquish control of the processor to other tasks on a regular basis.

VII

Parameter	Default	Acceptable Range	AUTOEXEC. NCF	STARTUP. NCF	Description
REPLACE CONSOLE PROMPT WITH SERVER NAME	ON	ON or OFF	YES	YES	Specifies whether you want the server's name to be used as the console prompt or if you want the older style colon prompt (:).
DISPLAY INCOMPLETE IPX PACKET ALERTS IPX	ON	ON or OFF	YES	YES	Specifies if you want NetWare to display an error message on the console whenever it receives an incomplete packet. Errors of this nature can be a result of several problems, such as bad NIC drivers, a faulty NIC, or cabling problems.
DISPLAY OLD API NAMES	OFF	ON or OFF	YES	YES	Specifies if you want NetWare to display the names of older APIs that an NLM uses when it loads.
MAXIMUM SERVICE PROCESSES	20	5 to 40	YES	NO	NetWare uses a "service process" to receive and process all requests on the server. Specifies the maximum number of tasks that can be completed at any one time. This value should be increased when the number of service processes that are currently in use (viewable from the main screen of MONITOR.NLM) are equal to the maximum setting.
ALLOW CHANGE TO CLIENT RIGHTS	ON	ON or OFF	YES	YES	Allows the server to assume the rights to a job of the client who submitted it.

SET TIME

From the server's console, you can change the date and time maintained by the server with the SET TIME command. For detailed information on using the SET TIME command, refer to "Changing the Server's Date and Time from the Console" in Chapter 10, "Miscellaneous Commands for Environment Management."

SPEED

When you type **SPEED** from the file server prompt, NetWare provides you with its speed rating for your server's CPU. Following are the approximate values you may get:

Type of machine	Speed rating
80386 16MHz CPU	120
80386 25MHz CPU	150
80386 33MHz CPU	250
80486 25MHz CPU	600
80486 33MHz CPU	900
80486 50MHz CPU	1200
80486 66MHz CPU	1800

If your results are considerably lower than these values, you may not have your server's PC configuration settings set on the highest mode. Refer to your hardware documentation for further details.

TIME

You can check the time being maintained by the file server by typing **TIME** from the file server prompt.

TRACK ON

To those who are unaware, the network may seem like a peaceful place, but the fact is there is a constant flurry of information traveling between servers across the network cabling. While reviewing all of this information requires a tool such as a protocol analyzer, NetWare provides you with a command that can be used to review some of the basic information crossing the wire.

When you type **TRACK ON** from the file server prompt, NetWare presents you with the router tracking screen (see fig. 22.3). From this screen, you can monitor the network for the various advertising packets that are used between servers and the GET NEAREST SERVER REQUESTS issued from the workstations.

```
OUT [00010000:FFFFFFFFFFFF] 11:28:06pm   DOUG-SERVER      1   DOUG-SERVER      2
IN  [00000050:000000000001] 11:28:12pm   DOUG-SERVER      1
OUT [00000050:FFFFFFFFFFFF] 11:28:36pm   00010000   1/2       00008022   1/2
OUT [00008022:FFFFFFFFFFFF] 11:28:36pm   00010000   1/2       00000050   1/2
OUT [00010000:FFFFFFFFFFFF] 11:28:36pm   00008022   1/2       00000050   1/2
IN  [00000050:000000000001] 11:28:40pm   DOUG-SERVER      1
OUT [00000050:FFFFFFFFFFFF] 11:29:05pm   DOUG-SERVER      1   DOUG-SERVER      2
OUT [00008022:FFFFFFFFFFFF] 11:29:05pm   DOUG-SERVER      1   DOUG-SERVER      2
OUT [00010000:FFFFFFFFFFFF] 11:29:05pm   DOUG-SERVER      1   DOUG-SERVER      2
IN  [00000050:000000000001] 11:29:07pm   DOUG-SERVER      1
IN  [00008022:02608C40CCB5] 11:29:31pm   Send All Server Info
OUT [00008022:02608C40CCB5] 11:29:31pm   DOUG-SERVER      2
IN  [00008022:02608C40CCB5] 11:29:34pm   Route Request
OUT [00008022:02608C40CCB5] 11:29:34pm   00000050   1/2
IN  [00008022:02608C40CCB5] 11:29:34pm   Route Request
OUT [00008022:02608C40CCB5] 11:29:34pm   00000050   1/2
IN  [00000050:000000000001] 11:29:35pm   DOUG-SERVER      1
OUT [00000050:FFFFFFFFFFFF] 11:29:35pm   00010000   1/2       00008022   1/2
OUT [00008022:FFFFFFFFFFFF] 11:29:35pm   00010000   1/2       00000050   1/2
OUT [00010000:FFFFFFFFFFFF] 11:29:35pm   00008022   1/2       00000050   1/2
IN  [00000050:000000000001] 11:30:02pm   DOUG-SERVER      1
OUT [00000050:FFFFFFFFFFFF] 11:30:05pm   DOUG-SERVER      1   DOUG-SERVER      2
OUT [00008022:FFFFFFFFFFFF] 11:30:05pm   DOUG-SERVER      1   DOUG-SERVER      2
OUT [00010000:FFFFFFFFFFFF] 11:30:05pm   DOUG-SERVER      1   DOUG-SERVER      2
<Use ALT-ESC or CTRL-ESC to switch screens, or any other key to pause>
```

Fig. 22.3 NetWare router tracking screen that is shown after using the TRACK ON console command.

Tip

Whenever a workstation loads the DOS requester or workstation shells, the workstation issues a GET NEAREST SERVER REQUEST that appears on the server's router tracking screen. If a station is having trouble connecting to the server, check the router tracking screen to see if the GET NEAREST SERVER REQUEST is coming through by typing **TRACK ON** from the console prompt.

Tip

If you are seeing multiple GET NEAREST SERVER REQUESTs from a workstation when no one can attach to the server, make sure the REPLY TO GET NEAREST SERVER configuration parameter is set to YES.

The NetWare router tracking screen can be broken into two basic sections, IN messages and OUT messages. Depending whether you are looking at the IN message (signified by the IN field) or OUT message (signified by the OUT field), the fields that follow differ.

Following is a description of the different fields associated with the inbound message. The values shown below will differ for your server depending on your specific configuration.

IN This field indicates that the message is inbound to the server.

[00000050:000000000001] This field shows you the network number (00000050) and the node address (000000000001) of the server or station that sent the message.

DOUG-SERVER This field shows you the name of the server that issued the message.

1 This field shows you the number of hops from the server sending the message to the current server.

00008022 This field shows you the network number that is known by the server sending the message.

1/2 This field shows you the relative distance of the sending server. The 1 indicates that the server is 1 hop away, and the 2 indicates the number of *ticks* (1 tick equals 1/18s) that it takes for a packet to reach this server from the sending server.

Following is a description of the different fields associated with the outbound message. The values you see for your server will differ depending on your own server configuration.

OUT This field indicates that the message is outbound from the server.

[00008022:FFFFFFFFFFFF] This field shows you the network number (00008022) and that the message is a broadcast intended for all nodes (FFFFFFFFFFFF).

VERSION

When you type **VERSION** from the file server prompt, NetWare displays a few lines of text detailing the version of NetWare in use and licensing information such as the maximum number of users that can access the server concurrently.

VOLUME

When the file server is up and running, you can check which volumes and name spaces are currently loaded by typing **VOLUME** from the file server prompt. NetWare displays a two-column listing that shows each of the mounted volumes in the first column, and the name spaces that are loaded for each in the second column (for example, DOS, MAC, NFS).

Chapter 23

The MONITOR Console Management Utility

Of all the utilities that are provided with NetWare, MONITOR is probably the most robust. When you use this utility, you can perform a wide variety of tasks that assist you in the management of your server and the diagnosis of potential problems.

In this chapter, you learn about the MONITOR utility in detail and specifically:

- Connection information
- File status information
- Memory usage information
- Resource utilization
- Securing the file server console with a password

Loading MONITOR and the Main Menu

Like any other NLM on the server, the MONITOR utility is loaded with the help of the LOAD console command. But, before you continue, you have the option of loading it with one of three specialized parameters:

/NS	Use to load MONITOR without the screen saver (also known as "the snake").
/NH	Use to load MONITOR without help screens, thus saving RAM.
/P	Use to load MONITOR and enable you to select the Processor Utilization option.

If you choose to use one of these parameters, you can use them simply by appending them to the end of the LOAD command. For example, to load the MONITOR utility without the help screens, type **LOAD MONITOR /NH** from the server console prompt.

When you first load MONITOR, NetWare displays a screen divided in half. The upper half provides basic statistical information about the server and the bottom half is a menu of the various tasks that you can perform (see fig. 23.1). For your reference, each of the fields shown in the upper half of the screen is desribed in the following bulleted list.

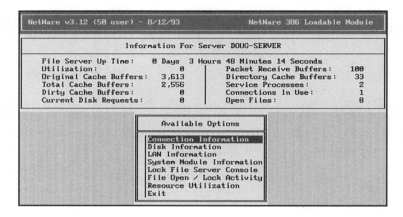

Fig. 23.1 The main menu of MONITOR.

- `File Server Up Time`: This field tells you how long the file server has been up and running.

Tip
If your server's CPU utilization is consistantly above the 40 percent mark, it may be time to start looking at upgrading some of your server's hardware.

- `Utilization`: This field provides you with the current CPU utilization of the file server.

- `Original Cache Buffers`: This field informs you of the number of cache buffers (in blocks) that were available when the file server was first booted. Each block is equal to the cache block size used on the server. For example, if your cache block size is set to 4K and this field shows you 2,000 cache buffers, you have 8M of cache buffers when the server first boots.

- `Total Cache Buffers`: This field shows you how many cache blocks are currently available. The value shown here decreases as additional NLMs are loaded.

Tip

If the number of dirty cache buffers is consistently high, and if your Service Processes are maxed out, try increasing your maximum Service Processes. This may reduce the number of dirty cache buffers and improve the performance of your server.

- `Dirty Cache Buffers`: The field shows you the number of blocks that are sitting in memory waiting to be written to disk.

- `Current Disk Requests`: This field shows you the number of disk requests that are sitting in the server's memory waiting to be processed.

Tip

If the number of Packet Receive Buffers shown reaches your maximum setting, you must increase your maximum. When maxed out, errors such as LAN receive buffer limit reached all buffers are in use. Possible causes: disk channel bottleneck or buffers have been lost can and will appear. In situations like these, users may get various errors on their workstation or their PC may appear to be hung until the maximum is increased.

- `Packet Receive Buffers`: This field shows you the number of buffers that are available to handle requests from stations.

Tip

If the number of Directory Cache Buffers shown reaches your maximum setting, you should increase the maximum if users are experiencing a decrease in performance when performing directory searches.

- `Directory Cache Buffers`: This field shows you the number of buffers that are available to handle the caching of directories.

Tip

If the number of Service Processes shown reaches your maximum setting and you are noticing a decrease in performance, try increasing the maximum by five processes.

- `Service Processes`: This field shows you the number of tasks NetWare is currently capable of handling at any one time. Once processes have been allocated by NetWare, the only way to bring them back down is to reboot the server.

■ `Connections In Use`: This field shows you the number of nodes that are currently connected to the server. A connection is considered to be any workstation that has loaded all of the workstation drivers. A user does not have to log in from the station for this field to increment.

> **Note**
>
> A station that has loaded the workstation drivers but has not logged into the file server appears in MONITOR's Connection Information listing as "NOT-LOGGED-IN."

■ `Open Files`: This field shows you the number of files that are currently opened by the file server, its processes, and all attached users.

Managing Users

With the MONITOR console utility, you can review and manage the various connections currently in use on the server by selecting Connection Information from the Available Options menu. After selecting this option, NetWare displays the Active Connections window that you can scroll through to check which connections are currently in use. From this window, there are several alternatives that are available to you, each of which are discussed within the following sections.

> **Note**
>
> From the Active Connections window, any connections that display NOT-LOGGED-IN and not a user name are workstations that have loaded the network shell or DOS Requester but no one has logged in from them yet.

Clearing a User Connection

When you use the MONITOR console utility, you can clear a specific connection by selecting Connection Information from the Available Options main menu. Next, NetWare displays the Active Connections window which lists each of the connections that are in use. From this window, you can scroll through the listing, and by highlighting the desired ID and pressing the Delete key, you remove the connection.

Reviewing Statistics and the Open Files for a Specific User

After you have selected the desired connection from the Active Connections window, the MONITOR display changes from the previous screen. Like the previous screen which was divided into two halves, this screen displays statistics information in the upper half of the screen while the bottom half provides you with a listing of the files currently opened by this station (see fig. 23.2). For your reference, each of the statistical fields are described in the following bulleted list.

```
┌─────────────────────────────────────────────────────────────────────┐
│ NetWare v3.12 (50 user) - 8/12/93          NetWare 386 Loadable Module │
│  ┌────────────────────────────────────────────────────────────────┐   │
│  │              Connection Information for DOUG                     │   │
│  │  Connection Time:      0 Days  3 Hours 47 Minutes               │   │
│  │  Network Address:      00000022:0260BC40CCB5:4003               │   │
│  │  Requests:                1,432      Status:        Normal       │   │
│  │  Kilobytes Read:            860      Semaphores:          0       │   │
│  │  Kilobytes Written:           0      Logical Record Locks  0      │   │
│  └────────────────────────────────────────────────────────────────┘   │
│       ┌──────────────────────────────────────────────────┐            │
│       │                   Open Files                      │            │
│       │ SYS:PUBLIC/RCONSOLE.HLP                           │            │
│       │ SYS:PUBLIC/SYS$ERR.DAT                            │            │
│       │ SYS:PUBLIC/SYS$MSG.DAT                            │            │
│       │                                                   │            │
│       └──────────────────────────────────────────────────┘            │
└─────────────────────────────────────────────────────────────────────┘
```

Fig. 23.2 Connection statistics that can be reviewed using the MONITOR utility.

- Connection Time: This field shows you how long the user has been logged into the server.

- Network Address: This field shows you the user's network address (that is, the network number), the MAC layer address of the workstation (the physical address of the NIC), and the socket address being used.

- Requests: This field shows you the total number of requests the station has made to the server since it first logged in to the server.

- Kilobytes Read: This field shows you the number of kilobytes the workstation has read since it logged in to the server.

- Kilobytes Written: This field shows you the number of kilobytes the workstation has written to the server disks since it logged in to the server.

- Status: This field displays the current status of the workstation. One of the following status types is shown:

    Normal: The workstation is logged into the server and functioning normally.

    Waiting: The workstation is waiting for a file to be unlocked.

    NOT-LOGGED-IN: The workstation is connected to the file server but no one has logged in yet (when the status has loaded the network drivers but no one logged in).

- Semaphores: This field shows you the number of semaphores in use by this station. A semaphore is used to control how many tasks can control the server resources at one time and how many workstations can run a program at any one time.

■ Logical Record Locks: This field shows you the total number of record locks this station currently has in use. A record lock flags a file as being in use so no other connection can access the file.

On the bottom half of the screen, a window entitled Open Files appears that lists all the files currently opened by the selected user. When you highlight one of these files and press the Enter key, NetWare displays an additional window that lists the record locks in use for the selected file. The fields used for this window are described below.

■ Start: The offset in the file at which the record lock begins.

■ End: The offset in the file at which the record lock ends.

■ Record Lock: This field displays the type of record lock that is being used and will show one of the following types:

Locked Exclusive: The record is locked so no other user can read or write to the record.

Locked Shareable: The record is locked so other users can read from the record but cannot write to it.

Locked: This lock type is shown when the record lock is complete.

TTS Holding Lock: This lock type is shown when the record lock has been released by the application but there are still transactions outstanding for TTS to write to disk.

■ Status: This field displays the status of the lock, which could be one of the following settings:

Logged: The file server is preparing to lock the file.

Not Logged: The "normal" status which shows that there are no outstanding requests for the locks.

Managing Disk Drives

When you use the MONITOR console utility, you can manage the disk drives in your file server by selecting Disk Information from the Available Options main menu. Next, NetWare displays a listing of the disk drives that are currently accessible. To review detailed statistics for a specific drive, highlight the drive and press the Enter key.

After selecting a disk drive, the MONITOR screen changes to provide you with detailed statistics for the selected drive on the upper half of the screen and the Drive Status window that can be used to modify the drive's status in the bottom half (see fig. 23.3). Each of the statistics shown on the screen are described below.

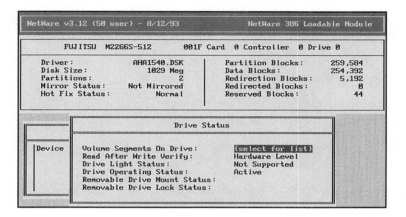

Fig. 23.3 Disk information screen shown with the MONITOR utility.

- **Driver:** This field shows you the name of the driver being used for the selected disk.

- **Disk Size:** This field shows you the total size of the selected disk.

- **Partitions:** This field shows you the number of partitions, NetWare and non-NetWare, on the selected disk.

- **Mirror Status:** This field shows you the current status of the selected disk's mirroring, which could be one of the following:

    Mirrored: The selected disk drive is mirrored to another disk drive.

    Not Mirrored: The selected disk is not mirrored or has been unmirrored due to an error.

> **Caution**
>
> If you selected a disk drive that was initially mirrored but now shows a mirror status of Not Mirrored, a critical error has caused the drive to unmirror. Refer to the heading "Mirroring and Duplexing Problems" in Chapter 27, "Disk Problems," for further information.

    Remirroring: The selected disk is currently being remirrored. This status is shown when NetWare is remirroring disks after a failure or when drives are being mirrored for the first time.

- **Hot Fix Status:** This field shows you if Hot Fix is enabled for the selected disk drive.

> **Caution**
>
> If the status Not-Hot-Fixed appears, this means the hot fix facility has failed and the drive should be replaced.

■ Partition Blocks: This field shows you the total number of blocks on the selected hard disk's NetWare partition.

■ Data Blocks: This field shows you the number of blocks on the selected disk's NetWare partition that are available to store data.

■ Redirection Blocks: This field shows you the total number of blocks that have been allocated for NetWare's Hot Fix feature for the selected disk.

■ Redirected Blocks: This fields shows you the number of bad blocks that were found by Hot Fix and placed in the redirection area.

■ Reserved Blocks: This field shows you the number of blocks that are reserved for Hot Fix's tables.

Tip

If you are noticing that the number of Redirected Blocks is increasing steadily, or fast approaching the number of Redirection Blocks, consider replacing the drive before the server actually fails.

Caution

When the number of Redirected Blocks plus the number of Reserved Blocks equals the total number of Redirection Blocks, NetWare's Hot Fix has failed and the drive should be replaced.

Checking Partitions on a Drive

You can check which NetWare partitions are on a specific disk drive by following these steps:

1. From the Available Options main menu of MONITOR, select Disk Information and then the desired disk drive from the listing of System Disk Drives.

2. After selecting the drive, you can review which NetWare partitions are on the drive by selecting the option Volume Segments on Drive from the Drive Status Window.

Modifying Read After Write Verification

To ensure the integrity of the data on your server disk, you can use what is known as Read After Write verification. The purpose of this feature is to instruct the system that a read should be performed immediately after a write to ensure the correct information was written to disk.

> **Note**
>
> Most disk drivers have a default method they use for read-after-write verification and adjust NetWare's setting appropriately.

You can change the method by which NetWare handles the read-after-write verifying of a drive by following the steps below:

1. From the Available Options main menu of MONITOR, select Disk Information and then the desired disk drive from the listing of System Disk Drives.

2. After you select the drive, NetWare displays the Drive Status window. Within this window, the field Read After Write Verify shows you how NetWare currently handles this task. If you want to change the method for how this verification occurs, highlight the field and select one of the following options:

    Software Level: Instructs NetWare to handle the read-after-write verification.

    Hardware Level: Instructs NetWare to let the disk controller handle the read-after-write verification. You should check your controller documentation before using this option.

    Disable Verify: This option can be selected when the disk drive that you are using can handle its own read-after-write verification. You should check your disk drive documentation before using this option.

Making the Disk Light Flash

While a seemingly trivial task, MONITOR's capability of making a specific disk light flash can make your life that much easier if you are planning on taking a server down to swap out a faulty drive. For example, if you are having a problem with your disks and NetWare statistics information points to drive number 2, you can use the Flash Light feature to find out which drive in the server is actually number 2.

You can use MONITOR to make one of the disk's lights flash by following the steps below:

1. From the Available Options main menu of MONITOR, select Disk Information and then the desired disk drive from the System Disk Drives listing.

2. After you select the drive, you can make the disk's light flash by highlighting the Drive Light Status option and pressing Enter.

> **Note**
>
> This option is only available when your disk driver supports it.

Disabling and Enabling a Disk Drive

Using the MONITOR utility, you can enable or disable a disk drive by following the steps below:

Caution
Disabling a disk drive that is currently in use by the NetWare operating system causes the server to crash.

1. From the Available Options main menu of MONITOR, select Disk Information and then the desired disk drive from the System Disk Drives listing.

2. After selecting the drive, you can enable or disable the drive by selecting the Drive Operating Status option and either selecting the Activate Drive or Deactivate Drive option.

Managing LAN Drivers

When you use the MONITOR console utility you can manage the LAN driver(s) in use on your file server by selecting LAN Information from the Available Options main menu. Next, NetWare presents you with a listing of the LAN drivers that are currently loaded on the server. By selecting one of the LAN drivers from the screen, NetWare displays an additional screen listing detailed statistics for the selected card (see fig. 23.4). Each of the statistics available from this screen is described in the following bulleted list.

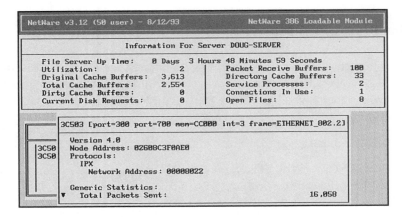

Fig. 23.4 NIC statistical information displayed with the MONITOR utility.

> **Note**
>
> Due to the varying characteristics of NICs, each model of an NIC can have several statistics that are specific to itself. Unfortunately, it is not possible to list every statistic you might see, so the following statistics are considered to be "generic."

- `Driver Name And Configuration`: The top line of the LAN driver's statistics screen displays the selected driver's name and configuration information such as the interrupt and memory addresses in use.

- `Version`: This field shows you the version number of the selected NIC's driver.

- `Node Address`: This field shows you the MAC layer/physical layer address of the selected NIC.

- `Protocols`: This field shows you the communications protocols currently in use for the selected NIC.

- `Network Address`: This field shows you the network address (that is, the network number) to which the selected NIC connects.

- `Total Packets Sent`: This field shows you the number of packets that have been sent by the file server through the selected NIC.

> **Tip**
>
> If you are noticing the `Packets Received` and `Packets Sent` counters are only incrementing by 1 every couple of seconds, there is most probably a problem with your cabling, the NIC, or the NIC's driver.

- `Total Packets Received`: This field shows you the number of packets that have been received by the file server through the selected NIC.

> **Tip**
>
> If the `No ECB Available Count` field is increasing steadily or on a frequent basis, try increasing your `Maximum Packet Receive Buffers` setting.

- `No ECB Available Count`: This field acts as a counter for the server that increments each time a packet is received when there is no packet receive buffer available.

- `Send Packet Too Big Count`: This counter monitors the number of times the server tries to transmit a packet that is too big for the NIC to handle.

Tip

An excessive number of `Packet Too Big` or `Packet Too Small` errors could be indicative of a corrupt or faulty NIC or driver or a cabling problem.

- `Send Packet Too Small Count`: This counter monitors the number of times the server tries to transmit a packet that is too small for the NIC to handle.

- `Receive Packet Overflow Count`: This counter monitors the number of times a packet is received that is too big to store in a cache buffer. This counter should not increase unless you are using an application that cannot negotiate the appropriate packet size.

- `Receive Packet Too Big Count`: This counter monitors the number of times the server receives a packet that is too big for the NIC to handle.

Tip

When the server is receiving an excessive number of packets from the network that are too big or too small, it could indicate a problem with a workstation's NIC, driver, or a potential cabling problem.

- `Receive Packet Too Small Count`: This counter monitors that number of times the server receives a packet that is too small for the NIC to handle.

- `Send Packet Miscellaneous Errors`: This counter monitors the number of times an error occurs when sending a packet.

- `Receive Packet Miscellaneous Errors`: This counter monitors the number of times an error occurs when receiving a packet.

- `Send Packet Retry Count`: This counter monitors the number of times the server must re-transmit a packet due to errors in previous transmissions.

Tip

An excessive number of errors in the Send Packet Retry Count counter could be a result of a faulty driver or NIC.

- `Checksum Errors`: This counter monitors the number of times packets are received with errors due to its checksum problems.

- `Hardware Receive Mismatch Count`: This counter monitors the number of times a packet is received by the NIC when the length does not match the length specified within the packet.

Reviewing Detailed Information on System Modules

When you use the MONITOR console utility you can review the modules that are loaded on your server as well as the memory and resources they are using. Using this information, you have a better understanding of how each module works and how it affects your available RAM and resources.

By selecting System Module Information from the Available Options main menu of MONITOR, a window entitled System Modules appears, listing each of the loaded modules. From this window you can select the desired module to review the different resource tags in use (see fig. 23.5). Finally, you can check which NetWare tracked resources are in use for each resource tag by highlighting the selected tag and pressing the Enter key.

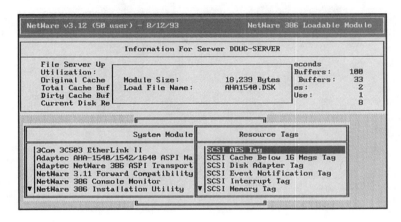

Fig. 23.5 Resource tags in use by a system module shown with the MONITOR utility.

Note

For detailed information on each of the NetWare tracked resources, refer to the heading "Reviewing the Resources Tracked by NetWare," later in this chapter.

Reviewing File Status Information

If you have ever logged into the server, tried to update a file, and then gotten an error message telling you the file was in use, this feature of MONITOR will be invaluable to you.

When you use MONITOR you can review statistical information about any file on the server by selecting the File Open/Lock Activity option from the Available Options main menu. After you select this option, NetWare displays the Select an Entry window that displays all the volumes on the server. All you have to do to review the file information is select a volume, then the directories, and finally the desired file name from the listing provided. Once you select the file, NetWare displays two new windows (see fig. 23.6). Each of the fields within these windows is described in the following bulleted list.

Shortcut
Instead of scrolling through the listing of files to find the desired file, you can type the first few characters of the file name, and MONITOR automatically moves the cursor to the appropriate location (you must be in the same directory as the file before trying this).

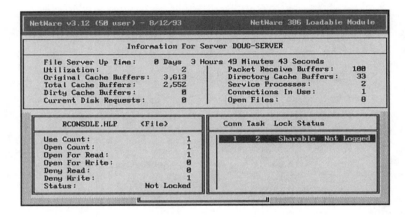

Fig. 23.6 File status information that can be reviewed with the MONITOR utility.

- Use Count: This field shows you the number of connections currently accessing the selected file.

- Open Count: This field shows you the number of connections that currently have the file open.

- Open For Read: This field shows you the number of connections that currently have the file open to read.

- Open For Write: This field shows you the number of connections that currently have the file open to write to.

- Deny Read: This field shows you the number of connections that have the file open to read and are restricting access to the file from other connections.

- Deny Write: This field shows you the number of connections that have the file open to write to and are restricting access to the file from other connections.

- Status: This field shows you the locking status for the file. When locked, additional users are not allowed to access the file.

- Conn: This field shows you the connection numbers of the users accessing the selected file.

- Task: This field is the task number assigned by the shell.

- Lock Status: This field shows you the detailed record locking status of the file. Within this field, one of the following variables is shown:

     Exclusive: No other users are allowed to access the record.

     Shareable: Additional users are allowed to read but not write to the record.

     TTS Holding Lock: The file has been unlocked, but NetWare's TTS system still has some transactions pending.

     Logged: The file server is preparing to lock the file.

     Not Logged: There are no requests outstanding to lock the file.

Reviewing File Server Memory Utilization

On the NetWare server, one of the most important resources is the memory. Because it is so important, you should be checking the server on a regular basis to ensure there is enough free RAM to handle all of the necessary tasks. You can review your memory statistics with MONITOR by selecting the Resource Utilization option from the Available Options main menu. Once you select this option, a window similar to the one in Figure 23.7 appears.

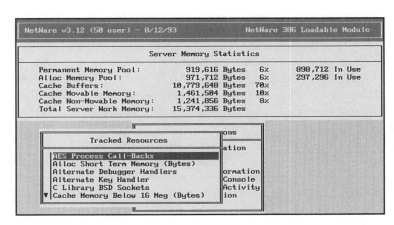

Fig. 23.7 The MONITOR resource utilization window.

Within the Server Memory Statistics window, MONITOR provides you with the following information:

■ The amount of memory allocated per memory pool

■ The percentage of the total server memory that each pool uses

■ For the permanent and alloc pools, MONITOR tells you how much of the pool is actually being used

Each of the fields in the Server Memory Statistics window is described in the following bulleted list.

■ Permanent Memory Pool: This memory pool is used by the server for the long-term memory needs such as the requirements of a disk driver and packet receive buffers. Once memory is allocated to this pool from the Cache Buffers it is not returned until the server is reset.

Tip

By default, the maximum size of the Alloc Short Term Memory pool is 8,388,608 bytes. If the size of this pool reaches this setting, you can increase the maximum using the SET command. Refer to Chapter 10, "Miscellaneous Commands for Environment Management," for information on setting this parameter.

Tip

If the amount of memory allocated to the Alloc Memory pool is significantly higher than the amount of memory actually shown as being in use, you may want to reboot your server to refresh the pools.

■ Alloc Memory Pool: The Alloc Short Term Memory pool is used to provide short term memory requirements, such as the windows of different NLMs, users' drive mappings, broadcast messages, SAP information, and miscellaneous user connection information. Once memory is allocated to the pool from the Cache Buffers, it is not returned until the server is reset.

Tip

If your Cache Buffers are running low, as a temporary fix until you can purchase more RAM, unload any unnecessary NLMs, use the REMOVE DOS command to return some extra RAM to the OS, and reboot the server to refresh the other memory pools.

■ `Cache Buffers:` Cache Buffers provides you with the memory information for the file cache buffer pool. This pool is the total amount of RAM left over for caching files after the other pools have taken their share of the server's total RAM. You should never let this pool run below 50 percent and ideally, it should be a minimum 60-70 percent.

■ `Cache Movable Memory:` NetWare uses this section of the file cache buffer pool to store system tables that change in size, such as the hash tables. When memory is used for this purpose, it is returned to the file cache buffer pool when it is no longer needed.

■ `Cache Non-Movable Memory:` This section of the file cache buffer pool is used for NLMs that are loaded in memory. When memory is used for this purpose, it is returned to the file cache buffer pool when it is no longer needed.

■ `Total Server Work Memory:` This field shows you the total amount of memory that is installed in the file server minus the memory used to run DOS, SERVER.EXE, and the server's ROM BIOS.

Reviewing the Resources Tracked by NetWare

The NetWare server controls the various tasks it must perform by using different "resources." Essentially, a resource is a name for a specific task the server can perform. These resources can be assigned by NetWare to NLMs and other drivers to complete their own tasks.

Using the MONITOR utility, you can review the different resources that are tracked by NetWare by selecting the option Resource Utilization from the Available Options main menu. From the window that is presented next, you can scroll through the listing of tracked resources, and by pressing Enter on the desired resource, you then can scroll through its listing of resource tags.

Each of the resources tracked by NetWare is described in the following bulleted list.

> **Note**
>
> Disk drivers and NLMs can actually have their own resources that can be tracked by NetWare and are added to the listing when they are loaded. As such, the list of tracked resources on your server will most probably have some additional entries.

■ `AES Process Call-Backs:` This resource is used by an NLM to schedule events that will take place in the future. For example, a virus-scanning NLM may use the resource to plan the next time it will perform its scan.

■ `Alloc Short Term Memory (Bytes):` The server's Alloc Short Term Memory pool is used by NLMs for short term memory requests such as storing screen information from a menu. By selecting this resource, you can view all of the NLMs and other drivers using this pool.

Next, you could view the amount of memory that is being used by each NLM or driver by highlighting the driver name and pressing the Enter key.

- `C Library BSD Sockets`: This resource is used to track the number of Berkley UNIX sockets in use on the server.

- `Cache Movable Memory (Bytes)`: The server's Cache Movable Memory pool is used by the server to store information such as DETs, FATs, and various other tables. When you select this resource, NetWare displays a listing of all drivers and NLMs using this pool. You then can select a specific resource to determine how much memory it is actually using.

- `Cache Non-Movable Memory`: The server's Cache Non-Movable Memory pool is used by the server to store modules in memory. When you select this resource, NetWare displays a listing of all drivers and NLMS that are using this pool. You then can select a specific resource to determine how much memory it is actually using.

- `Console Command Handlers`: This resource tracks the modules loaded on the server that add additional console commands. For example, the CDROM NLM provides several additional commands that can be used from the console prompt.

- `Disk Adapter Locks`: This resource tracks modules that need to gain access to information pertaining to the server's disk drive adapters.

- `Disk Drive Locks`: This resource tracks modules that need to gain access to information pertaining to the server's disk drives.

- `Disk File System Partition Locks`: This resource tracks modules that need to gain access to information pertaining to the NetWare partitions on the server.

- `Disk Raw Partition Locks`: This resource tracks a module's access to the server's disk partitions.

- `Event Notification Call-Backs`: This resource tracks when a major system event has occurred. For example, your disk driver may use this resource to track the status of the disk controller channel.

- `Hardware Interrupt Handlers`: This resource tracks the hardware and modules that are using interrupts in the server.

- `Interrupt Time Call-Backs`: This resource tracks modules that process tasks on a regular basis. For example, a virus-scanning NLM might scan the server's hard disk every hour on the hour.

- `IPX Sockets`: This resource tracks modules that use socket connections between two or more devices.

■ LSL AES Event Call-Backs: This resource is used by the NIC driver to schedule future events.

■ LSL Default Protocol Stacks: This resource tracks protocol NLMs that are configured to accept packets not acceptable by other protocol NLMs.

■ LSL Packet Receive Buffers: This resource is used by NetWare to determine which modules are using specific packet receive buffers so it knows which buffers can be freed up when the module is unloaded.

■ LSL Pre-Scan Protocol Stacks: This resource tracks the protocol NLMs that have been configured to scan all packets to see if they belong to them before they are accepted.

■ LSL Protocol Stacks: This resource tracks the different NLMs that are registered with the operating system as being a protocol stack.

■ NCP Extensions: This resource tracks the different modules that use their own NetWare Core Protocols (NCPs).

■ Network Management Managers: This resource tracks NMAGENT and the number of managers it has allocated.

■ Network Management Objects: This resource tracks NMAGENT and the number of objects it has allocated.

■ Network Management Triggers: This resource tracks NMAGENT and the number of triggers it has allocated.

■ Permanent Memory (Bytes): The server's Permanent Memory pool is used by the operating system to track a variety of information such as users' disk space restrictions. By selecting this resource, you can view each of the modules using this resource. Then, by selecting the desired modules, you can determine how much memory is being used.

■ Poll Procedure Call-Backs: This resource tracks modules that process certain tasks at set intervals.

■ Processes: This resource tracks modules that initiate any process when they are loaded.

■ Processor Exception Handlers: This resource tracks modules that attempt to perform a task not allowable on the server.

■ Registered Disk Adapters: This resource tracks the configuration of the various loaded disk drivers.

■ Registered Hardware Options: This resource tracks the NIC and DISK drivers that make requests to different interrupts or memory and I/O port addresses.

■ Registered MLID Boards: This resource tracks the NIC drivers loaded on the server.

■ Remote Server Sessions (Instances): This resource tracks the remote servers that have a minimum of one connection established.

■ Screen Input Call-Backs: This resource tracks modules which use a method for displaying information on the server's console without requiring keyboard input.

■ Screens: This resource tracks the number of screens a module has opened. For example, the MONITOR NLM may have several screens opened at any one time.

■ Semaphores: This resource tracks modules that use semaphores to grant and restrict a user's ability to access a resource.

■ Semi-Permanent Memory (Bytes): The server's Semi-Permanent Memory pool is used by modules that are planning to use a section of memory for an extended period of time (that is, disk drivers). When you select this resource, you can review the modules using the resource. Then, by selecting the module, you can review how much memory is being used for this pool.

■ Service Advertising (Instances): This resource tracks the number of times a module broadcasts its presence across the network.

■ Service Connection Tasks Numbers: This resource tracks a module's task numbers for use by a connection. For example, a backup software NLM might automatically login to a file server and use a connection on the server.

■ Service Connections: This resource tracks all the connections between the server and the attached workstations.

■ Settable Parameters: This resource tracks any modules that add parameters that can be used with the server's SET command.

■ STREAMS: Active Stream Handles: This resource tracks the communications streams in use.

■ Tracked Resource Types: This resource tracks the modules which add additional tracked resources to the server. By selecting this resource, you can view a listing of each of the modules that has added a tracked resource to the server. Then, by selecting the module, you can view the number of resources that the module added.

Locking the File Server Console with a Password

If you want to ensure that only authorized personnel can issue commands from the file server's console, you can use the MONITOR utility to lock the console with a password.

Tip
If you ever forget the password you entered to lock the console, the password for the SUPERVISOR ID also works.

When you select Lock File Server Console from the Available Options main menu of MONITOR, NetWare prompts you to enter a password that is used to lock the console. After entering the password, your server's console is locked until the password is entered.

Viewing the Processor Utilization

If you loaded MONITOR with the *-p* option, you can select the option Processor Utilization from the Available Options main menu of MONITOR. Once selected, MONITOR presents you with a window entitled Available Processes & Interrupts where you can select the process or interrupt you want to view. After making your selection, MONITOR presents an additional screen where you can view the amount of time and the percentage of time the CPU spends servicing the selected process or interrupt.

Chapter 24

Miscellaneous NLMs

Aside from the various NLMs that are discussed throughout this book, there are a few others you may find of use when managing your NetWare file server.

In this chapter, we examine a few of these NLMs and how they can be used in your environment.

Logging what Happens on the Server Console

Commands issued at the file server console and information that is displayed on the console only remain visible for a brief period of time. As more information is sent to the server's display, previous commands and errors scroll off the screen, never to be seen again, unless you use CONLOG.NLM.

CONLOG is a fairly new utility available with the NetWare OS that is used to track what actually occurs on the console. When NLMs are loaded on the console, CONLOG tracks the displayed information; when commands are entered on the console, CONLOG tracks the commands.

When you type **LOAD CONLOG** at the file server console prompt, NetWare begins logging the console display to a file called SYS:\ETC\CONSOLE.LOG. The log file remains open until you unload the utility by typing **UNLOAD CONLOG** at the console prompt.

> **Note**
>
> Before you attempt to load CONLOG, make sure you have a directory called ETC off the root of the SYS volume; otherwise, you get an error.

Unfortunately, since CONLOG tracks the logging information in the server's memory, you cannot view the actual log until you unload CONLOG, which then forces NetWare to write the data to disk.

> **Tip**
>
> When the server is first being booted, the commands stored in the AUTOEXEC.NCF file load fairly quickly and then scroll off the screen. Because it is difficult to see any potential errors in time, you can place the LOAD CONLOG command near the beginning of the AUTOEXEC.NCF file to track everything that happens when the server boots.

> **Caution**
>
> When CONLOG is loaded on the server, it uses roughly five percent of the CPU's time while commands are being entered or data is scrolled across the screen.

Creating and Modifying ASCII Text Files from the Console

Throughout this book, you have seen examples of ASCII text files called NCF files that can be used on the console just like a DOS BAT file. While in many cases you use a DOS editor to create or modify these files, NetWare provides you with a utility, known as EDIT.NLM, that can perform the same task from the server's console.

When you type **LOAD EDIT** from the file server prompt, NetWare presents you with a window asking for the file's name. Within this window, type in the file name, including the full path to the file, that you want to create or edit. Alternately, you can supply the same information from the command line. For example, to create the file ABC.TXT in the SYSTEM directory, you could type **LOAD EDIT SYS:\SYSTEM\ABC.TXT**.

After entering the file name, NetWare presents you with a full-screen window displaying the file's contents. From this screen, you can make any necessary modifications. When finished, press the Esc key and confirm whether or not you want to save the file.

Changing the Console's Default Keyboard Language

NetWare 3.12 provides you with the capability of supporting different keyboard language types on the console such as:

- Germany
- France

- Italy

- Spain

- United States

To change your current keyboard type from the default United States, type **LOAD KEYB** *country* from the file server's console prompt.

Clearing NOT-LOGGED-IN Connections

When the network shells or the DOS Requester are first loaded on the workstation, a request known as a "Get Nearest Server Request" is issued from the workstation onto the network. This request travels throughout the network cabling, looking for the first server that it finds. If the server is operational and able to accept users, a reply is sent to the workstation confirming its presence and the station then has a logical attachment to the server.

From the time the station receives its reply until the time that a user actually logs into the server, a connection known as a NOT-LOGGED-IN connection is held open on the server. These connections can be viewed from the Connection Information screen of the MONITOR utility.

While these types of connections are necessary to enable the user to log in, they can cause a potential problem with regard to your server's user count. If the maximum number of users in your company exceeds the maximum number of concurrent users that can be supported by your file server, someone trying to log into the server may be denied access due to insufficient connection slots being available because of an excessive number of NOT-LOGGED-IN connections. Previously, your only options were to manually delete these types of connections or ask users to turn off their PCs if they were not going to use the network. Thankfully, Novell came out with a utility that can automatically remove NOT-LOGGED-IN connections after a settable period of time: NLICLEAR. You can use NLICLEAR by typing the following from the command line:

```
LOAD NLICLEAR [poll=x] [conn=y] [notify]
```

Based on the preceding syntax, replace:

> *x* with the period of time, in seconds, that you want NLICLEAR to scan the server for NOT-LOGGED-IN connections. When the poll parameter is left out, NLICLEAR defaults to 60 seconds, but you can change this value to anywhere between 15 seconds and 3,600 seconds.

> *y* with the number of connections you want NLICLEAR to scan starting from the last possible connection. For example, if your server supports 100 connections and you use the CONN=25, NLICLEAR scans connections 75 to 100 for NOT-LOGGED-IN connections.

The *notify* parameter is included when you want NLICLEAR to display a message on the console each time it clears a connection.

EXAMPLE: To clear the NOT-LOGGED-IN connections every five minutes and force NLICLEAR to display a message on the console every time it clears a connection, type the following from the file server's console prompt:

LOAD NLICLEAR POLL=300 NOTIFY

Tip

Do not set your polling value too low. If a user turns on their PC and does not log in within the polling period, NLICLEAR clears their connection and they either have to reboot their PC or reload the shell or DOS Requester.

Monitoring Protocol Statistics

PROTO is a NetWare NLM utility that can be used to track statistics for the protocols in use on your file server. By typing **LOAD PROTO** from the file server's console prompt, a menu appears, listing each of the protocols currently in use. By selecting one of these protocols, PROTO provides you with a variety of statistics you can use to determine what is occurring on the server and network.

Note

To fully understand all of the statistics PROTO displays, you must have a thorough understanding of how the protocols work.

Chapter 25

Accessing and Working on the Console

Working on the NetWare console is a fairly straightforward task, but there are a few things you should know about how you can access the console in the first place and what to do when you're there.

In this chapter, you examine console access and specifically:

■ Learn the various keystrokes that can be used at the console

■ Use RCONSOLE and ACONSOLE to access the console remotely

■ Use NCF files to automate commands

Maneuvering around the Console

When you are working directly on the file server console, the following special keystrokes can be used to maneuver around the screens and through the different commands:

Keystroke	Description
Alt+Esc	Scrolls through the various active screens. Can only be used when working directly on the server console.
Ctrl+Esc	Selects an active screen to view from a menu listing. Can only be used when working directly on the server console.
Up Arrow	Scrolls backward through the last commands you typed from the command line.
Down Arrow	Scrolls forward through the command listing.

(continues)

Keystroke	Description
Home	Returns your cursor to the beginning of the prompt line.
End	Places your cursor at the end of the prompt line.
Alt	When held down, displays the name of the current screen. Can only be used when working directly on the console.

Remote Console Management

Most of the configuration and a fair amount of the monitoring facilities are initiated from the file server console. Unfortunately, depending on your proximity to the server, sitting right in front of the console may not always be an option to you. In cases like this, two utilities are available with NetWare that enable you to access the server console from across the floor, from a different building, or even from another city or country.

RCONSOLE and ACONSOLE are NetWare's remote management utilities that are used to provide you with a virtual console at your desktop. When you use the instructions in this section, you can use one of these two utilities to access the server console at your workstation and issue any of the commands as if you were sitting right at the server.

Accessing the Console over a Dedicated Link
NetWare's RCONSOLE utility is used when you want to remotely access the file server console from a station that has a direct communications link with the network. Before you jump in and try to use RCONSOLE, there is a little bit of preparation that must take place at the file server.

While RCONSOLE is run from the workstation, it relies on two files that must be loaded on the console:

- *REMOTE.NLM.* This loadable module manages inbound and outbound information from the keyboard and monitor.

- *RSPX.NLM.NLM.* This loadable module acts as the communications driver that is used to advertise the server's ability to accept requests from RCONSOLE. This module also interacts with REMOTE.NLM to provide support for the SPX protocol.

Using the NetWare LOAD console command, you can load these NLMs by typing the following from the file server console prompt:

```
LOAD REMOTE [password]
LOAD RSPX
```

Note

These NLMs must be loaded in the order shown.

Tip

If you add these commands to your AUTOEXEC.NCF file, it is highly recommended that you include the password on the LOAD REMOTE load line. Without it, NetWare pauses while it is booting to prompt you for a password.

Tip

If you have NetWare 3.11 servers on your LAN, you should update their RCONSOLE.EXE, REMOTE.NLM, and RSPX.NLM programs with the ones you got with NetWare 3.12. The files that shipped with 3.11 do not enable you to access the 3.12 servers properly.

Including the password on the same line as the LOAD REMOTE command is optional. If you do not specify a password, NetWare prompts you for one after you type **LOAD REMOTE**. When prompted, you either can enter a password or press the Enter key. If you did not enter a password, NetWare prompts you for one the first time you try to run RCONSOLE.

After loading these two NLMs, the next step is to gain access to the RCONSOLE utility and its associated files. To use the files shown below, you must either be logged into the server with the rights necessary to access the directory, or these files can be run from the workstation's hard disk.

File	Directory
RCONSOLE.EXE	SYSTEM and PUBLIC
RCONSOLE.HLP	SYSTEM and PUBLIC
IBM$RUN.OVL	PUBLIC
SYS$ERR.DAT	PUBLIC
SYS$MSG.DAT	PUBLIC
SYS$HELP.DAT	PUBLIC

Tip

When the files are placed on the workstation, you do not have to be logged into the server. As long as you have loaded the network shells or the DOS Requester, you can use RCONSOLE successfully.

Note

NetWare 3.12 places the RCONSOLE.EXE program in the SYSTEM and PUBLIC directories, but previous versions only placed it in the SYSTEM directory.

With these files in your current directory or path, you then can type RCONSOLE to get a listing of the various servers currently available for remote access. From this listing, you then can highlight the desired server and enter the password when prompted.

Tip

If you do not see the server you are looking for in the listing of available servers, make sure RSPX has been loaded on the server in question.

Note

If you did not specify a password when you loaded REMOTE, NetWare asks you for a password when you select the desired server. You must enter a password. That password is then used by NetWare for all future RCONSOLE sessions until the server is rebooted.

Accessing the Console over an Asynchronous Line

Accessing the server's console when your workstation is directly attached to the network is a nice feature, but what if you are at home or on the road somewhere and you get a call from one of your users notifying you of a problem with the server? While accessing the server with RCONSOLE may not be an option, you can use NetWare's ACONSOLE utility to call the server from a remote location with a standard asynchronous line, such as your phone line.

Preparing Your ACONSOLE Installation

NetWare's ACONSOLE utility is used when you want to remotely access the file server's console from a station using a dial-up asynchronous communications line and a modem. Before you jump in and try to use ACONSOLE, there is a little bit of preparation that must take place at the file server.

Because ACONSOLE is a utility used to access the console asynchronously, the first thing you need is two modems. One modem must be attached directly to the server that you are accessing and the other modem is used on the workstation from which you are accessing the server.

Next, while ACONSOLE is run from your PC, it relies on two files that must be loaded on the console:

- *REMOTE.NLM.* This loadable module is used to manage inbound and outbound information from the keyboard and monitor.

- *RS232.NLM.* This loadable module acts as the communications driver used to activate the server's serial port transfer monitor and keyboard information from the remote PC to the REMOTE.NLM module.

Note

These NLMs *must* be loaded in the order shown.

Using the NetWare LOAD console command, you can load these NLMS by typing the following at the file server console prompt:

```
LOAD REMOTE [password]
LOAD RS232 [serial_port] [modem_speed]
```

Based on the preceding syntax, replace:

password with the password you want to use for remote access. Entering the password at the same time as the LOAD REMOTE command is optional. If you do not specify a password, NetWare prompts you for one after you type **LOAD REMOTE**.

serial_port with the serial port (for example, COM1) that the modem is attached to on the server. If you do not enter this parameter on the load line, NetWare prompts you for it.

modem_speed with the maximum baud rate the modem supports. If you do not enter this parameter on the load line, NetWare prompts you for it.

Note

If you add these commands to your AUTOEXEC.NCF file, it is recommended that you include each of the parameters shown. Without them, NetWare pauses while it is booting to prompt you for each parameter.

After loading these two NLMs, you must ensure that the following files are accessible from your workstation. Beside each file name, their locations on the server are provided. If you are going to be using ACONSOLE from a workstation that does not have access to a server, you must copy these files to your PC's local disk.

File	Directory
ACONSOLE.EXE	SYSTEM
IBM$RUN.OVL	PUBLIC
SYS$ERR.DAT	PUBLIC
SYS$MSG.DAT	PUBLIC
SYS$HELP.DAT	PUBLIC

Configuring Your ACONSOLE Installation

After you have gone through all the preparatory work, you now are ready to configure your ACONSOLE installation with the appropriate modem settings and the phone numbers you call to access the servers. The actual configuration has two parts—the server side and the workstation side.

The Server. During the ACONSOLE preparation, the RS232 module was loaded to enable the server operating system to interact with the modem attached to the serial port. Once this module was loaded, two additional commands were made accessible from the console—*RS232* and *MODEM*.

To view the current serial port settings, you can type **RS232** at the command line and press the Enter key. NetWare then tells you the serial port, interrupt, port address, and speed of the server's modem.

To send a command to the modem, you can use the MODEM command in one of three ways:

- MODEM: When you type **MODEM**, NetWare enables you to interact directly with the modem and enter the specific commands from a special prompt.

- MODEM *filename:* Instead of issuing commands from the server, you can create a basic ASCII text file. When you append the name of the file after the MODEM command, NetWare sends the contents directly to the modem.

- MODEM *commands:* When you use this method, you can append the required modem commands directly after the MODEM command.

The Workstation. With the necessary files in your current directory or path, when you type **ACONSOLE**, NetWare presents you with a menu containing two options—Connect to Remote Location and Configure Modem. When you select Configure Modem, NetWare presents you with a window listing the current modem configuration (see fig. 25.1). From this window, you can modify each field to suit your modem's specific requirements. Refer to your modem's manual for the appropriate settings.

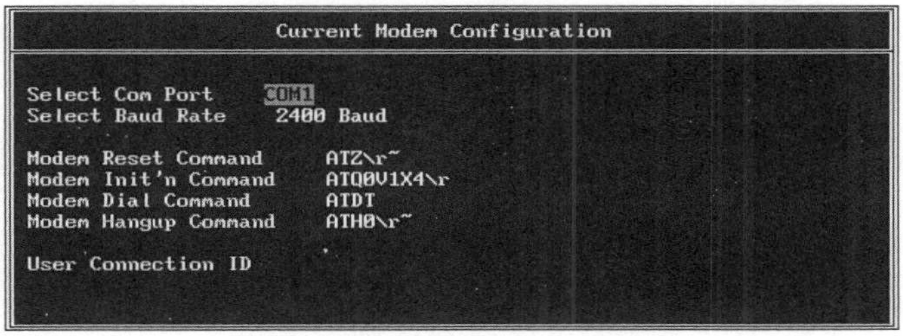

```
                      Current Modem Configuration

    Select Com Port        COM1
    Select Baud Rate       2400 Baud

    Modem Reset Command     ATZ\r~
    Modem Init'n Command    ATQ0V1X4\r
    Modem Dial Command      ATDT
    Modem Hangup Command    ATH0\r~

    User Connection ID
```

Fig. 25.1 Configure modem window used with ACONSOLE to configure your modem's communications parameters.

Once your modem settings for the workstation have been set, you can create a listing of the various servers you can call by selecting the Connect To Remote Location option from the main menu. NetWare then presents you with a window listing all the servers currently in your calling list. To add a server to this listing, press the Insert key and enter the server name and phone number as prompted, and then press Esc to update your listing.

Connecting to a Server with ACONSOLE

After you have completed the preparatory work and configuration, accessing the server with ACONSOLE is a breeze. After you select Connect To Remote Location and then the desired location from the listing provided, ACONSOLE automatically initializes your modem and dials the desired server.

Once the modem establishes a connection with the server, you must enter the remote console password you specified when you loaded the REMOTE module on the server.

Tip

If you forget the password you used when loading REMOTE, the password used for the SUPERVISOR ID also works.

Special Keys and Commands Used During Remote Console Access

Whether you accessed the console remotely with RCONSOLE or ACONSOLE, there are several special keystrokes you should know, and a few additional commands that are available to you.

Once connected to the console remotely, the following keystrokes are used to maneuver around the console:

Keystroke	Description
+	Scrolls forward through active screens
-	Scrolls backward through active screens
Shift+Esc	Clears the remote console session and returns the listing of servers
* (from the number pad)	Calls the Available Options menu

If you pressed the * key on your numeric keypad, NetWare displays a menu similar to the one shown in Figure 25.2. From this menu, you can perform the following tasks:

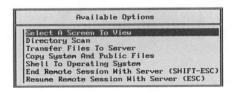

Fig. 25.2 Available Options menu presented when accessing the console remotely.

■ *View active screens:* To view other active screens on the console, select the Select a Screen To View option and then the desired screen.

■ *View a directory listing:* To view a directory listing of the server's local drivers or the NetWare volumes, select the Directory Scan option and then insert the name of the directory you want to scan.

■ *Copy files to the server:* By selecting the option Transfer Files To Server, you can copy files from your workstation's local disk to the server's DOS or NetWare partitions.

■ *Copy the NetWare system and public files:* When you select the Copy System And Public Files option, NetWare enables you to reinstall the system and public files from the workstation's local drives. If your current directory contains subdirectories for each NetWare disk, you can install the system and public files from these subdirectories instead of the local floppy drive.

■ *Shell to DOS:* When you select the Shell To Operating System option, a DOS shell opens so you can perform any DOS-related commands. You then have to type **EXIT** to return to the console screen.

■ *Close your remote console session:* You can select the End Remote Session With Server option to close your remote console session and return to the server listing.

Automating Console Tasks

Managing a LAN can be such a time-consuming task that anything you can do to automate your responsibilities can really make your life that much easier. While NetWare 3.12 does not provide any specific automation tools, you can save yourself a bit of time by creating your own NCF files.

In NetWare terms, an NCF file is like a DOS batch file that can be used on the file server console. By using a basic DOS ASCII file editor, you can create NCF files listing the various commands you want executed. For example, when your server first boots, an NCF file, AUTOEXEC.NCF, loads all the drivers necessary for initializing your NICs and other modules. Feel free to experiment creating and using your own NCF files.

> **Note**
>
> The NCF file should be stored in the SYSTEM directory or within one of the directories that were defined in the server's search path.

> **Shortcut**
>
> You can create an NCF file that can be used to automatically reboot the file server. Using an ASCII file editor, create a file named RESET.NCF that contains the following commands (you can call the file anything you like, but it must have the NCF extension):
>
> ```
> REMOVE DOS
> DOWN
> EXIT
> ```
>
> With your newly created NCF file, you can type **RESET** either directly from the console or through a remote session; NetWare automatically shuts down the file server and reboots it!

Chapter 26

Debugging and Resolving File Server Abends

With all the tasks an administrator does, one of the most important ones is troubleshooting problems with the server. While there are a variety of problems that could arise in a networking environment, file server abends are the most critical. When a file server abends, it is not accessible by any user on the network; as such, the problem must be resolved as quickly as possible.

Using the NetWare DEBUG Feature

When the file server abends, the abend message and a hexadecimal stack appears on the file server console. At this point, you have the option of turning off your server, dumping the memory contents to disk for diagnosis by Novell (known as a *coredump*), or gathering some information with Novell's DEBUG utility.

Using DEBUG, you can gather a variety of information, such as:

- The modules that were loaded when the server abended

- The processes that were running when the server abended

- The screens that were loaded when the server abended

- The version of NetWare in use

- The reason for the abend

From the file server prompt you can access DEBUG by using the following keystroke combination:

```
Shift+Shift+Alt+Esc
```

Caution

This keystroke combination *will* work when the server is operating. Do *not* attempt to access DEBUG when the server is up as this disrupts users accessing the server.

After you have entered the special keystroke combination, NetWare presents you with several lines of hexadecimal stack information and a pound (#) prompt. While most DEBUG functions prove to be of little use unless you are a programmer who knows the inner workings of NetWare, there are several commands that can provide you with some helpful insight to resolving your server abend. Table 26.1 provides you with a listing of these special commands and a description of what each one does.

Note

These commands must be issued from the debug prompt (#).

Table 26.1 Commands that are of use within NetWare's DEBUG utility.

Command	Description
.A	Displays the cause of the abend.
.C	Instructs DEBUG to perform a coredump.
.H	Displays the DEBUG help menu.
.M	Displays the names and addresses of the modules that were loaded when the server abended.
.P	Displays all of the processes that were running on the server when it abended.
.R	Displays the specific process that was running at the time of the abend.
.S	Displays the names of the screens that were loaded when the server abended.
.V	Displays the version of NetWare in use.
H	Displays a detailed help screen.
G	Returns to the screen you were on prior to entering the DEBUG facility.
Q	Returns to the DOS prompt.
V	Displays each of the screens that were loaded when the server abended.

> **Tip**
>
> When your file server abends, NetWare only gives you the option of rebooting the server if you want to reset NetWare. Unfortunately, this means you must wait while the server restarts as if a cold boot was run. To reset the server quickly, access DEBUG and use the Q command to return to DOS. NetWare then returns you to the DOS prompt on the server where you can type SERVER to reload NetWare.

Common Abends and Reparative Actions

In this section, we examine the two most common abends—General Protection Processor Exceptions (GPPEs) and NMI Parity Errors—and the various methods you can use to resolve these problems.

There are hundreds, if not thousands, of possible error messages you may encounter on your NetWare server. Some of these errors are extremely rare, while others are far more common. This section introduces you to two of the most common types of server errors, and offers some advice for counteracting these problems.

General Protection Processor Exception (GPPE)

One of the most common errors, and one of the most annoying to troubleshoot, is the General Protection Processor Exception (GPPE) file server abend. The GPPE error halts all operations with the file server and thus requires your immediate attention.

When you are trying to troubleshoot a GPPE error, it is imperative that you know as much about your server as possible. GPPE is an acronym for General Protection Processor Exception and it is just that: general. In the majority of cases, it means that some conflict has caused the problem, either conflicts between two devices configured with the same settings, or a server-based software conflict.

Identifying Causes of GPPEs

Since the GPPE can be so difficult to resolve, knowing where to look can be a critical factor to resolve these errors. To assist you in troubleshooting your server, following is a listing of the most probable causes of GPPEs:

- *Improperly configured or conflicting hardware:* Conflicts with the configuration of your server hardware are probably the most probable cause of most GPPEs. When you are installing and configuring your hardware (such as adapters, disk drives, and memory), it is critical that you ensure everything is set up properly. Never assume that, if the server boots, then the configuration is correct. Some configuration-related errors can take days or even months to appear.

■ *Faulty or corrupt NLMs and drivers:* Using poorly written or corrupt NLMs or drivers can get you on the fast track to abending your server. Since these programs run directly on the file server and interact with the NetWare operating system, problems with these programs almost certainly abend your server.

Tip
If you suspect that a certain NLM is causing you problems, try recopying it from a reliable source, such as the master diskettes. The NLM could have been corrupted somehow and thus will not function properly.

Tip
When having problems with GPPEs, check which versions and revisions of NLMs and other drivers you are using. With this information at hand, consult your vendors to make sure you are running the latest versions/revisions. When vendors find problems with one of their drivers/NLMs, they correct the problem, but don't always notify all their clients.

■ *Faulty memory and other hardware:* While not as common as software-related problems, it is quite possible there is a faulty memory module or other piece of hardware in the server causing you grief. If you have confirmed that the configuration of the server is in order and you are running the latest and greatest NLMs and drivers, look to running the diagnostic programs that came with your hardware.

■ *Faulty utilities:* There are some third-party utilities on the market that can be loaded on the file server but are accessed from the workstation. If these utilities interact with any of the NetWare files (such as the bindery), GPPEs could arise if there is a programming problem in the utility.

■ *Poorly conditioned power:* Probably one of the most overlooked problems with servers regards the power being fed into the server. Poorly conditioned power or inconsistent power supplies can restrict your hardware from operating properly, thus the possibility of the GPPE.

Tips for Resolving GPPEs

As you are trying to resolve your server GPPE problems and carefully working through the points noted under the previous heading, there are several questions you can ask yourself to speed up the troubleshooting process. By asking yourself, or your server's administrator, the following questions, you will be in a better position to resolve the issue at hand:

1. In the server GPPE abend message, was there any specific reference to a utility or file? While this may not solve your problem immediately, it may lead you to the source of the problem. If a utility or file is mentioned in the abend message, start your troubleshooting by taking an in-depth look at what the utility or file does.

2. Were there any critical errors before the GPPE occurred? In some cases, a GPPE is a cause, not an effect, of the server abending. Checking the file server's error log (SYS$LOG.ERR) may provide you with some insight about what happened before the GPPE.

3. What was happening when the server abended? Knowing what users were doing at the time of the abend may be just the thing that you need to know to resolve the problem. In certain cases, accessing a corrupt file or using a poorly designed or corrupt program may cause the server to abend.

4. Can you re-create the abend? You should try to re-create the abend that occurred. By pinpointing the process that causes the abend, you and Novell are in a better position to clear up the problem once and for all.

5. Are you using any patches? Periodically, Novell issues patches for the operating system or another one of its utilities. If you are not using these patches, you may want to check into using them as they may be just the thing you need to fix your problem.

VIII

> **Caution**
>
> Before using any patches, carefully review the accompanying documentation. Some patches are only meant for use in certain situations and others should only be run in place of some other utility or patch.

Non-Maskable Interrupt Parity Error

The Non-Maskable Interrupt Parity error is a NetWare abend that, for the most part, is generated due to the failure of some memory component of the file server. Unfortunately, isolating this problem is not as simple as just replacing all the memory in your server.

Identifying Causes of NMI Parity Errors

If you are familiar with PC hardware, you know there is a variety of components that have some type of RAM. The following listing provides you with just a sample of what hardware could cause these abends:

- SIMMs or memory modules

- Memory boards

- System boards

- Network Interface Cards (NICs)

- Video controllers

Troubleshooting

- Disk adapter boards and SCSI cards

- Miscellaneous adapter boards

To make this error even more interesting, even though it is a memory-related problem, it does not necessarily imply that the memory is bad. Configuration conflicts or incompatible hardware could also generate an NMI.

Because the NMI can be caused by such a wide variety of situations and problems, to trouble-shoot these errors, you should follow the same steps and procedures that were outlined for troubleshooting the GPPE abends.

Tips for Resolving NMI Parity Errors

Along with the procedures outlined for troubleshooting the GPPE, there are a few additional steps you can follow to resolve these abends. Following are some tips on where you should look for the cause of the NMI and how to resolve it:

- *Run extensive tests on your SIMMs and other hardware:* Use the diagnostic software that came with your server hardware or a third-party diagnostic package to run the diagnostic tests on your server with several passes for the SIMMs. Some memory problems may be intermittent and require several passes with a diagnostic program to pick them up.

Tip

If you can afford it, there are a few hardware-based memory testers that provide a much more thorough examination of your SIMMs.

- *Don't buy cheap memory for the server:* Since the memory in the server is so crucial, this is not the place to try and save a little money by buying cheap SIMMs or memory modules. These products may be satisfactory for your workstations, but the server's dependency on memory demands high quality.

- *Don't mix and match memory vendors:* A SIMM is a SIMM is a SIMM, right? Wrong. While SIMMs should be fully compatible with each other, there may be slight differences that could cause your server to abend.

- *Don't mix different memory speeds in the server:* Mix different speed RAM in your server and you're just asking for trouble. If you are currently using 70 ns memory, stick with 70 ns.

- *Check your server hardware documentation on memory configurations:* Some PC hardware enables you to mix and match different sized SIMMs in the server (such as using 2M SIMMs and 4M SIMMs in the same box), while others require consistency between SIMMS.

Chapter 27

Disk Problems

It's a sad truth, but as a NetWare administrator, you encounter disk problems that are simply a fact of life and must be resolved as quickly as possible. When problems arise with a disk in the server, depending on the measures of protection used (for instance, mirroring or duplexing), users may not be able to work. Therefore, it is imperative that these problems are resolved as quickly as possible.

In this chapter, we look at topics related to disk problems, in particular the following:

- Solving problems with disk mirroring and duplexing

- Unmirroring your disks

- Remirroring after replacing a faulty disk

- Solving drive deactivation errors

- Preparing for drive problems

Mirroring and Duplexing Problems

In Chapter 3, "Installing the File Server," you saw how you could use NetWare's disk mirroring or duplexing facilities to provide disk-drive dependability even when a drive fails completely. Should a single drive fail, the mirrored drive continues to operate without any interruption of service. Once you have the opportunity to replace the faulty drive, the drives can be remirrored without interrupting service to the users.

When a drive error occurs, a message is displayed on the file server console and is written to the server's error log (SYS$LOG.ERR). Since monitoring the server console on a regular basis is not feasible, it is extremely important that you check the disk status on a regular basis. When mirroring is disabled and the situation is not resolved promptly, your server could be exposed to additional downtime should the other drive fail as well.

Reviewing Mirroring Status

To assist you in determining the status of your server's drive mirroring, there are several areas you can look to:

- *Server Error Logs:* The file server's error log SYS$LOG.ERR is located in the SYSTEM directory of the SYS volume. This error log contains notes about any disk problems or failures.

- *The MONITOR.NLM Console Utility:* MONITOR can be used to review the status of your server's disk drives by selecting Drive Information from the main menu and then the desired drive. Once the drive has been selected, NetWare displays a window with various statistics. From this screen you can check the Mirror Status field to ensure the drive is still mirrored (see fig. 27.1).

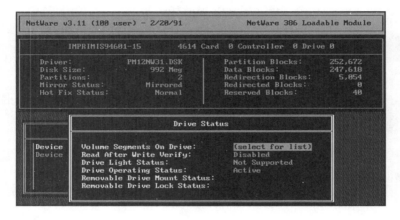

Fig. 27.1 Drive status information window of MONITOR.NLM.

- *The INSTALL.NLM Console Utility:* Using INSTALL, you can review the current mirroring status by selecting Disk Options from the main menu and then Mirroring from the Available Disk Options menu. NetWare then displays a window entitled Partition Mirroring Status that lists the various partitions on your server. When you select a mirrored partition, NetWare displays the status of each of the partitions that make up the mirrored pair in a window entitled Mirrored NetWare Partitions. If all is well, the status of both partitions says *IN SYNC* (see fig. 27.2); otherwise, a mirroring error has occurred.

- *The MIRROR STATUS Console Command:* When you type **MIRROR STATUS** from the file server console prompt, NetWare checks the server's disk systems and displays the current status of the disk mirroring.

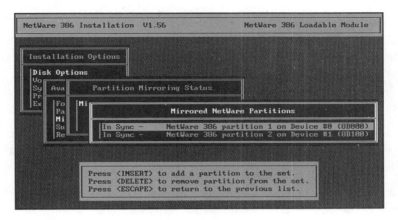

Fig. 27.2 Reviewing the status of the mirrored paritions using the INSTALL.NLM utility.

Identifying Causes of Mirroring Problems

Once you have identified that a mirroring problem has occurred, you must determine what caused the problem in the first place. Unfortunately, there is no single answer why drives would unmirror, but the most common causes are:

- *Improperly dismounted volumes:* There are only two acceptable ways a volume should be dismounted: by using the DISMOUNT console command to dismount a volume or by using the DOWN command that downs the file server and automatically dismounts all volumes. If the file server is turned off without being brought down properly, the chance of mirroring problems is extremely high.

- *Cable problems:* The cabling used to connect the drives within the server must always be tight and secure. Loose or improperly fitting cables can cause intermittent drive problems that are difficult to detect.

> **Caution**
>
> Always be extra careful when placing the cover on the server. In many cases, it is very easy to catch a disk cable while closing the cover; this could either loosen the cable or even crimp it and cause damage. When the integrity of a cable is in question, replace it. At $10-$20 per cable, it's really not worth risking it.

- *Power problems in the server:* One thing most people fail to consider before mirroring their disk drives is whether or not the server's power supply or disk chassis can handle the load. While the disk drives may physically fit within the server or chassis, the power requirements of the drives may be too much for the power supply. Overloading the power supply can cause intermittent drive problems which could result in the drives being unmirrored.

VIII

Troubleshooting

■ *Uncertified disks, disk adapters, or drivers:* Novell has a fairly extensive certification program used by third-party software and hardware vendors to ensure their products meet NetWare's requirements. During Novell's testing procedure, it may uncover certain bugs that make the product unsuitable for use in the server. Before making any purchases, check to see if the product has been certified for use with NetWare. While this will not guarantee an error-free environment, it puts you one step closer.

■ *Improperly installed disk adapter:* A disk adapter that has not been installed correctly and firmly seated in the bus of the motherboard can, and most probably will, cause intermittent or complete failures.

■ *Disk or disk adapter failure:* While not as common with modern technology, it is still possible for a disk drive or adapter to fail for no particular reason. When intermittent mirroring problems occur, swapping out the adapter or disk for a new one may resolve the issue.

Voluntarily Disabling Drive Mirroring and Removing a Faulty Drive

While you are performing your regular daily or weekly review of the server statistics (hint, hint), you may discover a potential problem with your disk system. The drives may still be mirrored, but if there is an excessive number of errors on a particular drive, the prudent action is to remove the drive and have it replaced *before* a critical error occurs. Instead of downing the server and just pulling out the drive, ideally you should disable the server's drive mirroring first to ensure the least amount of problems. By using the following steps, you can disable and remove the drive and bring the server back on-line:

1. From the main menu of INSTALL.NLM, select Disk Options and then Mirroring from the Available Disk Options menu. Then select the desired mirrored partition from the Partition Mirroring Status window.

2. After selecting the mirrored partition, NetWare lists all the partitions currently being mirrored in a window entitled Mirrored NetWare Partitions. From this window, select the faulty partition and press the Delete key to disable the drive mirroring. NetWare will then update the Partition Mirroring Status window to show you the two separate partitions. The status of one is Not Mirrored while the other is shown as Out Of Sync (see fig. 27.3).

3. With the drive mirroring disabled, the server can be downed and the faulty drive removed.

4. If the remaining drive was the primary drive of the mirrored pair, the server can be rebooted without any further intervention.

5. If the remaining drive was the secondary drive in a mirrored pair, you encounter the following error as the server reboots:

```
There are no accessible disk drives with NetWare Partitions. Check to see that the
needed disk drivers have been loaded and that your disk drives are properly cabled.
```

You get this error because the secondary drive is flagged "OUT OF SYNC." To return the drive to proper operating status, proceed with the following steps.

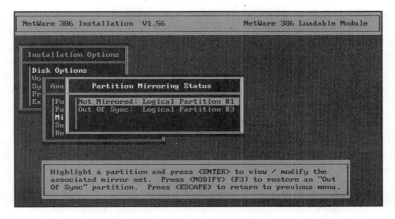

Fig. 27.3 Partition Mirroring Status window after the partitions have been unmirrored.

6. From the main menu of INSTALL.NLM, select Disk Options and then Mirroring from the Available Disk Options window to review a listing of the currently available partitions.

7. Highlight the partition marked "OUT OF SYNC" and press F3. NetWare then presents you with the error There are no accessible disk drives with NetWare partitions. You should ignore this message and press Esc.

8. Next, NetWare presents you with a simple question, Salvage Volume SYS Segment 0? If you want to bring your server back up with this drive as the SYS: volume, answer Yes.

Caution

If you answer No, NetWare deletes the volume's definition table, destroying all data contained on the volume. Once deleted, you cannot recover the volume except from a recent backup tape (you are backing up your server regularly, right??!!).

---

9. With the volume recovered, you can down the server and reboot.

Remirroring Drives after Replacing a Drive

After a drive in a mirrored pair has been removed because of a critical error that forced the drives to unmirror or you unmirrored them yourself, at one point you will want to reinstall a drive and establish mirroring. Before proceeding, you should determine which of the following situations you are in:

■ *Situation A:* A drive was removed from the server and is being replaced with a brand-new drive.

■ *Situation B:* A drive that was previously the secondary drive of a mirrored pair was removed from the server. After examination, you found the drive is sound and the problems were caused by something else, so you want to reinstall the drive.

■ *Situation C:* A drive that was previously the primary drive of a mirrored pair was removed from the server. After examination, you found the drive is functional and the problems were caused by something else, so you want to reinstall the drive.

If you are in Situation A or B, the new drive can be added to the server and mirroring can be established as done initially during the server installation. Refer to the heading "Preparing the File Server's Disks" in Chapter 3, "Installing the File Server," for further details.

Note

If you are using disk duplexing, make sure your disk driver is being loaded twice, once for each disk controller, or NetWare will not recognize the second drive when it is reintroduced.

If you are in Situation C, there are several additional steps you must follow carefully or else critical problems with your volumes could arise. When you are reintroducing the drive that used to be the primary partition, NetWare will be in a state of confusion as the server has two primary partitions, the old and the new. As such, you can expect to see an error similar to the following when the server boots:

```
Volume SYS could NOT be mounted; some or all volume segments cannot be located.
```

Since you introduced two drives that are both configured as the primary partition, you must reconfigure one of the drives as the secondary before you can proceed. By working through the following steps, you can redefine one of the drives as the secondary and get your server back online.

Caution

Since the error noted a problem with a volume, some people may load INSTALL.NLM and select Volume Options from the main menu to view the status of the volume. At this point, NetWare displays several errors, eventually asking you `Delete The Invalid Volume Segments?` You must answer No. If you answer Yes, NetWare cannot determine which duplicate volume is invalid and therefore deletes both.

To successfully reinstall the drive and establish drive mirroring, there are a few short steps to follow. For the purpose of the following instructions, the drive being reintroduced into the server will be known as drive 1, and the drive still installed will be drive 0.

1. Unload the disk driver for drive 0.

2. Load the disk driver for drive 1 and mount the volume.

3. Using INSTALL.NLM, delete the NetWare partition on drive 1.

4. Unload the disk driver for drive 1 and then load the disk drive for drive 0. Once loaded, reload the disk driver for drive 1.

5. Using INSTALL.NLM, re-create the server's disk mirroring with drive 0 as the primary.

6. From the console prompt, mount the volume.

NetWare now goes through a remirroring process to synchronize the data between the two drives. If the NIC drivers and other necessary NLMs have been loaded, users can log into the server, but unless it is critical that users log in immediately, do not let anyone log into the server until the remirroring process is completed. The amount of time required to resynchronize your NetWare partitions can be severely impacted when the server must also service requests from users.

Tip

You can make sure no one logs into the server by using the DISABLE LOGIN console command. Just be sure you use the ENABLE LOGIN console command when the remirroring is completed.

Tip

Using the MIRROR STATUS command from the console prompt, you can review the current status of the drive mirroring and the percentage of remirroring that has completed.

Drive Deactivation Problems

If you have been working with NetWare for some time, you most probably have had the misfortune of encountering your fair share of "Drive Deactivation" errors. If you're new to the field, don't worry, the fun is just beginning!

Of all the drive problems you can have, the Drive Deactivation error is probably the most annoying and most difficult to resolve. In general terms, errors of this nature are caused when there is some critical communications error between the disk, the disk driver, and NetWare. It is essential that the disk driver software and the disk drive can communicate fluently. If the drive does not respond to driver commands, several retries will occur. Eventually, the OS will deactivate the drive.

Reviewing Drive Status

When a disk drive has been deactivated, there are several ways you can be notified as noted below:

- *Error On Console:* When NetWare deactivates a drive, an error message similar to the following appears on the console:

  ```
  Device #0 FUJITSU M2266S-512 deactivated due to drive failure
  ```

- *Entry In Server Error Log:* When NetWare deactivates a drive, a message is noted in the server's SYS$LOG.ERR error log stored in the SYSTEM directory of the SYS volume. Because you cannot monitor the server's console at all times, by checking the error log on a regular basis, you can keep up with any drive problems.

> **Note**
>
> If the deactivated drive contained the SYS volume partition, depending on the cause of the deactivation, an error may not make it to the server's error log as the log is stored on this volume.

- *Change In Drive Status Shown Using MONITOR.NLM:* When you use the MONITOR console utility, you can review a current drive's status by selecting Disk Information from the main menu and then the desired disk. By examining the Drive Operating Status field within the window provided, you can determine if a drive is active or inactive. Refer to Figure 27.1 for an example of this window.

> **Tip**
>
> From the same screen, examine the Redirected Blocks field in the upper window. If the number of redirected blocks has increased dramatically or is approaching the number of Redirection Blocks, drive failure is imminent. At this point, start planning to swap out the drive with a new one.

- *Unhappy End Users:* If the deactivated drive was not mirrored, the volume contained on that drive is inaccessible to users logging into the server. If you don't use that volume, don't worry. Someone on the server does and if you are the administrator, they will be paying you a visit shortly.

Identifying Causes of Drive Deactivations

If you are one of the unfortunate who currently have a deactivated drive, you won't be happy to find out there is no surefire solution to fixing this problem. While troubleshooting these errors is difficult, following are several suggestions that could provide you with the answer you need to fix the problem.

Improper SCSI Configuration

The biggest problem many people have when using SCSI drives is improper configuration. In almost every way, SCSI drives are easier to manage than other drive technologies, but they *must* be configured properly. Here are a few SCSI rules that you should adhere to:

- The SCSI adapter card always uses a SCSI ID of 7.

- When using the MCA bus architecture (PS/2s) and some HP systems, the first drive in the SCSI chain should always be set to the SCSI ID of 6.

- When using the ISA or EISA architecture, the first drive in the SCSI chain should always be set to 0.

- No two drives in a single SCSI chain can have the same SCSI ID.

- When you are using the internal and external ports of the SCSI card, you *must* disable termination on the adapter card. If you are only using one of the ports, the adapter card must be terminated.

- Only one drive per SCSI chain should use a terminator. If you are using the internal and external ports of the SCSI card, a terminator is used on the internal *and* external chains.

- The terminator should always be on the last drive in the chain.

> **Tip**
>
> When you are using an external cabinet for your drives, where possible, terminate the cabinet and not the individual drives. This makes your life easier when you are adding drives later.

> **Caution**
>
> While the disk subsystem may work when the terminator is *not* on the last drive in a chain, there is no guarantee that it will continue to function normally. Do yourself a favor, stick with specifications. It only takes a few seconds to set the terminators properly!

> **Tip**
>
> When the SCSI card is used for disk drives and a CD-ROM or tape backup drive, you may have to set the "SCSI Disconnect" configuration parameter if your drives are being deactivated. Consult your SCSI card documentation for further details.

VIII

Troubleshooting

Tip

If you are using ADAPTEC cards, try changing the default transfer speed of the card from 10Mbps to 5Mbps. Consult your SCSI card documentation for further details.

Configuration Conflicts

Ensure that all adapter cards are properly configured and do not conflict with any other devices. Server-based backup systems or other devices (such as CD-ROM drives) can cause drive deactivation. When a conflict is present, it may not show up until the device is activated.

Faulty Hardware

Compared to configuration problems, faulty hardware or improperly installed hardware runs a close second as the leading cause of drive deactivation errors. If you have confirmed that the equipment is properly configured, here are several areas that you should examine:

- *Disk Cabling:* Examine the cabling of all disk devices to ensure a tight fit and that no cables have been damaged. SCSI cables are subject to electromagnetic interference and should be adequately protected and isolated if problems occur. Good quality cables should be used, especially for Fast SCSI (SCSI-2). You should immediately replace any cables where signs of damage are evident.

Tip

Compared to other computer hardware, cables are cheap. Since cables are the medium used to carry data between the drives and NetWare, *don't* buy poor quality cables!!!

- *Improperly Seated Adapters:* All adapter cards in the server must be firmly seated in their buses. As a precaution, try removing the adapter and reseating it. It may have come loose when the server was being moved around.

- *Inadequate Power Supply:* It is unfortunate, but in most cases, disk drives are added to a server without considering if the power supply can handle the load. While most power supplies can comfortably handle one or two drives, going beyond this could place too much stress on the power supply, resulting in inconsistent output.

- *Defective Parts:* Even if you are not 100 percent sure that a particular component is faulty, consideration should be given to swapping out parts in the attempt to isolate the problem. In some cases, the amount of time you spend trying to fix the problem could end up costing you more in downtime than just replacing the component in the first place. Unless you are positive that a particular component is faulty, leave this suggestion to last.

> **Caution**
>
> If the adapter is replaced with a different make or model, it may be necessary to reformat your hard drive. Not all adapters access the data in the same fashion; as such, a different adapter may not be able to read your current data.

Driver and Firmware

Your drive system relies on two key software components—the disk driver and the firmware. On occasion, new releases of these components are released by the manufacturer. While it is not necessary for you to always have the latest driver and firmware, when drive deactivations are occurring, using a newer driver or firmware could resolve your problem.

Unforuntately, vendors generally don't notify users of their driver or firmware updates, registered or not. Therefore, it is your responsibility to contact the vendor to find out what revisions have been released and what problems they corrected.

> **Tip**
>
> If you have recently upgraded your server from NetWare 3.11 to NetWare 3.12, check with the manufacturer of your disk controller to see if your current driver supports 3.12. Not all drivers on the market support 3.12 and can cause intermittent errors.

> **Tip**
>
> Some users have had problems after upgrading their ISADISK.DSK driver dated 02-15-92 to the updated driver dated 07-08-92. The new driver only attempts to write to the drive three times, whereas the older driver would continue these attempts. If the request is not successful by the third attempt, the drive is deactivated. Should your drive deactivate after upgrading, try going back to the old driver.

Tips to Help Prepare You for Drive Problems

While no one wants to be a pessimist, drive-related problems are a fact of life. Whether it is your disk drive or controller that fails, being prepared for the inevitable can drastically reduce the amount of time it takes you to resolve the problem. Following is a series of tips that can help you to be prepared!

- Document the manufacturer of your disk drives. Make sure you know its full name, address, fax number, address, and when available, BBS number.

- Document the makes and models for each disk drive in your server.

- Document the characteristics for each drive (number of cylinders, heads, and so on).

- Document the firmware levels for disks and disk controllers.

- Document the configuration information for each disk drive and controller. Documented information should include memory addresses, I/O ports, interrupts, and IDs (such as SCSI IDs).

- Carefully read the manufacturer's instructions for the installation of your disk or controller.

- If possible, try to keep a spare cable, disk, and controller on the shelf for swapping out faulty components.

Chapter 28

NetWare Utilities for Resolving Problems

NetWare comes equipped with three key utilities that are used to resolve some of the more common problems you encounter with your server. In this chapter, we discuss some of these problems, specifically:

- Using VREPAIR for volume-related problems
- Fixing the binderies with BINDFIX
- Recovering deleted files with SALVAGE

Repairing Problems with the Server's Volumes Using VREPAIR

NetWare's volume repairing utility, VREPAIR, resolves problems with the server's partitions and file system under certain maintenance situations. While the likelihood of problems with NetWare's partitions is minimized due to Novell's Transaction Tracking System, they still can occur.

The following listing provides you with the various circumstances when you would want to run VREPAIR:

- When removing NetWare Name Spaces
- When a volume will not mount
- When file-related errors are reported as the server boots
- When file-related errors appear on the file server console during regular operation
- If/When file-system corruption is suspected

If your server is in any of the preceding situations, running VREPAIR may return the server to proper operating order.

Running VREPAIR

You can run NetWare's VREPAIR console utility by typing the following from the file server prompt (replace *path* with the directory path leading to the VREPAIR utility):

```
LOAD [path]VREPAIR
```

> **Note**
>
> You must dismount the volume on which you intend to run VREPAIR before you can run VREPAIR.

> **Tip**
>
> If you have to run VREPAIR on the SYS volume, you may be unable to load VREPAIR from the server partition since it is stored in the SYSTEM directory of the SYS volume. If your SYS volume will not mount, your only recourse is to load VREPAIR from an alternate site. Therefore, keep a copy of VREPAIR on the server's DOS partition.

Once loaded, VREPAIR presents you with a menu containing three options—Repair A Volume, Set VREPAIR Options, and Exit. Before commencing the volume repair, you should review the settings in the Set VREPAIR Options to customize VREPAIR for your specific requirements. For your reference, each of the available options is described as follows:

- *Remove Name Space Support from the volume:* The default value for this option is "Quit If A Required VREPAIR Name Space Support NLM Is Not Loaded." When you select this option, NetWare removes name space support from the selected volume.

> **Caution**
>
> When VREPAIR is used to remove Name Space support, attributes maintained by the Name Space Support you are removing are lost. The only way to recover these attributes is to recover the files from a tape backup system that supports the storage of these attributes. You are backing up your server regularly...right?

- *Write All Directory and FAT Entries Out to Disk:* The default value for this option is `Write Only Changed Directory And FAT Entries Out To Disk`. The default setting updates the current FAT and DET with the necessary changes due to errors. Changing this setting causes VREPAIR to rebuild the FAT and DET and then write the new tables to disk.

> **Caution**
>
> You should only change this option as a last resort to recover the volume. Instructing VREPAIR to rewrite the entire DET and FAT could result in data loss.

■ *Write Changes Immediately To Disk:* The default value for this option is "Keep Changes in Memory for Later Update." Using the default setting instructs VREPAIR to store all corrections in memory. When the repair process is completed, VREPAIR asks you if you want changes written to disk. When you use this option, VREPAIR makes corrections to the partition as they are found.

> **Tip**
>
> Telling VREPAIR to Write Changes Immediately To Disk could save you a significant amount of time from running VREPAIR. If there are only a few errors on the partition, writing immediately to disk may slightly increase the running time, but when there are a lot of errors, writing immediately can cut the run time almost in half. Since the default stores errors in memory, as the memory fills up with errors to be written latter, the entire process can slow down drastically.

■ *Purge All Deleted Files:* The default value for this option is "Retain Deleted Files." Changing this setting forces VREPAIR to delete all purged files from the volume. You cannot salvage any files after running VREPAIR if the default is changed.

> **Caution**
>
> Telling VREPAIR to Purge All Deleted Files can add a significant amount of time to the repairing process.

After you have made the desired changes, you can select option 0 to return to the main menu of VREPAIR where you then can initiate the repair process by selecting Repair A Volume.

> **Note**
>
> If you are using name spaces on your server, you must load a special NLM for the name spaces you are using before you can initiate the repair process. From the main menu of VREPAIR, press Alt+Esc and load one of the following NLMs: V_MAC for Macintosh, V_OS2 for OS/2, and V_NFS for UNIX. Once the NLM is loaded, you can return to the main menu by pressing Alt+Esc and then run the repair process by selecting Repair A Volume.

VIII

Troubleshooting

As VREPAIR runs, there are three additional options available to you by pressing the F1 key. For your reference, each of these options is described as follows:

- *Do not pause after each error:* The default for this option is "Pause After Each Error." If left at the default, VREPAIR pauses after every error that is encountered in order to display detailed information on-screen. When you select this option VREPAIR runs automatically without displaying information on each error.

Tip

Instructing VREPAIR not to pause after each error can significantly reduce the amount of time taken to repair the volume. When there are a lot of errors, the default value forces VREPAIR to stop whenever an error is found; it does not continue until you tell it to.

- *Log errors to a file:* The default is "Do not log errors to a file." If you want a record of the errors that occurred for the purposes of analyzing what went wrong, you can log all the errors to a file on the SYS: volume (if you are *not* repairing SYS) or a local drive on the server.

- *Stop volume repair:* Select this option to stop the VREPAIR process and return to the main menu.

When VREPAIR completes, if you configured the options to write changes immediately to disk, you can press any key to clear the screen and return to the main menu. Otherwise, you must confirm that you want VREPAIR to write the necessary changes to disk. Figure 28.1 shows you what the final VREPAIR screen usually looks like.

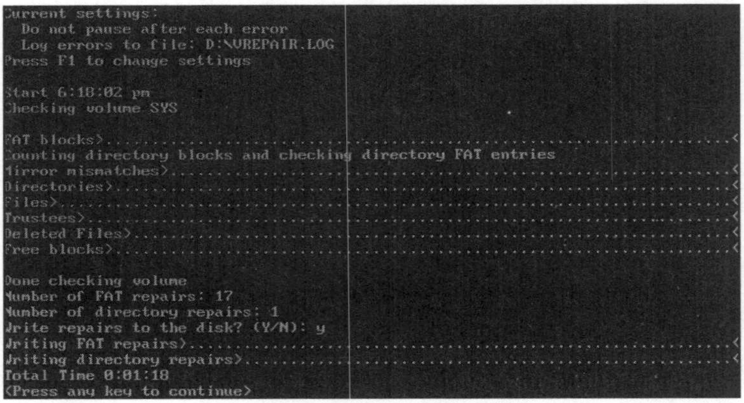

Fig. 28.1 The final screen shown in VREPAIR.

Caution
If you do not tell VREPAIR to make the desired changes, any errors it has found will *not* be corrected.

Tip
When you run VREPAIR and errors are found, after the first pass is completed and you are returned to the main menu, you should select the Repair A Volume option again. When VREPAIR writes errors to disk, there is a chance it will uncover or cause additional errors. You should keep running VREPAIR until no errors are found.

What VREPAIR Does while Running

When VREPAIR is running, it goes through a series of processes. The progress of each task is noted by a string of dots that stretches toward the edge of the screen.

VREPAIR displays the following messages while running tests:

- *Checking FAT Blocks:* On each NetWare partition, FAT tables are mirrored to ensure that if one fails, NetWare has another to fall back on. During this process, the two FATs are checked for any differences. Initially, VREPAIR validates the FAT tables by looking at both FAT blocks and repairing any differences. If VREPAIR finds problems in the first FAT table but not the other, it repairs the first table using information from the second. Upon successful completion, VREPAIR has a good copy of the FAT table stored in memory.

Caution
If the damage to the FAT is so severe VREPAIR cannot repair it, the operation is halted with the error "Volume Repair Was not Possible." At this point, your only alternative is to rebuild the partition and restore your data from the most recent backup tape (hint, hint).

- *Checking Mirror Mismatches:* During this phase, VREPAIR checks the mirrored copies of the Directory Entry Table for any differences. When errors are found, VREPAIR uses the same process to repair the DET as it did for the FAT.

Caution
In some instances, VREPAIR cannot fix a file link. Should this occur, affected files must be restored from a backup tape.

VIII

Troubleshooting

- *Checking Directory Entries:* During this phase, VREPAIR ensures that each entry in the DET is valid against the directories actually on the server. Invalid entries that cannot be fixed are freed for later use.

- *Checking File Entries:* During this phase, VREPAIR looks at the DET and FAT to ensure that the file listings are valid by running a mirror mismatch check on the FAT chains for all files on the volume being repaired.

> **Caution**
>
> Errors found when checking file entries could result in a file being truncated. Therefore, affected files have to be restored from a backup tape.

- *Checking Trustee Entries:* To ensure the integrity of the trustee entries for files, VREPAIR checks the entry that contains the first eight trustee assignments. If there are more than eight trustees, VREPAIR examines the "tnode structure" that is an additional file listing containing a pointer to the original file entry.

- *Checking Deleted Entries:* During this phase, VREPAIR confirms that the pointers assigned to a deleted file, the file's name, trustee entries, and name space are all valid. When files are deleted on NetWare, they are placed in a deleted file listing. Using this listing, NetWare can recover these files using the SALVAGE utility. The file entries for these files are moved into a delete file or directory block that only contains deleted files. Finally, the deleted file blocks use a pointer to tell NetWare from what directory the file originally came.

> **Caution**
>
> If VREPAIR cannot confirm the entries for a deleted file, it is removed from the system. Once removed, the file is not available for salvaging.

- *Checking Invalid Entries:* During this phase, VREPAIR checks the link between a DOS entry pointer and the corresponding Name Space entry to ensure it is valid. VREPAIR attempts to repair problems with these links. If the problem cannot be resolved, the entry is altered so it is only accessible to DOS.

- *Checking Free Blocks:* During this phase, VREPAIR checks the FAT and DET for listings of blocks that no longer exist on the server. When found, VREPAIR marks these blocks as free so they can be reused.

Repairing Bindery Related Problems

Note

RIGHTS REQUIRED TO COMPLETE TASK: YOU MUST BE A SUPERVISOR EQUIVALENT TO RUN BINDFIX OR BINDREST.

The NetWare bindery is made up of three database files (NET$OBJ.SYS, NET$PROP.SYS, and NET$VAL.SYS) that are used to store a variety of information such as the user IDs and groups that are on the server. Periodically, a problem that has to be repaired may arise with these programs. Using the BINDFIX utility, a SUPERVISOR EQUIVALENT can correct these problems before they become too severe. Following is a listing of the situations you could be in when you should run BINDFIX:

- When printing, "unknown server" errors appear

- A user cannot change their password

- User IDs cannot be deleted

- User or Group IDs cannot be modified

- Trustee rights cannot be granted, revoked or modified

To run BINDFIX, from the SYSTEM directory on the SYS volume, type **BINDFIX** and press Enter.

As it runs, BINDFIX examines several areas of the bindery, confirming their integrity and validity against what is actually on the system. While running, there are three questions you may be asked:

- *Delete mail directories of users that no longer exist?* If you answer Yes, BINDFIX deletes the mail directories of users you deleted from the system. This is an excellent way to do a bit of housecleaning on the server!

- *Create mail directories if they don't exist?* If you answer Yes, BINDFIX creates a mail directory for any ID on the server that does not already have one. Normally, all IDs are assigned a personal mail directory when they are created. But, there is always the possibility that someone inadvertently removed their mail directory.

- *Delete trustee rights for users to no longer exist?* If you answer Yes, NetWare scans all mounted volumes on the server and removes trustee rights and ownerships to files where the user no longer exists.

VIII

Troubleshooting

After BINDFIX has completed, it displays a message confirming the completion and states that the older bindery files were renamed with the extension OLD. Once you confirm the integrity of the fixed bindery files, you can delete these files.

> **Note**
>
> If BINDFIX failed or if you are having problems with your binderies, you can restore your bindery files from the backups BINDFIX made (NET$VAL.OLD, NET$PROP.OLD, and NET$OBJ.OLD) by typing BINDREST within the SYSTEM directory.

Recovering Deleted Files

When a file is deleted from the NetWare server, it is only removed from the listing of available files and remains available for recovery until one of the following conditions is met:

- NetWare requires the space in use by the file

- You use the PURGE utility to purge the file from the system

- The console setting IMMEDIATE PURGE OF DELETED FILES is set to ON

If one of these conditions has not yet been met, you can recover a deleted file by typing **SALVAGE** from the command line and working through the menuing interface.

The main menu of SALVAGE presents you with several options you can use to recover your deleted files, each of which is described below:

- *Salvage From Deleted Directories:* When files and the directory structures that held them are removed, NetWare stores the deleted files in a hidden directory called DELETED.SAV off the root of every volume. If you deleted the directory as well as the file, you can choose this option to view which files are available for recovery.

> **Tip**
>
> If you choose the Salvage From Deleted Directories option and NetWare tells you you have insufficient rights, this is not always the case as even SUPERVISOR IDs can get this error. Should this occur, make sure the directory DELETED.SAV was not deleted. If someone removed the directory by accident, you should recreate it and use the FLAGDIR command to flag it as hidden.

- *Select Current Directory:* By default, SALVAGE tries to recover files in the current directory. If the file you want to recover is not in the current directory, you can use this option to select any directory or volume on the server to which you have rights.

■ *Set Salvage Options:* When there are a lot of files available for recovery in the directory, finding the one you want can be difficult. When you use this option, you can tell SALVAGE how you want the listing of recoverable files to be displayed by sorting them in a certain order.

■ *View/Recover Deleted Files:* This is the option you use to actually recover the deleted files. After selecting this option, SALVAGE asks you to specify the name pattern to which you want it to match the file names. By default, SALVAGE provides you with a listing of all recoverable files but by using this field, you can specify a certain filename or pattern for which you are looking.

After you have selected the View/Recover Deleted Files option and specified the search pattern, SALVAGE presents you with a screen similar to the one shown in Figure 28.2 that you use to pick out the files you want to recover.

Fig. 28.2 Files available for salvaging.

From this window, you can highlight individual files you want to recover, or you can flag several files in one of the following methods:

■ When you want to flag multiple files, you can highlight each filename and press the Enter key.

■ Using the F6 key, you can specify a certain file name pattern you want to be marked for recovery.

Whatever method you chose, after the files have been flagged or highlighted, you can press the Enter key to tell SALVAGE you want to recovery them. When asked, confirm that you want to recover the files.

Note

If the file you are trying to recover has the same name as a file in the directory to which you are doing the recovery, SALVAGE asks you to rename the file you are trying to recover.

Alternately, from the window of files available to recover, you also can purge them by highlighting or flagging each one and pressing the Delete key or change the sort order by pressing the F3 key.

Using the PURGE Utility to Make Files Un-Salvageable

If you want to make sure a file(s) cannot be recovered with the SALVAGE utility, you can use a utility known as PURGE by using the following syntax:

    PURGE *[filename]* *[/all]*

Based on the syntax above, replace:

   filename with the name of the specific file you want purged, including the full path to its location.

The /ALL option is used when you want to purge all files in the current directory and all files in each of its subdirectories.

Note

Typing PURGE on its own purges all files in the current directory but not its subdirectories.

Tip

PURGE accepts wildcard entries for the filename. For example, to purge all files in the current directory with the extension EXE, type **PURGE *.EXE** from the command line.

Chapter 29

Miscellaneous Common Problems

While it is virtually impossible to discuss each of the errors you could possibly encounter while administering your network, there are several fairly common problems that could arise. In this section, we examine these common errors, specifically:

- Lost Hardware Interrupt errors

- NOT-LOGGED-IN connections

- Problems with unencrypted passwords

- User problems logging into the server

Handling Lost Hardware Interrupt Errors

A "Lost Hardware Interrupt" error occurs when a request is made by a driver with an interrupt call but it is dropped before the file-server CPU can respond. When this happens, the OS generates the following message on the file-server console:

```
Primary Interrupt Controller Detected A Lost Hardware Interrupt
```

Identifying Causes of Lost Hardware Interrupt Errors

There are several reasons why you may get Lost Hardware Interrupt errors on your server, but for the most part, they can be classified within one of the following causes:

- *Processor speed incompatibility:* When an adapter in your server is too slow for the CPU, intermittent Lost Hardware Interrupt errors may be generated since the board cannot respond as fast as the CPU wants it to.

■ *Faulty hardware:* If one of the adapter boards in the server is faulty, it may not be able to respond quickly enough to requests it receives and thus, a Lost Hardware Interrupt error is generated.

> **Note**
>
> This error is common with IDE drives and usually can be ignored.

■ *Bad drivers:* Poorly-written or poorly-designed drivers may not be able to make optimal use of the hardware, thereby not allowing it to keep up with the requests it is receiving.

■ *High utilization:* If your server is being subjected to an extremely high amount of of traffic, it may not be able to keep up with the requests it is receiving. In cases like this, the Lost Hardware Interrupt error is generated.

Resolving Lost Interrupt Errors

While not usually critical, Lost Hardware Interrupt errors can signify a performance problem on the file server. Following are several tips you can use to help you resolve these errors.

■ *Isolate the offending hardware or driver:* To isolate which driver or piece of hardware is causing this error, you should down the file server and reboot it without using the AUTOEXEC.NCF file. By issuing each of the commands contained within the AUTOEXEC.NCF file manually, you may be able to determine which driver or piece of hardware is causing the problem.

> **Note**
>
> Unless the problem is severe, this method may not uncover the cause of the Lost Hardware Interrupt error. Without users logged into the server and creating a load, there may not be any problem evident.

> **Shortcut**
>
> After downing the file server, you can reload NetWare without loading the AUTOEXEC.NCF file by typing **SERVER -NA** from the DOS prompt.

■ *Check for driver and firmware updates:* The manufacturers of your hardware and drivers may have issued updates since your purchase; using the updated versions may resolve certain performance problems.

■ *Reload NIC and disk drivers from your master copy:* It is possible your NIC or disk drivers were corrupted somehow. By reloading them from the master diskettes or CDs, you will be working with a fresh, untainted copy.

■ *Check for faulty hardware:* Use your server's or third-party diagnostic programs to examine the server for any faulty hardware. Faulty NICs and disk controllers are leading causes of these errors.

■ *Check the network infrastructure:* A faulty NIC or cable on the network can cause heavy bursts of traffic that may be flooding the network adapter in the server. As you check the network, examine the NIC drivers being used on the workstations. They may not be operating properly, thus causing some communications problems. When possible, update the NIC drivers to the latest version.

If you have worked through each of these tips and still cannot find the source of these errors, try to determine if your server appears to be suffering from severe performance or integrity problems. If the server seems to run a lot slower than it should, acquiring the assistance of an expert may be your best alternative, but if there are no secondary problems, you can disable these messages by typing the following from the file server prompt:

```
SET DISPLAY LOST INTERRUPT ALERTS=OFF
SET DISPLAY SPURIOUS INTERRUPT ALERTS=OFF
```

VIII

Troubleshooting

Tip

You can add these commands to the AUTOEXEC.NCF to ensure they are set each time the server is loaded.

Clearing NOT-LOGGED-IN Connections

When a workstation on the network is first turned on and the shells or DOS Requester are loaded, a logical connection is established between the workstation and the server. This connection, even though a user has not logged in yet, uses up one of the available connections on your file server. While this usually does not create a problem for a company that purchased NetWare with a user count that exceeds their number of employees, if your NetWare server's maximum user connections is less than the number of employees, you will most probably run into problems.

To illustrate, assume you purchase a 100-user version of NetWare but you have 150 people who access it from time to time. Since your estimates showed no more than 50 people would be using it at any one time, this should not be a problem, but it will. In this scenario, if 100 of the 150 people turned on their PCs, 100 connections known as NOT-LOGGED-IN connections would be established. Of these 100 people, assume only ten login. Even though there are only ten people logged in, if the 101st user turns on their PC to try and use the server, NetWare denies them access because there are not enough licenses. Remember, all those PCs that are turned on but are *not* being used are wasting a user connection.

To resolve this problem, Novell has a utility called NLICLEAR.NLM you can load on the file server. NLICLEAR.NLM checks the file server on a regular basis for connections that are classified as "NOT-LOGGED-IN" and deletes them. Refer to the heading "Clearing Not-Logged-In Connections with NLICLEAR.NLM" in Chapter 24, "Miscellaneous NLMs," for detailed instructions on using this module.

While effective, NLICLEAR can create problems for users who are using the older ODI/NETX implementation as opposed to the DOS Requester. When a user is using the NETX shell and NLICLEAR cuts their connection, they either have to unload NETX and then reload it (not always possible) or reboot their PC. With the new and improved DOS Requester technology, the user can re-establish a connection with the server merely by trying to access the network drive (such as by typing **F:**).

Dealing with Unencrypted Password Errors

When checking your file server console or the error log, you may see notice an error similiar to the following:

```
Station 2: Attempted To Use An Unencrypted Password Call
```

NetWare uses an encryption routine when sending and receiving passwords. By default, NetWare does not accept passwords that have not been encrypted first. Should a workstation or node attempt to send a password that has not been encrypted, NetWare logs the error noted above and denies access to the server.

While these types of errors are becoming more and more rare as people upgrade their software to recent versions, if you get this error, chances are you have a NetWare 2.x server on your network.

Novell NetWare 2.x cannot encrypt passwords for access to the 3.x server. As such, whenever you have a 2.x server on your network, you should upgrade its LOGIN and PUBLIC programs with those from the 3.x server. By doing so, you provide the users of the 2.x server with the utilities necessary to perform the approriate encryption.

Another possible cause of these errors is software from third-party developers. If these developers are not working with Novell's Application Programming Interfaces (APIs), their products cannot handle the necessary encryption. While most of the current products can handle encryption properly, if you are using older software and choose not to upgrade, you accomodate these systems by typing the following from the server console prompt or adding it to your AUTOEXEC.NCF file:

```
SET ALLOW UNENCRYPTED PASSWORDS=ON
```

Resolving Problems when Users Cannot Log in

One of the most common problems people run into with networks is users who cannot log into the server. When a user cannot login to the file server, in most cases, NetWare usually provides them with a detailed message telling them why. But in some cases, if they are logging in with some type of login shell (for example, using the Saber Menu login program), the exact error may elude them. Following is my personal top ten listing that resolves the majority of problems that could restrict a user from logging into the server:

1. Make sure the user is in the LOGIN directory of the file server. In NetWare 3.11, the DOS prompt for the first network drive was usually F:\LOGIN> but in NetWare 3.12, they will only see F:\>. To confirm that they have access to the LOGIN.EXE program, the user types DIR LOGIN.EXE. If it is not in the current directory or in a directory specified in the PATH statement, they cannot login.

2. Check to see if the user is entering the file server name correctly.

3. Check to see if the user is entering their ID correctly.

4. Check the command syntax they are using to login.

5. Check that the user actually has an ID on the file server to which they are trying to login.

Tip
If the user is not specifying the file server name when trying to login, NetWare attempts to log them into the server to which they currently have an attachment (the server of the LOGIN directory where they are). If they do not know which server this is, they can type **SLIST** to view a listing of the servers on the network. From the output, you can determine which server they are attached to by examining the STATUS column and finding the server which is the "DEFAULT."

6. Make sure the ID is not disabled. When you select User Information from the main menu of SYSCON and then the desired ID from the listing provided, NetWare presents you with a window of options specific to the selected ID. From this window, you can select Account Restrictions to see if the ID is still active.

Tip
If the ID was disabled and you re-enable it from the Account Restrictions screen, check the Account Expiration Date field to see if the date has been exceeded. If it has, the account locks out again as soon as they try to login.

7. Make sure the user is not trying to access more stations at one time than they are allowed. When you select User Information from the main menu of SYSCON and then the desired ID from the listing provided, NetWare presents you with a window of options specific to the selected ID. From this window, select Account Restrictions to review the maximum number of concurrent sessions. Then, from the DOS prompt, type **USERLIST *userid***, replace *userid* with the desired ID. NetWare then checks the connection information to see if the ID is logged in to the server and how many times it is logged in.

8. Make sure the account has not been locked out by the Intruder Detection system. When you select User Information from the main menu of SYSCON and then the desired ID from the listing provided, NetWare presents you with a window of options specific to the selected ID. From this window, select Intruder Lockout Status to see if the ID has been locked out.

9. Make sure the user is not trying to log in from an unauthorized station. When you select User Information from the main menu of SYSCON and then the desired ID from the listing provided, NetWare presents you with a window of options specific to the selected ID. From this window, select Station Restrictions to see if this ID has been restricted to logins from a specific network or node.

10. Make sure the user is not trying to log in during an unauthorized time. When you select User Information from the main menu of SYSCON and then the desired ID from the listing provided, NetWare presents you with a window of options specific to the selected ID. From this window, select Time Restrictions to see if this ID has been restricted to logins during certain times of the day.

Aside from problems logging into the server, users may also encounter problems attaching to a server when their PC is first turned on. When the network drivers are first loaded at the workstation, the workstation attempts to establish a logical connection with a file server. Once this connection is established, the user then can use any of the programs stored in the LOGIN directory. Unfortunately, at times, the user may get an error such as "File Server Not Found" when the network drivers are loaded or, at other times, they attach to a server but cannot get to the LOGIN directory on the server. When this happens to you, try working through the following tips to resolve the problem:

■ Make sure all the necessary files are being loaded on the workstation to access the server and there are no errors when they load.

■ Check the connection between the workstation and the network connection. It must be a good tight fit to work properly.

■ Check to make sure the workstation's NIC is operating properly by using the diagnostic software provided by the NIC manufacturer.

■ Check the workstation's CONFIG.SYS file to determine if a LASTDRIVE command is being used. When the workstation is using the DOS Requester, the CONFIG.SYS file must contain the line LASTDRIVE=Z:. If the workstation is using the older ODI/NETX or IPX/NETX implementation and LASTDRIVE=Z is in the CONFIG.SYS, the workstation will not be able to access a network drive. When old methods are being used to access the server (such as IPX/NETX), the first network drive is the first drive letter after the LASTDRIVE statement. For example, if LASTDRIVE=F: is used in the CONFIG.SYS, the first available network drive letter is G:.

■ Check if the workstation can communicate with the server. From the file server console prompt, type **TRACK ON** to view the requests being received, then reboot the workstation. As the workstation loads the network drivers, you should see a single GET NEAREST SERVER request appearing on the TRACK ON display followed by a single GIVE NEAREST SERVER response from the server. If you don't, the problem is either at the workstation or somewhere on the network (for example, a cabling or hub problem). If you see multiple GET NEAREST SERVER requests without any GIVE NEAREST SERVER replies, the server may not be configured to respond to this request, thus the workstation is not allowed to log in. By typing SET REPLY TO GET NEAREST SERVER from the console prompt, NetWare tells you if it will reply to this request. To log in directly to the server, this setting must be set to YES. If you see multiple GET NEAREST SERVER requests that are each followed by a GIVE NEAREST SERVER reply, the problem could be with the workstations NIC or the driver being used.

VIII

Troubleshooting

Appendix A

NetWare Command/ Utility Reference

Item	Class	Task
ABORT REMIRROR	CONSOLE	Instructs NetWare to abort the remirroring of the partitions.
ACONSOLE	UTILITY	Establishes remote console connections to the file server over an asynchronous phone line.
ADD NAME SPACE	CONSOLE	Sets up a NetWare volume to store *non*-DOS files such as Apple or OS/2.
ALLOW	COMMAND	Sets the inherited rights mask for a given file or directory.
ATOTAL	COMMAND	Provides summary accounting reports for your server(s) when used in conjunction with NetWare's accounting features.
ATPSQUERY	CONSOLE	Checks an AppleTalk PostScript (ATPS) printer for a listing of fonts.
ATPSV	CONSOLE	Activates or deactivates ATPS console screens.
ATTACH	COMMAND	Establishes a connection to a file server without executing any scripts. This command can be used from the command line and is also one of the basic login script commands.
BIND	CONSOLE	Allows a network interface card and a communications protocol to communicate together.
BINDFIX	COMMAND	Stored within the SYSTEM directory, BINDFIX corrects any problems within the NetWare binderies and makes a backup copy of the bindery files.

(continues)

Item	Class	Task
BINDREST	COMMAND	Stored within the SYSTEM directory, BINDREST restores the NetWare binderies from backups created by BINDFIX.
BROADCAST	CONSOLE	Sends a message to all attached nodes from the console.
CAPTURE	COMMAND	Redirects printing from your local printer ports to a NetWare print queue.
CASTOFF	COMMAND	Stops messages sent to your station from appearing on your monitor.
CASTON	COMMAND	Allows messages to be sent to your station, overrides the castoff command.
CHKDIR	COMMAND	Reports on the amount of space available and being used within the current directory structure.
CHKVOL	COMMAND	Reports the total amount of space free on the volume and how much of this space is available to a given user.
CLEAR STATION	CONSOLE	Clears a station's connection to the file server.
CLS	CONSOLE	Similar to the DOS CLS command, it clears the screen leaving the prompt at the top left.
COLORPAL	UTILITY	Changes the colors used in the NetWare utilities and menus from their default settings. Will not change the screens of the menus you design in NetWare V3.12.
CONFIG	CONSOLE	Displays some of the current configuration settings such as the network interface card settings, the protocols in use, and the IPX internal network number.
DISABLE LOGIN	CONSOLE	Restricts any new users from logging into the file server.
DISABLE TTS	CONSOLE	Disables the Transaction Tracking System.
DISMOUNT	CONSOLE	Dismounts a NetWare volume. Commonly used when it's necessary to perform maintenance on a volume using the VREPAIR utility.
DISPLAY NETWORKS	CONSOLE	Shows all the networks known to the file server.
DISPLAY SERVERS	CONSOLE	Lists all known servers on the internetwork.
DOWN	CONSOLE	Clears all station connections, unloads any running processes, and shuts down the NetWare OS so the server can be rebooted or turned off.
DSPACE	UTILITY	Places space restrictions on volumes or directories globally or based on a user ID.
EDIT	UTILITY	Creates and edits an ASCII text file stored on the file server.

Item	Class	Task
ENABLE LOGIN	CONSOLE	Reverses the DISABLE LOGIN command and allows users to log into the file server. Also clears the intruder lockout status of the SUPERVISOR ID if it has been locked out.
ENABLE TTS	CONSOLE	Reverses the DISABLE TTS command.
ENDCAP	COMMAND	Reverses the CAPTURE command by breaking the connection between your station's printer ports and the NetWare print queues.
EXIT	CONSOLE	Used after the DOWN command has been issued to return the server to the DOS prompt. Causes the server to reboot automatically if the REMOVE DOS command was issued before DOWN was issued.
FCONSOLE	UTILITY	Offers some management facilities for the file server. This utility is severely crippled in NetWare 3.x compared to NetWare 2.X.
FILER	UTILITY	Moves, deletes, or modifies the attributes of files and directories and can be used to view and modify the Inherited Rights Mask.
FLAG	COMMAND	Changes or views a file's NetWare attributes.
FLAGDIR	COMMAND	Changes or views a directory's NetWare attributes.
GRANT	COMMAND	Grants rights for a file or directory to a user or group.
INSTALL	UTILITY	Installs and configures NetWare.
LISTDIR	COMMAND	Lets you view a directory tree of the current directory and its subdirectories.
LOAD	CONSOLE	"Runs," or rather, loads a NetWare console utility or driver.
LOGIN	COMMAND	Run by the user to log in and establish a connection to the NetWare file server.
LOGOUT	COMMAND	Run by the user to break the connection between the workstation and the file server.
MAKEUSER	UTILITY	Creates user IDs in large numbers at one time by using templates and a basic scripting language.
MAP	COMMAND	Lets you view, remove, or establish logical drive mappings to directories and volumes.
MEMORY	CONSOLE	Displays the amount of memory available on the file server.
MIRROR STATUS	CONSOLE	Displays the current mirroring status of the NetWare partitions.

(continues)

Item	Class	Task
MODULES	CONSOLE	Shows all the drivers and NLMs loaded on the server with information, such as their version numbers.
MONITOR	UTILITY	A console utility, MONITOR is the main utility used to view statistical information on the server regarding the current users accessing the server, and disk, memory, CPU, and NIC utilization and statistics.
MOUNT	CONSOLE	Mounts a NetWare volume to make it accessible to users logged into the server.
NAME	CONSOLE	Displays the name of the file server.
NCOPY	COMMAND	Advanced copying command used to copy files or directories. Improvement over the DOS COPY command because all the work is done on the server.
NDIR	COMMAND	Views file or directory information based on a wide variety of criteria.
NLICLEAR	UTILITY	A console utility, NLICLEAR automatically clears NOT-LOGGED-IN connections on a regular basis.
NMENU	UTILITY	NetWare's menuing utility based on Saber Menus.
NPRINT	COMMAND	Prints a file to a network printer.
NVER	COMMAND	Displays version information from the workstation on the shells/requesters and file servers to which you are currently attached.
OFF	CONSOLE	Same as CLS.
PAUDIT	COMMAND	Used in conjunction with NetWare's accounting feature, PAUDIT details the accounting logs to date.
PCONSOLE	UTILITY	Creates, deletes, or modifies print servers and print queues. PCONSOLE also checks the status of the current printing installation.
PRINTCON	UTILITY	Creates print job configurations on the server.
PRINTDEF	UTILITY	Creates printer definitions and forms with detailed information.
PROTO	UTILITY	A console utility, PROTO provides statistical information on the protocols currently in use on the server.
PROTOCOL	CONSOLE	Displays the protocols currently in use on the server.
PSC	COMMAND	A command line utility to manage network printers.
PSERVER	UTILITY	A console- or workstation-based utility that initiates the NetWare print server.

Item	Class	Task
PURGE	COMMAND	Permanently removes files that have been deleted from the file server.
RCONSOLE	UTILITY	Enables a user connected to the network to take over the file server console from their stations.
REGISTER MEMORY	CONSOLE	Allows the installer to configure the ISA server memory above 16M.
REMIRROR PARTITION	CONSOLE	Instructs NetWare to remirror partitions.
REMOVE	COMMAND	Removes users or groups as trustees of a directory or file.
REMOVE DOS	CONSOLE	Removes the portion of DOS stored in the file server's memory, thereby restricting access to any local drives on the server.
RENDIR	COMMAND	Renames a directory.
RESET ROUTER	CONSOLE	Resets/rebuilds NetWare's internal routing tables.
REVOKE	COMMAND	Revokes trustee rights to a directory or file from a user or group.
RIGHTS	COMMAND	Displays the rights a user has in the current directory.
RPRINTER	COMMAND	Allows a printer attached to a workstation to service NetWare print queues.
SALVAGE	UTILITY	Recovers files that have been accidentally deleted from the file server as long as they haven't been purged from the system.
SBACKUP	UTILITY	Used to backup files stored on the server.
SCAN FOR NEW DEVICES	CONSOLE	Checks for any new SCSI devices that have been added since the server was brought on-line.
SEARCH	CONSOLE	Lets you view and modify the directories NetWare searches when loading a module from the console.
SECURE CONSOLE	CONSOLE	Prevents anyone from loading drivers/NLMs not in the system directory or the directories established in the server's search path (see the SEARCH console command).
SECURITY	COMMAND	Checks the NetWare binderies for users or other objects that have potential security risks associated with them, such as IDs without passwords.
SEND	COMMAND	Sends a message to a specific user or group. Can be used from the file server console prompt or a workstation.
SESSION	UTILITY	Lets you view or modify some of the current environment settings such as server attachments or drive mappings.

(continues)

Appendixes

Item	Class	Task
SET	CONSOLE	Views and modifies a series of parameters that can be adjusted to configure the file server.
SET TIME	CONSOLE	Sets the server date and time.
SET TIMEZONE	CONSOLE	Sets which time zone you are in.
SETPASS	COMMAND	Changes a user's current password and also can be used by the SUPERVISOR to change another user's password.
SLIST	COMMAND	Displays all known NetWare servers currently available.
SMODE	COMMAND	Sets the search mode of an EXE file.
SPEED	CONSOLE	Rates the file server's performance as a speed rating.
SPOOL	CONSOLE	Assigns queues to printers from the console.
SYSCON	UTILITY	Creates users, login scripts, and various time and account restrictions.
SYSTIME	COMMAND	Displays the time maintained by the file server and synchronizes the the workstation's time to the server.
TIME	CONSOLE	Displays the date and time.
TLIST	COMMAND	Displays the trustees to a directory or file.
TRACK OFF	CONSOLE	Stops the tracking of broadcast information.
TRACK ON	CONSOLE	Displays broadcasts sent from other servers and certain requests from workstations.
UNBIND	CONSOLE	Unbinds a protocol for a network interface card driver.
UNLOAD	CONSOLE	Unloads (removes from memory) a driver or NLM.
USERDEF	UTILITY	Creates new users.
USERLIST	COMMAND	Views the users currently logged into the file server.
VERSION	COMMAND	Displays version information of a NetWare file.
VOLINFO	UTILITY	Displays up-to-date information regarding the amount of space available on the server's volumes.
VOLUMES	CONSOLE	Displays which volumes are currently mounted and their name space information.
VREPAIR	CONSOLE	Repairs problems with a NetWare volume.
WHOAMI	COMMAND	Provides information to the users regarding the servers they are logged into, group memberships, and security equivalences.
WSUPDATE	COMMAND	Updates drivers, shells, requesters, or other files on the workstation.

Appendix B

Important Keys and Key Combinations

Throughout the NetWare utilities and on the console, there are several "special" keystrokes that can be used to make your life a bit easier. In the following table, these keystrokes are listed along with a brief description of each.

> **Note**
>
> Every key or key combination listed in this table does not work in every utility. When in doubt, experiment with them!

Keystroke	Description
Esc	Returns to the previous menu or exits a program.
Enter	Accepts the information entered or accesses the selected option.
End	Sends the cursor to the end of the line.
Home	Sends the cursor to the beginning of the line.
F1	Provides basic on-line help.
F3	Renames or modifies an object.
F5	Marks (flags) or unmarks (unflags) an object within a listing.
F6	Establishes a pattern used to mark objects.
F7	Cancels changes you have made.
F8	Establishes a pattern used to unmark objects.

(continues)

Keystroke	Description
+	Scrolls forward through active screens in remote console sessions.
−	Scrolls backward through active screens in remote console sessions.
* (from the number pad)	Calls the Available Options menu in remote console sessions.
Up Arrow	Recalls the last command(s) issued at the server prompt when accessing the server console.
Del	Deletes the highlighted object.
Ins	Inserts an object.
Alt	Views the current screen name when working directly on the server console.
Shift+Esc	Clears the remote console session and returns the listing of servers in remote console sessions.
Shift+Shift+Alt+Esc	Loads the NetWare debug feature.
Alt+Esc	Toggles between the different screens when working directly on the server console.
Alt+F10	Presents you with the Exit prompt to exit a menu utility no matter where you are within the menu.
Ctrl+Esc	Calls up a menu listing of the screens currently loaded so you can select which one you want to view when working directly on the server.
Ctrl+PgDn	Goes to the bottom of the document, script, or menu.
Ctrl+PgUp	Goes to the top of the document, script, or menu.

Appendix C

Hexadecimal Memory Conversion Table

Following is a chart of the hexadecimal values used for each M of RAM up to 128M. Using the REGISTER MEMORY command in conjunction with these values, you can use more than 16M of RAM in your ISA server. For further information on the REGISTER MEMORY command, refer to the heading "Using More Than 16M of RAM in an ISA Server" in Chapter 3, "Installing the File Server."

Memory	Hex Equivalent	Memory	Hex Equivalent
1M	100000	13M	D00000
2M	200000	14M	E00000
3M	300000	15M	F00000
4M	400000	16M	1000000
5M	500000	17M	1100000
6M	600000	18M	1200000
7M	700000	19M	1300000
8M	800000	20M	1400000
9M	900000	21M	1500000
10M	A00000	22M	1600000
11M	B00000	23M	1700000
12M	C00000	24M	1800000

(continues)

Memory	Hex Equivalent	Memory	Hex Equivalent
25M	1900000	52M	3400000
26M	1A00000	53M	3500000
27M	1B00000	54M	3600000
28M	1C00000	55M	3700000
29M	1D00000	56M	3800000
30M	1E00000	57M	3900000
31M	1F00000	58M	3A00000
32M	2000000	59M	3B00000
33M	2100000	60M	3C00000
34M	2200000	61M	3D00000
35M	2300000	62M	3E00000
36M	2400000	63M	3F00000
37M	2500000	64M	4000000
38M	2600000	65M	4100000
39M	2700000	66M	4200000
40M	2800000	67M	4300000
41M	2900000	68M	4400000
42M	2A00000	69M	4500000
43M	2B00000	70M	4600000
44M	2C00000	71M	4700000
45M	2D00000	72M	4800000
46M	2E00000	73M	4900000
47M	2F00000	74M	4A00000
48M	3000000	75M	4B00000
49M	3100000	76M	4C00000
50M	3200000	77M	4D00000
51M	3300000	78M	4E00000

Memory	Hex Equivalent	Memory	Hex Equivalent
79M	4F00000	104M	6800000
80M	5000000	105M	6900000
81M	5100000	106M	6A00000
82M	5200000	107M	6B00000
83M	5300000	108M	6C00000
84M	5400000	109M	6D00000
85M	5500000	110M	6E00000
86M	5600000	111M	6F00000
87M	5700000	112M	7000000
88M	5800000	113M	7100000
89M	5900000	114M	7200000
90M	5A00000	115M	7300000
91M	5B00000	116M	7400000
92M	5C00000	117M	7500000
93M	5D00000	118M	7600000
94M	5E00000	119M	7700000
95M	5F00000	120M	7800000
96M	6000000	121M	7900000
97M	6100000	122M	7A00000
98M	6200000	123M	7B00000
99M	6300000	124M	7C00000
100M	6400000	125M	7D00000
101M	6500000	126M	7E00000
102M	6600000	127M	7F00000
103M	6700000	128M	8000000

Appendixes

Basic MHS and FirstMail

Included with NetWare 3.12 is Basic MHS and FirstMail. This is an electronic mail package that performs message delivery within a single-server environment. You cannot use Basic MHS to communicate with other servers or workgroups if they are not using this file server.

In this appendix, you learn the steps necessary to install, configure, and test Basic MHS and FirstMail.

Installing Basic MHS

Following are ten steps to a successful Basic MHS installation:

1. At the file server console prompt, type **LOAD INSTALL** and press Enter.

2. From the Installation Options menu, choose Product Options.

3. At the Currently Installed Products screen, press the Insert key.

4. Insert the disk labeled BASICMHS_1 into your floppy drive, type the drive letter at the prompt, and press Enter. (The default drive is A; if you are using drive B, change it to B:.)

> **Note**
>
> Basic MHS comes on two disks, labeled BASICMHS_1 and BASICMHS_2. If you are installing from the NetWare 3.12 CD-ROM, the path is VOLUME:NETWARE.312\ENGLISH\BASICMHS.

5. Enter **Y** to accept the workgroup name; enter **N** to establish a new one (see fig. D.1). Note that by default, the file server name is used as the workgroup name. If you choose to use a new workgroup name, you are prompted for a long name and a short name.

   The workgroup names are used to identify your particular group. Since Basic MHS does not communicate outside of the one server, you can use any name you want.

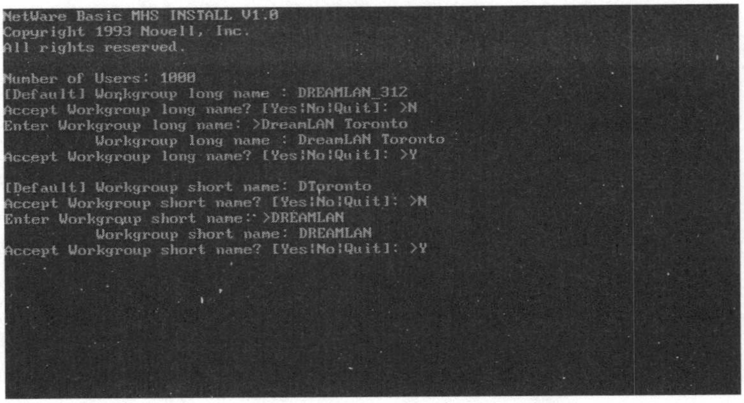

Fig. D.1 Specifying workgroup long and short names.

Caution

If you expect heavy e-mail usage, it is strongly recommended that you install Basic MHS on a separate volume. This reduces the chances of SYS running out of disk space, resulting in an inoperative server.

---

6. You are next asked if Basic MHS is to be installed (by default) to SYS:MHS. Enter **Y** if you want to. Otherwise, enter **N** and specify a volume and path of your choice. The installation program creates the necessary directory structure and assigns the necessary NetWare rights. You are prompted to insert Disk 2 at this step.

Tip

To simplify the administration task of Basic MHS, it is best that you add all users to the bindery before installing Basic MHS. This saves you from having to enter the user information twice.

---

7. Enter **Y** to add existing users from the NetWare bindery to the MHS database. Enter **N** to skip this step (see fig. D.2). You can manually define the users later on.

Caution

If you answered Y in step 7, all users in the EVERYONE group are added to the MHS database. If you have any users not listed in the EVERYONE group but want them to have access to MHS, you need to add them manually by using the ADMIN utility described in the next section.

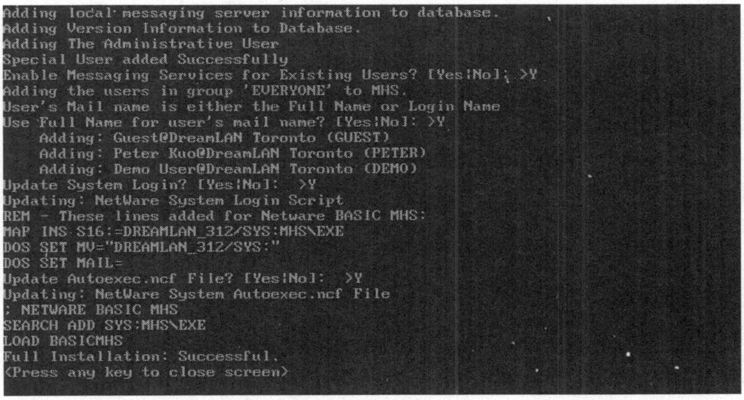

Fig. D.2 Add users defined in the NetWare bindery to the MHS database.

Tip

If you want to use users' full names for their mail IDs, you need to fill in the Full Name section in SYSCON when creating the users.

---

8. Enter **N** if you want to use NetWare logon names as mail IDs. Depending on the e-mail application, you may or may not be able to use the users' full names as mail ID. If your e-mail application supports (Standard Message Format) SMF-71 long name, you can use the users' full names as mail IDs. FirstMail supports the SMF-71 naming format.

9. Enter **Y** to allow the installation program to update your system login script. This sets up the necessary search drive and DOS environment necessary for MHS to function.

Note

Note that the lines are added at the beginning of the login script. You may want to move them.

---

10. Enter **Y** to allow the installation program to update the AUTOEXEC.NCF file so Basic MHS is loaded every time the server is brought up.

Upon installation completion, restart your server to ensure that Basic MHS loads correctly. If you encounter any errors during installation, it is best to remove Basic MHS and reinstall it from scratch. Located on the BASICMHS_1 disk is a file called MESSAGE.DOC you can refer to for any error messages you encountered.

Appendixes

If the Basic MHS NLM is loaded successfully, you find a Basic MHS status screen similar to the one shown in Figure D.3. During normal operation, the status screen displays message delivery status (see fig. D.4).

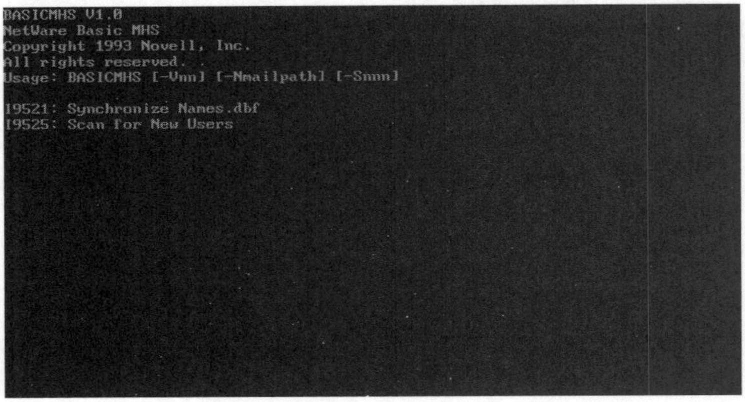

```
BASICMHS V1.0
NetWare Basic MHS
Copyright 1993 Novell, Inc.
All rights reserved.
Usage: BASICMHS [-Vnn] [-Nmailpath] [-Smnn]

19521: Synchronize Names.dbf
19525: Scan for New Users
```

Fig. D.3 Basic MHS server status screen.

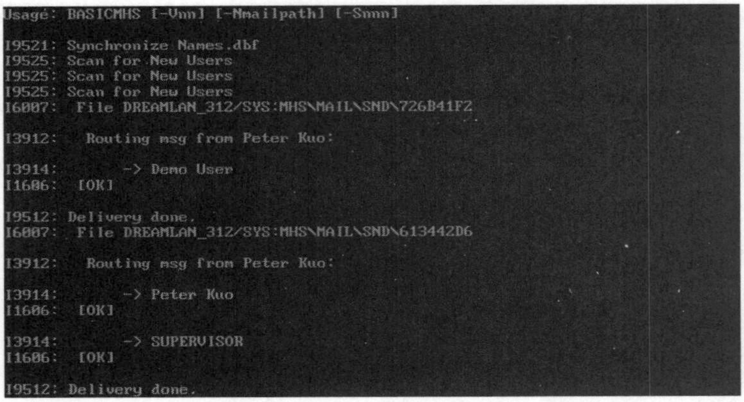

```
Usage: BASICMHS [-Vnn] [-Nmailpath] [-Smnn]

19521: Synchronize Names.dbf
19525: Scan for New Users
19525: Scan for New Users
19525: Scan for New Users
16007:   File DREAMLAN_312/SYS:MHS\MAIL\SND\726B41F2

13912:    Routing msg from Peter Kuo:

13914:        -> Demo User
11606:   [OK]

19512: Delivery done.
16007:   File DREAMLAN_312/SYS:MHS\MAIL\SND\613442D6

13912:    Routing msg from Peter Kuo:

13914:        -> Peter Kuo
11606:   [OK]

13914:        -> SUPERVISOR
11606:   [OK]

19512: Delivery done.
```

Fig. D.4 Basic MHS message delivery status.

If you have installed Basic MHS to a different volume, you must inform the NLM where this new location is. For its syntax and other load options, consult ADMIN.DOC on the BASICMHS_1 disk or your \MHS\SYS directory on the file server.

You are ready now to configure Basic MHS.

Configuring Basic MHS

There are a number of parameters you can change to better optimize the performance of Basic MHS, for example, the message delivery frequency. Make these changes using the ADMIN utility. It is copied to \MHS\EXE during the installation. ADMIN requires the Btrieve requester (BREQUEST.EXE in SYS:PUBLIC) loaded on the workstation.

Caution

Make sure you load BREQUEST.EXE before running ADMIN. It is possible to have your workstation lock up without any error messages if you try to run ADMIN without first loading BREQUEST.

From the ADMIN utility (see fig. D.5), you can do the following:

- Create, modify, and delete Basic MHS users

- Create, modify, and delete global distribution lists

- Define e-mail applications that are permitted to use Basic MHS

- Configure Basic MHS

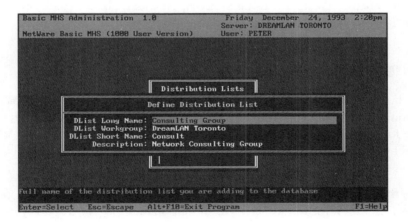

Fig. D.5 ADMIN.EXE's main menu.

In most cases, you only need to use ADMIN to perform maintenance on global distribution lists. On rare occasions, you add or remove users from the MHS database.

You need to log into ADMIN as SUPERVISOR or a SUPERVISOR EQUIVALENT in order to perform any maintenance tasks; otherwise, you can only view the information.

Appendixes

The only Basic MHS operating parameter you really have to change, if any, is the frequency with which Basic MHS does message delivery. It is the Delivery Message Every setting in the Configuration menu.

Tip
You should not make the frequency so short the server spends most of its time checking for pending mail, nor make the frequency so long that users have to wait for a long time to get their e-mail.

MHS User Maintenance

Use the Users selection from the Admin Functions menu to add, delete, or change user information. When you select the action, a list of currently defined users is shown.

To add a user to the list, simply press the Insert key. To remove a user, highlight the user name, and press Delete. To remove multiple users, use the F5 key to mark them all before pressing Delete. To modify a user's information, highlight the user's name and press Enter.

If you create a user using ADMIN, a corresponding NetWare bindery user account is also created. But if you create a new NetWare user using SYSCON, the user is not automatically added to the MHS database.

MHS Distribution Lists

Use the Distribution Lists option from the Admin Functions menu to define and maintain mailing distribution lists for your users. To create a new distribution list, press the Insert key. You are prompted for the necessary information (refer to fig. D.5). Notice that the Dlist Workgroup name is that of your workgroup. This is the same name as you specified in the installation Step 5 previously.

After creating the distribution list, you must specify the list of users to be included in the list. Highlight the distribution list you just created, and press Enter. Use the Insert key to bring up a list of defined users. Highlight the user you want added to the list. If there are multiple users you want to select, use the F5 key to mark them all before pressing Enter.

To modify the member list of the distribution list, highlight the list and press Enter. Use the Insert key to add new members and the Delete key to remove users from the list.

To delete a distribution list you no longer need, highlight the name and press Delete.

Defining MHS Applications

As MHS applications use a unique directory name to store their messages, it is important for Basic MHS to know the names of the applications used so messages are routed correctly. Normally this is done as part of the MHS application installation. However, if a particular application does not do that, then you must use the Applications selection from the Admin Functions screen to define it manually.

Using FirstMail with Basic MHS

FirstMail is not installed as part of the Basic MHS installation. It is located on a single disk labeled FirstMail v1.0 for DOS. To install it, simply copy the contents of the disk to a directory on the file server. There is no configuration necessary to use FirstMail with Basic MHS.

> **Note**
>
> If you want to reconfigure FirstMail or know more about FirstMail, consult the three text files on the FirstMail disk: README.TXT, ADMIN.TXT, and USER.TXT.

To make FirstMail available to your users, make sure you allow the Read and FileScan trustee assignments to the directory to which you installed FirstMail, and add a search map to it.

To start FirstMail, simply type **MAIL** at the DOS prompt. A screen similar to one shown in Figure D.6 appears. If there is new mail waiting for you, the opening screen looks slightly different (see fig. D.7).

Fig. D.6 First Mail's opening screen.

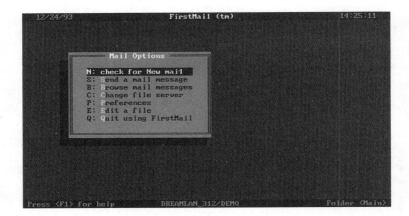

Fig. D.7 FirstMail's opening screen when there is new mail waiting.

You easily can test the installation of Basic MHS as well as the operation of FirstMail by sending e-mail to yourself. If everything is installed and configured correctly, shortly after you send the message, you see the message delivery status from Basic MHS on the file server.

You can configure the system login script to notify users automatically of any new mail message when they log in. Add the following to your system login script:

```
#newmail
if error_level  > "0" then begin
pause
end
```

If there are new messages pending, NEWMAIL displays on-screen the number of new messages.

Glossary

Active hub: Acting as a central point in a star topology, the active hub has multiple ports for workstation connections and can amplify LAN transmission signals.

Address: A unique identifier assigned to networks and nodes to ensure that each device can operate independently. In networking, an address is used just as you use the address of your house.

Advertising: The process by which a service on the network announces itself to the rest of the network. By doing so, it can make itself available for use by other nodes. See also *Service Advertising Protocol*.

Application layer: The seventh layer of the OSI Reference Model, the Application layer is responsible for the interface between computer and user for systems such as E-MAIL and Network Management.

Architecture: Frequently confused with the word topology, architecture defines how nodes of a network can communicate, restrictions of the network such as the maximum speeds and distances, and the protocols used. Examples of modern architectures would be Token Ring, Ethernet, or ARCnet.

Archive: An archive is a redundant or backup copy of a computer program, file, or database. Archives are typically made to store information for extended periods of time.

ARCnet: Developed by Datapoint Corporation, ARCnet defines a network operating at 2.5Mbps over UTP or coaxial cable. Generally wired as a star (though it is possible to configure it as a bus), ARCnet provides a cost-effective networking solution for the small LAN.

Asynchronous: Asynchronous communications is a method of transmitting data one bit at a time where clocking (the amount of time between each character) is not used. To ensure the proper transmission of data, start and stop bits are used to signify the end of a section of information.

Attachment Unit Interface (AUI) cable: Within a thick Ethernet environment, an AUI cable connects the workstation's network interface card with the Medium Attachment Unit (MAU). The AUI cable is also known as a transceiver cable.

Attenuation: As signals travel, their power, or amplitude, decreases over distance. This reduction in power is known as attenuation. In networking, it is important to remain within the set distance boundaries for a particular architecture or cable type. Extending beyond these distances usually results in network problems as the signal is attenuating so much it can no longer be read properly.

Backbone: The backbone is a main segment of a network to which smaller networks attach in some fashion. The backbone usually, but not always, operates at a higher speed than the networks that connect to it. By linking smaller networks into a backbone, nodes on either one can share information freely.

Balun: A small device used to connect cables with different electrical specifications, such as co-axial cable and twisted pair.

Bandwidth: The term bandwidth signifies the amount of data that can be passed through a medium within a given amount of time. For example, a Token Ring network can offer bandwidth levels of 4M or 16M.

Beacon: A beacon is a signal used in the Token Ring environment that indicates a serious problem on the ring such as a broken cable, a faulty NIC, or an NIC attempting to access the ring at the incorrect speed.

Blackout: A blackout is a complete loss of electrical power for an extended period of time.

BNC connector: Used specifically for coaxial cables, BNC connectors can either be crimped or screwed onto the end of the cable.

Boot image file: Boot image files are required when diskless workstations, or PCs that have NICs equipped with boot proms installed, are accessing the file server. Stored in the LOGIN directory of the file server, the Boot image file provides information to the PC such as DOS versions and the drivers to access the network.

Bridge: Operating within the Data Link layer of the OSI reference model (layer 2), the bridge connects networks of the same architecture, such as Ethernet to Ethernet or Token Ring to Token Ring. Since the bridge resides at the Data Link layer, it can read the MAC layer addresses within a packet to determine where the packet is destined.

Broadcast: A message that is sent across the network to all attached nodes.

Brouter: The brouter is more or less a hybrid mixture of a bridge and a router. Although not necessarily as functional as a bridge or router, a brouter usually offers both routing and bridging features.

Brownout: A temporary decrease in power line voltage.

Bus: A network topology where nodes are connected to a straight run of cabling. The ends of the main cable do not connect together and are usually terminated on both ends and grounded on one.

Campus network: The campus network is one in which nodes are spread throughout a limited area such as one between buildings a block or two apart.

Cheapernet: A nickname given to 10Base2 that reflects its historically lower-cost networking solution compared to other architectures such as Token Ring.

Cladding: Used within a fiber-optic cable, cladding is a plastic or glass covering surrounding the inner core of the cable. In addition to protecting the fiber, the cladding reflects the pulses of light down the run of cable.

Class A station: See *Dual attached station.*

Class B station: See *Single attached station.*

Client: The client is a node on a network that submits requests to a host, such as a mainframe or file server, for services.

Concentrator: Another name for a Hub or Multiport Repeater, the basic role of the concentrator is to act as a central wiring area for LANs of a star topology. Modern concentrators have come a long way from the initial versions by implementing bridge/router and management type functions.

Connection-Oriented Protocol: A protocol that is said to be "connection-oriented" relies on two-way communications. After a station transmits its data it waits to receive an acknowledgment from the receiving station. If/when an acknowledgment is not received, the sending station assumes the data was not transmitted properly and it will attempt to resend.

Controlled Access Unit (CAU): Pronounced "cow," the CAU is the Token Ring equivalent of the intelligent concentrator or a manageable MSAU. Acting as a central wiring center to the network, the CAU also is capable of providing management functions to the LAN such as notification of node failures.

Crosstalk: A potential problem with twisted pair cabling. When wires carrying electrical signals are placed close together, the signal on one wire can "corrupt" the signal on the other wire. Essentially, crosstalk is a spillover of information from one wire to another within the sheath. To minimize the effects of crosstalk, the wires are twisted a certain number of times per foot.

Data Link layer: The second layer of the OSI Reference Model, the Data Link layer deals with information in groups known as frames. The Data Link layer is capable of reading the physical address of the network card and can determine if a packet that it receives is for a particular station.

De facto: "By Fact." Used to refer to something that has become a standard not by law but instead, by widespread user acceptance. A perfect example of a de facto standard would be TCP/IP, the protocol of choice on the Internet.

De jure: "By Law." Refers to something that has become a standard based on law or regulation of an official standards body.

Disk driver: A small program that is used to allow the operating system to interact with and recognize the hard drive controller and disk subsystem.

Disk duplexing: Disk duplexing provides a high degree of fault tolerance for the disk subsystem should any physical errors occur. Two controllers are installed in the file server and assigned a unique channel. Once installed, a disk drive is added to each controller. Any data kept on the file server is saved on both disks. Since the controllers are on separate channels, and the data is kept in two locations, the file server continues to function should any single component fail.

An added benefit to having two separate channels is that each can complete requests independently of each other. Therefore, if one disk is busy reading or writing, the other disk can fulfill any outstanding requests.

Disk mirroring: With disk mirroring, a single controller is used with two or more disk drives. Any write requests to the file server are made to both drives. Should one drive fail, the system continues to operate until it can be repaired. While disk mirroring offers a degree of fault tolerance for the server similar to disk duplexing, it can cause a slight degradation in performance as multiple requests must be made through the same channel.

Distributed computing: Distributed computing relies on the resources of the client and the server computers. Data is broken up between the two and running applications will access both areas. By dividing the data into different locations, performance gains can be achieved by making use of the processing power at the workstation.

DIX: DIX stands for Digital, Intel, and Xerox. This group of organizations developed the earliest forms of Ethernet.

DIX connector: A 15-pin connector found on an Ethernet card. This connector is used with 10Base5 (thick Ethernet) with an external transceiver.

Dual Attached Station (DAS): Found in the FDDI environment, a Dual Attached Station—a Class A Station—is one that maintains a connection to the primary and secondary rings of an FDDI network. Should a failure occur on one of the rings, the DAS station autosenses this failure and reroutes data onto the other ring.

Electromagnetic Interference (EMI): A form of electrical noise that can affect the integrity of data being transmitted over electrical media such as cabling.

Enterprise network: An enterprise network is one that encompasses the entire organization. All attached nodes and servers are included within the network. Unlike a LAN or WAN, the enterprise network knows no physical or geographical boundaries.

Ethernet: One of the oldest networking architectures, Ethernet is a 10Mbps network that uses the CSMA/CD protocol. Certified within the IEEE's 802.3 specifications, Ethernet is capable of transmitting over coaxial, twisted pair, or fiber-optic cabling.

Fault: A break or failure within any given point of a system that can affect the availability of some or all functions.

Fault tolerance: The act of protecting the system functions against failure. Generally, fault tolerance is achieved through the use of redundant hardware within the server.

Fault tolerant: A system that is said to be fault tolerant is capable of remaining operable after an error or hardware failure occurs.

Fiber Distributed Data Interface (FDDI): Developed by ANSI, FDDI is a 100Mbps network architecture using fiber-optic cabling. While it is currently expensive to implement on a wide scale, it is commonly used for backbone or point-to-point connections between floors or buildings.

Fiber-optic cable: Made of a glass or plastic core, fiber-optic cable uses beams of light instead of electricity to transmit data. Surrounding the core, a thick layer of plastic cladding is used to protect the core from breaks and to reflect the beams of light down the length of cable. Fiber optics may offer bandwidth levels that are significantly higher than copper-based cabling; however, it is not a cheap solution. The main benefit to fiber-optic cable is that it is not susceptible to EMI interference. Therefore, fiber-optics is ideal for situations where there is a lot of higher machinery around such as in factories.

Hop: A hop is a measurement of distance that a packet travels through the network. Each passage through a router is considered to be one hop.

Hub: Another name for *concentrator*.

IEEE: Institute of Electrical and Electronics Engineers.

IEEE 802.1: The IEEE's interoperability group, the 802.1 committee is responsible for dealing with issues surrounding the interaction between other standards within the 802 project, systems management, and internetworking.

IEEE 802.2: For the purposes of the IEEE, the Data Link layer of the OSI Reference Model has been divided into two segments, the Medium Access Control (MAC) layer and the Logical Link Control (LLC) layer. It is the 802.2 specification which defines the LLC and its workings.

IEEE 802.3: The 802.3 committee is responsible for network implementations of the CSMA/CD protocol. Their previous work included such things as 10Base2 and 10Base5 but most recently, the 802.3 took on a new assignment known as 100BaseX (or Fast Ethernet), a 100Mbps architecture using the traditional CSMA/CD protocol.

IEEE 802.4: The 802.4 specification defines a deterministic token bus topology over broadband or single-channel media.

IEEE 802.5: The Token Passing Ring specification 802.5 is based on IBM's development of Token Ring. This standard defines a network with a maximum of 250 nodes per ring with transfer rates of 4 or 16Mbps.

IEEE 802.6: To develop a cost-effective and fast solution to connecting LANs across a city when using packet switching networks or T-1 lines is not an option, the 802.6 (Metropolitan Area Networks) committee selected the Distributed Queue Dual Bus technology from the University of Western Australia.

IEEE 802.7: The 802.7 committee is responsible for setting standards for the use and implementation of broadband technology.

IEEE 802.8: The 802.8 committee was formed to find alternatives to the cabling of the earlier specifications. Their focus is on fiber-optic cabling and its implementation.

IEEE 802.9: The goal of this committee is to produce a standard compatible with the 802.2 specifications and ISDN. They are looking at the different interfaces for voice and data communications available for the desktop.

IEEE 802.10: The LAN Security workgroup is responsible for dealing with issues such as secure wireless communications and encryption.

IEEE 802.11: Acting closely with the 802.10, the 802.11 Wireless Communications workgroup is dealing with various issues surrounding wireless communications such as bandwidth restrictions, protocols, and interface standards.

IEEE 802.12: The most recently created workgroup, the 802.12 is responsible for investigating a proposal put forth by Hewlett-Packard that defines a 100Mbps network architecture called 100VG-AnyLAN and a new protocol called Demand Priority.

Impedance: Impedance is the resistance of an AC current traveling down the cabling. The actual impedance of a network cable affects the propagation delay of the network transmissions. If/when the impedance of the cabling is not properly matched to the specifications of the network in question, communications can be unreliable or even impossible.

Internetwork Packet Exchange (IPX): IPX is a network layer protocol based on Xerox Network Systems (XNS) Internetwork Datagram Protocol (IDP). As a connectionless protocol, it relies on its other half, SPX, for any connection-oriented communications. IPX is the protocol responsible for addressing and routing functions such as packet forwarding.

Jacket: Also called a sheath, the jacket is the outer covering of a cable.

Local Area Network (LAN): The LAN is a small- to medium-sized network that generally does not encompass a very large geographic area. The LAN usually does not extend off of the floor of a building, or the building itself. Compared to WANs, LANs are higher speed networks with fewer users.

Mbps: Megabits per second.

Media: The plural for medium; media are entities—such as cabling—used to carry data from one point to another.

Medium: Whatever is used to transport data back and forth. While in many cases the medium is a physical entity such as a cable, it can also be an intangible such as a microwave or radio wave. When the medium is a tangible object it is called a *bounded medium*, meaning the data is bounded between the confines of the object. When the medium is not a tangible object, it is said to be an *unbounded medium*.

Medium Attachment Unit (MAU): Also called a transceiver, the MAU is used in 10Base5 networks and acts as a tap into the thick Ethernet cabling from the workstation.

Network: A network is a group of computers and other devices that communicate with each other through some type of medium.

Network Interface Card (NIC): A computer adapter used to connect a workstation to the network. The adapter usually plugs directly into the workstation motherboard and has a connector on the back of the card to attach to the network's cabling system.

Network layer: The third layer of the OSI Reference Model, the Network layer is capable of reading the Network layer address and routing packets as needed.

Node: Any workstation, printer, file server, or other type of hardware that attaches directly to the network in some fashion.

Open DataLink Interface (ODI): ODI is a specification from Novell that provides a generic method of accessing the network. In the past, logging into the NetWare server involved loading two files, IPX and NETX. With the ODI implementation, the IPX.COM file has been broken into separate files such as LSL.COM, IPXODI.COM and a file for the network interface card, known as the MLID. When different cards are used on two PCs, the ODI stack can remain the same except for the MLID. This affords the user much more flexibility when upgrading drivers on the network. Another added benefit to using ODI is that it is capable of supporting multiple protocols from the same workstation.

Open Systems Interconnection reference model (OSI): Developed by the International Standards Organization (ISO), the OSI reference model defines how a computer system should operate through the use of seven layers; Physical, DataLink, Network, Transport, Session, Presentation, and Application.

Packet: The packet can be viewed as a group of bits that contains information used to control the flow of the packet as well as the data being transmitted from one node on the network to another.

Peer to peer: The peer-to-peer network is one where any node can communicate with any other node directly. Unlike the typical client-server environment where the client requests resources from the server, nodes on a peer-to-peer network can request resources from any other node on the network.

Physical layer: The lowest layer of the OSI Reference Model, the Physical layer provides guidelines for the electrical specifications of the cabling and how the cabling is accessed. At the Physical layer, information is dealt with in bits.

Plenum: The space found between the ceiling and the floor above. It is commonly used for air ducts and to run cabling.

Presentation layer: The sixth layer of the OSI Reference Model, the Presentation layer translates data into a format mutually acceptable to both the sender and receiver.

Propagation delay: The propagation delay is the amount of time it takes for a single bit to travel from the sending and receiving stations. Network architectures have maximum allowable propagation delays which ultimately determine the overall size of the network.

Repeater: Within the OSI model, the repeater is a Physical layer device that can be used to extend the length of a network by regenerating the signal it receives and then amplifying it down the other section of the network.

Ring: A topology where the ends of the cabling have been closed together to form a circle, or ring.

RJ-11: RJ-11 is a 4-wire connector used on common phone cabling.

RJ-45: An 8-wire connector, the RJ-45 is commonly used in unshielded twisted pair networks such as 10BaseT.

Router: A Network layer device, the router is used to connect networks that use the same Network layer protocol, such as IPX.

Sag: A short-term drop in voltage below 80 percent. Used interchangeably with *brownout*.

Segment: A segment is an electrically isolated section of the network. For example, in a 10Base2 bus topology network, a straight run of cabling must have a terminating resistor placed at both ends. In this case, the segment would be the area between the two terminators.

Sequential Packet Exchange (SPX): The other half of the IPX protocol, SPX is a connection-oriented protocol developed by Novell but based on work from Xerox Network Systems (XNS).

Server: The server is some type of computer on the network that services requests from nodes and provides shared resources such as printers or disk storage. In most cases, the server is a very powerful computer that has high speed and/or multiple CPUs, high-capacity disk systems, and memory.

Service Advertising Protocol (SAP): As defined by Novell, the Service Advertising Protocol is used by servers to announce their presence on the network to other servers.

Session layer: The fifth layer of the OSI Reference model, the Session layer is responsible for establishing and terminating connections between nodes of the network. Once established, the Session layer manages the communications process and directs problems from the upper layers of the OSI model.

Shielded Twisted Pair (STP): Shielded Twisted Pair is a type of cable usually used in Token Ring networks. Depending on the type of STP, there are several pairs of copper wire surrounded by layers of wire mesh that act as a shield against external influences such as EMI.

Single Attached Station (SAS): The SAS, also known as a Class B station, is a node on the FDDI network that attaches to the medium through a single connection.

Star: The star is a topology where nodes are connected into a central point such as a hub or concentrator.

Star-Bus: The star-bus is a topology where the network is laid out as a star (nodes wired into a central point), but electrically, it operates as a bus (for example, 10BaseT).

Star-Ring: The star-ring is a topology where the network is laid out as a star (nodes wired into a central point), but electrically, it operates as a ring (such as Token Ring).

Surge: A short-term increase in the voltage power level. The opposite of a sag.

Tap: The point where a break in the normal flow of data has been redirected. A perfect example of a tap is a Medium Attachment Unit in 10Base5.

T-Connector: Usually used in thin Ethernet implementations over coaxial cabling. This connector has three different ports. One is connected directly to the node's Ethernet card and the other two are used to connect the node to the nearest upstream and downstream neighbors.

Thicknet (thick wire): A common term for 10Base5 Ethernet using thick coaxial cabling.

Thinnet (thin wire): A common term for 10Base2 Ethernet using thin coaxial cabling.

Token: A token is a 24-byte packet used to control when nodes can transmit. Nodes on the network sit idle and wait until they are in possession of the Token. Once in possession, the node has the opportunity to transmit any data it has ready to go. After sending the packet, the token must be passed on to the next node. The station cannot transmit on the network until the token has gone through the network and returned.

Token Ring: A 4Mbps or 16Mbps architecture, Token Ring is a token-passing network developed by International Business Machines (IBM) and has been duly noted in the IEEE 802.5 specifications. While wired physically as a star, it operates electrically as a ring. Token Ring works with UTP, STP, or fiber-optic cabling.

Topology: Defines how a network is physically laid out. The difference between the term topology and the term architecture is that topology does not place any restrictions on the number of nodes or cable distances.

Transceiver: Another term for a Medium Attachment Unit.

Transport layer: The fourth layer of the OSI Reference Model, the Transport layer ensures that data is sent and received properly over the network. Acknowledgments are generated at this layer within the receiving station to confirm that a packet was received properly.

Unshielded Twisted Pair (UTP): Mainly used in 10BaseT and 4Mbps Token Ring networks, UTP cabling consists of one or more pairs of copper wire where each pair is twisted a certain number of times per foot (the value changes depending on the classification). UTP cable is certified by several organizations such as the Underwriters Laboratories, IBM, and the EIA. While it is lighter and less expensive than Shielded Twisted Pair cabling, it is more susceptible to EMI.

Wide Area Network (WAN): A network that spans a large geographic area, sometimes extending between provinces, states or countries.

Workstation: A node equipped with a processor—such as a PC—that is used to access data from a network.

Index

M